THE
EAST INDIA
COMPANY

THE
EAST INDIA
COMPANY

A History

by Brian Gardner

THE McCALL PUBLISHING COMPANY
NEW YORK

Library of Congress Catalog Card Number: 73-154262
ISBN 0-8415-0124-6

The McCall Publishing Company
230 Park Avenue, New York, New York 10017

PRINTED IN THE UNITED STATES OF AMERICA

'It is the strangest of all governments, but it is designed for the strangest of all empires.'

Macaulay, 1833

CONTENTS

ILLUSTRATIONS

All the illustrations are from the India Office Library, by permission of the Secretary of State for Foreign Affairs, except for the following: Clive, Hastings, Ellenborough, Hardinge, Dalhousie, which are from the National Portrait Gallery, by permission of the Director.

MAPS

NOTE

A government which, through might of arms, was the most powerful in Asia; a government, the revenue of which was greater than that of Britain; a government which ruled over more people than the present government of the United States; a government owned by businessmen, the shares in which were daily bought and sold. As Macaulay said, 'It is strange, very strange.' The days of the East India Company seem remote, prodigiously remote, and so they are in every way except in the real passage of time. Even in my own lifetime there were former servants of the Company still alive. Although it receives little attention now, this remarkable institution was a matter for constant comment and controversy not so long ago. It is nearly seventy years since the last history of it was published in its own country.

What was so special about this Company? Well, at the end of its powers it was responsible, directly or indirectly, for nearly one-fifth of the world's population. Dr C. Northcote Parkinson made it seem straightforward enough, in his admirable definition:

How was the East India Company controlled? By the Government. What was its object? To collect taxes. How was this object attained? By means of a large standing army. What were its employees? Soldiers, mostly, the rest, civil servants. Where did it trade to? China. What did it export from England? Courage. And what did it import? Tea!

That is fair enough. But lurking behind the shelves upon shelves of correspondence in the India Office Library, London, with their intricate records of the public company which ruled over territories from St Helena to Singapore and beyond, there is an ambiance less easy to define and peculiar to the Company. R. H. Mottram expressed it eloquently:

> There was always something magic, queer, unaccountable about it. Clive knew perhaps what it was. But he died mysteriously and never said what he knew. The facts can always be collected. The ledgers and Minute books are all extant and can be read. Great modern cities, Calcutta, Bombay, even Delhi can be visited. The evidences of the Company lie scattered about Europe and Asia. Yet one has an odd feeling that the Company was not exactly that, and that the attempt to make the East mercantile on the European model ended by altering Europe and leaving the East, under the surface, untouched.

It is a story of fantastic endeavour, and the Company does have a special attraction of its own. This book has no pretensions of important original research, although, where it seemed useful, published sources have been garnished here and there with documents and material from primary sources in the India Office Library. Neither does it attempt to present any mystique. The story is set largely where most of it happened, i.e. in India, although not forgetting elsewhere, and, from Warren Hastings, mostly in the framework of the men whose task it was to activate or control what happened, i.e. the Governors-General. This latter method is no more perfect than any other, but it seemed more convenient than others both for reader and writer. Despite the efforts of its directors, from the time of Clive the East India Company was more a military power than it was a commercial concern, and it is in this setting that I have presented a subject too varied and vast for full treatment in one volume.

The place-names are those in common use under the British raj. I have used 'royal' rather than 'King's' or 'Queen's' to differentiate between those forces and the Company's own troops. To prevent a plethora of footnotes in what is intended as a popular, not an academic, history, I have documented quotations only where it seemed specially necessary.

The bibliography of British India before 1857 is not inconsiderable, and an exhaustive list can be found in the *Cambridge History of India*, Vol. V. Many of the Company's documents, particularly of the early period, have been published in various series, among them the *Fort William – India House Correspondence* (National Archives of India), the Oxford *English Factories in India* and *Court Minutes of the East India Company*, and *Letters Received by the East India Company* (London, 1896–). The Company's servants were a literate band themselves, producing many of the greatest histories and memoirs of Anglo-Indian literature, in particular perhaps the works and reports of Elphinstone, Edwardes, Outram, and Malcolm. Other long-established classics are *History of the Sikhs*, J. D. Cunningham, Sir W. H. Sleeman's *Report on the Thugs* (Calcutta, 1840), J. Z. Holwell's *Narrative* of the Black Hole of Calcutta (London, 1758), and the *Memoirs* of William Hickey (London, 1913–25). There have been three modern histories: *Ledger and Sword*, Beckles Willson (London, 1903), *Trader's Dream*, R. H. Mottram (New York, 1939), *The East India Company and the British Empire in the Far East*, M. E. Wilbur (New York, 1945). More specialised works are headed by *The East India Company 1784–1834*, C. H. Philips (Manchester, 2nd edn 1961), the indispensable source book for the Company's activities in London during its hey-day. The other great work in this field is *The East India Company in 18th Century Politics* by Lucy Sutherland (Oxford, 1952). The most essential work on the Company in India is *The Central Administration of the East India Company 1773–1834*, B. B. Misra (Manchester, 1959). There are numerous other specialised books on the Company, of which *The English East India Company 1600–40*, K. N. Chaudhuri (London, 1965), *John Company at Work*, H. Furber (Harvard, 1948), *The Government of India*, Sir C. Ilbert (London, 1916), *The Nabobs of Madras*, H. H. Dodwell (London, 1926), and his *Dupleix and Clive* (London, 1926), *Haileybury Since Roman Times*, C. M. Matthews (Haileybury, 1959), *Sirajuddaulah and the East India Company*, B. K. Gupta (Leiden, 1966), *The British in West Sumatra 1685–1825*, J. Bastin (Kuala Lumpur, 1965), *The Old East Indiamen*, E. K. Chatterton (London, 1914), *The Administration of the East India Company*, J. W. Kaye (London, 1853), and Sir John Foster's articles should be mentioned. *The Founders*, Philip Woodruff, is an impressive tribute to East India Company personalities in India, famous and forgotten. The other most moving and unreserved tribute of recent times to these men is Lord Radcliffe's Reith Lectures, 1951, *The Problem of Power*. Less uncritical is another modern historian of India, Percival Spear, among whose works is *A History of India* (Penguin, 1965), a useful and fresh analysis from the earliest to the present times, remarkably concise; his *The Nabobs* (Oxford, 1963) is also valuable. An Indian view is to be found in *Britain in India*, R. P. Masani (Bombay, 1960). Another modern writer on British India, Michael Edwardes, has made his best contribution on the hitherto somewhat neglected social side of the British raj, apart from his useful military histories. Correspondence of some of the Governors-General has been published, and some have been exceedingly well-served by biographers, not least Dalhousie (by Sir W. Lee-Warner, 1904), Canning (by Michael Maclagan, 1961), and Warren Hastings (Keith Feiling, 1954). The Afghan question prior to the Mutiny has been well served by P. Macrory and J. A. Norris. Much unpublished material regarding the Mutiny was used for *Eighteen Fifty-Seven*, Surendra Nath Sen (Delhi, 1957), *The Ranee of Jhansi*, D. V. Tahmankar (London, 1958), *Nana Sahib and the Rising at Cawnpore*, P. C. Gupta (Oxford, 1963), and *Way to Glory: Life of Havelock*, J. C. Pollock (London, 1957). Sen has also written two important accounts of the Marathas. Aspects of the Company's activities outside India have received attention recently in the meticulously researched *Sultans of Aden*, G. Waterfield (London, 1968), and in *Raffles*, M. Collis (London, 1966). This list of useful books could be continued for many pages, but I hope I have named enough to indicate that I am aware of my debt to the many writers who have passed this way, or parts of it, before me. I also wish to express my gratitude to the staffs of the British Museum, the India Office Library, the London Library, to Miss Doris E. Gregory for her careful and constructive typing, and to Chatto and Windus Ltd. and Mrs A. Cooke for permission to quote from *Memoirs of a Bengal Civilian* by J. Beames, MacGibbon & Kee Ltd. for permission to quote from *The Ranee of Jhansi* by D. V. Tahmankar, and Macmillan & Co Ltd. for permission to quote from *'Clemency' Canning* by Michael Maclagan.

Part One ACQUISITION
OF INDIA

1   THE SPICE LANDS

Elizabeth I, Queen of England, had been on the throne for more than forty years, the most English monarch in blood since her distant ancestor, Harold, more than five centuries before. She read the document which had been placed before her. It was New Year's Eve, 1600. The last hours of the sixteenth century were passing away. Elizabeth was by no means unused to giving her decision, and she was certainly not afraid to do so. She was a woman not only decisive but also shrewd. As she read that charter, could she have foreseen all that it foreshadowed? On the face of it, it did not seem a particularly remarkable document. It had been carefully prepared: had been preceded by a petition with which she was familiar:

> Whereas our dear and most loving cousin, George Earl of Cumberland and other of our well-beloved subjects...have of our certain knowledge been petitioners unto us for our Royal assent and license to be granted unto them, that they, of their own Adventures, costs and charges, as well as for the honour of this our realm of England as for the increase of our navigation and advancement of trade of merchandise...might adventure and set forth one or more voyage, with convenient number of Ships and Pinnances, by way of traffic and merchandise to the East Indies.

'Honour of our realm'...'Adventure'...They were revealing terms. Never before had Englishmen been so patriotic and so proud. The founding of the great East India Company, which was to become the most powerful company the world has ever known, was a typical expression of its time.

Various forces, coming together, had brought it into being. By decree from the Church in Rome, the extra-European world had been divided between Spain and Portugal. But Europe was in a ferment of rising capitalism. 'Companies' of merchants had been formed to develop trade. The Dutch were particularly active and had rounded the Cape; they had made contact with the archipelago of South-East Asia. The whole area around the Indian Ocean had been considered the preserve of Portugal – and Portugal was now a satellite of Spain. In the west, fifteen years before, an Englishman had actually attempted to found a colony in North America, to which the Spanish laid claim – but Spain had been defeated at the Armada in 1588. Perhaps most important of all, Philip II, king of both Spain and Portugal, the most powerful ruler in the world, had died in 1598. With Philip's death, the bonds which had been half restraining the urge of Europeans to expand round the world finally broke.

The east was important because from there came the supply of pepper and spices; spices, such as cloves, nutmeg, cinnamon, and also ginger, were of value and great importance as partial preservatives of food, and additives to a European population accustomed to fresh meat for only a few months in the year. Meat eaten at that time would have been largely unacceptable to modern palates, but without spices much of it would have been virtually inedible. Spices had a considerable place in life; men were prepared to die in search of them, and many did; no gift was more acceptable, and to be well supplied was a mark of status; wealth could be measured in spices. They were also the basis of many medicines. But the east was also widely believed to contain fabulous wealth and riches apart from spices, and it was this also which tempted the more adventurous and ambitious merchants in Lisbon, Amsterdam, Antwerp, and London. The more down-to-earth merchants were concerned also. London merchants had formed the Levant Company as a source of supply from the east. They had bought supplies of spices, silks, and luxuries from the middlemen of the eastern Mediterranean. They had even tried to open up a land-route from the Middle East across Russia. But now the Dutch, allies of the

English in the war against Philip, were importing direct from the east, round the Cape.* The Levant Company could not compete and was in mortal danger. For this reason, many members of the company began to agitate for a new company which would trade direct with the east, as the Portuguese had long done and the Dutch were now doing; it would have, among the subjects of the Queen, an exclusive right to do so; it was a time when Elizabeth was granting monopolies almost every time she raised her pen.

It was not the first time such a plan had been mooted. It had been suggested to Henry VIII. Englishmen had ignored the Portuguese and had visited India, as they had flaunted Spain in visiting the New World. Four merchants had left for India in 1583, travelling via Persia. But such expeditions were not invariably popular in England. The Queen's advisers, the Privy Council, were not anxious to rile Spain unduly – indeed, attempts were being made to conclude a peace treaty; not all Englishmen were as adventurous as Raleigh. Moreover, there was controversy about the very companies themselves. Was monopoly a good thing? Those excluded thought not. Those who risked life and fortune, and who clung together for safety almost as much as anything else, thought it was. London was the home of the increasingly popular 'joint stock' type of company, and the London merchants were not without power. Their moving spirits at this time were Richard Staper and Sir Thomas Smyth, first Governor of the East India Company to be, ex-Ambassador to Russia, and closely concerned with the Muscovy trade and the settlement of Virginia. Many of the merchants interested in investing in the east were the same as those who were interested in investing in New England.

The Queen had already met some of the London merchants concerning their plan to establish a direct trade with the east – at Hampton Court, on 16 October 1599 – and she was enthusiastic about the idea. The Company had, in fact, begun its formation in the previous month of that year. It had continued its arrangements with quiet confidence. Already preparations had been made for the first voyage. The merchants knew that the Queen's assent was something of a formality; they knew well that her enthusiasm was partly due to the vast customs dues she would receive if the stories of the riches from direct eastern trade were only half true. The exact

* Anglo-Spanish War, 1587–1604.

nature of their charter had been worked out with the Privy Council. Now all was ready for the signature of the Queen.

In 1580 the English people had been astounded by the return of Sir Francis Drake after a voyage around the world – regardless of the fact that the feat had been achieved by the Portuguese more than half a century previously. Eight years later, Philip's débâcle in his attempt to invade England – defeated by the weather – gave further confidence to the English. They were a remarkable people. Among other Europeans, they had an exceedingly poor reputation. Unaffected and unreserved, they were considered to be unmannered and rough; the Queen's court was seen as crude compared to that of Philip. In appearance the English were said to be uncouth and in dress inelegant, as compared to the aristocracy of continental Europe. In commerce they were not considered a match for the Dutch. The Channel kept them at a distance from the rest of Europe, and the rest of Europe was not sorry. It had to be admitted that they were good sailors and navigators, but only in a piratical and ruffianly sort of way. The hearty Tudor English were the rough diamonds of Europe. And they were about to burst out into the world in a most uncompromising way. In three hundred years they would rule over the greatest empire the world has ever known, or is ever likely to know. They would be famed for their reticence in style, their reserve, and their polish. It was a fate none could have foreseen.

But did Queen Elizabeth not have some inkling of the current she was about to release? Not the great cities that she could hardly have imagined, Calcutta, Aden, Bombay, Singapore...Not the details, of course. Not even the Bengal Lancers, and Rudyard Kipling, and the Campbells are Coming, and Clive and Hastings, and the pukka sahib, and Mahatma Gandhi product of the Inner Temple, and Jawaharlal Nehru product of Harrow, and the polo-players of Poona, and the Viceroy with his 700 servants, and the world's largest railway system, and her descendant George V accepting the homage of the Indian princes at the Durbar of 1911, and the cavalry jingling through the Khyber Pass, their lances glittering in the sun, and Lord Louis Mountbatten driving through the crowds, and the memsahibs with the silver muffin dishes, the lace napkins and honey of afternoon tea in the gabled, lattice-windowed houses of Simla...Not these; but it would be satisfying to think that she knew she was starting something important, and that it would be something which would bring more fame to her country than anything else in its history.

The Queen signed the charter 'Elizabeth', assigning a monopoly to the Honourable East India Company. It was marked with the royal stamp of England. It was valid for fifteen years.

India — vast, sprawling with humanity, superstition, religion, fear, and dangers to men of all kinds — was unaware of the activity in Europe which was to determine its fate. The Emperor was Akbar, third in line of the so-called 'Mughals' (who had no more than tenuous links with the Mongols). He was a foreigner, a Turk, spoke Persian, and was a Muslim, whereas Hinduism was mostly the religion of the ordinary people. He ruled over all northern and central India south from Afghanistan, and from the island of Bombay across to Bengal. It was not a neat and tidy empire, in the way of the Romans, that could be well understood by Europeans; it was, in the way of India, complicated, involved, beset with numerous differences and exceptions, and in some of its aspects beyond the understanding of Europeans of the time. But one thing was certain: it was all held together by the military might and power of Akbar, and to some extent by his understanding in ruling his polyglot and varied subjects. There were three main religions, with numerous sects: Hindu overall, Muslim in the towns, and Sikh in the Punjab (a sect which was in the process of breaking away from Hinduism). As elsewhere in the world, it was a time of religion: culture, education, and intellectual activity were centred on religion. Akbar, although of Muslim background, managed to make himself acceptable to all sections, although perhaps somewhat more through force than through the diplomatic skill which historians claim for him. India had had its firm and ruthless rulers before, but few had been as firm and ruthless as Akbar. He was something of a legend in his own time, and the legend persists: felling potential assassins with his own hand, jumping about on fighting elephants, as wise as he was tough. He was certainly deeply interested in religion, and studied every one he came across without becoming devout in any. Two Jesuit priests who had visited him in 1580 had come as near to converting him as most. His son wrote of him: 'His whole air and appearance had little of the worldly

21

being, but exhibited rather divine majesty.' By 1600 he had completed most of his conquests, and he lived at his court at Agra in great splendour. His court was, indeed, the most magnificent in the world.

Anyone who had visited Akbar's court, and several Europeans had, would have been impressed with the show of wealth and grandeur. It was partly this display which had led Europeans to associate the east with riches. It was misleading. India was a poor country, heavily taxed, and always on or over the brink of famine. Society was dominated by the hideous and sometimes terrifying system of caste, with the Emperor at the top and the 'untouchables' at the bottom. The typical community was the village, with land held in common; tax or rent was collected from it by Akbar's agent, who taxed certain areas for himself as salary. The whole system of administration was based on the collection of revenue and, where it was most easily operable, the system was harsh. Military chiefs were also administrators. It has been claimed that the lot of the Indian peasant was no worse than that of his counterpart in Europe, but famine and disease and lawlessness were all on a larger scale, year by year, than was customary in Europe.

The Empire was split between areas ruled directly by the Emperor and the associated states which recognised his supremacy. In the latter, there were princes and rulers who also lived in considerable grandeur. Little of the vast amount of wealth collected in India was put back into the country. Internal trade was limited by transport difficulties. External trade, of cotton, indigo, saltpetre, spices, was largely organised by the Portuguese who lived uneasily on the coast; gold, silver, ivory, and opium arrived on camels over the passes of the north or into Bengal and up-river from the east. The rich were fabulously rich: the rest were all poor. In 1605 Akbar died and was succeeded by his son Jahangir.

Everywhere there was fear and insecurity, dramatically illustrated by the hill-top citadels with mighty and colossal fortifications that made the castles of Europe seem puny. The most trouble to the Empire of the great Jahangir was being caused by the Afghans in the north, the Marathas in the central-west, and the stubborn kingdoms of the south which remained independent of the Mughals.

The merchants of London had no intention of sending out their own ships to Asia; it was too risky and too expensive. Each man paid in what he was willing to risk, and the total sum was used for buying four ships and filling them with cargo to sell in the east. At the end of the voyage, after the return cargo was sold, the profits, if any, would be shared out to each in proportion to the amount he had contributed, in addition to the original contribution, which was returned; it was known as 'joint stock' and was the forerunner of the modern company. The system was later changed in that the capital was not returned after each voyage. They were not princely gentlemen; they were ordinary city tradesmen and merchants prepared to take a gamble:

Nicholas Barnsley, Grocer, £150
Henry Bridgman, Leatherseller, £200
James Deane, Draper, £300
Thomas Farrington, Vintner, £200
Leonard Halliday, Alderman, £1,000
Ralph Hamer, Merchant Tailor, £200
Edmond Nicholson, Grocer, £200
Sir Stephen Seame, Lord Mayor of London, £200
Thomas Smithe, Haberdasher, £200
Sir Richard Saltonstall and his Children, £200
Richard Wiseman, Goldsmith, £200...
and nearly two hundred others.

The projected voyage was prepared in a business-like manner. Committees were selected from the subscribers to select and buy the vessels and to equip them. The largest ship, twice the size of the next biggest, was the *Red Dragon*, 600 tons, and with a crew of 200, which cost £3,700; the three other ships were the *Hector*, the *Susan*, and the *Ascension*; there was also a supply ship, to accompany the fleet, the *Guest*. During preparations, the workmen on the *Red Dragon* were allowed a barrel of beer a day to keep them out of the ale-houses. The sailors received two months' wages in advance (a mate's wage was fifty-six shillings a month). The inventories included '1 pease pot', '40 muskets', '18 swords', 'a paire of bellowes', 'a standinge bed with pillers vallens and curtaynes', '6 small baskets for bread', '8 barrells of powder', '3 old brasse ladles', '1 sheepskin', '26 sponges'...

The commander was the veteran mariner James Lancaster. He

had already sailed in the East Indies and was one of the most experienced English sailors. He was given special powers by the Queen herself to regulate and punish the 400 crew and officers, even with the right to establish martial law. 'We graciously approve and allow of the Company's choice of yee with all fitt power to rule and govern all and every subject employed.' On board each ship was a merchant, representative of the rest of the Company, to look after commercial affairs at the destination – for these city merchants were not afraid to risk life as well as capital in their patriotic and competitive quest for profits (the beds 'with pillers and curtaynes' were for them).

On a cold, murky day in January 1601 the small fleet of five vessels pulled away from Woolwich and, gathering wind in their sails, proceeded slowly down the Thames to the open sea. On each, overhead, flew the red-and-white flag of St George and England.

England was still at war with Spain and Portugal, and no landing was to be made on the Indian coast. The object of the company was to reach the islands of the East Indies, with which the Dutch had been trading on a comparatively large scale since 1595. Roughly speaking, the East Indies, or the Spice Islands, consisted of five main groups of islands between the Indian Ocean and the Philippines (which belonged to Spain): Sumatra and a few islands around it; Java and its string of islands to the east; Borneo and off-shore islands like Labuan; the Celebes Islands; and, farthest east, the Molucca Islands. The Portuguese, and now the Dutch, were interested in all these islands, and in the Malayan peninsula of the Asian continent which pointed down to meet them, the narrow waterway between the peninsula and Sumatra, the Malacca Straits (not to be confused with the Molucca Islands, fifteen hundred miles away), was the best passage from the Indian Ocean to China.

Lancaster, a bluff, hearty type of Englishman, had with him six letters from Queen Elizabeth for presentation to oriental kings; each was exactly the same, with a blank space for the name of the king to be filled in. He also carried – as well as his cargoes of iron, lead, and Norwich and Devon garments – items which it was hoped were suitable for presentation to eastern potentates.

It was 9 September before Table Bay was reached, in considerable misery. The crews were stricken with the dread disease of scurvy, brought about through the lack of fresh vegetables, a constant scourge of mariners for centuries; it induced haemorrhages from the nose, gums, and under the skin, and the teeth to drop out; the only cure was a diet of the missing foods, and this was impossible. Already The *Guest*, her crew decimated, had been abandoned. Only on the *Red Dragon* had the disease been kept away, Lancaster administering lemon juice to the crew of his flagship as a preventative. (There were at this time incidences of 'ghost' ships being found drifting in the oceans, all the crew gaving died from scurvy.) But by Madagascar even the crew of the *Red Dragon* were dying; 'the master's mate, the preacher and the surgeon with some ten other common men', were taken ashore for burial, and two men going ashore for the funeral were accidentally killed by the ceremonial salute.

Eighteen months after leaving London, the little fleet arrived at the principality of Achin in northern Sumatra, with which the Portuguese, and latterly the Dutch, had already traded. Two Dutchmen were among the first to welcome the unexpected arrival of English competitors. The local ruler was delighted. He had heard, much to the Englishmen's astonishment, of the defeat of the Armada, and was anxious to meet these representatives of a power that had defeated the allies of Portugal, the Portuguese being unpopular throughout the east. Two huge elephants were sent to the shore. On one of them was 'a small castle like a coach upon its back covered with crimson velvet. In the middle thereof was a great basin of gold and piece of silk exceedingly richly wrought to cover it'. Into this receptacle was put one of Elizabeth's letters. Lancaster mounted the other elephant. On arrival at the palace, the Company's presents, supposedly from Elizabeth, were presented to the ruler: a silver cup, a looking-glass, a sword belt, a feather fan, and other items. The chief seemed tolerably pleased. He heard Elizabeth's letter in translation (presumably via Portuguese); it explained that the English were better friends than the Portuguese, who were 'pretending themselves to be monarchs and absolute lords of all these kingdoms and provinces as their own conquest and inheritance, as appeareth by their lofty title in their writings'. The letter then asked for permission to start a warehouse and for protection for anyone left to manage it. The chief said the request would be considered; meanwhile, he granted a freedom to trade.

25

The King asked our Generall if our Queene were married, and how long she had raigned, which when the Generall had answered by his interpretor, the King wondred. The King likewise told the Generall, if the words in her Majesties letter came from the hart, he had cause to think well thereof. Dinner being ended, the King caused his Damsels to dance, and his women to play Musicke unto them, who were richly adorned with Bracelets and Jewels, and this was a great favour: for he dooth not usually let them be seene to any.

Lancaster received lavish presents from the ruler, and much-needed supplies. It was noted that envoys from other European nations in Achin were not receiving such attention. Trading, however, was another matter; it seemed the Sumatrans did not require the skilfully wrought iron, the East Anglian woollen vests, the hard-wearing Devon trousers, and the other items in the cargo; and the price they asked for pepper (in Spanish currency) was far higher than had been expected. Lancaster arrived at a solution typical of the English mariner of those times. He outwitted the local Portuguese envoy, lay in wait for a great Portuguese galleon that was expected, defeated her, and looted her cargo. She was a rich prize — one of the largest ships of the time — full of merchandise, jewels, and plate. With three of his little ships crammed full of loot, he left for Java, confident that he now had a better chance of successful trading. The fourth ship returned to London, which it reached on 8 May 1603 ('God be praised for it, and send the rest home in safety'). The Dutch were well established at Bantam, in Java; nevertheless, Lancaster made a good impression. An exchange of cargoes was made. But here Lancaster lost, through disease, his second-in-command, John Middleton, member of a family that was to play a worthy part in the early days of East India Company adventure. A certain William Starkey was left to look after the Company's interests, and the fleet set sail for home.

On the return journey, at St Helena, they met with French and Dutch vessels.

We delivered unto the Frenchmen and unto the Hollanders such victualles to relieve them as we could spare, which was six hogsheades of Porke, two hundred of Stockfish, one hogshead of Beanes, and five hundred of bread, whereof the Hollanders were in great want.

26

The *Red Dragon* lost a rudder in a tremendous storm. Lancaster ordered the remainder of the fleet to continue without him, taking a message to the Company's shareholders: 'And thus fare you well,' he wrote, 'desiring God to send us a merry meeting in this world if it be His good will and pleasure. The passage to East Indies lieth in 62½ degrees by the N.W. on the American side.' Fortunately, the storm died down, a new rudder was fixed, and the fleet arrived in the Thames on 11 September 1603, more than two and a half years after it had left on its mission. Of the 460 men who had left London, 182 had not returned.

In commercial circles in London there was some excitement. First news of the return had come from Plymouth, a horse-rider from the city being awarded £5 for bringing the message. Warehouses suitable for the cargo were quickly prepared. Six pounds were paid for pilotage, and £917 to the sovereign for customs. After these and other expenses had been accounted for, it was clear that the venture had been a success. No one had been certain that this could be, and the financial risks had been considerable for the larger investors. The fleet had brought with it 1,030,000 pounds of pepper, which was sold at a good profit.

Lancaster was a hero and was knighted. The merchants of the Company were delighted at the additions to their purses. Valuable experience of the eastern trade had been gained. The best route had been discovered, the leading market contacted and tested, and knowledge gained of the local princes and customs. Lancaster became a proprietor of the Company, and organised the next voyages. He never went overseas again, and died in 1618.

During the absence of the fleet, 'Good Queen Bess' had died after her long reign. She had been succeeded by James I, who was also King of Scotland. He was a very different man to the last of the hearty and ebullient Tudors. He was inclined to be cautious. He had been crowned only seven weeks before the return home of the East India Company fleet, but he soon showed that he was inclined to side with the critics of the Company's monopoly. He lacked Elizabeth's enthusiasm for probing the distant parts of the world. In 1604 the war with Spain ended.

The next voyage of the East India Company round the Cape was made under the command of Henry Middleton, who had been one of Lancaster's officers. With the same ships he returned to Bantam, and also visited the Molucca Islands, returning home with the loss of one ship. Once again a huge profit was made, bringing in just under 100 per cent to those who had raised the capital of £60,000. The East India Company and its adventurous voyages was the talk of the City of London. The third expedition left in March 1607, under a Captain Keeling. Of the £53,000 raised from the company members, £7,280 was spent on goods to take east, for selling and bartering, a far higher proportion than hitherto. Those incredible little ships, the *Red Dragon* and the *Hector*, which had already rounded the Cape of Good Hope four times, made up the fleet, together with the *Consent*, 105 tons. The *Consent* left a few days before the two hardy old vessels, and reached the Moluccas separately. Keeling was unable to obtain a cargo at first, owing to the competition of the Dutch, with whom Henry Middleton had also had difficulties. However, he bought a cargo of cloves, being carried in a junk for £2,948. Keeling sailed for home, and his cargo of cloves sold for £36,287. Meanwhile, the *Red Dragon* had been visiting Sumatra and Bantam, and the *Hector* had been exploring a new market for the Company. Profits from the third voyage were 234 per cent.

The East India Company had quickly established for itself an important position in English commerce. Its charter, granting an English monopoly, had been for fifteen years. But by 1609 the Company was seeking a new charter, with greater powers, although the original charter still had six years to run. In order to compete successfully with the Portuguese and Dutch, more ships were required, and more shareholders with capital were needed; the latter were increased from 218 to 276. The Crown was given the power to repeal the charter after three years' notice. By the time of the sixth voyage, the Company was able to fit out three completely new ships, at a cost of £82,000. This voyage was also under the command of Henry Middleton, now Sir Henry. His flagship was a magnificent new vessel, aptly named the *Trades' Increase*.

The *Trades' Increase* was the largest ship to be made in England up till that time, and the largest yet used for the East India run by any nation. It was 1,293 tons. The King, other members of the royal family, and many noblemen, as well as the members of the Company, attended the launching; it was a great social event. After the ship was afloat, the King and other guests were entertained to

28

a great feast on board, at the Company's expense, served on the wonderful dishes and plate which the Company had brought back from the east, which had hardly ever been seen before in England. But the English were not inspired shipbuilders of large craft, and the *Trades' Increase*, clumsy and unwieldy, was not a success. It was eventually set ablaze at Bantam.

The East India Company had a great influence on English shipping. Before the Company, nearly all English vessels were built for coastal or fishing work. The Portuguese, the Spanish, the Venetians, and the Genoese, had been the builders of ocean-going ships. Some of the few ocean-going ships owned in England had been bought by the Dutch, since the start of the Spice Islands boom. All this meant that ship prices were very high. The Company, needing more ships but unble to afford the high prices, decided to build its own. In 1607 a shipbuilding yard was leased at Deptford. The first two ships built there, the *Trades' Increase* and the *Peppercorn* went out to the east with Sir Henry Middleton in 1610. This enabled the Company to build its ships at £10 a ton instead of £45 a ton. About 500 men were soon employed in the Deptford yard, among them carpenters, painters, riggers, coopers, joiners, and the carvers who decorated the ships' hulls with their fantastic designs. During the period the Company had its own timber yards at Reading. The yard was very useful to the Company, as it also saved money on refitting and repairing ships between the gruelling voyages. At the same time, the upkeep of the yard itself was becoming increasingly demanding of the Company's financial resources. So after only twenty years it was decided to abandon it, and to hire ships, often built to the Company's specifications. During that short period of twenty years, however, some of the most impressive merchant ships in Europe had been produced at Deptford. By 1621 the East India Company still employed 2,500 seamen, although it had given up direct ownership of its 10,000 tons of shipping. Some idea of the importance of the new company can be appreciated from the fact that about one in every 2,000 of the population of England was in the Company's service at this time. The Company was often looking for marines, who had to be 'able men unmarried and approved saylors'.

By November 1621 the East India Company had exported woollen goods, iron, lead, tin, etc., to the value of £319,211. It had spent £375,288 on its cargoes in the east. These cargoes had in turn been sold in England for £2,044,600. The first twelve voyages had brought in an average profit of 138 per cent. There was, however, a very long wait for returns, as the round voyage had never been completed in a year, and sometimes took three or even four years. Shipping expenses also had to be deducted. But there was no doubt that the Company was a profitable one, although some of the members protested its profitability was exaggerated. In 1609 the Company ended the policy of financing each voyage separately; from then on the shareholders' funds were used for the general operation of the Company and profits were distributed in proportion to the capital invested.

Trade with the East Indies was not easy for apart from the distance involved, there was the bitter and intransigent competition of the Dutch. The Dutch East India Company had been founded in 1602, through an amalgamation of several smaller interests in Holland. It had begun with a capital of £540,000, compared to the £30,000 of the English Company. Up to 1610, the English company had sent 17 ships to the East Indies: the Dutch had sent out 60. The Dutch Company was a mighty military and naval organisation, and it looked upon the English company as an impertinent but potentially dangerous intruder into a trade which it considered was a monopoly belonging to itself. The Dutch established forts at all the best trading places, and attempted to dominate the local rulers in a more determined way than the Portuguese had done. Bearing in mind the importance of the two Companies in their respective home countries, the situation was potentially explosive. As the directors of the English Company said:

If the present misunderstandings between the two nations should ferment to an open war, it would be thought by the vulgar but a war for pepper which they think to be [a] slight thing, because each family spends but a little [on] it. But at the Bottom it will prove a war for the Dominion of the British as well as the Indian seas, because if ever they come to be sole masters of that Commodity, as they already are of nutmegs, mace, cloves, and cinamon, the sole profitt of that one commodity pepper being of general use, will be more to them, than all the rest and in probability sufficient to defray the constant charge of a great navy in Europe.

The fight to break the Dutch hold in the pepper trade was fierce, and in the end it was the Dutch who more or less won. But the East India Company's reading of the situation was unnecessarily pessimistic. The Dutch Company never had a secure monopoly of any product from the East Indies for any length of time. An Anglo-Dutch agreement of 1609 was meant to provide a settlement, but it decided nothing, for the Englishmen would not give up their journeyings to the Spice Islands and the two nations could not agree as to what were the Dutch spheres of interest and what were not. The Dutch Company eventually distinguished between three territorial categories: first, areas over which the Dutch Company had unchallenged control due to cession or outright conquest — i.e. fortified trading posts; second, areas where the Dutch Company had acquired exclusive trading rights from local rulers; three, free trade areas where the Dutch Company had no special privileges. Even in the second half of the seventeenth century this only provided a monopoly for the spices of the Moluccas; in other commodities — pepper, silk, coffee, tea — the Dutch Company had to face severe competition in purchase, and in sale to Europe. The Dutch Company, while instructing its servants not to use force in 'the neutral places belonging to free nations', was ready to maintain its control of the Moluccas trade by force. Its servants on the spot were even more aggressive. The founder of Batavia, Jan P. Coen, wrote in 1614: 'Your Honours should know by experience that trade in Asia must be driven and maintained under the protection and favour of Your Honours' own weapons...we cannot carry on trade without war nor war without trade.' A later governor, Antonio van Diemen, wrote, 'We are taught by daily experience that the Company's trade in Asia cannot subsist without territorial conquests.' The Company in Holland was not always backward in stating similar views, and exhorting its servants to 'ride the natives with a sharp spur'.

The London East India Company kept up its pressure in the Far East. It even associated itself with an abortive attempt to reach China by way of the North-West Passage, a route which would avoid the Dutch altogether, and which had intrigued and lured English navigators for more than a century. With the Dutch in such strength in the East Indies, the Company had begun, reluctantly, to look elsewhere. Ships had called at Persia, at Arabia, with which the Dutch were too fully occupied to develop trade, and at India.

❧

It is not too much to claim that the East India Company harnessed and organised that spirit of adventure and that firmness of purpose on which the British Empire was slowly constructed. A man like William Hawkins would have achieved little outside the framework of the Company, and Thomas Pitt, who came later, was no more than a rogue till he joined the Company.

It was in August 1608 that the first East India Company ship arrived off India, after a voyage of seventeen months. She was the Company's *Hector*. On board was the hardy, beer-swilling, jocular William Hawkins, bearer of a letter from James I to the Mughal asking for trade with India. Hawkins was no stranger to the east. He was an extraordinary character, determined, conceited, and ambitious. The Portuguese at Surat (the chief port linking Europe and India at the time) did everything they could to keep him from coming ashore, and took some of the British crew prisoner. When Hawkins protested, the Portuguese commander 'most vilely abused his Majesty, terming him king of fishermen and of an island of no importance'. Hawkins, getting ashore, tried to trade his cargo, but the local ruler accepted most of it as presents. The Mughal's viceroys, of course, were used to taking what they wished in form of payment, and enjoyed considerable autonomy. The Portuguese continued to threaten Hawkins. 'I could not peep out of doors,' he wrote, 'for fear of the Portugals, who in troops lay lurking in the by-ways to give me assault to murther me.' Leaving two men behind at Surat to attempt to improve trade, Hawkins set off with a large hired retinue for Agra, the Mughal capital.

It was two and a half months before he reached the city. Jahangir was managing to hold together the precarious links of his dominions, but by all accounts he was a cruel and unattractive ruler. The discipline and authority of his magnificent court was maintained by the lash. He was an alcoholic and a slave to opium. Hawkins, however, pleased him – although the Englishman had few presents to offer. Hawkins was able to converse directly with the Emperor in Turkish, and he rapidly became a favourite at court. The Emperor was impressed with the hard drinking of the Englishman and his robust humour. The Portuguese were alarmed. 'The Portugals were like madde dogges,' Hawkins wrote, 'labouring to work my passage out of the world.' Jahangir was so pleased with him that – according to Hawkins – he insisted on him joining his staff in a senior position (rank under the Mughals was regulated by the command of cavalry, and Hawkins was offered the command of 400 horse). Hawkins was not the man to turn this down, particularly as an enormous salary went with the position. As he explained to the Company, with commendable frankness: 'I should feather my nest and doe you service.'

Jahangir – again according to Hawkins – insisted that his new officer should take a wife; he offered him 'a white maiden out of his palace'. Hawkins, believing it would be impossible to find a Christian woman in Agra, said he could only marry a Christian. The Great Mughal promptly produced a Christian girl from Armenia. Hawkins was 'married' by his English servant Nicholas (the marriage was later legalised by a chaplain at Surat).

Jahangir proved to be fickle. Hawkins had the greatest difficulty in persuading him to come to a firm agreement with the Company. The Company, and perhaps Hawkins also, did not understand that a Mughal emperor had no time for agreements; he believed himself above such common matters, for if he should want to break such an agreement there was no reason why he should not do so; such a thing was therefore almost meaningless to him. The Emperor, for his part, had no idea of the importance that the English attached to such things. At length, Jahangir tired of Hawkins; the Englishman returned to Surat. He left on a Company ship for Bantam, but died on the journey home. He had achieved something in opening a direct dialogue between the East India Company and the Emperor.

Mrs Hawkins arrived in London, made a considerable nuisance of herself to the Company and married Gabriel Towerson, a senior servant of the Company.

After a slack period, the East India Company was apparently thriving; but it was deceptive. It employed permanent staff at Bantam and elsewhere in Sumatra and Java, and at Surat. Contact was also being made with the Celebes, the Moluccas, Siam, Persia, Japan, and soon to China. But for over fifty years the main depots, called 'factories', were still at Bantam and Surat. Between 1612 and 1616 £429,000 was raised for the Company; profits on individual cargoes were at times still exceeding 100 per cent. At candle auctions, in which bids could only be made while one wick of candle burned, lots of spices were sold at £100,000. But over longer periods the profits could be seen in a truer light; in the ten years of one stock, ending in 1642, for instance, the annual yield was only 3½ per cent; for several years in that period there were no dividends at all. Between 1621 and 1632 12½ per cent was the highest dividend paid. Considerable quantities of spices were still being imported via Holland; only in cloves and pepper was the Company having conspicuous success; for a time the Company was granted a monopoly in the sale of pepper.

The least favourable market still seemed to be India. Everywhere else the Dutch were the main difficulty; on the Indian coast, the Company had to contend with the Portuguese as well, who were desperately anxious to cling on to that part of their distintegrating empire and interests in the east. In 1612 two of the Company's ships defeated a Portuguese fleet of four galleons, the Company's commander appealing to his men as 'Englishmen famous over the world for trew valour, to put their trust in God and not fear death'. Jahangir was impressed with the victory. Command of the Arabian Sea was vital to many Indians, being the pilgrims' route to Mecca, and Indians – some through inclination, some through religion – had not the means to protect this route themselves. For long – too long, as they thought – they had relied on the whims of the Portuguese. They had already been impressed by English voyages; now the English seemed to have real sea-power. A *firman*, or edict, came to Surat from Agra. At last the Company had the piece of paper which it had sought so long. The Emperor, delighted with the rebuff to the Portuguese and impressed by the English display, had hurriedly decided to grant to the English the thing which they evidently considered most important. It was difficult for him, in Agra, to weigh the relative power and importance of European nations hovering around his coasts. In point of fact the edict gave away very little except the right to trade, which the English were already doing anyway.

Shortly afterwards, the Emperor declared war on the Portuguese. But his new allies were in no position to help him. The Company's fleet had departed for England, with the edict; only a few employees of the Company remained at Surat. At last four vessels (including the *Hector*, which had been on the Company's first voyage) arrived

34

off Surat, under the command of Nicholas Downton. To oppose them, the Portuguese assembled a fleet of six large galleons, two smaller ships, and about fifty sundry craft. On the galleons were some of the flower of the Portuguese nobility. One of the English ships was boarded, but the enemy were repulsed and lost many of their smaller craft. The Portuguese fleet withdrew. It was a significant engagement in the history of India. Portuguese power in the Arabian Sea and Indian Ocean never fully recovered.

Jahangir, however, was as fickle as ever. Another Company emissary to his court had brought with him an English mastiff as a gift. This mastiff had been pitted against a leopard, had savaged it and killed it. This had impressed the Emperor almost as much as the victories at sea. But the English were unpopular at court among the influential advisers; to them one foreigner was as suspicious as another; the English, with their incessant harping on trade, were no better than the Portuguese. Jahangir sent a son to govern Surat, where it was feared the English were becoming dominant, and he caused many difficulties.

The East India Company's directors in London now realised that their affairs in India had reached a critical state. The situation in the East Indies was deteriorating; the Dutch company there was proving too strong for them. They urged the court, with some wisdom, to send out to Agra a far superior Ambassador to the adventurers the Company had had to rely on hitherto. The man chosen was Sir Thomas Roe, himself a merchant and traveller – a grandson of a former Lord Mayor of London. He was a big man, with immaculate moustache and goatee beard. His mission was 'to reside at Agra, to prevent any plottes that may be wrought by the Jesuits'. He was to receive £700 a year, a considerable sum, together with his own chaplain and surgeon. He was empowered by James to conduct full negotiations, and was to stress with the Mughal the strength of English naval power. He was to carry a message from James seeking 'quiet Trade and Commerce without any kind of hinderance or molestation'.

Roe arrived at Surat, in great style, to a salute of forty-eight guns (from the Company's ships). Roe began as he intended to continue: with haughty pride, the representative of a nation that was the equal of the Mughal Empire. He refused to be searched on landing, and returned to his ship until the order was revoked. This caused something of a sensation among the small European community, who had suffered many indignities for years.

Roe had been carefully selected for his role. He was tall, had a commanding presence, and a loud voice; he had a strong personality and was shrewd and intelligent; he had courtliness of manner equal to that of the Portuguese nobles. When he was brought before Jahangir he was told that he must touch the ground with his head. This he declined to do, saying he had not come as a servant.

> So I passed on until I came to a place railed in right under him with an ascent of three steps where I made him reverence and he bowed his body; and so went within it. I demanded a chair, but was answered no man ever sat in that place, but I was desired as a courtesy to ease myself against a pillar covered with silver that held up his canopy. Then I moved for his favour for an English factory to be resident in the town [i.e. Agra], which he willingly granted and gave orders for the drawing up of the firman.

Roe's presents were the most magnificent that had yet been sent out by the Company. King James's message to the Emperor concluded, 'for confirmation of our good inclination and well-wishing toward You, We pray You to accept in good part the Present, which our said Ambassadour will deliver unto You. And so doe commit You to the mercifull protection of Almightie God.' The main present was a coach and four, complete with a coachman. Jahangir took great pleasure, in the succeeding months, in trying to out-countenance Roe. Roe had presented him with an original painting, claiming that such a masterpiece could only have been painted in Europe by someone trained in the European tradition. Not long afterwards the Emperor showed him six pictures on a table, all of them identical to Roe's gift. The Englishman was asked to pick the original, and was only able to do so with some difficulty. The Mughal was delighted at his indecision: 'he was very merry and joyful'. He gleefully presented Roe with one of the copies, wrapping it up in paper himself, and remarking: 'You see, we are not so unskilfull as you esteem us.'

The Emperor's fascination with Roe – he was for ever asking him how much he drank, and about his way of life – did not extend to his court. Roe's apparent arrogance, his distaste for the atrocities at Agra, and his constant harping on commerce, did not endear him to the Great Mughal's entourage. That Roe survived was a tribute to the growing reputation of England as a power as much as to his own skill. He continued to argue for a written trade treaty granting the Company virtual monopoly rights in Euro-Indian trade. Jahangir was as bored by the subject as ever. Roe became increasingly frustrated. He wrote to the Company advising against a permanent representative in Agra. 'I would sooner die than be subject to the slavery the Persian [Ambassador] is content with...A meaner agent would better effect your business.' He suggested an Indian should be appointed the Company's agent at Agra, with a subordinate at Surat.

Jahangir began to tire of the Englishman. Roe irritated him. He confiscated a fresh batch of presents without waiting for them to be presented (as, of course, he felt quite entitled to do). Roe, meanwhile, became involved in court politics in order to further the Company's cause. A musician – a cornet player – was sent out from England to amuse the Emperor, but was not entirely successful. Other employees of the Company at the Indian capital were Richard Steele, who tried to establish trade, Edward Terry, Roe's chaplain, a doctor, and William Hensell, the coachman. The Company asked Roe to extend his service by one more year, but this he refused to do, pleading ill health.

Before departure, Roe at last gained a new edict. It was more substantial than the *firman* granted after the naval defeat of the Portuguese. Its main provisions were for improving the lot of the Company's staff at the depots at Surat and Agra; for instance, they could not carry arms, build a headquarters, or settle their own disputes. Its importance was that it gave the East India Company a basis of self-government in India. Roe had established in India that the British trading ambition there was not a temporary adventure; the British were there to stay.

Roe was received at Hampton Court in private audience. The Company gave him £1,500. He lived comfortably for another quarter of a century, but never returned to the east. He was the first of a long line of Englishmen in India who combated the difficulties of the east with courage, confidence, and aplomb. But, unlike those who came much later, his interests were solely to serve the East India Company and, through it, his country; in that he was typical of the coming regime of the East India Company; the notion of service to India and the Indians was to come much later.

Although many were to follow him, few were to bring such understanding to India as Sir Thomas Roe. He told the Company:

A war and traffique are incompatible. By my consent you shall no way engage yourselves but at sea, where you are like to gayne as often as to lose. It is the beggering of the Portugall, notwithstanding his many rich residences and territoryes that hee keeps souldiers that spendes it: yet his garrisons are meane. Hee never profited by the Indyes since he defended them. Observe this well. It hath also been the errour of the Dutch, who seek plantation here by the sword...Lett this be received as a rule that if you will profitt seek it at sea and in quiett trade for...it is an errour to affect garrisons and land warrs in India.

The rivalry between Dutch and English in the 'Spice Islands' archipelago had become intense and clashes had become almost inevitable with each voyage. Nathaniel Courthope, Sir Thomas Dale, John Jourdain, all led expeditions to the East Indies and had to fight the Dutch, although the two nations were supposedly at peace. Jourdain, the Company's first President in Java, was killed in a naval battle with the Dutch in 1620. The Dutch were extremely jealous of their new acquisitions, for which they had fought bitterly with the Portuguese. Although the English ships were often able to hold their own, the Company was being defeated in its efforts to establish itself in this region — more highly prized than India — by sheer weight of numbers. The Dutch East India Company, an amalgamation of interests, was much richer and more powerful than its London counterpart. At length the Dutch settled the matter by a simple expedient; they massacred most of the Englishmen at the East India Company's main depot.

The new trade with Europe had now moved beyond Java and Sumatra to the Moluccas (now all part of Indonesia). The most important British depot in the East Indies was at Ambon, which was also the capital of Dutch interests in the Moluccas. A treaty had been signed between the Dutch and English, in 1619, on a live-and-let-live basis; the British were to be allowed one-third of the trade, and would contribute the same proportion to the cost of the forts, which were, however, to be manned by the Dutch; the treaty had solved nothing. 'Chief Factor' of the English in the area was Gabriel Towerson, who had married Hawkins's Armenian widow, and had succeeded to the post once held by William Starkey, of the Company's first voyage. He was a jolly, breezy sort of man; he disliked the Dutch.

What happened at Ambon is one of the most horrible stories of Europeans in the east. A Japanese mercenary in the Dutch garrison was suspected of spying for the English. The Dutch were extremely sensitive about their position, and deep feelings of insecurity were common to all Europeans in the east. The Japanese mercenary had been asking questions about the guard system at the Dutch fort. He insisted that his questions had only been out of curiosity, but he was put to torture and 'confessed', having 'endured pretty long', according to the official Dutch report. At first he said there was a conspiracy of the Japanese to overthrow the Dutch. But after further torture he said the English were involved. 'Extremely surprised when I heard of this conspiracy,' wrote the Dutch governor; there were very few Japanese in the area, and even less English. As one account says: 'The ever-present dread of revolt, however, lent a powerful stimulus to the official Dutch imagination.'

The Japanese soldiers were disarmed and imprisoned. There was also one Englishman in the fort, who had been arrested for arson; he was evidently the English Company's surgeon. He confessed ('After little or no torture,' according to the Dutch report), and told a detailed story of conspiracy to gain control of the fort, led by Towerson. Orders were immediately issued for the arrest of the other English in the Moluccas, seventeen in all, all in the Company's service. The Dutch authorities then began the methodical torture of the group, each unfortunate victim being subjected to water ordeal and burning until he confessed. This lasted for several days, some of the men continuing to protest their innocence, 'with deep oaths and protestations', between bouts of torture. Towerson himself does not seem to have been put to the ordeal, but the 'confessions' of others were enough to condemn him.

The Dutch later admitted torture had been used, but denied its extent. It should be remembered that torture was customary at that time, the curious notion being that it was the one certain way of extracting the truth. Guido Fawkes had been tortured in London only a few years before. On the Company's own ships, forty strokes of the lash were not unusual.

Only two of the prisoners were reprieved. The remainder were assembled in the courtyard for execution. One of them drew from a pocket a piece of paper, which he read; it was a prayer and a final declaration of innocence. Finished, he threw the paper to the ground, where it was retrieved by an official. The executioner began the beheadings. 'And so, one by one, with great cheerfulness, they suffered the fatal stroke.'

When news of the executions reached England, the country was outraged. For several months the affair was discussed with fury, in London and other cities, and at court. A deep sense of indignation against the Dutch remained for years. The King was shocked, but did little. The Company demanded 'real restitution for damages, justice upon those who had in so great fury and tyranny tortured and slain the English, and security for the future'. The dispute became bogged down in diplomatic exchanges.

Whatever their justification, the executions had achieved what the Dutch had wished for so long – the virtual elimination of the English from the Moluccas; but it is most unlikely that this was the calculated intention of the executions. The executions, and the Company's lobbying, were among the pressures that finally led to an inevitable Anglo-Dutch war; for the Dutch and English were rivals around the globe, having clashed in the Americas as well as in the east.* In that war, the Dutch secured the Cape of Good Hope, so strategically placed on the route to India and the east; they were to hold it for nearly a hundred and fifty years. The English were successful in the war, but the English company never recovered in the East Indies from the Ambon massacre. For a few years the 'factory' at Bantam lingered on; it finally closed in 1667, after a second Dutch War (it was this war which resulted in the exchange of New Amsterdam, renamed New York, for Surinam).†

In India, meanwhile, the Dutch and English had worked together a little better. For a while they had been allies against the Portuguese: the English warring at sea and the Dutch on land. In the Arabian Gulf, the East India Company strengthened its interests by means of a treaty with Persia, a naval victory, and the capture of the

* Anglo-Dutch War, 1652–4.
† Anglo-Dutch War, 1665–7.

40

important Portuguese bastion of Hormuz after a ten-weeks' siege. But soon the Dutch and English were at loggerheads in India, full of suspicions and accusations. In mid-century, the Dutch took Ceylon from the Portuguese by force.

The East India Company's wide interests stretched — by the standards of those days — over enormous distances, and financially it was often in extreme difficulty. The expense of its operations was frequently greater than its income, and it was often in debt. But a new generation of directors was as ambitious as the founders. They persisted in increasing the operations, except in the East Indies.

In 1640 Francis Day, one of the Company's representatives in Southern India, in the lands independent of the Mughal, obtained from a local sovereign a grant of land on the east coast. Upon this, the Company built the trading post of Fort St George — around the walls of which grew an increasing settlement — to become one day the great city of Madras. It was the first land to be held by the British in India. By 1670 the post had developed to about 300 English, with some 3,000 Portuguese living under their protection. It was mostly famous for its laxity of morals. The Company's chaplain wrote to the directors on 31 January 1676:

I have the charity to believe that most of you have so much zeal for God, and for the credit of religion, that your heads would be fountains of water, and eyes rivers of tears, did you really know how much God is dishonoured, his name blasphemed, religion reproached amongst the Gentiles, by the vicious lives of many of your servants...I do earnestly wish there may be more inspection taken what persons you send over into these places; for there come hither some thousand murderers, some men stealers, some popish, some come over under the notion of single persons and unmarried, who yet have their wives in England, and here have lived in adultery; and some on the other hand have come over as married [couples] of whom there are strange suspicions they were never married... Others pride themselves in making others drink till they be insensible, and then strip them naked and in that posture cause them to be carried through the streets to their dwelling place. Some of them, with other persons whom they invited, once went abroad to a garden not far off, and there continued a whole day and night drinking most excessively, and in so much that one of the number died within a very few days after.

The Company was not finding it easy to recruit staff, and it had to take what it could get. Prospects were not good, mortality from sickness high, and the Company forbade private trading by its employees. In 1665 two factions at Fort St George fought each other in rebellion, and the Company was obliged to send out a fleet and troops to settle the matter. Rough as Fort St George was, its foundation was a most important step in the history of British rule in India. At last the officials of the East India Company were able to barter, trade, and negotiate with Indian rulers from an independent base of their own. And the place was not without its humanitarian outlook; although slavery was countenanced, the slave trade, which was abolished there in 1683, was not. In 1653 it was made a 'presidency', and five years later was given authority over the Company's posts on the Coromandel coast and in Bengal.

The Company's territory was increased by the acquisition, in 1667, of the island of Bombay, which Charles II had received six years earlier as part of his dowry on marrying the Infanta of Portugal. Charles, like most of his contemporaries, had not previously heard of the place, but he was a good friend to the Company and he gave it the island for a loan of £50,000 at 6 per cent, charging a rent of £10 per annum (which the Company paid till 1730). The Portuguese had held it for nearly a hundred and thirty years, and the Company was quick to appreciate its importance.

Bombay and Surat were in the west. Fort St George was in the south. The Company was also showing interest in eastern India — the populous, dank, sweltering, tempting lands of Bengal. This was not surprising. The main trade-routes of India, from the north, east, and central districts, had always been down the mighty Ganges and its tributaries. A constant traffic followed the river's course, with many trading places on its banks, eventually concentrating at the many small ports where the river debouched into the ocean in a complicated maze of numerous channels. Such trade and commerce as existed in the interior of India relied to a great extent on the Ganges. At the delta of the river, where it met the Brahmaputra, was Bengal, nominally in the Mughal Empire.

From 1633 the Company had attempted to institute trade with this area, but without success. After concessions from the Emperor, the Company set up a 'factory' at Hooghly. Cromwell, and Charles II, showed interest in the Company and its affairs, and the war with the Dutch had improved the English position in Bengal; but difficulties with local rulers brought confusion and sometimes despair; the Bengal traders and the Company's merchants were not attuned to the practices of each other, and thus there was an almost continuous failure in communication and trust. The East India Company had been empowered to raise its own military forces — a fateful decision in Indian history — and a more aggressive policy in Bengal was decided upon. In 1686 an expedition was sent to Bengal; the reason was officially to exact satisfaction for alleged wrongs by the Mughal and his subordinate rulers.* This enterprise was left to a singularly ruthless individual, Job Charnock, who became a legend in Anglo-Indian history. He had with him over 300 men, formed in companies on the model of the royal army, and also Portuguese mercenaries and Rajputs. The Mughal's forces, over 12,000 strong, slowly assembled to meet the English. The years of wearisome talk and argument and misunderstanding were over. The years of the sword were beginning.

The Nabob of Dacca, the supreme Mughal authority in Bengal, was incensed at the insolence and perfidy of the foreigners in challenging the Emperor. The Indian forces had some success in brief skirmishes, and their artillery bombarded the British forts; the English evacuated Hooghly. Charnock, having decided on an unlikely village called Kalikata as his chief post in the area, much against the Company's wishes, was recalled. A general evacuation from Bengal was undertaken. To the west, the Mughal had seized Surat.

Then a most unexpected thing happened. The Mughal emperor, Aurangzib (Jahangir's grandson), offered peace. It was an extra-ordinary act of goodwill because the English appeared to have lost much of the influence they had been so slowly accumulating for half a century and more; but Aurangzib was concerned about the pilgrim route across the Arabian Sea, which the English had kept fairly peaceful with their command of the seas. The Nabob of Dacca was told to re-admit the English to Bengal. The terms were very humiliating for the Company, but soon Charnock was back, establishing a fort at Kalikata. The climate was dreadfully un-healthy, the place was surrounded by jungle and swamp; the Eng-lishmen died off like flies. But Fort William, at Calcutta, was

* Anglo-Mughal War, 1685–8.

to become the headquarters of the Company's third presidency, and eventually to take precedence over the other two and to become the capital of India. (The third presidency was officially established by the East India Company in 1699, six years after Charnock's death.) Charnock ruled, with the Brahmin widow he had rescued from the funeral pyre, like a Raja, and a fairly refractory Raja at that. He died in Calcutta, but his descendants played a prominent part in city life for many years to come; an elaborate mausoleum was erected over his tomb; the city he had founded from a collection of huts at the water's edge grew to be a vast metropolis of some 3,500,000 people; for many years it was to be second only to London in the British Empire.

At this time important changes were made in the structure of the Company. The English headquarters in the west were moved down the coast from Surat to Bombay; a few years later the Bombay presidency became the seat of administration for all British forts and depots in India. In 1685 Sir John Child, a prominent member of the Company, became the first 'Captain-General and Admiral' for India – a post which developed into the 'Governor-General' of later years. He had considerable powers, which negated the previous necessity for frequent but slow correspondence with London. The Company was empowered to coin its own money in India. All this without any reference to the Great Mughal whatever. Most important of all, in 1689 the East India Company issued a formal declaration of intent in India. It declared that the Company 'must make us a nation in India. Without that we are but a great number of interlopers, united by His Majesty's royal charter, fit only to trade where nobody of power thinks it their interest to prevent us.' It was a significant declaration, for it revised the aims of the founders, which had been purely commercial: it foreshadowed the era, not of merchants but of administrators. But the purpose of the whole operation was still trade, and trade alone.

❧

From time to time during the seventeenth century the Company's charter was renewed, notably under Cromwell in 1657.* This was not accomplished without a great deal of opposition. Throughout the century the Company's activities were the subject of controversy and were the centre of economic debate in England. In only two

* Cromwell's grandson, John Russell, became Governor of Fort William in 1711.

44

years between 1601 and 1640 did it export goods to a value greater than its payments abroad. The basic weakness of the Company was that the peoples of tropical and semi-tropical areas did not require English products, in particular they did not require wool; what had been founded as an export-import company was therefore always exposed to the vagaries of the market at home. In the first twenty-three years of its operation the Company exported £753,336 of bullion to the east. The merchants of India, China, and Japan were, to a man, more interested in English gold and silver than they were in woollen garments. In the later years of the century the situation was aggravated by the Company's policy of actually importing manufactures from India, the unprocessed products of which were not so easily importable to Europe as the spices of the East Indies had been. Even as early as 1621 it was recognised that over 50 per cent of exports *ad valorem* from India would have to be silks and cotton cloth; the 26 per cent hoped for from pepper was not achieved. By 1675, the Company's imports had risen to £860,000.

In 1628 the Company had presented a 'Petition and Remonstrance' to the House of Commons, a remarkably early discourse in the science of economics:

Some men have alleadged that those countries which permit money to be carried out, doe it, because they have few or no wares to trade withall: but we have great store of commodities, and therefore their action ought not to be our example.

To this the answer is briefly: That if we have such a quantity of wares, as doth fully provide us of all things needfull from beyond the seas, why should wee then doubt that our monies sent out in trade must not necessarily come back againe in Treasure, together with the great gaines which it may procure in such manner as is before set down? And on the other side if those Nations which send out their monies, do it because they have few wares of their owne, how come they then to have so much Treasure as we ever see in those places, which suffer it freely to be exported at all times and by whom so ever? We answer *even by trading with their monies*. For by what other meanes can they get it, having no mines of gold or silver?

Thus may we plainely see, that when this waighty businesse is duely considered in its end (as all our humaine actions ought well to be weighed) it is found much contrarie to that which most men esteeme thereof, because they search no further than the beginning of this work, which misinformes their judgements and leades them into errorr. For if wee only behold the actions of the husbandman in the seede time, when he casteth away much good corne into the ground, we will rather account him a madd man than a husbandman: but when we consider his labours in the harvest, which is the end of the endeavours, we finde the worth and plentifull increase of his actions.

But by the end of the century, the harvest still had not come. And Indian manufactures were entering Britain. Henry Martyn,* in his *Considerations Upon the East-India Trade*, complained:

There is no reason, that the Indians will take off any of our manufacturers, as long as there is such a difference in the price of English and Indian labour, as long as the labour or manufacture of the East Indies shall be valued there at but one-sixth part of the price of like labour or manufacture here in England...Therefore, unless now and then for curiosities, English manufactures will seldom go to India. Without the help of laws, we shall have little reason to expect any other returns for our bullion, than only manufactures, for these will be most profitable; for the freight of unwrought things from India is equal to the freight of so much manufacture; the freight of a pound of cotton is equal to so much callico, the freight of raw silk to that of wrought silk; but the Labour by which this cotton or raw silk is to be wrought in England is a great deal dearer than the Labour by which the same would be wrought in India. Therefore of all things which can be imported thence, manufactures are bought cheapest; they will be most demanded here, the chief returns will be of these, little then will be returned from India besides manufactures. And when these shall be imported here they will be likely to stay; in France, Venice, and other countries, Indian manufactures are prohibited, the great consumption must be in England. It has been proved by arguments that bullion and chiefly bullion is carried into India, that chiefly manufactures must be returned, and that these must be consumed in England. But instead of all other arguments, is matter of fact: cargos of bullion are every year carried into India, while almost every one at home is seen in Indian manufactures...The next

* Not to be confused with an East India Company chaplain of the same name who, in the early nineteenth century, translated the New Testament into Hindi and the Prayer Book into Hindustani.

complaint against this trade is of the Labourer: that he is driven from his employment to beg his bread; by the permission of Indian manufactures to come to England, English manufactures must be lost.

Fortunately for the Company, it did not trade only with India. With remarkable persistence, and despite many set-backs, it had been trying to trade with Japan, China, Siam, and Formosa – the four great nations of the Far East. It was partly forced to this by the Dutch domination of the Spice Islands (East Indies). The Portuguese had already reached Japan, and had run a depot on the China coast, at Macao, since 1557. In Japan, they had spent much effort in attempts to convert the population to Christianity, not without some initial success. The arrival of Spanish missionaries, however, and fierce rivalry between Portuguese and Spanish priests, had brought about an unholy situation. The English, spearheaded by a remarkable adventurer, Will Adams, were less devout and at first were welcomed; they were intrigued to find that their doubtful reputation had preceded them. An early English master reported: 'Our English nation hath long been known by report among them, but much scandalled by the Portugals Jesuites as Pyrats and Rovers upon the seas...[tales of which] they terrifie and skare their children.' The Dutch, however, had narrowly got there before the English, as at so many other places in the east. Dutch competition was ruthless. The Japanese, accustomed to fine and beautifully coloured silks, were not impressed with the coarse and dull English woollens. The English factory on Hirado Island was abandoned in 1623.

In China, also, the main problem was that the Chinese were not overwhelmed with the desire to purchase merchandise sent out from London. Queen Elizabeth had twice sent letters to the Emperor of China, but neither had reached him. For many years the urge to contact China was behind the quest for a North-West Passage, a challenge which obsessed English mariners for centuries. (Not surprisingly, for it was estimated that of the first 3,000 Englishmen to round the Cape, 2,000 never returned.) Many merchants connected with this quest were also members of the East India Company. Failing to discover this route, a number of voyages rounded the Cape for China, both privately backed and by the East

India Company. The Chinese authorities, however, were more than reluctant to have anything to do with Europeans. The Dutch overcame this problem by pirating their junks, and the masters of Company vessels asked the directors to permit the same, but this the Company declined to do. Factories were established at Amoy, Tonkin, and in Formosa, but none of them came to much. The Portuguese, with their well-established base at Macao, were nearly as formidable rivals in China as the Dutch had been in Japan. It was not until the sixteen-nineties that East India Company trade with China became really established; some lead and woollen goods were sold, and tea, spices, and silk bought; unfortunately the Chinese demanded at least two-thirds payment in silver. The first highly profitable voyage from China was in 1700. The Company began importing the new beverage of ch'a, or tea, from China, which had first been sold at a London coffee-house in 1657. The Company also began to export opium to China from India.

The second half of the seventeenth century was a time of consolidation for the East India Company, as well as the search for new markets in the Far East. Cromwell had set the Company up again, after its associations with royalty had nearly ruined it during the early days of his rule, and the Restoration of 1660 saw the start of prosperity for it. From 1657 to 1663 it was allowed to use the British stations in West Africa as calling places. James II, like Charles II, was the Company's friend. During the last years of the century, the Company's annual dividend averaged 25 per cent. This, coupled to the fact that the trade was financed by the export of bullion rather than of goods, did not make many friends for the 500 shareholders of the Company. There was jealousy, as well as economic doubts.

One obstacle to the Company was the activity of 'interlopers', following the example of Sir William Courteen (who eventually gained a licence), thirty years before. Many of these men based themselves on the American colonies and engaged in smuggling and in piracy. The East India Company was unable to check the bargain sale of merchandise from the east in New England, much of it commandeered from their own ships. This was the start of a long history of bad relations between the East India Company and North America. The one bright spot was the career of Elihu Yale, a second-generation American, who joined the Company's service, became Governor of Madras, and made a fortune through private trade. He was the benefactor of the university named after him.

Even more serious was the establishment, in 1698, of a rival English company; the two Companies were forced to outbid each other in the east, and prices rose to such an extent that for a time the London market was almost stagnant. This new company had come about with the fall of James II and the Stuarts in 1688. The East India Company had always fostered close links with the Stuarts, and that hard Dutchman, William of Orange, was quite glad to grant a new Whiggish company the right to trade with India and the east (especially when it promised to raise a £2,000,000 loan for the Government) – and so was Parliament, which had long been nagging about the Company's monopoly and trade – as had the ports of Bristol, Liverpool, and Hull, outraged by their exclusion from the trade. 'The old East India Company,' said Samuel Pepys, 'lost their business against a new company by ten votes in parliament, so many of their friends being absent going to see a tiger baited by dogs.' The new company was called the English East India Company (as distinct from the London East India Company). After only four years of competition, which proved ruinous to both, it was decided that monopoly was better after all; this took some time to undertake, but amalgamation was completed in 1709 – in the form of the United East India Company.* In almost every way this was merely the original company; the new company had never established a wide network of posts and administration, or employed a considerable body of employees scattered about a large part of the world.

The Company's headquarters in London graduated from three rooms at the residence of its first Governor, Sir Thomas Smyth, to the more spacious Crosby House, belonging to a later Governor, until finally it got its own offices, custom built in Leadenhall Street in 1648. A home for old sailors and a chapel, which survived until 1866, were beside the Company's former docks at Blackwall; but control of the East India docks and dockyard, still to be used by the Company's ships for generations, was in the hands of a

* The full title of the Company was 'The United Company of Merchants of England Trading to the East Indies'; this it remained until the Act of 1833, abolishing its trading function, renamed it the East India Company, which it had always been known as, anyway.

succession of separate companies. Apart from the organisation of voyages in what was becoming to be considered one of the finest fleets in the world, administering pay and minor appointments, and merchandising returning cargoes, one of the main tasks of the London staff was constant litigation against employees, particularly in India, who had been engaged in private trading – something against which the Company was adamant but about which it could do little.

Another bane of the Company was the activity of the merchant interlopers. It was exceedingly difficult to deal with these men, as the only remedy was long and wearisome litigation, into which the Company was reluctant to enter. The Court Minutes of the Company had referred to the interlopers as early as 22 February 1615 – 'to examine all suspected personnes that intend interlopinge into the East Indies'. Sometimes the Company received little or no support at home in maintaining its position, but in 1685 the Company mounted 48 prosecutions for interloping. In 1701, the notorious Captain Kidd was executed for piracy in the Indian Ocean. Even with illegal perquisites, life abroad in the Company's service was seldom a happy one, which no doubt accounted for the heavy incidence of alcoholism and opium-taking. One early employee complained:

> At home men are famous for doing nothing; here they are infamous for their honest endeavours. At home is respect and reward; abroad disrespect and heartbreaking. At home is augmentation of wages; abroad no more than the third of wages. At home is content; abroad nothing so much as grief, cares and displeasure. At home is safety; abroad no security. At home is liberty; abroad the best is bondage.

The various 'factories' differed in size from a complement of less than a dozen to one or two of fifty or more staff. The men lived in rooms over a hall beneath; not till near the end of the century were women allowed, and then employees rented or bought houses in the town. Many of the factories were proud of their gardens, on which much trouble was spent by the more sober inmates, and the garden at the Company's house at Surat was considered to be a considerable achievement. Five-year contracts of employment gave way to longer engagements, anticipating a lifetime's career in the service of the East India Company. The hierarchy was –

Apprentice (until 1694)*
Writer
Factor
Junior Merchant
Senior Merchant (or Chief Agent)
Councillor
President and Governor
There were also Chaplains, Surgeons and Masters.

Life in the factory building was continued as much as possible in the traditions of home. Members sat at table in strict precedence, toasts were drunk to the Crown, the Company, and to wives at home. The main meal was midday, especially on Sundays. Brandy and wine were drunk to excess. English dress, heavy, tight-fitting, and utterly unsuited to the climate, was almost invariably worn.

The most conspicuous member of the Company's staff in India at this time, the late seventeenth century, was Thomas Pitt. He started his career in the east as an 'interloper', with some success, and to the fury of the Company, so jealous of its monopoly. Despite attempts to seize him, peremptory warnings and legal action, Pitt obtained trading privileges from local rulers. Returning to England, he was arrested and fined £1,000, which he could well afford (it was later reduced to £400). After a brief career as a Member of Parliament, he returned to India to replenish his fortune. The Company wisely decided to engage him on its staff rather than have him as a rival, and he became Governor of Fort St George in 1697. The incipient Madras, already described, was a place well suited to his tastes, and he made a popular Governor. For thirteen years he supervised the rapid growth of the place. He treated Indians with some disdain, and insisted that Englishmen be treated with, at the least, respect. 'Those within our reach I keep in pretty good order by now and then giving them a pretty good banging.' For years Englishmen had felt themselves humiliated and scorned in India by numerous petty restrictions, and by laws and customs they did not understand or care about. Thomas Pitt was the first of many senior administrators of the Company who believed he had the right answer. Like so many of his successors, however, he could not resist the temptations of the country, even when in the Company's

---

* Many of them, by special arrangement, from Christ's Hospital School, which almost alone among leading schools provided a commercial education.

service. He added to his personal wealth with singular concentration. On the famous Pitt Diamond, which later became one of the French Royal jewels, he made a profit of over £100,000 – a quite staggering fortune at the time. He was not without his good qualities, and under him British influence on the east coast of India suffered none of the periodic setbacks it had known hitherto.

By 1700 the English in India had taken the place of the Portuguese. The East India Company, beset with difficulties in its East Indies, Persian, and even China trade, was to make India the centre of its operations. It had, it seemed, no serious rivals among Europeans in trading with the vast, populous and ostensibly rich subcontinent. In 1707 Aurangzib died; he proved to be the last of the great emperors, for within months of his death the Mughal Empire, so delicately held together, began to disintegrate. Chief among the claimants and trouble-makers were the Marathas and the Sikhs. But something even more immediately important for the English had happened. The *Compagnie des Indes Orientales* had been founded in 1664. The French had been late on the scene. There was not much yet to indicate that they would be even more dangerous rivals than the Dutch had been.

2 THE CARNATIC

The United East India Company found itself trading with a sub-continent more turbulent and lawless than at any time since the first voyage. Under Aurangzib, the position of Hindus had deteriorated as compared to that of Muslims. The most formidable enemies of the Mugahl Empire were the Hindu Marathas. Originating in the hinterland behind Bombay, they roamed over the country in sprawling armies. In a fashion not uncommon in Asian history, they sought power through military pressure from one place to another rather than in permanent territorial acquisition; the Mughals themselves came under their sway.

For a century the British had traded as peaceably as they could. They had built up Bombay and Madras, and now also Calcutta was growing. Although not always heard by their employees in the field, the directors of the Company had endeavoured to keep on the best of terms with the local populations. 'Righteousness is at the root of our prosperity,' they claimed. They insisted:

> Let your ears be open to complaints, and let no voice of oppression be heard in your streets. Take care that neither the broker, nor those under him, nor your own servants, use their patron's authority to hurt and injure the people. Go into different quarters of the town and do and see justice done without charge or delay to all the inhabitants. This is the best method to enlarge our towns and increase our revenues.

Rivalry with the French had been keen, but when the two countries had been at war, as they had during the reigns of William III and Anne, hostilities had not extended to India; the French Company had not been able to afford them: the English in India had been more hostile towards their Dutch allies than towards their French enemies.* With the death of Aurangzib, conditions for trading became increasingly difficult. Rival factions and rulers fought for control of the Mugahl provinces. There was an obvious opportunity for the European powers to better their positions in India if a man prepared to act should appear on the scene. Such a man arrived in India in 1722 – Joseph François Dupleix, the greatest enemy the East India Company ever had.

The scene of the forthcoming drama in India, when the fate of India was to be decided for two centuries, was the Carnatic. This was the hinterland of the eastern, or Coromandel, coast. Its main towns were Trichinopoly and Arcot. Farther inland was the state of Mysore: to the north, the state of Hyderabad. On the coast itself there were three important trading posts, fortified and surrounded by their native towns: Madras (Fort St George), Fort St David, both British, and between them Pondicherry, the chief French town in India. The territory of the Europeans reached for only a few miles around their forts.

A career in India was not considered a highly prized ambition among European youth. The conditions were arduous in the extreme, the death-rate from disease acceptable only to the most adventurous gamblers or to those who had little choice in the matter. It was common practice to send unsatisfactory young men, who showed no signs of bettering themselves at home, to India. It was thought that the greater the scoundrel, the more likelihood there was of his returning with a fortune; on the other hand, if, after a few years, he joined the ever-growing cemeteries around the European stations, then the loss would not be great. Such a young man was Joseph Dupleix. Like many other frustrated youths, he was to find in India a challenge that would spur him to greatness.

By 1731 he had become the Governor of Chandernagore, which was not far from Calcutta and was the rival French establishment to the British in Bengal. Twice a year ships arrived, after the long voyage from France, with money to pay for the return cargo that had been collected. This did not demand a great deal of work and

* Anglo-French Wars, 1688–97, 1702–13.

there was little to do except engage in private trading – in which the staff of the French Company were allowed to engage provided they did not trade with Europe or China. Dupleix, however, was a man of considerable energy and even greater ambition. He threw himself into his work to such effect that he soon increased the trade at Chandernagore several-fold, and also began to accrue a personal fortune. He re-established two 'factories' elsewhere that had been abandoned through loss of trade. Although he worked hard enough in the tropical climate to be considered an eccentric by his more enervated Gallic colleagues, he found no satisfaction apart from financial. He detested India, loathed his fellow-officials, feared the terrible death-rate of Europeans in Bengal. After ten years the French company's trading at Chandernagore, under Dupleix, more than trebled. The rival East India Company did not know such prosperity, and its senior officials began to look upon the Frenchman with awe. He did not return to France on leave. He outlived many of his English, French, and Dutch fellow-traders in the fly-ridden little trading posts at the estuary of the Ganges, nearly a year's journey away from home. After twenty years in India, the formidable Dupleix was given command of Pondicherry.

Pondicherry, nearly a hundred miles down the coast from Madras had been French since 1683, apart from a short period of conquest by the Dutch. It had been heavily fortified, and enjoyed a busy commerce. Its hinterland had recently been threatened by a Maratha horde that had overrun much of the Carnatic. The Marathas had captured the Carnatic capital of Arcot.

Dupleix arrived at Pondicherry in January 1742. He was determined to restore order to the area and to increase commerce, for he had lost most of his fortune before leaving Chandernagore. His health was not good and he had even thought of resigning. But there was talk of war between Britain and France, and the opportunities in the Carnatic that would result from such a war were not lost on him.

There had been war in Europe between Britain and France since 1740, but it was not formally declared until 1744.* News of the declaration of war did not reach India till the following year. Thus began the long series of incidents between British and French in India that lasted nearly seventy years; an era of bitter and

* War of the Austrian Succession, 1740–8.

sometimes fierce rivalry, punctuated with periods of uneasy peace. As far as India was concerned, the final result was likely to be determined sooner rather than later. The French realised this more clearly than the representatives of the East India Company; neither power was in India in any force; the arrival of a ship with a few reinforcements was likely to sway the issue for many months; the locally raised Indian troops could not be expected to feel much loyalty to either side. First to hear of the declaration was the French island of Mauritius, in the Indian Ocean. The French governor there was Admiral La Bourdonnais, who made preparations to launch an expedition against Madras.

The directors of the French company had written to Dupleix urging him to avoid hostilities with the British in India. The French company was nearly bankrupt. The King of France was reluctant to send troops to India, being fully occupied in Europe and North America. Dupleix dutifully proposed to the English officials at Madras, Calcutta, and Bombay that there should be no hostilities east of the Cape of Good Hope. To Dupleix's satisfaction, the proposal was rejected. Only six weeks after the declaration of war, a squadron of four English men-of-war left the English Channel for India; these were Admiralty, not Company, ships. This fleet captured four French ships, an act which is supposed to have incurred Dupleix's wrath. He saw in this act the opportunity to disobey his superiors and attack the British. He accepted the assistance that had been offered by La Bourdonnais. The Nawab of the Carnatic was persuaded to join the French cause.

Madras was by now the richest and most populous town on the eastern coast. It had a population, with surrounding encampments and townships, of nearly 250,000. It was not well-protected, the East India Company having been as parsimonious as usual, and the Company had only about 200 hurriedly raised troops there, ten of them officers (two of whom were foreigners); officers in the new East India Company forces at this time were invariably drunks or felons who did not dare show their faces at home. There was also a force of ill-disciplined sepoys. Against this, the French were able to raise 1,000 Europeans. After a few hours' bombardment, Madras surrendered unconditionally, to La Bourdonnais. It was not a glorious moment in British history, and figures but little in British history books.

56

Dupleix had wanted the town to be spared on the payment of a large sum of Indian currency, the restitution of the captured French vessels, and a promise of no hostilities east of the Cape for the remainder of the war. Relations between Dupleix and La Bourdonnais were already bad: now they blazed into a furious row about what to do with Madras. La Bourdonnais even considered bombarding Pondicherry; his prime motivation at Madras seems to have been to increase his personal treasury. Eventually La Bourdonnais collected an enormous ransom, returned to Mauritius, was replaced, went back to France, and was thrown into the Bastille for three years, dying soon after his release.

Dupleix was left in supreme command of the French in India. He ordered the destruction of the East India Company fortifications at Madras and imprisoned the English garrison. He then set about the destruction of Fort St David, about fifteen miles south of Pondicherry. Among the garrison at Fort St David was a young officer, Robert Clive, only in his early twenties, but destined to be one of the two greatest and most famous names in the story of the East India Company.

⌦⌦

Clive was born into an impoverished family of squires in Shropshire, the kind of background from which many of England's greatest sons have come. As a child and youth he had been a good deal worse than the mere 'mischievous' assigned to him in so many accounts; he had terrified local shopkeepers and had organised a local 'protection' racket. At length he was sent to the Merchant Taylors' school in London, where he did not distinguish himself. India was the obvious place for such a rascal, and his father sent him off there, at the age of eighteen, as a writer in the service of the Company.

There is no doubt that there was a quality to Clive that distinguished him from the other ruffians, misfits, and adventurers who found themselves in the Company's service at that time. His employers considered him a model youth, industrious and sober: his colleagues considered him a riotous companion. He had an air about him, and he had the luck, perspicacity, or persistence to catch the eye of important superiors. He found the life of a writer deadly dull. Counting bales and adding up invoices were not his idea of a grand life, and the salary of £5 per annum was hardly enough to encourage him. He was depressed by the climate and the monotony; he was homesick. Twice he tried to shoot himself, but was less efficient in doing so than he evidently was in his work. He was impressed by these failures to kill himself and, on finding that there was nothing wrong with the pistol, he concluded that he was marked out for special things; with this in mind, he returned to his efforts to advance himself.

During the war with France, Clive had transferred to the military branch of the Company's service – an inevitable move for a young man of Clive's type and attitude. He was in the garrison of Fort St David, as an ensign (the junior rank among officers). The fort was vitally important to the Company, being its last foothold on the Coromandel coast, so far the most profitable area for trade in India. Fort St David was in a critical position because the Nawab, after hovering between British and French, had now gone over again to Dupleix.

The court of directors was well aware of the pressing need for troops in the Carnatic, and its letters at this time are full of references to its efforts to raise troops, not only at home but in Europe, especially Switzerland, and the difficulty it had in doing so. Some reinforcements did arrive from home, and also money, which was quite as important. Perhaps most important of all was the arrival of Major Stringer Lawrence to take up the command of the Company's troops at Fort St David. Six months later, a fleet under Admiral Edward Boscawen arrived to blockade and destroy Pondicherry. With Boscawen came a force of royal troops to help the Company's inadequate and frail forces.* With humble apologies to Lawrence, the directors explained that Boscawen would be commander-in-chief of all forces, land and sea, royal and Company, in deference to the Crown. The blockade and siege of Pondicherry was soon abandoned, due to Boscawen's incompetence and the determination of Dupleix, not to say of Madame Dupleix; Dupleix's wife was by all accounts a remarkable person, and the normally formidable Dupleix was said to be but putty in her hands.

Two months after the raising of the siege, the War of the

* These were the first troops of the British Army to serve in India. Arrived Fort St David 29.7.1748. The Company had raised a force in Madras in 1686, but the E.I.C. armies date from 1662 (Bombay), 1746 (Madras), and 1754 (Bengal).

Austrian Succession came to an end. Dupleix had become a Director of the French company, and received high honours. The treaty ending the war provided for the restoration of conquests; St Louis, in America, was therefore restored to the French, much to the fury of the New Englanders, and Madras became British once again. The Indians who had heard of all these doings, ostensibly on behalf of some distant throne thousands of miles away in Europe, may well have done so in some bewilderment. The situation seemed to be back much as it had been before; but really it was very different – for British and French had fought each other in India.

⚬⚬⚬⚬⚬

One vital factor demonstrated by the war was the ineffectiveness of native Indian forces against Europeans. Dupleix and the British had ignored the protestations of the Nawab of the Carnatic and had marched about over his territory. The Governor of Fort St David was soon to write to the directors, of India and the Indians: ''tis certain any European nation resolved to war on them with a tolerable force may overrun the whole country.' The vast, exciting, populous sub-continent lay ready for rape. The Mughal authority had completely collapsed in the area in which the French and British were rivals, and the name of the Emperor was used freely to justify any activity whatever. Neither the French nor the British could ignore this situation, although the directors in London did their best to do so. Owing to the slowness of communication with London, the local authorities had much freedom in practice. The English at Madras, pressed by Boscawen, agreed to back a contender for the kingship of Tanjore in the South Carnatic. As a result of fighting to this end, the East India Company received the grant of a tract of land at Devicotah, on the coast. It was their first act of territorial conquest in India, and it was due to the military capabilities of Major Stringer Lawrence. Lawrence was a 'stout hale man of fifty' who had been sent out by the British Government during the war with France to command the Company's troops, at the by no means inconsiderable salary of £820 per annum. He had moulded together the previously independent companies of infantry into battalions as in the British Army. He was not a man of great intelligence or perception, but he was a sound, sturdy soldier who understood conditions in India and acted according to common

59

sense more than to any shafts of brilliance. Accordingly he met with some success. It has often been said that Stringer Lawrence was the 'founder of the Indian Army', and for once what has been said often is perfectly true.*

The business of enthroning and supporting puppet kingdoms continued. Dupleix, with the help of his wife and a brother-in-law, expanded the French holding around Pondicherry and got the French into a predominant position on the Carnatic. The main conflict was over the throne of the Carnatic; after the War of the Austrian Succession, in India it was the War of the Carnatic Succession; the British candidate held the fortress city of Trichino-poly, around which there was periodic fighting for many years. The French and British kept up an awkward pretence of neutrality. Lawrence wrote:

> A messenger came to me from Mr d'Auteuil [Dupleix's brother-in-law] to acquaint me 'That although we were engaged in different causes, yet it was not his design nor inclination that any European blood should be spilt: but as he did not know our post, should any of his shot come that way, and hurt the English, he could not be blamed.' I sent him for answer, 'that I had the honour of carrying the English colours on my flag gun, which if he pleased to look out for, he might know from thence where the English were posted'; and I assured him I should also be very loth to spill European blood; but, if any shot came that way, he might be assured I would return them.

Dupleix's contenders proved more formidable than the English contender, and at length one was declared Nizam of the Deccan and another Nawab of the Carnatic – a combined area from near Trichinopoly in the south to Hyderabad in the north, which was, in fact, virtually all Southern India. The British candidate had nothing but his fortress at Trichinopoly, to which he promptly retreated. The French received considerable grants of land on the coast, to say nothing of an immense quantity of loot, mostly in the form of jewels. Dupleix was at the height of his power. His influence spread over all of Southern India, which that of the

---

* He became, in effect, the first commander-in-chief, India, when a letter from the court of directors, 23.3.1757, gave him authority to appoint the commander-in-chief for Fort William, in addition to his own responsibilities in the Carnatic.

Mughals had never done. The ruler of the Carnatic was his puppet. The French company seemed to have won complete domination of trade with India. The opportunities of extending French influence northwards and gaining all India for France were obvious. Dupleix adopted the dress of an Indian prince — 'cet appareil comique', as a colleague put it. In Hyderabad, the Frenchman Charles Bussy ruled indirectly over millions.

But the French company in Paris, determinedly modest in ambition, was having none of these grand schemes. And, in the end, neither were the British in India, still confined to Madras and Fort St David in the south. Lawrence, disgusted with British inactivity and official Company meddling in matters of military discipline, resigned and went home. His able young lieutenant, Robert Clive, returned to the wearisome chores of civilian life. In Madras, officers were so discontented that several had to be dismissed. It seemed that the East India Company had little or no future in India.

The British were roused to action by the sight of French flags planted round the boundary of Fort St David. The Governor at Fort St David was Thomas Saunders, a 'cold, austere and silent man'. Little known to history, Saunders was one of the most formidable Englishmen yet to have arrived in India. The authorities in India decided to make one last bid to improve their position, although England and France were at peace in Europe. Trichinopoly was besieged by Dupleix's allies. If it could be relieved, and the Nawab's forces defeated, French power and influence would suffer an immense blow in prestige — and prestige was nearly everything. Clive, back in the Company's army, suggested an attack on the important and prestigious Arcot, capital of Dupleix's puppet Nawab of the Carnatic, in order to draw off the besiegers of Trichinopoly.* It was an extremely bold plan. Considering the hesitancy and indecision of the past, it seemed unlikely that it would be accepted. But Clive's magnetic personality and his confidence evidently swayed the Governor, who remembered Stringer Lawrence's high opinion of Clive. The plan was accepted. It was seen to be the last throw. Every available man was supplied for Clive's column.

* Modern historians usually give credit for the idea to Clive, but there is some evidence that he knew nothing of it until the decision had been made.

The expedition marched out of Madras on 26 August 1751. Clive, an inexperienced young captain of twenty-five, commanded 200 English and 300 sepoys, with eight officers, half of whom were clerks who, fired by Clive's example, had joined the military arm. He had three pieces of artillery. Marching through severe tropical storms and drenching rain, the column was less than ten miles from Arcot, which was garrisoned by about 1,100 men, in five days. Hearing of the unexpected arrival of a British force, the enemy hastily departed without offering opposition.

The British were naturally delighted with this easy success. For the British to be occupying the French-puppet-Nawab's capital was the most humiliating set-back to French prestige since the Anglo-French conflict in India had started. Worse was to come.

Clive found the fort in a bad state of repair. He did not know what to do, and at one time seems to have considered retiring to Madras. He thought of scattering his force about several forts in the neighbourhood. Saunders wrote to him: 'Let me advise you not to grasp at too many things at once...Would it not be better to keep your force entire?' A member of the Council felt obliged to urge Clive:

> In regard to what you write the Governor of making Trimidi your sanctuary in case of an attack, instead of Arcot, though he had not mentioned it to you, I believe he thinks if the latter is tenable you should by no means quit...There is another thing that (Tho' I don't mind money myself) your expedition will make you a much better figure in history if it pays itself than otherwise. Take care of that and collect some of the rents before you return, for the Company's expenses are very great.

Saunders reinforced this advice two weeks later: 'The possession of Arcot is deemed of the utmost consequence.' Luckily for him, Clive stayed. If he had withdrawn to Madras, he might never have been heard of to history. Saunders and the Council at Fort St David pushed Clive into his destiny.

Clive may not have had much military knowledge, but he did have leadership and personality. Even his lack of military expertise had its advantages, for he decided on a night attack on the enemy encamped near the town. A night attack was considered the most difficult of all military operations, and few professional commanders would have risked one with inexperienced officers and troops. Clive risked it. He enjoyed another amazing success, routing the enemy without the loss of a single man.

The plan was beginning to work. Indian reinforcements from Trichinopoly were soon on the way. Altogether some 4,000 men were sent north for the recapture of the Nawab's capital, under the command of the Nawab's son.. Several thousand joined it on the way. Dupleix sent a force of 150 Frenchmen from Pondicherry. Clive's 500 men, now with five guns, prepared for siege in the fort.

Clive had several advantages. His two successes without loss of life were seen by the sepoys and local inhabitants not as luck but as the work of a brilliant and inspired soldier. The sepoys were therefore faithful to him. Clive, speaking hardly any of the native dialects, had gained a remarkable hold over his Indians. The days dragged on. The defenders fell ill with disease and malnutrition. The water supply was cut. Ammunition was running short. The diet was mainly grain and, although there was plenty of it, it was not suitable as a staple and unvaried diet for Europeans; they grew listless and sick.

The situation was saved by a Maratha band of 6,000 men, which had been plundering and fighting its way around Southern India. For no particular reason except apparent admiration for Clive's stand, they decided to come to the aid of the British. Hearing that the dreaded Marathas were riding for Arcot, the Nawab's son tried to persuade Clive to surrender — persuasion, as was the custom, being mainly through attempted bribery. Clive staunchly rejected all attempts to weaken him, and a large-scale offensive against the fort was launched. The Nawab's army was some 10,000 men.

Clive's force was now reduced to less than 350 men, all of them weak. Only about 80 of the English were fit for duty. They watched from the battlements and walls as the battering elephants lumbered towards the gates. They fired, apparently hopelessly, at the elephants, partly protected by iron armour. Even where the elephants were hit, the musket balls did not penetrate the elephants' thick hide. They did, however, sting and irritate them. The elephants panicked, rushing back over hundreds of tightly packed and screaming Indian troops, trampling many of them to death. Without the elephants, attempts to scale the walls, using ladders, were unsuccessful. Many hundreds of Indians had been killed by the quick-firing British infantry and the stampeding elephants. Clive had lost about half a dozen men. The siege had lasted fifty days.

The Nawab's son withdrew his army, and the Nawab himself was caught by the Marathas and executed. Some 600 French sepoys deserted to Clive. Mysore offered its support to the British. Stringer Lawrence returned as Commander-in-Chief.* With a force of 1,500, he marched to Trichinopoly and forced the combined Indian–French force to surrender; meanwhile, Clive defeated d'Auteuil. Trichinopoly was relieved. The British contender, who had waited so long, and apparently with only the slenderest chance of success, was proclaimed Nawab of the Carnatic. Dupleix, fuming at Pondicherry, had in only a few weeks seen all his dreams of fabulous power and wealth for France, for himself and for Madam, dashed to the ground. The East India Company, from being the holder of a mere couple of forts on the Coromandel coast, had become one of the most powerful forces in Southern India. The French company had lost nearly all it had gained. And the man responsible for it all seemed to be a young captain in his mid-twenties of whom previously no one had ever heard.

Nothing mattered more in India than prestige. And Clive had gained tremendous prestige. His exploits at Arcot spread for hundreds of miles. He became a legendary figure. He was, it was said, invincible in war; for people who were unwarlike, and most of the population were, it was a reputation which brought respect and not a little fear. Saunders told Clive that the local native writers were ensuring that 'you will be delivered down to future ages'.

The East India Company was begun on its long and painful journey into the interior of India.

⚬⚬⚬

The remaining fighting was inevitable, but superfluous. At first Dupleix seemed to have some success in recovering his position. He reacted with desperation. He had lost none of his diplomatic skill, if everything else. He detached Mysore and the Marathas

---

* Lawrence left India in 1759, a poor man unique among his contemporaries. Clive kept him till his own death in 1774; Lawrence died a few weeks later. There is a memorial to him in Westminster Abbey: 'For discipline established, fortresses protected, settlements extended, French and Indian defeated, and peace restored in the Carnatic.'

from their embrace with the British. He threatened Fort St David from the land. His forces captured 200 Swiss mercenaries travelling by sea from Madras to Fort St David. The British were appalled by this furious reaction of Dupleix. The two countries were meant to be at peace. The only excuse for their fighting hitherto had been their alliances with Indian princes; there was no legality for direct offensives against each other's holdings on the coast. Lawrence defeated the French force investing Fort St David after a fierce battle. Hostilities moved to Trichinopoly, the return of which Dupleix believed would solve all his problems. The armies of the two companies had discarded all pretences and were openly at war with each other in India, unbeknown to either government at home or to either company. When they heard of it, the two companies were so startled that they exchanged copies of their correspondence with India.

Pressure against Dupleix grew quickly in France when the state of Southern India was realised in Europe. Dupleix put forward a plan by which the French company could get rich independent of trade — by taxes in its territories. The idea did not appeal to the directors in Paris, who were already alarmed at their Governor's ambitious policies in India. Rumours of fantastic riches which Dupleix was said to have accumulated circulated in France. His independence of action was seen to be arrogant rather than, in the conditions and the difficulties of communication, inevitable. He was accused of accepting enormous bribes for himself and his wife. His despatches were said to be written in a disrespectful tone. They were charges which were all to be settled on Dupleix's British successors.

Not entirely undue to Dupleix's excesses, the French company was virtually insolvent. A replacement arrived at Pondicherry on 1 August 1754 with powers to arrest Dupleix if necessary. He immediately contacted Madras, stating his desire to establish peace between the two companies, and as a gesture of goodwill he sent back the Swiss prisoners. A truce was established. It began:

The two companies, English and French, shall renounce for ever all [Indian] government and dignity, and shall never interfere in any difference that may arise between the princes of the country.

Dupleix was at first well received in France, and he actually looked forward to returning to India. His return to his homeland, in 1754, was only the second time he had been out of Pondicherry in the twelve years since he had arrived there. He insisted that he had spent his private fortune furthering French interests; a lot of his wealth had gone back in the same way he had received it. He vainly tried to get some money back from the French company, and his remaining days were largely spent in litigation. His income from India was cut off, and he was hounded by creditors. He continually protested his poverty. When his wife died, he married again, but to a lady of no fortune. He died on 11 November 1763. Four years later there was a sale of his effects for the benefit of his creditors: included were a large and glittering collection of diamonds, rubies, emeralds, gold chains, pearls, and many articles set with precious stones. All his creditors were satisfied.

3 PRELUDE TO CONQUEST

While this struggle for prestige had been taking place in the Carnatic, far up the coast, in the Ganges basin of Bengal, the situation had been relatively calm. This had been due to an able Nawab, Alivardi Khan. He had withstood Maratha raids, and he still pretended some allegiance to the Mughal. He had tolerated the European companies rather than encouraged them, but trade had been increasing; cotton, silk, sugar, and saltpetre (for gunpowder) were exported. The chief French port was still Chandernagore. The East India Company was now well established at Calcutta, one of the most thriving and quickly growing trade centres in India. Outside the walls of Fort William, at Calcutta, on the banks of the Hooghly, over fifty buildings had been erected, including houses for Europeans, a church, jail, court, and warehouses. Over 100,000 Indians had settled around the European town in search of money, occupations, and security. The Fort was considered the finest European building in India.

In 1756, two years after the departure of Dupleix, there were two events which were to upset this delicate situation. The French and British returned to war; rivalry in North America had been even more intense than in India, and the two countries were on opposite sides in the struggle for power in Europe centred round Frederick the Great.* News of the war, however, did not reach India until the end of the year. By that time Bengal was

* Anglo-French War, 1756–63.

already the scene of disaster for the East India Company. In the spring, Alivardi Khan had died. He was succeeded by his grand-nephew, Siraj-ad-daula, a headstrong youth in his teens whose claim to power was anything but secure. He saw the Europeans, whose presence had seemed to cause so much unsettlement in the Carnatic, as threats to the peace of Bengal, which was essential for him in order to consolidate his power. At the same time, the French and British, aware that the Anglo-French peace might not last long, were looking to their fortifications. The British in particular were alarmed at the exposed position of the European town around Fort William. When the Nawab heard of these war-like activities, he demanded that they should cease. The French sent a mollifying reply. The British, fearing to lose face, resisted the demand – without, in the event, actually doing much to improve their fortifications. This lack of diplomacy precipitated a crisis. Siraj-ad-daula was thoroughly alarmed about British intentions (which, in fact, were nothing more than to trade). He gathered a large army and descended on Calcutta from his capital at Murshidabad, a hundred and sixty miles away.*

The Nawab's army arrived at Calcutta in June and promptly put the place to siege. Despite the fact that he had some 50,000 men and the British garrison was only 520, the British were not unduly alarmed. In the first place, the Bengal army was not expected to be particularly bellicose or efficient in leadership. Secondly, the broad Hooghly offered a life-line to safety; there were several Company ships at Calcutta, and the British had command of the river. The Governor was Roger Drake, a man of thirty-four, who enjoyed his position with some relish, but had done little to show that he deserved it (his promotion to Acting Governor and then Governor, at a young age, had been largely due to the heavy death-rate among his superiors and colleagues, to which the cemetery outside the fort bore eloquent witness). Siraj-ad-daula always insisted that his quarrel was against Drake rather than with the Company. The commander of the garrison was Captain George Minchin, who sweated out the days in his tight-fitting red tunic and dreamed of home. Drake and Minchin were neither intelligent nor industrious; many of their senior colleagues were similarly uninspiring; at home, few of them would have held comparable employment. The most

* Anglo-Bengal War, 1756–7.

competent of the Company's servants at Calcutta was John Zephaniah Holwell, the chief magistrate, whose reforms and heavy hand on abuses and frauds had increased the Company's income considerably; a serious man of forty-five, he had been trained as a doctor at Guy's Hospital, in London, before becoming a lawyer. He was a more temperate official than was usually found in the Company's service at the time, and was considered something of a sober-sides.

Minchin and Drake decided to try to hold some of the outlying buildings in a perimeter around the fort. The fighting was unexpectedly fierce. Hundreds of Indians fell before the British muskets. Much of the town was soon ablaze. Suddenly Madras seemed a long, long way off — as, indeed, it was. The vast horde closed inexorably in. With the loss of Calcutta, one of the three most important posts of the East India Company, the years of patient work in Bengal would be lost.

What followed was one of the most ghastly and terrible episodes in Anglo-Indian history. An episode usually written of as one of Indian atrocities, but which was a time, in some respects, of British shame, too. The quality of calmness in desperate situations, for which the British were becoming noted, was not to be conspicuous.

On the night of 18 June and in the early hours of 19 June, the situation had deteriorated sufficiently to call for the evacuation of the European women and children to the ships. It was almost the only decision Drake made, and that not without difficulty. About thirty children were safely taken out on small boats to the waiting ships. There were screams and tears when the coloured sixteen-year-old wife of a British sailor, Mary Carey, was not allowed to embark. Despite her protestations, and among scenes on her behalf by English women, she was returned to the shore. Colour-consciousness was evident in the Company's posts, although it did vary between the regimes of different Governors (some of whom married Indians themselves). It was partly a matter of sheer preservation, for a handful of English were scattered round the edges of a vastly populous sub-continent the inhabitants of which outnumbered them by almost millions to one; it was partly due to their insistence on retaining their own customs and way of life in a strange land. Some Company employees studied local history and other matters and became among the earliest European experts on Indian affairs,

TURKISH EMPIRE

PERSIA

Basra

Bushire
Gombroon
Ormuz

Kabul

MOGUL
EMPIRE   Agra

Surat

Bombay
English 1662

Calicut

Goa

Hooghly 1650

Balasore
1633

Masulipatam

Pulicat
Madras 1639
Pondicherry (French 1683)

Ceylon
Trincomali (1683)

Dutch conquest 1638-58

BURMA

SIAM

Penang

Achin

Sumatra

CHINA

Peking

Canton

Macao 1557

Manila

Philippine
Islands
(Spanish)

Formosa

_English factory abandoned
1623; trade thereafter in
Dutch hands_

JAPAN

Hirado

NEW
GUINEA

Ternate Moluccas

Amboyna
Pulo
Run 1616

Timor

Malacca
(Dutch, 1641)

Singapore

Borneo

Batavia

Java

Bantam 1596

NEW HOLLAND

_(Coast visited but interior
unexplored; no trade)_

Mocha

Aden

Mombasa 1505
Zanzibar 1508

Mozambique 1508

Delagoa Bay

Cape Town
1652

INDIAN OCEAN

Mauritius 1598

Assada

Madagascar

St. Augustine's Bay 1645-6
(Courteen's Coy)

Showing the principal depots of the English E.I.C. Dutch and Portuguese and respected Indian sensibilities; others — and they were in the majority — took little or no interest.

The two officers, one of them Charles Manningham, sent to supervise the evacuation of the women and children, had sent them to the *Dodaldy*, a ship in which they happened to be partners. They insisted on remaining on board, despite an instruction from Drake to return, saying that they could not leave the women and children unprotected. It was this act, whether cowardly or not, that began the thoughts of escape and the panic that was to come. In the council chamber of the fort, Drake, Minchin, and senior civilians argued for hours about what was to be done. Drake had almost collapsed, and seemed to have no will. There was no leadership. On the 18th fighting continued. The ships waited a safe distance from the bank. There was little food to be had, not so much because of shortage but because there were no cooks or cooking implements in the fort. A young Writer recorded the scene of disorganisation and chaos:

> It is almost impossible to conceive the confusion there was in the Fort, there being at least 2,000 [Indian] women and children, nor was there any method to prevent them coming in as the military and militia declared they would not fight unless their families were admitted...The enemy began now to fire very warmly upon the Fort from all quarters. Our garrison began to murmur for want of provisions...The whole garrison was quite fatigued, having been under arms a great part of the preceding night. Many of the military and militia having got at liquor began to be very mutinous and under no command, having drawn bayonets on several of their officers.

There seems to have been no effort to restore the morale of the men or to control the growing number of refugees, some of whom came in tatters and others in luxury, with servants and private stocks of food; the presence of these latter, mostly rich merchants, made the atmosphere even more tense.

Deliberations continued in the council chamber. How long would the powder last? Should they evacuate immediately? Should they not take off the Company's treasure first? Everyone 'was at liberty to give his opinion'. A direct hit from an enemy cannon ended the discussions for a few hours, the ball crashing into the chamber. According to one who was present, the meeting ended in 'the utmost clamour, confusion, tumult and perplexity'.

71

By the following morning, 19 June, Drake still had not decided what to do. 'In a dreadful situation,' he wrote. With bitter fighting all around, the Governor went down to the underground passages beneath the fort. Despite this abdication of leadership, and with half the European town crackling with flames and thudding with falling timber, the garrison, depleted, hungry, and frightened, fought desperately. Wounded were carried in to the hospital, where they lay on the floor in pools of blood, vomit, and excrement, groaning for help and tormented by the swarms of flies. The sound of gunfire was drowned by the screams of those being tended by the single surgeon, who was busy amputating throughout the day.

Drake was discovered sitting on a chest in an underground passage. He was told that the supply of dry powder had run out. Appalled, he rushed upstairs. Nothing he did allayed the rumour of the end of the powder; it spread through the refugees in minutes. Hordes of tearful Indian women and children rushed towards the shore. In the stampede, two sentries were trampled to death. There was complete panic. Craft of all kinds, dangerously overloaded, moved uneasily away from the blazing town. Europeans jostled among them. Leaning over the parapet of the fort, Drake and Holwell saw the almost unbelievable sight of Captain Minchin, the military commander, struggling aboard a boat. Then they saw other officers fleeing as well.

Drake rushed out, through a gate of the fort, and down to the river bank. Soldiers and civilians watched to see if he could get to Minchin in time to stop him and end the panic. They saw the Governor, gesticulating and apparently arguing with an officer beside a small boat. To the amazement of those watching, Drake waded into the water, clambered on to the boat, and was rowed out towards the *Dodaldy*. He did not once look back at Fort William, the walls of which grew steadily farther from him.

Only the sturdiest, and those still fighting unawares on the perimeter, now resisted the panic. Europeans and refugees fought for the last remaining craft as an armada set out for the *Dodaldy*. But that ship was already crowded to an almost impossible degree and its master, a tough and unemotional mariner named Young, was worried about its safety. Soon after Drake climbed aboard, the *Dodaldy* began to move slowly downstream.

About 170 of the garrison remained. With hardly any powder

left, and morale as low as it could be, their position seemed hopeless. Most of the Europeans crowded into the Council Chamber, where men in bloody bandages and battle-torn clothes argued feverishly, while a clerk, in the best tradition of the East India Company, carefully wrote down the minutes as best he could. Although Holwell was not the senior official, he was made emergency commander, apparently by pressure from the disillusioned military.* Although stern, self-righteous, and unpopular, they saw in him a leader, and they were right. Holwell immediately gave a number of orders, solved the food problem by commandeering utensils and supplies from wealthy refugees, and offered hope. Another Company vessel, the *Prince George*, was standing near by, only a mile and a half away. Holwell sent off a messenger telling the vessel to come close up to the fort after dark to take off the remaining Europeans. And, with a good understanding of the psychology of the average Company employee, he ordered some of the Company treasure to be shared out among the men and ordered officers to give liquor to the men. He also reorganised the remaining powder supplies to enable resistance for a few more hours.

Later in the day, the *Prince George* appeared in the river. The message had reached her safely. It was a wonderful moment for the watching survivors, who had believed themselves doomed. But the trials of the wretched garrison were not over. As they watched, the ship seemed to shudder and then come to a standstill. She had struck a sandbank and had run aground. The news utterly desolated the garrison. The master of the *Prince George* begged the *Dodaldy* for assistance, but Captain Young refused to give it, fearing that he might further endanger his human cargo. He held firm despite entreaties from the wives and officers on board his ship.

The *Prince George* could be clearly seen from Fort William as it was set ablaze by Indian fire arrows and as it disintegrated. The fate of the garrison seemed settled. They must fight to the death or surrender to the unknown mercies of the Bengal army, which had proved such an unexpectedly fierce enemy. Holwell called yet another meeting of all available Europeans. He urged the garrison to hold out till dawn, when he would open negotiations.

Next morning, the masts of the Company's ships were still

* The members senior to him who survived signed an affidavit after the war declaring Holwell had taken command with their assent.

visible. Although they all had guns and could have come nearer to the fort in safety, none of them moved in to help. Young convinced himself that Calcutta had already fallen. Almost incredibly, the garrison was left to its fate. Appalled by the sight of the masts which would not move to his aid, Holwell began to try to make contact with the Nawab. After furious fighting in the early morning, a truce was arranged.

During the heat of the afternoon, when most of the exhausted men were dozing or asleep, Indians began moving in among the buildings. They were joined by fifty-six Dutch mercenaries of the garrison, who had decided to change sides while there was still time. A vital gate was opened to the rushing Indians by one of the Dutchmen. The Nawab's colours were run up on the staff beside the Governor's House. Holwell protested to a Bengal officer at the breaking of the truce and tried to retain authority. It was no use. Groups of Company soldiers stood about, full of fear, as Indians tore the buttons from their jackets and the buckles from their shoes. Others plunged into the jungle (a few of whom reached safety) and some into the river.

Siraj-ad-daula himself entered Fort William, followed by a glittering procession. Holwell was brought before him. He expressed annoyance at the paucity of the Fort's treasure, at the stiffness of the fighting, and at the presence of Holwell and his men, who, he seemed to suggest, would have pleased everybody if they had joined the Governor in flight.

The prisoners were herded together while the town and fort were ransacked and the Governor's residence set ablaze. It seemed perhaps there was hope, after all. It looked as if the Nawab would withdraw, after teaching the Company a lesson. 'We even entertained hopes not only of getting our liberty, but of being suffered to re-establish our affairs and carry on our business.' Then a shot was heard. One of the Dutchmen, drunk, had fired at an Indian in a brawl.

There seems to have been some confusion about this shooting and the Nawab was advised that it was dangerous to have a body of Englishmen sitting openly in the fort, even under guard. It would be best to lock them up. The Nawab asked whether there was a prison in the fort. There was. It was a room built of solid masonry against one of the massive walls. It had been used as a temporary jail for soldiers and sailors, mostly for the common offence of drunkenness. Four, or at the most five, men had spent the night there. The real jail of Calcutta was a building outside the fort. Holwell and the others were pushed towards this room. Holwell was the first to be shoved through the door. At first all he saw was darkness. The pressure of others from behind pushed him farther inside.

The room had become known in Fort William as the Black Hole. It was about eighteen feet long and fourteen feet wide. Into this hot and stuffy little room were pushed 145 men and one woman — Mary Carey. It was 8.0 p.m. on the night of 20 June 1756.

◦≫◊≪◦

As the first prisoners stumbled inside, the darkness of the room blinded them. Then they could make out two small windows on the west wall, with iron bars across them. The dim light of these revealed a wooden platform across one side of the room, on which the drunken soldiers had slept. As the crush increased alarmingly, some men crawled into the space beneath this platform under the impression that they would find there more space. By the time the prisoners were all inside and the door was slammed shut and bolted, all were standing pressed together and there was no room to move. The temperature in the almost airless room was about a hundred degrees. A terrible claustrophobic panic overcame this tightly wedged mass of exhausted and frightened humanity.

Holwell, being first in, had managed to find a place near one of the windows. He realised that the positioning of the windows meant a totally inadequate circulation of air. He clung on to one bar desperately in order not to be swept away. The light of the fires outside flared up from time to time, giving a brief glimpse of the appalling scene all around him. Panting men were struggling and clawing at each other to reach the windows. Already the weaker were being pressed to suffocation in their efforts to survive; some of these slid to the floor, where the last breaths were trampled out of them; others died standing up, the dead bodies remaining upright, so great was the crush. Close friends became enemies to death in the struggle for air. Men shouted from underneath the platform as they tried to get out; reaching for their pocket knives, they lacerated the legs closing them in, but their captors could not move themselves.

Holwell, still keeping a grip on the bar, attempted to calm the panic:

> Observing every one giving way to the violence of passions, which I foresaw must be fatal to them, I requested silence might be preserved, whilst I spoke to them, and in the most pathetic and moving terms...I begg'd and intreated, that as they had paid a ready obedience to me in the day, they would now for their own sakes and the sakes of those who were dear to them, and were interested in the preservation of their lives, regard the advice I had to give them. I assured them, the return of day would give us air and liberty; urged to them, that the only chance we had left for sustaining this misfortune, and surviving the night, was the preserving a calm mind and quiet resignation to our fate; intreating them to curb, as much as possible, every agitation of mind and body, as raving and giving a loose to their passions could answer no purpose, but that of hastening their destruction.

The authority of Holwell and the urgency of his pleading had some effect. For a period there was comparative calm; in an effort to control their feelings, men stood and gasped patiently for air, trying to ignore the groans of the dying below. It was an achievement on Holwell's part, for he himself believed that death for all was 'inevitable' before long. Then he saw an Indian guard through the window, and begged him to tell the Nawab of their plight. He offered him a reward of a thousand rupees, a considerable fortune. But the guard soon returned, saying that nothing could be done. Holwell's entreaties were so great that he agreed to go once again. When he came back, he said that nothing at all could be done without the Nawab's permission. The Nawab was asleep, and no one dared to wake him.

Conditions in the Black Hole had become appalling. Sweat poured off the men. Many tried to drink their own urine. Others vomited over their neighbours. The stench was so vile that Holwell could only turn his head into the room for a few seconds at a time. All efforts to batter and shove down the great wooden door proved unavailing. Shouts for mercy to those outside had no effect. Some of the officers tried to maintain discipline and made desperate efforts to ease the communal torture. Holwell wrote:

76

Various expedients were thought of to give more room and air. To obtain the former, it was moved to put off their clothes: this was approved as a happy motion, and in a few minutes I believe every man was stripped [except for Holwell himself and three others]. For a little time they flattered themselves with having gained a mighty advantage; every hat was put in motion to produce a circulation of air, and Mr Baillie proposed that every man should sit down on his hams: as they were truly in the situation of drowning wretches, no wonder they caught at every thing that bore a flattering appearance of saving them. This expedient was several times put in practice, and at each time many of the poor creatures whose natural strength was less than others, or had been more exhausted and could not immediately recover their legs, as others did when the word was given to RISE, fell to rise no more: for they were instantly trod to death or suffocated. When the whole body sat down, they were so closely wedged together that they were obliged to use many efforts before they could put themselves in motion to get up again. Before nine o'clock every man's thirst grew intolerable.

At last the guards outside decided to get some water into the cell. For most, this only brought further misery. Skins full of water were brought up to near the window, and hats thrust through the bars to gain some of the precious liquid. But most of it was spilt or seeped away. The few drops that reached those inside only made their cravings worse. The guards crowded round the windows to peer in, in evident fascination, as the half-crazed, unclothed Europeans fought furiously to get nearer the windows and the water. Holwell wrote:

> How shall I give you a conception of what I felt at the cries and ravings of those in the remoter parts of the prison, who could not obtain a probable hope of obtaining a drop, yet could not divert themselves of expectation, however unavailing! And others calling on me by the tender consideration of friendship and affection, and who knew they were really dear to me. Think, if possible, what my heart must have suffered at seeing their distress, without having it in my power to relieve them; for the confusion now became general and horrid.

After several hours at the window, Holwell could no longer bear the pressure and the fight to maintain his position. 'I called to them and begged, as the last instance of their regard, they would remove the pressure upon me and permit me to retire out of the window to die in quiet.' He managed to reach the platform, after he had 'travelled over the dead'. Surrounded by the dead, and the moaning dying, he lay down to die. But the urge to live returned and somehow he struggled through the throng again to the window. There he, and one of the naked officers, sucked at the moisture in his wringing-wet shirt (he had already tried to drink his own urine). Once more he returned to the platform. He lay down beside Mary Carey, whose husband had just died in her arms. Not far away were an officer and his youthful son who had died clutching each others' hands. There Holwell lost consciousness.

By the time dawn lit the windows, less than forty captives were alive. A few officers remained by the windows beseeching the guards to inform their superiors of the plight of the European prisoners. The stink of vomit, urine, excrement, corpses, and sweat was overpowering; but even that foul air was accepted with gratitude by the living. It was only when Holwell was propped up against one of the windows, apparently dead, and was recognised, that an officer was brought. Seeing the situation, he ran off immediately to Siraj-addaula. The order was given for the release of the prisoners.

The press of dead bodies was so great against the door, which opened inwards, that all the efforts of the guards could not open it. It took twenty minutes for the tottering survivors to move the corpses and for the door to be opened.

It was about 6 a.m., ten hours after their incarceration, when the surviving prisoners – among them Holwell and Mary Carey – staggered out into the bright early morning sunlight. There were twenty-three of them. One hundred and twenty-three lay dead inside.

⟨❧⟩

Holwell's sufferings were not finished. While the recovering survivors were still lying in the square, he was brought before the Nawab and asked to reveal where the Company's treasure was. Holwell had no idea. For all he knew, the deserters had taken it with them. The Nawab and his advisers thought Holwell was bluffing, and in order to make him change his mind it was suggested he should be fired out of a cannon. At length it was decided that

Holwell and three others should be taken back to Murshidabad as hostages until the East India Company's Bengal treasure-chests were delivered to the Nawab. The other survivors of the Black Hole were freed and told to leave Calcutta immediately; seventeen of them eventually reached the nearest trading station down-river. Calcutta, a smouldering ruin, was re-created as a Muslim town. The French and Dutch in Bengal, observing what had happened to the British, handed over large sums of money to the Nawab. The latter wrote off to the Emperor in Delhi telling him proudly of his success against the insolent Europeans.

After a week's imprisonment in Murshidabad, the Nawab released his British captives, apparently showing genuine pity at last. Holwell and his companions, half dead, reached the other survivors.

When the news reached Madras of the Black Hole and the loss of Calcutta, there was a deep and strong demand for revenge against Siraj-ad-daula. Holwell stirred up a considerable controversy concerning the part played by Drake and Manningham, particularly in an enormous letter to the court of directors which contained the first reference to the Black Hole: 'A night of horrors I will not attempt to describe as they bar all description.' For a time Drake was suspended, but was later reinstated.* Holwell, deciding to attempt to describe the horrors after all, wrote an account on the voyage home, and when this was published in England the indignation was intense. His little booklet, originally written as a letter, had a small circulation, but its story remained in the national memory and was taken up by grateful Victorian historians in search of the heroes of empire over a century later.† The Black Hole, apart from its immediate effects on British policy in Fort St George,

---

* An attempt was then made to transfer him to the West Coast, but he refused to go, claiming ill health would not allow him to take the journey. He died soon afterwards.

† From over-stating the incident, some contemporary historians have claimed little, if any importance, for it, and have not even accepted Holwell's account. This is going to the other extreme. The sacking of Calcutta in general, and the Black Hole in particular, was the germ which led to the conquest of Bengal. There are at least four references to it in the Bengal–East India House correspondence, and also in the correspondence of the French and Dutch Companies for the same period, and many corroborating references in private correspondence. Holwell was a man of the highest principles.

poisoned the British view of India and the Indians; and it was to live on in British history when far greater tragedies, in terms of numbers, were forgotten. Unknown to the British, it had been no one's fault in particular, and had not been calculated at all; it had been the result of carelessness, thoughtlessness, and the fear of waking the Nawab of Bengal while he slept.

At the official enquiry, only Captain Minchin, among the deserters, was dismissed. Manningham and Frankland, who had left with the women and children, were both reinstated and promoted not long afterwards, despite the efforts of survivors to bring them to justice. Holwell returned to India and became Governor of Fort William, although, in an excess of righteousness, he icily asked to stand aside in favour of Manningham, who was technically next in line.* He lived till the age of eighty-seven. The only woman in the Black Hole, Mary Carey, was the last to die; she survived into the nineteenth century.

Of the Black Hole itself, there is now no trace. Until a few years ago the General Post Office in Calcutta, built on the site of Fort William, contained a plaque marking the spot. But the memory of that night in June 1756 cannot mean much in a country where human life has for so long been so multitudinous and so difficult to preserve from the moment of birth, and the plaque is no longer there.

* Court Minutes, 22.3.1758.

4 THE CONQUEST OF BENGAL

While Calcutta had been going through its agony, Robert Clive, the greatest British hero that India had so far produced, had been basking in the admiration of London society. On his return to England, with the girl he had married only a month before leaving Madras, he had been lionised as the man who had held Arcot and finished Dupleix. The English have always loved a successfully resisted siege. The East India Company had acknowledged him as perhaps its most successful servant. They wrote of 'the great regard they had for the merit of Captain Clive, to whose courage and conduct the late turn in our affairs has been mainly due'. Clive's trip home had been well judged. He had taken a house near Westminster. He had met and become friendly with many of the great of the land. He had stood for parliament. But when the new war with France had loomed up, it had been decided to send an expedition to the Coromandel coast in order to hold the newly won British power there and in the Carnatic. Clive, aged thirty-one, had been appointed Governor of Fort St David. So that he could command both royal and Company troops, he had been commissioned as a Lieutenant-Colonel in the Army; only six years before he had been an unknown and humble employee in the Company's service.

Clive's arrival at Fort St David was at a time when news of the loss of Calcutta and of the Black Hole dominated the thoughts of all the Company's servants in India. An expedition was raised for

Bengal, and Clive was appointed Commander-in-Chief. It is clear that even at this early stage he saw a great personal opportunity. Despite all the upheavals in Southern India, the Frenchman Bussy was still virtually ruling Hyderabad; no European could but admire him, and Clive certainly did. Perhaps an Englishman could do the same in the potentially even richer area of Bengal. However, Clive's mission was clearly stated to be the recapture of Calcutta, after which he was to return to the Coromandel. He was given supreme powers, much to the horror of the court of directors when they heard of it; they told the council at Madras:

> We cannot pass over one step which hath been taken by your Select Committee which we look upon as the greatest and most unheard of Assumption of Power, a Power which they were not Invested with, which we think ourselves not even authorized to delegate to you, nor could we ever have thought of Investing any one Person with on ever so extraordinary Occasion. You'll be at no loss to determine that can be no other than that uncomptroleable One Given to Colonel Clive, who is thereby not answerable...Had we not the highest Opinion of Colonel Clive's Prudence and Moderation there would be no end to the Disagreeable Reflections we might make in so extraordinary a Precedent, a Precedent tho' he is the object of we can but highly disapprove of, lest at any future time some Favourite might start up, of Integrity and Ability much inferior to him, who might be intruded upon us, and from Private views involve the Company and a whole Settlement in Trouble and Confusion. It is on his Candour and Justice we must also rely, and not in the Prudence of the Select Committee in the Disposal of no less than four Lakh of Rupees and a great Quantity of Stores to the Gentleman only...*

The expedition left for Bengal in a fleet of twelve ships, five of them royal men-of-war under the command of Vice-Admiral Watson, an experienced and able naval commander. With Clive were nearly 1,000 European troops, mostly belonging to the Company, there having been a dispute with the senior royal officer, and 940 sepoys. The fleet sailed up the Ganges basin. Command of the sea was established; this vital fact has sometimes been overlooked. Wat-

* India Office Records: 4/4/861. The E.I.C. repeated its strictures in a further letter on 1.11.1757, and also to Fort William ('extensive and dictatorial powers') on 3.8.1757.

son's attitude was simply expressed: 'While a Frenchman remains in this kingdom, I shall never cease pursuing him.'

However, first it was necessary to restore Calcutta to the East India Company. Clive increased his force by raising locally the 1st Bengal Native Infantry. But his column was still puny compared to what he knew the Nawab could put in the field; the defeat at Calcutta had dented the confidence of Europeans against Indian forces. Clive encamped his force just outside Calcutta. He had less than 2,000 men and 7 guns. Siraj-ad-daula's army of 12,000 men and 40 guns were well placed behind a low defensive ditch, originally built by the British, around the landward side of the town; he also had 18,000 cavalry, whereas Clive had none.

Remembering his success at Arcot, Clive decided on another night attack. It was not an unqualified success. It was launched too late, at 2.0 a.m. The guides lost their way. At dawn, Clive's force stumbled about in mist. By the time he had extricated them, he had lost 57 killed and some 150 wounded, about a tenth of his entire force. Enemy losses, however, were over 1,000. The Indian line was broken and Clive marched into Fort William, more through luck than judgement. In the evening he evacuated the fort and returned to his camp outside Calcutta. Despite this curious and muddled handling of the battle by Clive, the Nawab was sufficiently impressed to call for a truce.

When negotiations began, Clive, against the advice of Watson, offered peace. Like the directors, he wanted no more fighting, and the merchants wanted only to return to Calcutta. The battle was considered a victory by the British, and revenge could be said to have been exacted. Siraj-ad-daula also wanted peace. He had troubles in his own court. He assured Watson: 'As long as I have life I shall esteem your enemies as enemies to me.' A treaty was signed on 9 February 1757. The British returned to Calcutta and were soon at work rebuilding the town and re-establishing trade. The court of directors expressed their delight at 'the most welcome and agreeable News of an Accomodation with the Nabob greatly to the Company's Advantage'. Clive told them: 'Whenever...your Affairs call upon me to act either in a Civil or Military Station, in any other part of India, I shall with equal Readiness embrace the Opportunity.'*

* This letter took almost exactly a year to reach London.

It was now time to face the French, who showed every sign of using the war in Europe as an excuse to restore their former power in the Carnatic. Clive was ordered back to Madras. He had no intention of going. He argued, not without reason, that as soon as he and his force left Bengal, Calcutta would be as liable to fall as before. He disobeyed the order.

The Nawab made despairing efforts to keep the British and French from fighting for supremacy. On 4 March 1757 he wrote to Clive:

> It has given me the utmost satisfaction that you have wisely considered and reflected upon what I wrote you and that you paid a due regard to the established customs in desisting from your design against the French. I have likewise wrote to the French and made use of all necessary means to engage them to make peace with you, which I made no doubt of their complying with. I shall send a trusty person for both your agreements, which I will preserve among my own papers.

The main French station in Bengal was still Chandernagore, where Dupleix had begun his career. Clive sent a note to the French Governor on 14 March:

> The King of Great Britain having declared war against France, I summons you in his name to surrender Chandernagore. In case of refusal, you are to answer the consequences and expect to be treated according to the usage of war...R. Clive.

Its abrupt, no-nonsense style, unusual in that age, was typical of Clive. He waited only twenty-four hours for a reply. Not getting one, he marched on the French fort and began a siege. The siege of Chandernagore would not have succeeded without the aid of Watson, who prevented all traffic to it on the river. Watson was not the sort of man to mount a long and patient siege, and nor, indeed, was Clive. After a week the fort was subjected to a heavy bombardment, which was replied to from the besieged walls. Casualties on both sides were severe. The French surrendered before Clive mounted his attack from the land side.

It was an important conquest, which has in the past been underrated. The French company was very badly affected by the loss of its most prosperous station. When the news reached London, the stock of the East India Company went up 12 per cent.

84

More important, Britain now had complete command of the Hooghly and the Ganges basin; with that command, although they hardly knew it, went the command of Bengal.

～⋙⋘～

Siraj-ad-daula had lost a possible ally. What would the British ambitions be in Bengal now that they had dealt with their most dangerous rivals? Siraj-ad-daula did little except wait, and time was one thing he had little of, for intrigue against him was growing in his own court. One of the most active conspirators was Mir Jafar, who was a general of the Nawab's army as well as being his uncle. Through the Company's agent in Murshidabad, William Watts, Clive made contact with Mir Jafar, using a Hindu merchant named Omichand, who had already played an unsavoury part in Anglo-Bengali relations at the time of the sacking of Calcutta. Letters in a code devised by Roger Drake passed between Clive and Mir Jafar, sewn into the insides of travellers' shoes. Mir Jafar promised to pay the Company a million pounds in compensation for the ransacking of Calcutta, and he would also recompense the civilian population. The vast sums of money involved proved irresistible. What he wanted in return was British support in snatching the Nawab's position; and that Clive was not in the least reluctant to do.

Just when negotiations had reached their pitch, Omichand threatened to betray Mir Jafar unless he was bought off. A large sum of money, as well as 5 per cent of Siraj-ad-daula's treasure, would have to be guaranteed him in the actual treaty between Mir Jafar and the British. Clive himself thought of a plan that would outwit the rapacious Omichand (and that would enrage many of his contemporaries when they heard of it, and horrify future historians). Two treaties would be drawn up. One, with Omichand's demands included, would be a fake. No people in the world set greater store by the honour of treaties, and the East India Company in particular was obsessed by the integrity of treaties, which were not regarded as of such importance by those who claimed the omniscience of the Mughal when it suited them. There was probably not another European in India who would have dared make the suggestion that Clive blandly put forward.

The two treaties were duly drawn up, one on red paper, one on white. The white one gave Omichand nothing: the red one was the fake. Only Watson, of those whose signatures were necessary, refused to sign the red one. Clive was not concerned: 'We will sign it for him in such manner that Omichand shall not discover it.' Roger Drake was one of those who 'swore before God' to pay Omichand.

Omichand, at Murshidabad, remained silent. The ruse had worked. Clive decided to march. It was a tremendous gamble with the lives of his men to commit himself before Mir Jafar had attempted his coup. He has been criticised for recklessness, but it must be said that if he had waited for Mir Jafar to act he might have waited for ever. Watson was doubtful: 'You cannot be too cautious to prevent a false step being taken, which might be of very fatal consequences to our affairs.' Nevertheless, he agreed to loan Clive 150 sailors for the march, and to control the river.

It was a tense time for all concerned. Could the unscrupulous Mir Jafar be trusted? Behind the British lay the shadowy form of the directors of the Company. Nothing succeeds like success, but if failure awaited Clive there could well be a personal catastrophe for him, with his disobedience and his presumption, and for all those who had gone along with him. Clive was the most calm of all. He was exactly the right man for the task.

⌒⋙⋘⌒

Leaving Calcutta almost undefended and Chandernagore with only a tiny garrison, Clive and his troops marched out of the gates of Chandernagore on 13 June. Having been reinforced from Madras and Bombay, he had with him nearly 3,000 troops, over a third of them sepoys, but among the European troops was a battalion of royal troops, the 39th Foot (Dorset Regiment). There was considerable friction between this regiment and the Company's European troops. Clive had twelve pieces of artillery, but still had no cavalry. The Nawab had some 50,000 men and a small French column which had joined with him. His artillery, officered by Europeans, mainly French, was far more formidable than that of Clive.

The two forces moved towards each other. Still there was no word from Mir Jafar. Clive hesitated. His officers begged him to attack immediately. Major Eyre Coote asked him to 'come to an immediate action; or, if that was thought entirely impracticable, that we should return to Calcutta; the consequence of which must be our own disgrace, and the inevitable destruction of the Company's affairs'. But Eyre Coote did not fully appreciate Clive's dilemma. A message came from Mir Jafar:

> As yet you are now only designing, but it is not now proper to be indolent. When you come near I shall then be able to join you...Then the battle will have no difficulty...Let me have previous notice of the time you intend to fight.

Mir Jafar seemed to trust Clive almost as little as Clive trusted him. Clive replied:

> I am determined to risk everything on your account, though you will not exert yourself...If you cannot go even this length to assist us, I call God to witness the fault is not mine, and I must desire your consent for concluding a peace with the Nawab, and what has passed between us will never be known. What can I say more than that I am as desirous of your success and welfare as my own.

Clive took up a position on the river bank at a village called Plassey (or Palasi). Facing him, behind a carefully entrenched position, was the Nawab's army. The Nawab himself, despite his overwhelming superiority, was extremely apprehensive.

On the morning of 23 June 1757 the Nawab's army moved out of its position and formed a crescent of three divisions around the British force, threatening to push it back into the river. The Nawab could trust none of his division commanders; and one of them was Mir Jafar.

Clive waited for Mir Jafar's division to rebel. He wrote to Mir Jafar: 'Whatever could be done by me, I have done; I can do no more.' For a while nothing happened. Then the Bengal artillery opened fire. A gunnery duel took place for several hours. The Nawab could afford casualties; the Company could not, and Clive was forced to retire a short distance. He decided to hold on during the day and then to employ his favourite night attack.

The clouds had been rolling up all morning. At midday it began to rain. The British troops had been trained for such an eventuality; they quickly covered their ammunition with tarpaulins. The British were able to continue their bombardment; the enemy, with wet ammunition, were not. It was a dispiriting time for the Bengal infantry, soaked and defenceless against the British guns, with their own artillery silent. The Nawab's cavalry came up for the charge. Clive's guns belched out a fierce barrage as the cavalry came on. The elephants supporting the cavalry became unruly, and the charge began to break up. Clive's experience taught him that this was the time to strike. He sent Eyre Coote and the infantry to storm the entrenchments and strong points of the Nawab's original position; they met with quick and easy success.

The Nawab called for Mir Jafar and pleaded with him for help; but Mir Jafar kept his troops disengaged and despatched a message to Clive. Siraj-ad-daula mounted a camel and, with a small party, fled the battlefield for Murshidabad. Those remnants of his army which remained loyal followed him in a rout, pursued for several miles by the British.

It was the end of the Battle of Plassey, too often claimed to be one of the turning points in Indian history. The Nawab of Bengal had lost decisively to a British force less than a tenth of the size of his own. French support had made no difference to him. The British, whether they knew it or not, were masters of Bengal – the most strategically placed province in all India, at the Ganges basin. Perhaps Plassey was a turning point, but a lot had gone before, and much was to come. Before he retired that evening, Clive sent off a crisp message to Calcutta:

> Gentlemen – This morning at one o'clock we arrived at Placis Grove and early in the morning the Nawab's whole army appeared in sight and cannonaded us for several hours, and about noon returned to a very strong camp...upon which we advanced and stormed the Nawab's camp, which we have taken with all his cannon and pursued him six miles...and shall proceed for Murshidabad tomorrow. Mir Jafar [and other conspirators] gave us no other assistance than standing neutral. They are with me with a large force...Our loss is trifling, not above twenty Europeans killed and wounded.

Next morning Mir Jafar arrived in Clive's camp, somewhat apprehensive about the reception he would receive. Observing the formalities of a guard of honour, 'he started as if he thought it was all over with him'. Clive advised him to leave for the capital immediately; he himself followed soon after.

Clive entered Murshidabad, with an escort of 500 troops, with the object of 'settling the government'. He formally enthroned Mir Jafar.

Siraj-ad-daula, in disguise, was captured and brought to Murshidabad, where he was cut to pieces and his remains paraded through the streets on an elephant. His eventful reign had lasted only fifteen months. He was twenty years old.

Mir Jafar was obliged to keep his promises. Soon hundreds of boats were travelling down-river to Calcutta, loaded with treasure. Although the Bengal treasury turned out to have nothing like as much in it as had been expected, the Company received half the compensation promised immediately, much of it in jewels and plate. This was taken to Calcutta in great style, 'drums beating and colours flying' when French and Dutch settlements were passed. Now everyone could see that the affair of the Black Hole had been settled. Clive himself was not forgotten in this distribution of wealth. As a personal gift from Mir Jafar, he received £234,000.

Clive was supremely confident. The great gamble had come off. He accepted the grovelling congratulations of Drake and others with arrogance. He claimed the victory for himself, not without justification. He wrote to his colleagues in Calcutta, referring to a letter sent before the battle: 'I can put no other construction on it than an intent to clear yourselves at my expense, had the expedition miscarried.' He was beginning to taste the limitless extents of flattery that India can offer. He was treated with the greatest subservience by princes and generals; he was suddenly tremendously rich; the Nawab of Bengal was his puppet who would do whatever Clive told him; by deeds as well as personality, he had come to dominate his colleagues in the Company's service. First Arcot, now Bengal. He was treated as an emperor, for in India a man who ruled Nawabs was an emperor.

London was far, far away — in another world, it seemed.

<hr/>

Clive had been sent to India to protect the Carnatic from the French. In the absence of him and his army, the French at first did well. A considerable expedition arrived from France, under the command of one Tom O'Lally, a Franco-Irishman otherwise known as the Comte de Lally or Baron de Tollendal. Lally had been in the French Army since the age of nineteen — he was now fifty-six — and had gained an enviable reputation as a soldier in European wars. He knew nothing of India and cared less. He did, however, detest the English, and was glad of an opportunity to fight them anywhere. He despised the Indians, who were going to have to fight for him, and he despised the French officials and officers that he found in India.

Lally galvanised the Carnatic into activity. A few days after his arrival, he put Fort St David to siege, having decimated all the French garrisons in order to put a large force of Europeans into the field. He had at his disposal French Army troops as well as troops of the French company. His most important assets were artillery and a force of French cavalry. The garrison of Fort St David had no taste for a fight with Lally and his men — 'their movements were so sudden'. What they did have a taste for was the liquor in the stores. As a contemporary account, based on an official enquiry, put it: 'They were never in a condition properly to do their duty.' After a short bombardment, the garrison of Fort St David surrendered.

It was to be Lally's only success. He made the fatal error of bringing Bussy down from Hyderabad, which he had been overseeing since sent there by Dupleix, not without remarkable benefit to his own finances. The Nizam of Hyderabad believed that French power must be waning, and sought an alliance with the British. The result of this was that about eighty miles of coast north of the Carnatic, known as the Northern Circars, were given over to the East India Company. Clive sent an expedition from Bengal to claim this territory, and the British took possession after the defeat of the French at Masulipatam.

For this, Lally could blame only his own clumsiness. At Madras, however, which he put to siege, he could blame bad luck — and British command of the sea. Just when he was preparing to storm the place, a British fleet arrived with reinforcements. He had to abandon the siege and retreat.

Eyre Coote, now a Colonel, arrived from Bengal to take command. Lally had 2,500 Europeans, 10,000 sepoys, 20 guns, 3,000 Maratha allies. Coote had 1,700 Europeans, 3,500 sepoys, 1,500 cavalry, and 15 guns. But the British had Coote, who was as headstrong, or more so, than Clive. Despite warnings from Madras, he took on Lally, who was besieging a small British force at Wandewash. Coote proved the better commander. The French force was defeated; the British buried at least 200 French after the battle, and took 240 prisoners (including Bussy). The British lost 52 Europeans. It had been a brilliantly conducted battle, a far more desperate affair than Plassey, and almost as important.

Lally withdrew to Pondicherry, where, for a change, he became himself the victim of a siege. Coote starved him out. Lally surrendered in 1761. The other, smaller, French stations had already fallen. The British insisted that the Nawab of the Carnatic, who owed them his throne, pay for the defence of Madras on the grounds that it was the home of his friends, and for the siege of Pondicherry on the grounds that it was the home of his friends' enemies. The Nawab concurred.

For two years the French flag ceased to fly in India. By the Treaty of Paris, 1763, the French forts were returned to them, some of them having been razed to the ground. But the French never recovered, and only six years later the French East India Company collapsed, although the stations remained in the possession of France. Bussy returned to France with a vast fortune. Lally, taken prisoner at Pondicherry, was shipped to England, but was allowed to go to Paris when he heard that his enemies – who included almost every Frenchman who had ever been in the Carnatic – were accusing him of treachery in coming to a private agreement with the British at the surrender of Pondicherry. Friends in London advised him not to go, but he insisted on clearing his name. He was sent to trial, found guilty, and beheaded.

❧

In a few years the East India Company had grown into a vast concern. Its trade with China, now almost all in tea, had become one of the major trades of the day, with the East India Company disputing the trade with the Portuguese, the Dutch, and with interlopers. 'Cost what it will,' instructed the directors, 'we must try to make these interlopers sick of their voyages for tea.' By imperial ruling, Canton became the main entrepôt, and there the Company maintained a small staff in its own buildings. With government backing, the Company sent Lord George Macartney, a former governor of Fort St George, to Peking in an attempt to create better conditions for increasing trade. The mission was not a success. The Company's ships, formerly almost unladen on the India to China run, had been filling up with Indian opium. From

1729 the Chinese authorities had attempted to stop the trade (and in 1797 even forbade the sale of opium), but the Company continued to smuggle in large quantities. As the years went on, the import of opium to China, and the export of tea from it, became the largest part of the Company's trade, helping to finance the increasingly costly operations in India. Ships were bringing in up to half a million pounds in weight of tea each; there was a ready market for it, despite the tremendous duty of four shillings a pound. A lot of this tea was re-exported to Europe. No help came from the Chinese emperor. A Company official who attempted to trade outside Canton was imprisoned for three years, which brought forth an outcry of public indignation in England.*

During the war with France the Company lost a station in Sumatra, where their interests now revived, and in Persia, their other field of activity. The Persian trade was beset with difficulties, not the least of which were pirates; the persistent efforts of the directors to maintain this trade, through long periods of disappointment, were quite remarkable. The Company had established a depot at Pegu, in Burma, but this was abandoned after a massacre of the staff there; the Company had been unsuccessfully trying to trade with Burma since 1647.

It was in India that the East India Company's success had been so dramatic. The Company was no longer one of simple traders. It ruled Bombay, Calcutta, and Madras, the last two of which had been considerably enlarged with surrounding territory, several lesser stations, including Surat, where it had gained 'special favour' after an expedition from Bombay, had conquered Bengal and had retained its mastery of the Carnatic. And, perhaps most important of all, it had the man who could consolidate its position as a real, if unaware, contender for the Mughal legacy itself.

---

* The essential work is 'The Chronicles of the East India Company Trading to China,' H. B. Morse (Oxford, 1926).

5 THE AGE OF CLIVE

Bengal was the most important of the Company's acquisitions in India. Madras and the Carnatic had to be restored to a profitable state. Bombay, the most unpopular station of the three Presidencies, slumbered in mercantile routine. The chairman of the Company was an Irishman, Lawrence Sulivan. In his mid-forties, he had served the Company in Bombay; he knew little, and understood less, of the complications of Bengal. He was determined to keep the Company's activities confined to trade. But after Clive's king-making in Bengal, was that any longer possible? Clive wrote to Sulivan:

> Experience, not conjecture, or the report of others, has made me well acquainted with the genius of the people and nature of the country, and I can assert with some degree of confidence that this rich and flourishing kingdom may be totally subdued by so small a force as two thousand Europeans...[the Indians] are indolent, luxurious, ignorant and cowardly beyond all conception...I am persuaded you will believe I do not want to aggrandize the Company at the expense of all equity and justice; long may the present [Nawab] enjoy the advantages gained him by our arms, if he abides strictly by his treaties. But you, Sir, who have resided so long in India, are well acquainted with the nature and dispositions of these Muslims, gratitude they have none, bare men of very narrow conceptions, and have adopted a system of politicks more peculiar to this country than any other, viz. to attempt everything by treachery

rather than force. Under these circumstances, may not so weak a prince as Mir Jafar be easily destroyed, or influenced by others to attempt to destroying us? What is it, then, can enable us to secure our present acquisitions or improve upon them but such a force as leaves nothing to the power of treachery or ingratitude?

It was talk of imperialism, and Sulivan didn't like it; the Company, he believed, was an instrument for trade, not for territorial acquisition. Nevertheless, there was relief when Clive defeated an expedition from the Dutch East Indies which had come to re-establish the Dutch position in Bengal, despite the fact that the two nations were meant to be at peace. The defeat of the Dutch at Chinsura, in 1759, marked the end of Dutch power in India. Sulivan and the other directors were more concerned with reports of mismanagement and financial chaos in the Calcutta Presidency. A strong letter was sent out complaining of 'weak management, such gross neglects of our interest, that were the facts properly established would oblige us to animadvert upon your conduct in the severest terms'. One of the main troubles was that Clive had self-admittedly made a fortune out of Bengal, and other lesser servants saw no reason why they should not follow his example; they did not see the distinction Clive made between riches gained by the sword and otherwise. Matters did not improve, and after three years Clive returned to England. One act he had done during his governorship was to send a young Company servant as his permanent representative at Mir Jafar's court: a young man named Warren Hastings. Clive was succeeded at Calcutta by Holwell, the hero of the Black Hole, and then by Henry Vansittart, member of an East India Company family.

At thirty-five, Clive was reputed to be the richest man in England. He looked after his parents, his sisters, and his old mentor Stringer Lawrence. ('It gives me great pleasure that I have an opportunity given me of showing my gratitude to the man to whom my reputation and, of course, my fortune is owing.') Clive lived in style. He bought his way into the House of Commons. He was granted a barony. All this brought him few friends. There were rumours of corruption; to be paid for putting a man on a throne was not a noble exercise in contemporary Europe among people who had never been to India. Clive made matters worse by

his haughty bearing, proud attitude, and his notably grumpy appearance.

The situation in Bengal deteriorated. Many of the Company's servants were considerably less principled than Clive. Bribery and graft were commonplace, but it must be said that many Company servants did not feel any moral obligation in Bengal, did not even realise that the British were the most powerful force in the land; they saw themselves as a handful of foreigners adopting local customs in a vast, populous land over which they had little control. They had no feelings of duty towards India or the Indians. They were men who were gambling their lives, in a deadly climate, in the expectations of quick wealth. Many died. Many returned rich. Meanwhile the East India Company, with the expense of its establishment, was not making a comparable profit for itself.

The council at Calcutta deposed Mir Jafar and replaced him by his son, Mir Kasim, who paid them handsomely for it; there seems to have been no reason for this at all except greed of the officials at Calcutta. Mir Kasim, however, disappointed the council by showing no inclination to be a puppet ruler. He was defeated by the Company's forces and driven out of Bengal altogether. In 1764 he returned, in alliance with the Nawab of Oudh and with the backing of the Mughal emperor himself. This was a direct clash between the old Mughal authority in India and the East India Company.* The directors far away in London could do nothing to stop it. The two armies met at Buxar, a place with a commanding position on the Ganges. The Company's column, heavily outnumbered but far better trained and equipped, was under the command of Major Hector Munro. After three hours, the Indian army gave way. A rout was prevented by the sacrifice of a portion of the Indian army, which remained to be slaughtered or drowned after a bridge of boats over which the main part of the Mughal army had escaped had been destroyed. Munro was infuriated at the escape, for, as he said, the value of the jewels of the two Nawabs 'I was informed amounted to between two and three millions'.

There was now no doubt in anyone's minds, not even in the directors' in London: the East India Company was supreme in Bengal and dominated the neighbouring provinces of Bihar, Orissa, and Oudh. Mir Kasim was replaced by another son of

* Anglo-Mughal War, 1764.

Mir Jafar, who lined the pockets of the gratified Calcutta officials anew. All this news took over nine months to reach England, as the ships creaked and groaned in the long haul round the Cape of Good Hope.

The Company's ships had become the most famous mercantile fleet in the world. They were known as the East India Company's, although in fact the Company merely hired them. They had all too often been hired from the directors themselves, many of whom had been shipbuilders; they formed the powerful 'shipping interest' on the board. The opportunities for corruption had not been ignored, and in 1708 directors had been prohibited from hiring ships to the Company. But the 'shipping interest' still existed. Throughout the eighteenth century there was a running battle between the shipbuilders and the East India House. East Indiamen in the eighteenth century were of about 470 tons, with 90 crew, and 30 guns.

The master, or captain, of an East Indiaman was in a much envied position, as he was allowed to engage in limited private trade. After service as a mate, with at least three voyages' experience, a man might buy a mastership for £8,000 or £10,000 from a new ship's owner. After a few voyages the captain could sell his rank and situation for a similar amount. Officers had a special uniform, and were paid, suspended, or dismissed by the Company, not by the owners. They enjoyed a high rank in society (when the Company came to have its own navy, the mercantile officers took precedence of the naval officers). One eighteenth-century master mariner, Captain Eastwick, has left a valuable record:

These vessels were expecially built for the service, and were generally run for about four voyages, when they were held to be worn out, and their places taken by others built for the purpose, About thirty ships were required for the company every year... The captain of an East Indiaman, in addition to his pay and allowances, had the right of free outward freight to the extent of fifty tons, being only debarred from exporting certain articles, such as woollens, metals, and warlike stores. On the homeward voyage he was allotted twenty tons of free freight, each of thirty-two feet; but this tonnage was bound to consist of certain scheduled goods, and duties were payable thereon to the company... the gains to a prudent commander averaged from £4,000 to £5,000 a voyage, sometimes perhaps falling as low as £2,000, but at others rising to £10,000 or £12,000. The time occupied from the period of a ship commencing receipt of her outward cargo to her being finally cleared of her homeward one was generally from fourteen to eighteen months, and three or four voyages assured any man a very handsome fortune.

Towards the end of the century the Company began again to have larger ships built, the hiring charges having become exorbitant. Thus began the line of completely new East Indiamen: the magnificent ships that were still sailing in the second half of the nineteenth century. These were more than twice the size of the old ships, about 1,200 to 1,400 tons, and were used mainly for the China trade, and for passengers. They ploughed through the oceans in leisurely fashion (often heaving to at night) with their cargoes of silks, muslins, tea, and chinaware, and ambitious young men starting their careers in the east, or families returning from home leave. It was not until the advent of the formidable 'Yankee' Clippers that the great East Indiamen began to really hustle.

~~~

The situation in London was bringing the Company into ridicule. There were so many wealthy former employees from India in society that they formed a group known as the Nabobs. At the same time the Company's fortunes languished. A new office had been built on the site of the first East India House (1648–1726); it was more impressive than the Company's balance sheet. Shareholders were nervous. News had arrived from India of the slaughter of 170 British at the depot at Patna, the capital of the state of Bihar. Once again the Company's position in Bengal seemed in danger.

It is typical throughout British history that in time of danger the British turn to the right man for the hour, despite the disfavour and unpopularity he has often experienced. The East India Company turned to Lord Clive of Plassey. Would he return to Bengal? He pondered on it for some days. He had no personal desire to go. He detested Bengal, disliked the Indians, was in poor health, and abhorred the prospect of leaving his beloved family. However, there was his reputation to think of, and Clive had always thought about his reputation a great deal. If he went, people could not claim, as they already had done, that he was incapable of disinterested service to the Company without personal gain. There

98

was also the Company's position in Bengal to be considered; Clive had created that position, and if the British were to lose their predominance there, Clive's prestige would suffer greatly. He agreed to go – providing Sulivan resigned, for he could not work under the stubborn Irishman. Clive's return was seen to be so important that Sulivan was voted out of the chairmanship. It was of great satisfaction to Clive, and this opportunity to be rid of his old enemy may well have been his major reason for going back to India.

Lord Clive embarked on 4 June 1764. His orders were to restore the position in Bengal and to restrain private trade and corruption among the Company's employees. He arrived at Calcutta exactly eleven months later. Clive's second Governorship was a tempestuous affair, during which he expended enormous energy and determination in the most difficult circumstances. A Select Committee of four was appointed to keep him under some local control, but it had little restraint over him. To the pleasure of the directors at home, he decided to limit the Company's area of influence to Bengal and the neighbouring states, Bihar and Orissa, although a march to Delhi was well within the resources of the Company and would no doubt have been successful. Oudh was returned to its Nawab. Clive restored the so-called authority of the Mughal over the Company's areas, well aware that such authority had little real meaning; but he believed it gave the Company a legitimate appearance in its rule. The Nawab of Bengal was obliged to surrender such power as he had enjoyed. Clive forced him to disband his army. By accepting the 'Daweni', or sub-rule, of these areas, at the Treaty of Allahabad, 1765, the East India Company was empowered to raise taxes there for ever: a proportion to go to the Mughal and a proportion to the administration and defence of the area. This was soon being done to such good effect that a large surplus was gained. Much of this revenue was used for the purchase of the Company's tea supplies in China. To the grudging admiration of Muslim hierarchy, the British were turning out to be the most efficient tax-gatherers India had ever had. And, in India, more than anywhere, tax collection meant power. The Calcutta counting-house paid out a total of about £1,000,000 to the Nawab of the three provinces and to the Mughal. But the annual receipts were between three and four millions. Most of the difference, in the form of silver, went to China. Clive and the Select Committee wrote to the directors:

By establishing the power of the Great Mughal, we have likewise established His rights; and his Majesty, from principles of gratitude, of equity, and of policy, has thought proper to bestow this important employment on the Company, the nature of which is, the collecting of all the revenues…By this acquisition of the Daweni your possessions and influence are rendered permanent and secure, since no future Nawab will either have power or riches sufficient to attempt your overthrow, by means either of force or corruption.

The directors were not entirely dissatisfied, but, as usual, they were alarmed at any departure from the Company's business of trading. They wrote to Clive:

We conceive the office of Daweni should be exercised only in superintending the collections, and disposal of the revenues; which, though vested in the company, should officially be executed by our Resident at the Durbar [Court]…The ordinary bounds of which control, should extend to nothing beyond the superintending the collection of the revenues.

Clive was more realistic:

We are sensible that since the acquisition of the Daweni the power formerly belonging to the Nawab of these provinces is totally, in fact, vested in the East India Company. Nothing remains to him but the name and shadow of authority.

But he was adamant that the Company rule should be indirect and, for different reasons, was not entirely opposed to Company policy. In the same letter, he wrote:

The distribution between the Company and Nawab must be carefully maintained, and every measure wherein the country government shall even seem to be concerned must be carried on in the name of the Nawab and by his authority. In short, I would expect all the Company's servants, the [tax] supervisers excepted, confined entirely to commercial matters only… Every nation trading to the East Indies has usually imported silver in return for commodities. The acquisition of the Daweni has rendered this mode of traffic no longer necessary for the English Company; our investments may be furnished; our expenses, civil and military, paid; and a large quantity of bullion be annually sent to China, though we export not a single dollar.

Clive has been remembered as a soldier, although his military feats were nothing in themselves compared to his importance in the less glorious occupation of tax-collecting. The foundations for the greatest company the world has ever known were now well laid. But Clive and the directors were convinced that the Company's interest would remain snugly in Bengal, Bihar, and Orissa, with Oudh as a buffer state isolating them from the turmoil inland.

In the second part of his assignment, Clive was less successful. He replaced many corrupt officials. He tried to put into practice the new regulations demanded by the directors. But he had two difficulties which could not be overcome. In the first place, his own reputation as a man who had made a vast fortune out of India did not make his strictures convincing – a fact which distressed him, for he always maintained his own grant from Mir Jafar had not been comparable to commercial corruption. 'Corruption, Licentiousness, and Want of Principle seem to have possessed the minds of all the Civil Servants,' he wrote; 'they have grown callous, rapacious, and luxurious beyond conception.' Secondly, the employees of the Company were not sufficiently well paid to make a career in the heat and discomfort of India attractive without the prospect of a personal fortune. But Clive did make some improvement. From his second Governorship, bribery and private trading (except in salt, which was allowed for senior staff) was recognised as illegal, whereas before it had been carried on fairly openly; from then on it became more underground. There was some unrest among employees, but Clive managed to subdue it. More serious was a mutiny among military officers, who had also enjoyed financial privileges. With great tact as well as firmness, Clive put this down.

Lord Clive returned home in 1767. His achievements had been considerable, India would never be the same again, but it is possible to exaggerate them. F. P. Robinson wisely wrote, as far back as 1912:

> Clive's seizure of Arcot in 1751 was for a long time con-
> sidered to mark the beginning of the British conquest of India.
> It is impossible in reality to fix upon any date as that at which
> the success of the English definitely began. The wars of Clive
> and Warren Hastings, the discomfiture of Lally and Dupleix,
> and the acceptance of the Daweni of Bengal marked, indeed,
> a new era in the Company's history, but the way had been

paved by the less famous actions of such men as Job Charnock and Governor Pitt of Madras, who are equally responsible for the creation of the Indian Empire.*

Clive was still only forty-one, but he looked years older than his age. He was addicted to opium. He was actually poorer than when he had left London, for his expenses and gifts, and salaries to the personal staff that had accompanied him, were greater than the salary and expenses supplied by the Company. Sulivan and his many other enemies were waiting for him. His wealth, and the propriety of its origin, were the subjects of public debate, and were even raised in the House of Commons. A section of the press hounded Clive in print. But they all found it difficult to pin specific charges on him. At the debate in the House he defended himself with considerable, if aggressive, dignity. The House carried by 155 to 95 a motion that he had made a quarter of a million pounds during his first administration of Bengal. But in the early hours of that morning it passed another motion declaring 'that Robert, Lord Clive, did at the same time render great and meritorious services to his country'. It was a compromise. Clive complained that 'I have been examined by the select committee more like a sheep-steeler than a member of this House'. He was conscious that he was defending many others who had been to India and had been accused of wrongly enriching themselves – often with far better reason than the accusations made against himself. The debate had been a test case, compounded of widespread jealousy, indignation, and genuine moral concern directed against all East Indiamen. The result had been indecisive.

Clive died the following year, in mysterious circumstances, at his house in Berkeley Square, perhaps from an overdose of opium. His coach was waiting at the door to take him to Bath, for the waters there. It is tempting to believe that he committed suicide, for he'd had such mental and physical agony to contend with, and was a dark, moody man; it is a temptation few historians have resisted. He was buried at the little village church of his home in Shropshire. His reputation remained very much under a cloud. His widow survived him for forty-three years, living in the shadow of her husband's controversial career; she lived well into the nineteenth century. His son became Governor of Madras, and under him the

* *The Trade of the East India Company.*

barony was raised to an earldom. There was not a single memorial of any sort to Clive, in his own country or in India, until the twentieth century. He has only been rehabilitated in public esteem since a sympathetic and best-selling book published in 1931.

One thing Clive had done during his second Governorship had hardly been noticed. He had reorganised the Company's army in Bengal. It was now far better disciplined, better trained, and, since the unhappy officers' mutiny, in better morale. It was the constant amazement of the thousands of Indians who watched it marching in its neat uniforms, brasses shining, gun barrels glistening, the long columns of men reacting instantly to commands. The army was split into three brigades. Each one was planned to be able to defeat any Indian army on its own. The East India Company, without hardly knowing it, had made for itself in Bengal the most formidable military power in the east. It was a not unimportant fact.

6 THE AGE OF WARREN HASTINGS

It is not always wrong to take the human view of history and, when India is being considered, this is particularly so. Roe, Charnock, Stringer Lawrence, all had played their part. British India in the seventeen-seventies was largely how Clive had shaped it. Events had been engendered by him more than they had ruled him. Now another great Englishman had appeared on the stage, and he, too, was to take his place in Indian history.

Warren Hastings was seven years younger than Clive, but he also came from impoverished country stock. He had a wretched childhood, losing both his parents while a baby and being brought up first by an uncle and then, when his uncle died, by a very distant relative. Despite this experience, he was not a hard man, and, although he was ambitious, it was not ruthless ambition. He arrived in India, as a Company clerk, while still in his teens. He was given responsible posts early on. During the recovery of Bengal, he came to Clive's notice and was sent, as we have seen, as the East India Company representative to the Nawab of Bengal's court at Murshidabad. He held this difficult post for three years, without making a fortune. The officials at Calcutta began to see him more as an ally of the Nawab than as their representative, partly through his continual protestations at the plundering of the country by Company officials for personal gain. He was recalled to Calcutta, and after three years of squabbling in the council he resigned and sailed for England.

His fourteen years in Bengal had gained Warren Hastings private means considered modest by the standards of the returned 'Nabobs', and had lost him his wife and his two children. He was one of the Company's most experienced officials and his reputation for probity, although not universal, was strong among the Company's directors. Moreover, unlike Clive and others returned from India, he had not developed arrogance and impatience during his years abroad. After only two and a half years at home, he was offered the second senior position at Madras, which he accepted. On the voyage out he met, and apparently conquered, the wife of a noble German portrait-painter, who became his constant companion, and with whom he was to live.

Hastings added to his reputation at Madras by sound administration, by comparative integrity, and by working on a scheme to provide Madras with an all-important pier (men and goods had to be landed and embarked through the surf).

In April 1772, five years after Clive's departure, Warren Hastings took his seat in the council chamber at Fort William as Governor. It was not an enviable position for one whose main desire was not to enrich himself. But Hastings was still ambitious, and he was the sort of man who welcomed responsibility. The country had been swept by one of the most terrible famines it had ever known. There was a shortage of currency owing to the export of gold and silver to China to purchase tea. The administrative system of indirect rule set up by Clive had not proved a success. There was trouble with Oudh, and with the Mughal, both bolstered up by Company support.

In London there was a feeling that Bengal was too much for the Company to handle. There was great controversy, in Parliament and out of it, as to what should be done. The East India Company directors, remarkably in view of the disloyalty and unpopularity of so many of its senior servants in India, were determined to carry on; they had friends in the House of Commons, but they themselves were not above the bribery with which they so often charged their employees. In 1772 the Company was on the verge of bankruptcy. The millionaire 'Nabobs', grown fat in its service, would not come to its aid. The Company was obliged to seek a loan from the Government. The chief minister under George III was Lord North.

He was not a far-sighted man, but he was an able and shrewd politician; his view of the world began and ended at Westminster. He saw a chance to force some control on the ailing, controversial, and sometimes disreputable East India Company. He arranged for the Company to be loaned £1,500,000, and at the same time brought in the Regulating Act. The management of the Company's Indian possessions was brought under indirect control of Crown and Parliament. Recognising as it did that the Company's responsibilities were not only in trade, and that the nation was responsible for good order in Indian affairs, it was a most historic act.

A Council was to be set up in Calcutta consisting of a Governor-General and four officially appointed members. The Governor-General was to be Warren Hastings and, as suggested by himself, he was to have supreme power not only over Bengal but over the other two presidencies, Bombay and Madras, as well. All his reports, and those of the Council, would have to be shown to the Government within fourteen days of their arrival in England. There were restrictions on private trading by the Company's servants, and on the receipt of gifts. Finally, a Supreme Court was to be set up in Calcutta with all the legal paraphernalia of a high British Court. The Regulating Act was well-meaning enough, but it crystallised what had been the main problem for over a century — the great lack of understanding of India and its affairs that existed in London. From now on the East India Company, in its efforts to rule Bengal, and later India, was hampered by the views and whims of changing governments.

One of the new Calcutta councillors was Richard Barwell; loquacious, avaricious, and always loyal to Hastings. The other three were sent out from London and had not had any previous experience of Bengal. General Clavering, opinionated and arrogant, and Colonel Monson, a peppery bon viveur, were nominees of the anti-Nabobs and George III. They saw their duty as one of cleaning up the Company's administration. The final member of the Council was something of a mystery. When the names were announced, many had never heard of him. For years he had been a civil servant in the War Ministry, but at the time of his appointment he was without regular employment, without wealth, and with very little influence. Why this man was picked for such an important post has always been a mystery. Although he was certainly more able and intelligent than his three fellow-councillors, it was an age when influence was all. It has been suggested that he was the anonymous Junius, the author of scurrilous and vindictive letters in the *Daily Advertiser* about the Government, and that Lord North appointed him in order to get him out of London. His name was Philip Francis. He was, he declared, predisposed towards Warren Hastings in his difficult task.

Hastings awaited the arrival of the councillors with apprehension but without undue alarm. He was exceedingly proud to be Governor-General. Lord North, announcing the appointment in the House, had spoken of him as a 'person who, though flesh and blood, had resisted the greatest temptations – that, though filling great offices in Bengal during the various revolutions that had been felt in that country, never received a single rupee at any one of them'. It was not entirely true, but no one was more convinced of Hastings' integrity than was Warren Hastings himself.

The new councillors arrived at Calcutta on 19 October 1774. Philip Francis described their reception as 'mean'. There was, he complained, no guard of honour. The salute was of only seventeen guns, whereas his ears had been waiting for twenty-one. The council met next day. The three members from London, to be known as 'the Majority', immediately made it clear that before anything else they wanted an enquiry into past abuses, and Warren Hastings and Barwell had no doubt that they were to be included in the enquiries. There followed perhaps the most remarkable story of well-intentioned maladministration that even the history of the British Empire has to offer. While Bengal groaned under economic chaos, Francis and Hastings engaged in six years of personal squabbling, abuse, and vendetta that was to lead inevitably to physical violence between them. What was the reason for Francis's persecution, for such it was, of Warren Hastings? A clash of personalities is often cited, but more likely is Francis's conviction that the East India Company, and Britain, had no business in India except commercial business. Warren Hastings was basically an imperialist. Philip Francis was basically an anti-imperialist; 'Under a European government,' he wrote, 'Bengal cannot flourish.'

Most of Hastings's recent actions, including the unsavoury Rohilla war in which he had involved the Company, were condemned. Hastings was appalled. He had been in the country twenty years; his opponents had been in it less than twenty weeks. When the council began countermanding its measures – for he was usually outvoted 3 to 2 – he wrote in despair to Lord North that it was 'a declaration to all Indoostan that my authority was extinct and that new men and new measures would henceforth prevail'.

Five months after his arrival, Francis produced a letter at a council meeting from Raja Nand Kumar, a notorious intriguer of Bengal whom Hastings had offended. The letter contained charges of bribery against Warren Hastings, involving more than a third of a million rupees. Nand Kumar requested permission to appear before the council to establish his charges with written evidence. The Majority were delighted, for it was to investigate such charges, and to put the administration of Bengal on a basis that would satisfy the most meticulous London armchair traveller, that they had come to India. At first they were unaware of Nand Kumar's reputation. Hastings was outraged at the suggestion:

> I will not sit at this Board in the character of a criminal, nor do I acknowledge the members of the Board to be my judges... The chief of this administration, your superior, gentlemen, appointed by the Legislative itself, shall I sit at this Board to be arraigned in the presence of a wretch whom you all know to be one of the basest of mankind?...Shall I sit to hear men collected from the dregs of the people give evidence at his dictating against my character and conduct? I will not.

The hearing continued without him. Nand Kumar produced a document, probably forged, purporting to prove that Hastings had accepted money. The Majority decided that Hastings should be obliged to repay the money. However, the East India Company's legal advisers decided not to act, and the matter was not pursued. Hastings considered quitting 'this hateful scene before my enemies gain their complete triumph over me'. He told Lord North: 'the meanest drudge, who owes his subsistence to daily labour, enjoys a position of happiness compared to mine, while I am doomed to share the responsibility of measures which I disapprove, and to be the idle spectator of the ruin which I cannot avert'.

But Hastings was being over-pessimistic. Although Lord North could do nothing for him, Warren Hastings had his friends in India – not the least of which was the climate, which he understood and his enemies did not. In his years in India he had gained many friends and a good deal of respect from the local population. At length, a man came forward with a case against Nand Kumar. The charge was of forgery, and the penalty of local law for forgery was death. Hastings acted with speed. The matter was referred to the Chief Justice of the new Supreme Court. He was Sir Elijah Impey, an old schoolfellow of Hastings and a close friend. The legal formalities took some months, but at the end of them Nand Kumar was executed. The Governor-General had the power to stop the death sentence, but he did nothing, although he had frequently spoken against the barbarity of Indian penalties. He was never again bothered by Indian informers, genuine or feigned. It was a turning point in his fight against the Majority.

In 1776 Francis wrote home that both Clavering and Monson were in a 'woeful condition'. Francis himself was far from well. Hastings, he admitted, was 'much more tough than any of us'. Hastings, in fact, was not so much tough as sensible. 'I eat supper,' he said, 'go to bed at ten, abstain wholly from wine, and from every other liquid but tea and water.' The others were mostly addicted to drink, and went in for not a little gambling and wenching. Monson died soon after Francis's letter.

Warren Hastings decided to fight on. Clavering, he noted, hope-fully, was 'covered with boils'. 'I am determined that no less authority than the King's express act shall remove me, or death.'

In fact, the King was only too anxious to remove him. Various intrigues took place in London during 1776. The directors did their best to stand by Hastings. Eventually it was agreed that he should resign 'voluntarily', but before he could do so Clavering foolishly attempted to seize the Governor-Generalship, failed, and a legal decision in Calcutta obliged Hastings to stay on until fresh instruc-tions arrived from London. The following year his German Baroness, who had lived with him all these years, obtained a divorce, enabling her to marry, Clavering died ('after a delirium of many hours' noted Hastings), and Warren Hastings was in command in India again — for the rules of the council were that in the event of an indecisive vote the Governor-General should have the decision, and it was now Hastings and Barwell versus Philip Francis and Monson's replacement. Hastings still had two years of his five-year term to run. He stayed on.

Warren Hastings devoted himself during this period to improving the assessment and collection of taxes. In 1772 he had taken over an administration weighed down by debt; in 1777 he reported Company affairs to be 'in a more prosperous state than it has known'. He had encouraged and increased the profitable opium trade to China. He had made many economies, including nearly halving the cost of an expanding postal service, done by overland couriers from Calcutta to Bombay and Madras since 1775. The directors, however, thought his methods 'the meanest and the most corrupt', shareholders in London still being unable to believe that their servants could act in any but corrupt ways. Warren Hastings, by this time, was immune to such abuse. 'You hurt yourselves,' he said, 'and your own affairs, by treating with indignities the man whom you leave in charge of your interests.' Hastings could not relax. Once again there was talk of war with France.

❧

Britain was in trouble with her American colonies, and the East India Company was concerned. After Britain, the thirteen colonies, which now had a population of some 3,000,000, were the best market for tea. But the Company had always had the greatest difficulty in maintaining its monopoly in the American colonies through the activities of smugglers, pirates, and the many inhabitants of Dutch background in New York and Pennsylvania. High taxes made it also impossible for the Company to compete with its rivals in North America, and its agents were finding increasing reluctance to import. Republican tendencies were well to the fore in America, and it is absurd to suggest that they were much fanned by a tax on tea, especially when there was so much illicit tea already on the market, but the duty on tea, and other articles, of 1767 did act as a focus for rebellious thoughts. When all taxes were lifted three years later, except the revenue on tea, the latter became the centre of a crisis. The East India Company's tea remained unsold. In 1773 Lord North's government gave way, allowing the Company to send tea to America without the English tax, but still with an import duty; the Company's monopoly was confirmed. It was not enough, it was too late, and by then it was irrelevant. At Boston, and three other cities, the stocks of tea which the Company had hurriedly sent in at the new low price were destroyed or sent back to Europe. Tea had become a symbol of British authority, a 'badge of slavery', as it was described. The East India Company had become synonymous with English repression. A typical letter to the Company declared, 'The Americans will not be slaves, neither are they to be trapped under the notion of cheap teas. Death is more desirable to them than slavery – it is impossible to make the Americans swallow the tea.' It was true. In sixteen months the war of independence had begun, and a great republic was born with an inbred distaste for tea.

The outbreak of the bitter and prolonged war between Britain and her American colonies was almost certain to involve France sooner or later.* Louis XVI had watched with amused satisfaction as the English were embarrassed by their American cousins. French activity in India had been on the increase. Warren Hastings heard of a French representative who had been sent to the Maratha capital of Poona. Hastings was alarmed, for the Marathas were at the time the greatest rivals and threat to the Company's power in India. He wrote:

> I lay it down as a point incontrovertible that if a detachment of much less than 1,000 Europeans, with arms for disciplining a body of native troops in the European manner, shall have once obtained a footing in the Maratha country, or the allies of that Government, all the native powers of Indoostan United will lie at their mercy, and even the provinces of Bengal be exposed to their depredations.

Hastings now showed himself, what is often forgotten, that he could be a great war leader, decisive and strategically skilled, as well as a firm and wise peace-time administrator. His remaining years in India were to be dominated by war.

He collected a force of six battalions to march right across India, from Bengal to Bombay, something which no European had previously done. The Marathas, perhaps inspired by the French, had to be warned off Bombay.† It was a remarkably courageous decision, but Philip Francis was against the scheme from the start. 'We should stand on our defence, and not weaken or divide the force on which the safety of Bengal may depend.' Hastings argued that, as the news from North America was so bad (he had been shocked to hear of the surrender at Saratoga), it was 'incumbent on

* American War of Independence, 1777–83.
† First Anglo-Maratha War, 1775–82.

those who are charged with the interest of Great Britain in the east to exert themselves for the retrieval of the national loss'.

In July 1778 news reached Calcutta that France had finally declared war on Britain, in support of the colonists.* Warren Hastings captured Chandernagore within days and ordered the Company's forces at Madras to seize Pondicherry. He immediately raised further battalions of sepoys.

Philip Francis was predictably pessimistic. He declared: 'Our resources already exhausted, a French invasion certain and impending, and the country incapable of resistance.' There was, in fact, a serious set-back when the authorities at Bombay, impatient at the wait for the overland expedition from Bengal, decided to act on their own and sent a force to take Poona. This small force was easily surrounded and was obliged to sign a humiliating surrender. But prestige was restored when, to the astonishment of half India, the column of East India Company infantry from Calcutta arrived at last at Bombay, having slogged right through the unexplored jungle and hills of Central India. Said Warren Hastings: 'Its way was long, through regions unknown in England, and untraced in our maps.'

The war with the Marathas dragged on, but Hastings's strategy was almost certain to be successful; he divided the attentions of the Marathas by threatening them from the rear while they were engaged with Bombay. The fortress of Gwalior, believed to be impregnable, and one of the keys to Central India, was successfully stormed. The Marathas were a confederacy, and this was always their weakness. The expense of the war and the determination and superiority of the Company's forces led to disaffection and the eventual signing of a treaty. The treaty provided for the proud and fierce Marathas and the fully engaged East India Company to live and let live in India. The Marathas remained as formidable a threat as ever, but the French, still at war with Britain, had already turned their attention to another potential enemy of the Company in India, Haidar Ali of Mysore.

⟨⟩

During this warring with the Marathas, Warren Hastings had been continually harassed and pestered by his enemies in Calcutta, notably Philip Francis, as determined as ever to be the custodian of

* Anglo-French War, 1778–83.

the Company's integrity and its unblinking watch-dog; whereas in peace-time he had always suspected the Governor-General of the worse possible motives, in war he suspected inefficiency and inadequate direction.

Warren Hastings's original term of office had been for five years. But with all their other worries, the Government were glad to agree to the Company's keeping him on after that, from year to year, and Hastings, now that Clavering was dead, was prepared to stay. One of his most upsetting problems at this time was a row with his old friend Impey. 'I suffer beyond measure by the present contest,' he told Sulivan. The trouble was that Impey, naturally, was determined to preserve the independence of the judiciary while Warren Hastings was impatient of restraint. The controversy was settled by the courts being remodelled on Mughal forms and usage rather than on English, which was just what Hastings had wanted. Impey was awarded a new salary, and thus, when he eventually returned to England, there was the inevitable charge of corruption. 'I have undergone great fatigue,' he complained wearily, 'compiled a laborious code, restored confidence to the suitors, and justice and regularity to the Courts of Justice...without any reward, and for my recompense shall have lost my office, reputation and peace of mind for ever.'

Clavering's replacement on the council was Sir Eyre Coote, who had fought under Clive and had defeated Lally at Wandewash. He was an aseptic, irritable man of strong personality who had become famous for his hold over the sepoys. He was inclined to support Hastings, but was no cypher. With his arrival, the incredibly rich Barwell began to press for release in order to enjoy his wealth among the Nabobs at home. Because of his loyalty to Warren Hastings, he could only do this after an agreement with Francis that the latter would not take advantage of Barwell's absence in the council votes. The agreement was arranged by the Advocate-General in Calcutta, and was put on paper. Hastings considered it 'a deed of faith and honour, not of law'. But no sooner had Barwell departed than Francis began to obstruct Warren Hastings's measures. Perhaps Hastings was wilful and touchy, certainly Francis was stubborn. Hastings saw it as a matter of honour. After so many years of bitterness, it is perhaps not surprising that Francis decided the charge against his honour could only be settled by a duel (although duels seldom decided anything). There have been many accounts of this affair, and none of them better than that written by Warren Hastings himself:

Colonel Pearse [his second], by appointment, called on me, but before the time, at about a quarter after 4 [a.m.]. I laid down again on the couch half an hour. Then dressed and went with him in his carriage...Arrived at Belvedere exactly at the time proposed – at 5.30, found Mr F. and Colonel Watson walking in the road. Some time was consumed in looking for a private place. Our seconds proposed that we should stand at a measured distance, which both (taking a recent example in England) fixed at 14 paces, and Colonel Watson paced and marked 7. I stood to the southward. There was (as I recollect) no wind. Our seconds (Colonel W., I think) proposed that no advantage should be taken, but each chose his own time to fire – I should have said that Colonel Pearse loaded my pistols on the ground with two cartridges which he had prepared. I had resolved to defer my fire that I might not be embarrassed with his. He snapped, but the pistol missed fire. The Second put a fresh priming to it and chapped the flints. We returned to our stations. I still proposed to receive the first fire, but Mr F. twice aiming and withdrawing his pistol, I judged that I might seriously take my aim at him. I did so and when I thought I had fixed the true direction I fired. His pistol went off at the same time, and so near the same instant that I am not certain which was first, but believe mine was first and that his followed in the instant. He staggered immediately, his face expressed a sensation of being struck, and his limbs shortly but gradually went under him, and he fell saying, but not loudly, 'I am dead.' I ran to him, shocked I own at the information, and I can safely say without any immediate sensation of joy for my own success. The Seconds also ran to his assistance. I saw his coat pierced on the right side, and feared the ball had passed through him; but he sat up without much difficulty several times and once attempted with our help to stand, but his limbs failed him and he sank to the ground. Colonel W. then proposed that as we had met from a point of honour and not for personal rancour, we should join hands (or that Mr F. should give me his). We did so; Mr F. cheerfully, and I expressed my regret at the condition to which I saw him reduced ...As soon as I returned home, I sent Mr Markham to Sir E.

[Impey] to inform him of what had passed, and that I should wait the event, which, if fatal, I should instantly surrender myself to him, that the law might take its course against me.

Francis's wound was not serious, and he soon recovered. But he had lost heart for the battle, at any rate in Bengal, which he disliked intensely. A few months later he sailed for home, richer than he had arrived, but it seems through his skill and luck at cards rather than through any other means (at one time Barwell had lost £20,000 to him at whist). It seemed a great victory for Warren Hastings, but his joy was subdued. His problems were still many and great. The fighting against the Marathas had spoiled all his carefully balanced budgeting, and there was serious trouble in the Carnatic with Mysore. He wrote:

> What a victory!...an exhausted treasury, an accumulating debt, a system charged with expensive establishments, and precluded by the multitude of dependants and the curse of patronage from reformation...a country oppressed by private rapacity and deprived of its vital resources by the enormous quantities of current specie annually exported in the remittance of private fortunes...the support of [the languishing] Bombay...the charge of preserving Fort St George [Madras] and recovering the Carnatic from the hands of a victorious enemy...and lastly a war either actual or depending in every quarter, and with every power in Hindustan.

7 THE VICTORIES OF EYRE COOTE

Once more the British were being pushed back in the Carnatic to their strongholds at Madras and Fort St David. The state of Mysore had come under the rule of a Muslim adventurer, Haidar Ali, who had already fought the British more than a decade previously.* He was an unscrupulous, clever despot who was proving a more intelligent military foe than any adversary the Company had yet met. He had found the Madras presidency, which claimed much of the Carnatic and area, easy prey.†

The Governor, Lord Pigot, sent out to make necessary and urgent reforms at the notoriously inefficient Madras administration, had been outvoted by his council and thrown into jail. The Madras authorities, through tactlessness and lack of sympathy, had brought about such enmity to themselves that a coalition of the Marathas, the Nizam of Hyderabad, and Mysore had actually been formed, with the object of removing the presumptuous British out of the Carnatic and, possibly, out of India altogether. The Marathas were defeated, as has been seen, and the Nizam was disengaged from the alliance – both thanks largely to Warren Hastings, who had suspended the new Governor at Madras. But Haidar Ali, with a vast

---

* First Anglo-Mysore War, 1767–9, in which Haidar Ali had embarrassed the small Company contingent then in the Carnatic. The peace treaty had provided for Company aid for Mysore against the Marathas, but it had not been honoured, and Haidar Ali had been waiting for revenge ever since.
† Second Anglo-Mysore War, 1780–4.

force, had swept down from the mountains, on 20 July 1780, and began the systematic overrunning of the Carnatic in the excuse of coming to the assistance of the French, and encouraged by the help he expected to get from them. Under Haidar Ali's protection the French had established themselves on the West Coast, at Mahé.

Haidar Ali's horde of horsemen, coming down from the passes, spread out over the countryside in great clouds of dust. They spread terror across the Carnatic as they plundered, burned, and slaughtered. But it was not an indiscriminate rampage; it was carefully designed to provide supply and transport difficulties for the East India Company. Haidar Ali came behind, with his main force, occupying and placing garrisons in the towns. The Company had two armies, one in Madras and one, under Colonel Baillie, in the Northern Circars, at Guntur. In command was Sir Hector Munro. He made the error of delaying the joining of the two columns, which together would have amounted to over 8,000 trained troops. Seeing his opportunity, Haidar Ali sent his son, Tipu, to overwhelm the smaller column from Guntur. At first the British fought off Tipu's onslaughts, but a combination of indecisive command, lack of artillery ammunition, and inferiority of numbers were too much for them. The Company's line broke and the men were cut down in hundreds. By the time Munro arrived on the scene with reinforcements the battlefield was silent and Baillie's force virtually annihilated. In the early hours of the following morning, Munro, leaving all his heavy guns and stores behind, began the retreat to Madras.

The campaign had lasted only three weeks and had been a tale of disaster for the British from start to finish. The Company had met with its most formidable enemy yet in India. Most writers put the defeat down to bad command by Munro and Baillie, who, over the years, received condemnation from British historians amounting almost to vilification. What was much more likely was that Munro, an experienced and sound commander, was no match at all for Haidar Ali, who had high qualities of generalship that were overlooked then and have been since.

Hemmed in at Madras, Munro could do nothing to relieve the various sieges inland, the most important of which was at Wandewash. Arcot had already fallen. The Company had virtually lost the Carnatic. What was to be done? Once again it was the energy and determination of Warren Hastings — ineptly and condescendingly described as 'the clerk who sat on the Mughals' throne' — who made the vital and saving decisions. Sir Eyre Coote, that irascible Irishman on the council at Calcutta, was in bad health. He was fifty-three, which was old by Anglo-Indian standards. But he was, after Clive, the most prestigious commander that Britain had produced in India; he was also, which Warren Hastings probably knew, a far better and more experienced general than Clive had ever been. Hastings asked him to go to Madras and take up the challenge of Haidar Ali. Reluctantly, but with a strong sense of duty, ill-tempered and grumbling as always, Coote went off to take up command. Warren Hastings's position was clear: 'While I have a soldier, or a rupee, I will never abandon the Carnatic; for if we do not fight Haidar Ali in that country, we shall have to fight him here.'

Eyre Coote's main problem was one of transport. With the whole country in the hands of the Mysore forces, he could not raise animals or wagons, and it was two months before he moved out of Madras with the Company's army. There was some sharp fighting. Exactly twenty-one years to the day after he had won the great battle of Wandewash in the Anglo-French War of 1760, he again relieved the town. Plagued by lack of supplies, Coote was forced to return to the coast at Fort St David. It was five months before enough provisions had reached him by sea to allow him to move into the field again. Because of Haidar Ali's extremely effective laying-waste policy, Coote had to march along the coast, hoping to meet the main force of the enemy.

The two forces met near Porto Novo, on the coast road south from Fort St David. The British were supported by a fleet just off the coast which was able to supply covering fire and, even more important, four days' rations for the army. Sir Eyre Coote, quite as experienced as Haidar Ali in fighting in India, was no fool.

The Company's infantry, having fed on a few meagre ounces of rice, moved forward in battle order, in two lines, against the enemy lining the crest of a low line of hills. To Haidar's surprise, the British force left the line of the main road, where he had been preparing to meet them, and advanced straight at him through sand-dunes. The East India Company line continued to move steadily forward, although under heavy fire. Haidar Ali waited before sending his cavalry thundering down on the British and their sepoys. As if by magic, the first Company line neatly broke up and formed into tightly packed squares, a manoeuvre that had been perfected by the British Army to contend with cavalry in Europe. The cavalry continued to ride down in an apparently overwhelming mass, but as it neared the squares and charged aimlessly through the gaps, or was brought up against the glistening bayonets of the squares themselves, the whole vast mass of horsemen began to fall to the ground, amid screams from men and animals, and to disintegrate like swarms of flies against small red bricks. As further waves came on to join their confused and struggling comrades, they were met by disciplined volleys of musketry and by shot from the Company artillery. Suddenly the survivors of the Mysore cavalry began to turn and flee; within minutes it was a rout. From the British squares, faint cheering could be heard above the sound of battle drifting across the sandy hills.

The squares reformed into line and began again marching steadily forward. This display of faultless discipline unnerved the Mysore infantry and it began to fall back. But Haidar Ali was not finished. He had a strong force of cavalry and infantry, supported by guns, and these he now cleverly brought down on the British rear. They were met by the Company's second line, which so far had not been engaged. After fierce fighting, the Mysore troops were driven back; Haidar Ali, seeing the battle slipping away from him, supported them with all the cavalry he could muster, and once more tried to break the British rear. But the Mysore cavalry came under fire from a British warship, which had been alert for such an opportunity. It was too much for Haidar Ali's men. The Company infantry steadily advanced and took all the Mysore positions. The Mysore Army fled. The proud Haidar Ali was forced by his generals to leave the field.

It had been a great victory, consummately won by Eyre Coote, a classic illustration of infantry defeating cavalry, of trained troops defeating ill-trained, and of military and naval co-operation. The British were about 8,500 strong and lost some 300 killed or wounded. Haidar Ali's force had been 65,000 strong and he had lost about one man in six. Of all the great East India Company military victories in India, Porto Novo is the least known. But as a military achievement, Arcot, Plassey, Seringapatam, Lucknow, fall before it. Porto Novo, the finest victory the British ever won in India, had no immediate practical effect whatever, for Eyre Coote's men were half starving and could not follow up their victory. The psychological effect, however, was tremendous; the humiliations of the massacre of Baillie's column and the panicky retreat of Munro were avenged.

The two armies, both reinforced, met again nearly three months later, near where Baillie's force had been overrun. After hard infantry fighting, Haidar Ali was obliged to fall back, but this time there was no rout. A month later they met again. Haidar Ali, taken by surprise, resorted again to his cavalry, whose charges against the Company squares and shot-and-grape proved as ineffective as they had done at Porto Novo. After this, Eyre Coote returned his bedraggled, ravenous but victorious army to Madras. Haidar Ali still had his conquered territory, but he was never the same man again. He died the following year, aged about sixty. His rule passed to his son Tipu, the 'Tiger of Mysore'.

◦◦◦◦◦◦

By now the French were on the scene. Scenting the possibility of victory in alliance with their old allies of Mysore and the possibility of using their part in the American War of Independence to quietly regain their predominance in the Carnatic, they had sent out two of their most formidable commanders: Bussy, who had been virtual ruler of Hyderabad, and their famous Admiral Pierre André de Suffren Saint Tropez. Bussy was past his best and had never been an outstanding military commander. His French expeditionary force of 3,000 men was gratefully welcomed by Haidar and Tipu, but made little real difference. After one ferocious battle, in which honours were even, there were no major engagements. Eyre Coote had returned to Calcutta for a rest. His replacement, General Stuart, was a soldier of the royal army and would not take orders from the East India Company, a fact which led to his recall. Eyre Coote, travelling back to Madras from Calcutta, died on board ship.

Suffren, meanwhile, was plaguing the British at sea. The growing Company rule in India had been based on its command of the sea as much as on anything else. The large army maintained in Bengal had always been a factor of power in the Carnatic, and elsewhere along the coast, owing to the speed at which it could reinforce local garrisons, particularly that at Madras. Suffren's ambition was to change all this. He was a vehement leader, as fierce as he was fat. He had been appalled by the lack of vigour shown by French naval forces in the last two wars with England, and he was determined to restore the prestige of the French Navy. On the way out to India, he had met a British fleet and given some idea of what might be expected of him in the Bay of Bengal. His campaign was notable for the number and severity of the engagements that took place. Suffren lost no major ships and forced the surrender of several isolated British garrisons. He had no local port for refitting, but, with fourteen ships, he defeated a British fleet of eighteen vessels in his last major engagement of the campaign. On his return to France, he was greeted as the major hero of the war.

The arrival of news from Europe that peace had been concluded put an end to hostilities between French and English. Although by the peace treaty Britain had to return the French possessions in India, France was never again to make a serious bid for power in India. It was a matter of the utmost importance for the future of India; only thirty years previously it had looked as if France, not England, must become the master of southern India for many generations. But a treaty between Tipu and the British was not signed till several months later. Tipu agreed to retire to his own mountainous territory. But the Company was uneasy about him, to say the least. He was notoriously war-like, and dressed his army in garments with tiger stripes: a reminder of his proud title of 'the Tiger of Mysore'. He was cruel, vain, and arrogant, and unlike his father in almost every way except in military ability. During the war he had shown he was an able, if headstrong, commander. The British knew that he could send his army pouring down one of the valleys again, the numerous valleys from the Mysore highlands which led into the Carnatic, not all of which the Company could possibly guard.

One of Tipu's most damning aspects was his cruelty to prisoners. He refused to release several hundreds, including British officers and men (of whom over a thousand had been captured during the war); he needed them for training his own army in European methods.

The end of the war was a great boon to Warren Hastings, for the directors still expected him to make a profit and to finance the China trade, despite all the local expenses. He had had his own troubles in the Bengal area. His efforts to raise revenue became more and more desperate. He even dipped into his own fortune. His richest vassal was the Raja of Benares, and his most recalcitrant debtor the Begum of Oudh, both of whom enjoyed the Company's military protection. Warren Hastings left Calcutta to see if he could wring some money out of them. The Raja welcomed this pecuniary visit by rising against the Company and threatening Hastings with his life. Warren Hastings escaped from Benares just in time, the Raja's forces were soundly defeated, and his successor proved more forthcoming. The Begum, charged with helping the Raja, was forced to add more than a million pounds sterling to the Company's treasury in Calcutta. It was an ugly affair, and Warren Hastings, carefully collecting documentary evidence of the culpability of the Raja and the Begum, knew it.

In England, a Whig government had fallen largely through over-pressing its efforts to control the East India Company. A Bill, introduced by Fox, which would have deprived the Company of all its power and trading privileges, was rejected by the House of Lords. The young Pitt, great grandson of 'Diamond Pitt' of Madras, had become chief minister. To show his gratitude to the East India Company for its support during the political struggle, he cut the duty on tea from 50 to 12 per cent.

Soon afterwards, in 1784, Pitt introduced his famous India Bill, which was passed by Parliament. The Company once again owed the Government money, and it was obliged to accept a 'Board of Control' which could command the directors themselves. The Board of Control soon had its own offices, in Westminster, from where communications began to flow to Leadenhall Street. The President of the Board had a seat in the Cabinet (eventually the board consisted only of the president). It was described as 'dual control' between crown and company and tethered the Company to home politics even more than North's Regulating Act had done. A future Viceroy, Lord Curzon, said of it, over a century later: 'Had a Committee been assembled from the padded chambers of Bedlam, they could hardly have devised anything so extravagant in its madness.' It was another important step in the Government taking responsibility in India away from 'John' Company, as the East India Company was starting to be popularly known (in answer to Jan Company, the old name in the east for the Dutch East India Company). But it was a responsibility which confined itself to policy and appointments and not to accepting blame when things went wrong.

Warren Hastings was not surprised to learn that a provision of the Bill was that the private fortunes of Company servants could be investigated. It was a sop to the many parliamentarians who were still obsessed by the enviable fortunes of the Nabobs. With the Company's profits back again at over a million pounds, Warren Hastings felt he had served the East India Company long enough. After a second period of sixteen years spent in India, he sailed from Bengal for the last time in 1785. He was fifty-two years old and was to live another thirty-three years without honours or employment, during which he was to be almost constantly reviled by a public and a parliament which was as ignorant of him as it was of India. This courteous, serious, apparently mild little man had been, without any doubt at all, the greatest peace-time administrator, and the greatest war-leader as well, that the sub-continent had known since the mighty Akbar two centuries before. On board ship, he wrote:

I have saved India, in spite of them all, from foreign conquest ...Yet may I feel a regret to see that hope which I have too fondly indulged, and which I have sustained during thirteen laboured years with a perseverance against a succession of difficulties which might have overcome the constancy of an abler mind, of being in some period of time, however remote, allowed to possess and exercise the full powers of my station, of which I had hitherto held little more than the name and responsibility; and to see with it the belief, which I had as fondly indulged, that I should become the instrument of raising the British name, and the substantial worth of its possessions in India, to a degree of prosperity proportioned to such a trust; both vanish in an instant, like the illusions of a dream; with the poor and only consolation left me of the conscious knowledge of what I could have effected, had my destiny ordained that I should attain the situation to which I aspired, and that I have left no allowable means untried, by which I might have attained it.

8 ~ CORNWALLIS ~

Although they were continually engaged in fighting, all written evidence of the time points to the fact that the East India Company was a peace-loving power in India. But its peaceful intentions were complicated by two factors: it had an important trade and source of revenue to defend, and it was all too conscious of its responsibilities in the areas over which it ruled. Pitt's India Act contained a declaration that it was contrary to British policy to extend Company rule in India — but that took no account of the age-old condition of rule in India: conquer or be conquered.

Warren Hastings had set a high standard in India, although it was but little recognised at the time. His successor, the third Governor-General, was to be equal to the challenge.* Before he even arrived in India, he had achieved one of the most notable acts of his Governor-Generalship; he had insisted, as a condition of accepting the post, that the council should not have the power to overrule him. He thus freed himself in a stroke from the bondage under which Warren Hastings had suffered.

Lord Cornwallis, a tubby, rather sleepy-looking man with a squint, forty-eight years old, was not a likely choice for such a demanding post. He had no experience of India. He had recently been employed as a major-general in America, where he had had a mixed record against the rebel colonists, culminating in the capitulation of his force at Yorktown (his position there had been

* An interim Governor-General, John Macpherson, is well forgotten.

so 'precarious' that he had nobly recommended against help being sent him). He was, however, a good friend of the King, and Pitt thought well of him. Perhaps it was considered only just that a man who had helped lose one empire should have the task of consolidating another. Whatever the reason, Cornwallis had no desire to go. He was not by any means a fool, but he was a man who enjoyed English country pursuits and he was not known for his energy. But he did have a strong sense of duty towards his country. He wrote, wearily:

> The proposal of going to India has been pressed upon me so strongly, with the circumstance of the Governor-General's being independent of his Council...and having supreme command of the military, that, much against my will, and with grief of heart, I have been obliged to say yes, and to exchange a life of ease and content to encounter all the plagues and miseries of command and public station.

His salary, as Governor-General of the three presidencies and as Commander-in-Chief in Bengal, was £31,000, a very considerable sum (worth over $300,000 today), but even this did not tempt Cornwallis. It was duty, and duty alone, which spurred him on.

Cornwallis, like most other Englishmen who had never been to India, saw his duty as improving the conduct of the East India Company's servants and improving the administration. He succeeded in both. With the directors and Board of Control months away, he was all-powerful. He was a simple imperialist who believed that Indians should be ruled by Europeans for their own benefit. Indians, who had previously been ruled by foreign Muslims for centuries, were not surprised. Cornwallis's instructions had been explicit: no territorial acquisition. He tried hard to avoid interference in Indian affairs. His reforms included the raising of pay of the Company's employees, which gave them more self-respect and encouraged them away from illegal private trading; he tried to instil them with a sense of duty like his own, something which Clive and Warren Hastings, with their own questionable activities, had never really been able to do. The integrity of Cornwallis was unquestioned; he did not even draw all his salary. He improved the administration of justice in Bengal. Above all, he tried to get a fairer raising of revenue.

Warren Hastings had been so desperate to raise money for his wars against the Marathas, Mysore, and the French that his system had become overstrained. Cornwallis's act, designed and carried out by his civil servants, is known as the Permanent Settlement of the Bengal Revenue. Revenue gathering had revolved round the Zemindars; they had originally been the Mughal tax-collectors, but through custom and reforms the position had become hereditary and the descendants of the original Zemindars had become fixed in one district, for which they paid a set tax to the British while often raising a larger amount of revenue from the peasants, which they kept for themselves. Cornwallis ordered an enquiry into the land tenures of the Zemindars and the peasants. It was an incredibly complicated and difficult task. But, with much patience, it was done. Some order was arranged and proceedings were put on a more legal and documented basis. The amounts due from the Zemindars were reviewed and corrected, but their power to tax the peasants was left uncontrolled because Cornwallis felt the Company did not have the strength to abolish the system altogether and substitute its own. It was not the basic reform it was claimed to be, but it did get the Company's servants at closer grips with their responsibilities than they had ever been before. For the peasant it meant, all too often, a higher tax and an absentee landlord (for that is what the Zemindars were becoming in effect). The net profits of the East India Company, in Cornwallis's third year, 1789–90, were £2,807,444; this compares well with Pitt's revenue from the whole of Great Britain, in 1790, of about £16,000,000.

Cornwallis had a poor opinion of Indians. 'Every native of India, I verily believe, is corrupt,' he said. In another of his reforms he dismissed all high Indian officials in the Company's service and replaced them with Europeans. This Europeanisation of the Company's service was the most important action of Cornwallis's regime, and it would be difficult to underrate it.

More and more, under Cornwallis, the Company's men were engaged in administration rather than in trade, inevitably, owing to income from tax having become far more important to the Company in India than income from trade; under him the two tasks were for the first time made quite separate, done by different men; for the administrators to engage in private trade, or financial dealings, under Cornwallis was a very serious offence; under his

Governor-Generalship many men were sent home. It was the beginning of the Civil Service in India. Employment was organised in three quite different classes: judicial, revenue, and commercial. Under Cornwallis, as well, the Army grew more efficient. In this he was backed by Henry Dundas, who managed the Board of Control, a devious politician and a crony of Pitt. Recruiting in England, which had previously been done just before the departure of ships, was put on a more permanent basis.

Patronage became less prevalent under Cornwallis. In one letter home, answering a suggestion that he employ a friend, he wrote, curtly: 'Here, my lord, we are in the habit of looking for the man for the place, and not for the place for the man.' He even rejected the requests of the Prince of Wales to find suitable employment for the Prince's friends. Some just came out to Bengal, anyway, with letters recommending them. With the Nabobs still alive and well at home, the love of India as a place for quick riches was still strong. Cornwallis wrote to a friend:

> I think I told you how much Lord Ailesbury had distressed me by sending out Mr Ritso. He is now writing in the secretary's office for 200 or 250 rupees per month, and I do not see the probability of my being able to give him anything better, without deserving to be impeached. I am still persecuted every day by people coming out with letters to me, who either get into jail or starve in the foreign settlements. For God's sake do all in your power to stop this madness.

During his seven years in India, Cornwallis hardly left Calcutta once. Unlike Warren Hastings, he made few visits to the interior to see for himself. To his son, he described a working day:

> I get on horseback just as the dawn of day begins to appear, ride on the same road and the same distance, pass the whole forenoon after my return from riding in doing business, and almost exactly the same portion of time every day at table, drive out in a phaeton [light four-wheeled carriage] a little before sunset, then write or read over letters or papers on business for two hours; sit down at nine with two or three officers of my family to some fruit and a biscuit and go to bed soon after the clock strikes ten. I don't think that the greatest sap at Eton can lead a duller life than this.

Although Cornwallis himself lived simply – for years his spartan style was a legend in Calcutta — society life under him blossomed as never before. With an increase in shipping, the British were able to live as much like at home as possible. Whereas in the early days it had not been unknown for Company employees to wear Indian dress, and an Indian diet had often been the only one available, by now such betrayals of Englishness were viewed askance, although not yet with horror. Many employees married local women. The port of Calcutta had developed around the Fort into a town with substantial Georgian buildings. At the head of Calcutta society was the deceptively somnolent-looking Governor-General. The *Calcutta Gazette* reported an official entertainment:

> A very large and respectable company, in consequence of the invitation given by the Right Honourable the Governor-General, assembled on New Year's Day at the old Court House Street, where an elegant dinner was prepared. The toasts were, as usual, echoed from the cannon's mouth, and merited this distinction from their loyalty and patriotism. In the evening the ball exhibited a circle less extensive, but equally brilliant and beautiful, with that which graced the entertainment in honour of the King's birthday. Lady Chambers and Col. Pearse danced the first minuet, and the succeeding ones continued till about half after eleven o'clock, when the supper tables presented every requisite to gratify the most refined epicurean.

Gone were the rough and rowdy days of Governor Pitt at Madras. And as for Job Charnock, how amazed he would have been to hear the strains of the minuet drifting over the waters of the Hooghly, where he had built his settlement of clay and straw huts a hundred years before.

⚬⚬⚬

In London, the headquarters of the Company, the signs of increased British activity in India were not so obvious. The East India Company hid behind its unpretentious four-storey building in Leadenhall Street; the property extended over 300 feet to the rear. It was not until 1796 that work was begun on a far more imposing frontage, suitable for what was now as great a company as any in the world. There were offices, rooms for the directors, and warehouses. The docks at Blackwall had been expanded over the years, and East Indiamen, with their three masts and black and white hulls, were a

*...he East India House, 1648-
...26.*

*...rt William, Calcutta, in 1754, two years before its overthrow by the Nawab
...Bengal.*

Robert Clive, Servant of the Company, 1743-60, 1765-7.

Warren Hastings, Servant of Company, 1750-85.

Fort St George, Madras, about the time of Clive.

rd Wellesley being enter-
ned at breakfast by the
wab of Oudh.

The East Indiaman, 'Earl of Abergavenny', off Southsea, 1801.

Lord Auckland, Governor-General, 1836-42, holding a durbar while on to

Company troops in Rangoon in 1825, during the first Burmese War.

Lord Ellenborough,
Governor-General,
1842-4.

Lord Hardinge,
Governor-General,
1844-8.

Lord Dalhousie,
Governor-General,
1848-56.

Anglo-Indian dinner, mid-nineteenth century.

The Company's headquarters at the East India House in Leadenhall Stre 1833.

A meeting of shareholders in the Court Room, as depicted by Rowlands

Passengers crossing Egypt, on the short route from England to India.

The 1st Bengal Fusiliers, East India Company Army, on the march during the Revolt.

The Residency at Lucknow after the relief.

Gwalior, the last stronghold of the great revolt.

familiar sight on the Thames, and considered to be among the finest ships afloat.

Down to the India Act of 1784, the East India Company had been governed by the proprietors, or stockholders, of its stock and by the twenty-four directors of the 'court'. There were usually about 2,000 proprietors. Any owner of stock could attend the meetings, but only those with £1,000 or more could vote in a ballot (a holding of £10,000 and upwards would give four votes). About fifty proprietors held stock of over £10,000, and nearly all these lived in London. (The Company was as exclusive to London as it always had been.) These were the most powerful proprietors, and they consisted almost entirely of the members of two groups: those representing the banking, commercial, and shipping interests of the Company: and the Nabobs, anxious to gain influence in the company for which they had once worked. Under Pitt, dividends were fixed at 8 per cent in 1784; they were raised to $10\frac{1}{2}$ per cent in 1793.

The proprietors met quarterly in the General Court Room of the East India House. After Pitt established the government-run Board of Control, they had little real power, but these voluble meetings served to express public disquiet about the Company's affairs. Many proprietors were keen critics, and of one such it was said his 'mental vision was microscopic and whose nature's plague it was to spy into abuses'.

The proprietors were empowered to elect the directors, but the directors in practice held so many votes between them that they voted each other in for terms, going in and out of office by strict rotation; in this way directors were invariably voted back in after a year out of office, or could pass the privilege on to sons and relatives. About half of them knew India. It was almost impossible to break into this closed circle, except through death or disqualification. When the death of a director occurred, competition among the proprietors for his place was fierce. A proprietor described the scene on a polling day for a director:

> From the portico to the balloting glasses the passages were stuffed with persons who had nothing to do with the election. Butlers and servants of all descriptions so crowded the way that the Proprietors could hardly get in. Here stood a rank of footmen in embroidered liveries — there a collection of butlers —

and, in another quarter, a party of miserable, venal parasites – men whom the Proprietors knew to be such. One pressed forward and said that his friend or his master...was perfectly calculated to fill the office of Director; and intimations were regularly given to ladies, as they passed, how very handsome they were, as the means of procuring their suffrages. I defy anyone to deny that the scene is not more like that which occurs at the election of a parish beadle than that which should appear when the Directors of a great Company are about to be elected.

A directorship brought with it great prestige and influence for patronage and other perquisites within the Company. A further attack on the court of directors was the official establishment of the Secret Committee (which had existed unofficially before). The cabinet did not always want the directors to know of their decisions, and thus three directors – the Secret Committee – who were sworn to secrecy, were empowered to transmit instructions direct to India without the assent of the full court of directors. However, sometimes the Secret Committee would contain at least one director, such as Sir James Hogg in the eighteen-thirties, who refused to be dictated to by the President of the Board of Control. The flow of command – to President of the Board, to Secret Committee or court of directors, to the secretaries or examiners at the India House, to the Governor-General – was so set with hurdles that it could easily be sluggish and impaired. Until 1834 the court of directors was divided into twelve major committees, the most powerful of which was the committee of correspondence; its chairman, and the chairman of the court of directors (i.e. the chairman of the Company), enjoyed some power. Noting this awkward system, the court of directors itself was later (1829) to declare: 'Were the Indian government as constituted (comprehending under that term the established authority in this country as well as in India) to be characterised by a single word, it might with no impropriety be denominated a government of checks. Now whatever may be the advantage of checks, it must always be purchased at the expense of delay.'

Dundas, President of the Board, was the most powerful man concerned with the Company since Sulivan. He wrote instructions and guide-lines of policy to Cornwallis. He was an old enemy of Warren Hastings, although, ironically enough, he had been in favour of strong Governor-Generalship. He now played a sinister part in the long and distasteful story of Warren Hastings's impeachment.

ᗒᗊᗕ

Impeachment implied accusations of misconduct by public figures being brought before the House of Lords. This is what now happened to the unfortunate Warren Hastings. Whether it would have happened without Philip Francis is difficult to say; perhaps it would, for prejudice against the ex-Governor-General was widespread. But there is no doubt that Francis activated the movement. It was an ungenerous act, to say the least, for inevitably the two men had lived closely together in Calcutta, despite their enmity, had even had times of sociability, and Francis must surely have known that Warren Hastings was not the man so many imagined him to be. One can only put it down to vindictiveness or to blind prejudice. Francis now lived in St James's Square, renowned for his caustic wit, his gallantry to ladies, and his constant protestations of penury.

At first Warren Hastings had been fairly well received in London. Pitt had little interest in him, one way or the other; even the King was quite favourably disposed. Unfortunately, Francis was an old friend of that formidable parliamentarian, Edmund Burke. A week after Hastings had landed, Burke ominously gave notice in the House of Commons that he 'would at a future date make a motion respecting the conduct of a gentleman just returned from India'. Burke was also being primed by his cousin, an official in India. Burke, understanding little of India, had rushed blindly into defence of the Indians, presenting himself as the gallant defender of a gentle people oppressed by rapacious conquistadors like Warren Hastings. Although the Company and many of its servants was certainly greedy, the Indians of Bengal and the Carnatic had not been better ruled for centuries, if ever. In the light of history, Burke's seems a foolish posture, but he believed it a brave and distinguished one. Francis supplied the details of prejudice: Burke set them alight with mighty rhetoric. The matter came before the House of Commons. It was a terrific occasion. The Whigs followed Burke; Richard Brinsley Sheridan and Charles James Fox spoke witheringly of matters about which they knew little and understood less. Warren Hastings replied, typically, with the most boring, detailed, and long-drawn-out reply that the House could remember. Pitt (influenced by Dundas) dithered, but inclined the Government towards impeachment.* Burke won the debate.

The trial before the Lords did not begin until two years later. It opened in a blaze of publicity, as a fashionable entertainment, and seats at Westminster Hall, where it was held, were impossible to get. The prosecution, managed by Burke, Fox, and Sheridan, was long-winded and prone to all the exaggeration beloved of the day. The audience was delighted by such a display of dazzling rhetoric. Said Burke:

> I impeach him in the name of the people of India, whose rights he has trodden under foot, and whose country he has turned into a desert. Lastly, in the name of human nature itself, in the name of both sexes, in the name of every age, in the name of every rank, I impeach the common enemy and oppressor of all.

Such rubbish continued for two years – during which the court sat for only fifty-four days. Warren Hastings became so depressed with the length of the proceedings that he said he would have pleaded guilty if he had foreseen them. He offered to waive his defence. But it was decided the trial had to go remorselessly on. The public had lost interest. The Hall was half empty. Sometimes only just enough peers were present to allow the proceedings to continue. It was over three years from the start before Warren Hastings could begin his defence. He had lost heart, and was disgusted by what he had heard. Burke insisted on cross-examining his witnesses at extraordinary length. There were lengthy arguments as to the admissibility of evidence...

It was seven years and two months before a verdict was reached. Despite all distractions, despite all prejudice, despite all ignorance, despite extreme boredom and weariness, the peers gave a resounding verdict of Not Guilty. With the verdict, Philip Francis lost his high hopes of the Governor-Generalship, and his seat at the general election of 1798. He lived unobstrusively for another twenty years.

Hastings had engaged in profuse pamphleteering, and the assembly and presentation of the defence had cost him £100,000 –

* Ironically enough, Dundas himself was to suffer impeachment years later, when First Lord of the Admiralty, for misappropriation of public funds. His son, Robert Saunders Dundas, M.P. for Rye, became, like his father, President of the Board of Control for India and then First Lord of the Admiralty.

rather more money than he had. He asked the Government for his costs, and was rejected. But the East India Company came to his aid and enabled him to live his retirement comfortably in the country. He seldom visited London. Honours were few, and were slow coming. In 1813 he was called to give evidence on Indian affairs before both Houses of Parliament. In a quiet but impressive tribute to him, both Houses stood as he entered. He survived till 1818, when he died aged 85. Mr Warren Hastings, first Governor-General of India, was not buried in one of the great places of the nation, but, like Clive before him, at a parish church in the English countryside from which he had come.

❧

Cornwallis proved himself an able administrator for the Company. But basically he was a soldier. He had arrived in India with strict orders from Dundas and the Board not to become involved in any aggression or conquest during his term of office. He tried to follow this policy loyally, and kept the Company out of Indian affairs as much as he could.

In 1790 Tipu's army came thundering down into Travancore, in the south-west, which was under the Company's protection, from Mysore. Tipu claimed territorial and other grievances.* Cornwallis was furious, not so much with Tipu as with the Madras Government, which he held responsible. He told Dundas: 'I still think that he would not have ventured to do it if he had not been encouraged by the weakness of the Madras Government.' The acting Governor, John Holland, was so energetically criticised by Cornwallis that his career was ruined. It was decided that an army under Colonel William Medows, commander-in-chief at Madras, was to probe Mysore from the far south. He was to be supported by a column of troops from Bengal. So unenviable was the reputation of Tipu, son of the upstart who had grabbed the Mysore throne, that the more traditional authorities of Hyderabad and the Marathas were glad to co-operate with Cornwallis. But Medows was easily checked by Tipu as he left the plains and entered the passes which led to Mysore. Tipu then struck out across the Carnatic, which he and his father had conquered ten years before. Medows, having heard nothing from the column from Bengal, had to withdraw hurriedly in order to protect Madras, the

* Third Anglo-Mysore War, 1790–2.

fall of which to an Indian army would have been a calamity to Company prestige.

Not surprisingly, Cornwallis — who fancied himself as a commander — decided to come down from Calcutta and take up the command. In 1791 he pushed his main army into Mysore, his objectives being Bangalore and Seringapatam, Tipu's capital. The former place was besieged and stormed. Ten thousand cavalry from the Nizam of Hyderabad arrived to join Cornwallis, and the latter rashly decided to make a dash for Seringapatam. When he got there, he found Tipu and his army awaiting him. The town was situated on an island in the Cauvery river. On one side, up against the river, was an immensely strong fortress. It seemed an almost impregnable position. Cornwallis, as Medows before him, was becoming increasingly worried about his lines of communication and his supplies. Destroying his siege artillery, he fell back to Bangalore. He decided that Seringapatam could only be taken after a careful and meticulous advance. He spent the rest of the year preparing for this. Tipu, meanwhile, utilised the time to improve his position.

In early 1792 Cornwallis, with 22,000 of the East India Company's troops and 18,000 of the Nizam's, was once more encamped near Seringapatam. On 6 February he struck with three attacks; two of these successfully forced an entry into the city and Tipu withdrew into his fortress. Reinforcements for the Company arrived from Bombay and Tipu asked for terms. Cornwallis was determined to be harsh. Tipu was obliged to hand over almost half his lands to the alliance of the Company, the Nizam, and the Marathas. He had to pay a huge indemnity. And he had to release all his prisoners. Cornwallis had no misgivings at all about taking a large chunk of southern India for the East India Company. He wrote to Dundas:

> I request that you will be pleased to assure His Majesty that, although the formidable power of Tipu has been so much reduced by the event of a war into which we were forced by the ungovernable ambition and violence of his character, as to render it improbable that he can be able, for many years to come, to give any material disturbance to the British possessions in India; yet that in the selection of the countries that are to be ceded to us, my primary object shall be to fix upon those districts, to the extent of our rights by the present treaty, that

may be from the local situation best calculated for giving us a strong defensive frontier against the future attacks of any Power whatever.

To ensure that his demands were carried out, Cornwallis took two of Tipu's sons as hostages. The two boys, aged eight and ten, passed through the gate of the fort on elephants while Tipu watched dejectedly from the ramparts above. They were dressed in all their finery. Cornwallis wrote:

> They had several rows of large pearls round their necks, from which was suspended an ornament consisting of a ruby and an emerald of considerable size surrounded by large brilliants; and in their turbans each had a sprig of rich pearls. Bred up from their infancy with infinite care, and instructed in their manners to imitate the reserve and politeness of age, it astonished all present to see the correctness and propriety of their conduct.

Cornwallis took a close interest in the welfare of the two boys and insisted that they should be treated with the greatest consideration. He had already decided to return home, feeling he had fulfilled his duty in India. There was a great deal of talk about Tipu withholding European prisoners at Seringapatam, and stories circulated in London, Calcutta, Madras, and Bombay of the atrocities which Tipu was meant to have inflicted on them. Tipu insisted he had no more prisoners, and Cornwallis, well aware of the malicious intent of the rumours, was inclined to believe him – as he told him in a letter (in which he wrote of the boys' 'good manners and disposition during the period that I had the happiness of being in their company'). Before he left for home in October 1792, Cornwallis gave the order for the release of Tipu's sons.

On his return to England, Cornwallis continued to busy himself with Indian affairs, particularly in the reorganisation of the East India Company's forces (a plan which infuriated the officers of the Bengal Army). He was well received by people of all factions – court, Parliament, Company – a remarkable achievement in itself.

Before Cornwallis had left India, an event had occurred in France that had shaken every regime in Europe. On 21 January 1793 King Louis XVI had been guillotined. The French Revolution had set ablaze ideas that had been smouldering for centuries, the heat and energy of which were even to reach India.

135

9 THE WELLESLEYS

With Lord North's Regulating Act, Pitt's India Bill and the trial of Warren Hastings, the East India Company had been in the forefront of the public scene for twenty years. India was a constant topic of discussion. When it was to be debated, the House was filled, rather than quickly emptied as it was to be in future generations. Warren Hastings and Cornwallis, in their different ways, had taken an imperialist view of their tasks, and this had made the controversial old East India Company as admired and as hated as ever before. Cornwallis's successor, Sir John Shore, was a man with whom the directors of the Company felt far more comfortable. Like Hastings, he had spent his entire career in the Company's service, starting as a humble 'writer' and becoming Cornwallis's right-hand man in revenue matters. He was mild, courteous, respected, and even more insistent about his personal integrity than Warren Hastings had been. 'For one sinecure place in Bengal, there are ten in England,' he wrote. Shore was fortunate in that his Governor-Generalship did not have war thrust upon it. He tinkered with and mulled over his beloved revenues. He played cricket on the Calcutta lawns. He translated Persian classics into English.

Shore practised a policy of non-intervention. 'Our reputation for justice and good faith stands high in India,' he proudly claimed. 'And if I were disposed to depart from them, I could form alliances that would shake the Maratha Empire to its very foundations.

I will rather trust the permanency of our dominion to a perseverance in true principles.'

What would have happened if the Company's raj had continued along the modest lines of Sir John Shore and the commercially minded directors? It will never be known. For the next Governor-General was a very different man indeed – there had been no one like him in India since Clive.

Richard Wellesley, Earl of Mornington, was thirty-seven years old and he was one of the most ambitious men in London. From a family of minor English and Irish squires which had risen from nothing in half a century by way of the Irish Parliament, during which it had changed its name twice, he had enjoyed the curious privilege of being educated at both Eton *and* Harrow (having been expelled from the latter place for rioting). Feeling restricted by the Dublin Parliament, he had settled on India as his vehicle to power. His maiden speech at Westminster had been on the subject.

On 28 June 1793 he became a member of the Board of Control for the affairs of India, under Dundas. He was an extremely conscientious member, taking a close interest in all Indian affairs. However, he thought the position unworthy to one of his talents. 'I cannot bear to creep on in my present position,' he said. He frequently asked Pitt to give him a more important post. Wellesley had an extremely high opinion of himself, and the haughty, arrogant air with which this young Anglo-Irishman faced the world did not endear him to everybody. Sheridan described him in the House with his 'sonorous voice, placid countenance, leaning gracefully on the table'.

Wellesley had become friendly with Cornwallis, and when the latter was persuaded against his will to return to India, because of new threats from France, Wellesley agreed to take the Governorship of Madras. France and England were again at war, on account of the French Revolution; the French had declared war 'on all kings, and on behalf of all peoples'.* At the last minute Cornwallis was sent to Ireland, where there were even greater problems, and Wellesley was appointed Sir John Shore's successor in Calcutta. That such an ambitious careerist had accepted the post of Madras shows the importance that India, and the East India Company, had come to take in British affairs. Wellesley, now Lord Wellesley in the English

* Anglo-French War, 1793–1802.

peerage, went to Walmer Castle, in Kent, where Pitt and Dundas gave him his instructions.*

Under the cold, austere mask of Wellesley, there was a passionate man known only to his friends, who were alarmed that his indiscretions might harm his career. Wellesley's only regret at his appointment was that he felt unable to take his wife with him. They had only been married three years, but she had had five of his children before that. Wellesley's friends advised him that such a situation might cause embarrassing difficulties for the new Governor-General, even in the loose moral climate of Calcutta. Wellesley adored his children (two of the sons were to have distinguished careers). He told a friend, named as guardian in his will: 'Whatever may have been the folly which produced these little children, I am sure you have too much real feeling not to agree with me that they are a charge as dear and as sacred as if they had been born under the most solemn engagement.' He decided to leave his wife and family at home, although he was to regret having done so. 'The voyage, the climate, might injure her health,' he explained, 'and it is my duty not to separate her from her children.'

Wellesley's ship made the usual call at the Cape of Good Hope, and there he met several officers of the Company returning home, who spoke to him with many grievances. The feeling among many of the East India Company's servants in India was that a more positive, aggressive policy was needed. They also spoke of French intentions, making an alarmist case out of the fact that the Nizam of Hyderabad and Tipu of Mysore had both hired French adventurers to train their armies. Wellesley listened to all this probably with rather too much care. It was true that General Bonaparte was advancing towards Egypt, but there was very little French activity in India.† Pondicherry had been seized at the start of the new war, and France had no base from which to mount a threat to the Company.‡ The main danger was the old enemy Tipu, once more

* Wellesley was usually known as the Earl of Mornington, an Irish title, until his marquessate in 1799.

† The French fleet was defeated by Nelson in August 1798, but Napoleon managed to get back to France, where he was hailed as a hero, the conqueror of Egypt.

‡ The mercurial history of Pondicherry is a constant background to the history of the East India Company. It is as follows: 1683–93, French; 1693–7, Dutch; 1697–1761, French; 1761–3, British; 1763–78, French; 1778–83, British;

making war-like gestures. He had become infected with ideas of the Revolution, more probably as he recognised in it a powerful enemy to the East India Company than for ideological reasons; this despotic potentate now liked to be referred to as Citizen Tipu, and he made attempts to copy the system of the French Directory. He was supported by a small contingent from France. To complicate matters, the Marathas were dispirited and were less inclined to join with the Company against Tipu. In the north, the Afghans always threatened.

Wellesley spent several months at Madras on the way to Calcutta, and was appalled by the difficulties facing him. He wrote home: 'I can anticipate nothing but the most baneful consequences of a war with Tipu. The situation, I fear, is bad beyond the hope of remedy.' The Company's army, made up of criminals, deserters, sailors, and others with reasons for leaving Britain, did not impress him. He found the same situation in Bengal. Financial affairs, as usual, were also far from satisfactory. Wellesley protested, as others had before him, of the vast sums leaving India to pay for the Company's purchases of China tea. Soon after his arrival at Calcutta he wrote home to Lord Grenville, Foreign Secretary, about the lonely life which every Governor-General was obliged to experience, but which Wellesley inflicted upon himself as a matter of policy:

> Without [my wife], I fear, I shall not have fortitude to remain here long enough to accomplish all my grand financial, political military, naval, commercial, architectural, judicial, political reforms, and to make up a large treasure...All this might be effected within five or six years from the day of my embarkation at Cowes. But I leave you to judge of the necessity of her society while I give you some idea of my private life. I rise early and go out before breakfast, which is always over between eight and nine. From that hour until four (in the hot weather) I remain at work, unless I go to the Council, or to church of Sundays; at five I dine, and drive out in the evening. No constitution here can bear the sun in the middle of the day at any season of the year, nor the labour of the business in the evening. After dinner, therefore, nobody attempts to write or

---

1783–93, French; 1793–1802, British; 1802–3, French; 1803–16, British; 1816–1954, French.

read, and, in general, it is thought necessary to avoid even meetings on subjects of business at that time; for in this climate good or ill health depends upon a minute attention to circumstances apparently the most trivial. Thus, in the evening I have no alternative but the society of my subjects, or solitude. The former is so vulgar, ignorant, rude, familiar, and stupid as to be disgusting and intolerable; especially the ladies, not one of whom, by-the-bye, is even decently good-looking. The greatest inconvenience, however, arises from the ill-bred familiarity of the general manners...The effect of this state of things on my conduct has been to compel me to entrench myself within forms and ceremonies, to introduce much state into the whole appearance of my establishments and household, to expel all approaches to familiarity, and to exercise my authority with a degree of vigour and strictness nearly amounting to severity...It required some unpleasant efforts to place matters on this footing, and you must perceive that I am forced to fly to solitude for a large portion of the twenty-four hours, lest I should weaken my means of performing my public duty.

Wellesley's brother Henry, whom he had brought with him as his personal secretary, was his only close human contact. After Wellesley, the Governor-Generalship was not to be the same again. It was he who turned this post, later the Viceroyalty, into one of remote power and grandeur, almost like that of the past Mughals themselves. Wellesley furthered Cornwallis's policy of keeping Indians out of public service by also banning all Indians and Eurasians from official social occasions, an act which would have horrified many of the early Governors, not least Warren Hastings.

The Mysore question occupied much of Wellesley's time. He decided that war, after all, was inevitable, providing he could restore the alliance with Hyderabad. He wrote home: 'I trust that the Court of Directors...will be ready to sacrifice with cheerfulness something of present commercial profit to the Company for the preservation of the main sources of our wealth and strength.' This came as something of a shock in London, because Parliament and the Company had been under the impression that Wellesley would continue the policy of non-intervention which they preferred. Now, it seemed, they had unknowingly sent out another Clive. As the Governor-General was now all-powerful in the Company's affairs

in India, only controlled by a correspondence from London which took months to reach Calcutta, there was little they could do. But from then on there was frequent friction between Wellesley and the East India House (that 'most loathsome den', as he called it). The directors replied that if a war was to be fought, they would suggest the western seaboard of southern India, from Goa to Travancore, as a suitable acquisition. The Company's armies in Bengal and the Carnatic were enlarged and improved.

Wellesley successfully concluded negotiations with the Nizam of Hyderabad, who expelled his French advisers in return for the protection of Company forces. Wellesley found Tipu, as expected, less amenable. Tipu refused to expel his French advisers. He was proud of his independence and claimed he could employ whatever European advisers he pleased. Word had reached Calcutta of Napoleon's landing in Egypt, apparently threatening India. Wellesley began preparations for war.

◠◦◠

By February 1799 the Fourth Anglo-Mysore War was imminent. Preparations, more extensive than any the East India Company had made before, had been proceeding for months under the Governor of Madras, Clive's son, and the commander-in-chief at Madras, Lieutenant-General George Harris. Harris was a protégé of Medows; he had had a dangerous head operation after being wounded at Bunker's Hill in the American War of Independence, but it had not impaired his ability. Also at Madras was Wellesley's brother Arthur Wellesley, nine years his junior, and recently appointed to the command of the 33rd Foot, a royal regiment sent from Europe to reinforce the Company's troops. Arthur had arrived in India only a few months before Wellesley. Two more forceful men could hardly have been let loose on the sub-continent. Both were tough, stocky, and short (in contrast to the flattering portraits of later years). Arthur had an aloof, cold manner like his brother, but he does not seem at this period to have had quite the driving ambition of the head of the family. 'My highest ambition,' he said, 'is to serve His Majesty as a major-general.' He had taken a keen dislike to India, particularly – as had his elder brother – to the traditionally coarse, ebullient, and hard-living society of the Company's employees. 'A miserable country to live in,' he said. 'I now begin to think that a man deserves some of the wealth which is sometimes brought home for having spent his life here.' As for the Indians: 'They are the most mischievous, deceitful race of people I have ever seen or read of. I have not yet met with a Hindu who had one good quality, even for the state of society in his own country, and the Mussulmans [Muslims] are worse than they. Their meekness and mildness do not exist.' Such was the state of understanding between British and Indians in the late eighteenth century – as stated by one of the least meek and least mild British officers of the day.

Arthur used his family connection to advise Wellesley and to approach him direct, but as he said: 'I can't expect to derive any advantage from it [his brother's position] which I should not obtain if any other person were Governor-General.' Wellesley, however, was not a man to be put off using an officer in order to avoid charges of nepotism. He believed his brother was an extremely able young officer, far more studious about his profession than was usual in the Army – and he was perfectly correct. Wellesley had decided to accompany the invasion of Mysore himself, and Arthur, as a professional, was appalled at the arrogance of his brother, a mere civilian, intending to virtually take the command of a difficult military operation. 'I am entirely ignorant what you may have in coming,' he wrote from Madras, 'which may certainly counterbalance the objection which I have to the measure; but it appears to me that your presence in camp, instead of giving confidence to the general, would in fact deprive him of the command of the army. All I can say on the subject is, that if I were in General Harris's situation and you joined the army, I should quit it.' This led to a temporary coolness, and for a time the brothers addressed each other in the coldest terms (Arthur headed his letters 'Your Excellency'). But Wellesley did decide to stay in Calcutta.

The correspondence between Wellesley and Tipu had been dragging on for months. Wellesley's letters were of considerable length, containing involved arguments to support his demands. Tipu replied, when he did, briefly, in a courteous, placatory tone. When a mission left Mysore for the French island of the Île de France (Mauritius), Wellesley saw his chance. He sent off a long accusation of French-Mysore collusion and demanded an immediate reply. When none came, he ordered his army to advance.*

* Fourth Anglo-Mysore War, 1798–9.

143

The invasion of Mysore was to be in two thrusts. Harris, with Arthur Wellesley's regiment and the Nizam's cavalry guarding his supply train, was to advance towards Bangalore from the Carnatic. Another army, under Lieutenant-General James Stuart, which had come from Bombay, was to advance from the Malabar coast. With Harris were about 37,000 fighting men, including 6,000 of the Hyderabad cavalry. Stuart had 6,420 men, of whom 1,617 were Europeans. As Wellesley's aide-de-camp pointed out, it was 'most completely equipped, and most amply and liberally supplied; and as well appointed, as perfect in point of discipline, and as fortunate in the acknowledged experience and ability of its officers in every department, as any that ever took the field in India'.

Harris's ponderous force moved at a snail's pace up into Mysore. There was little Tipu could do about it, for his infantry, he knew, were no match for this vast column, which stretched for several miles as it advanced, and with its baggage train for a further seven miles to the rear. (According to one reliable source*, the entire column, with camp-followers, exceeded a quarter of a million souls.) Tipu's cavalry watched from the hills, in some dismay, at the magnificent spectacle moving ever slowly forward; occasionally they charged down in an attempt to disrupt the march, but disciplined musketry volleys sent them thundering off again, leaving many dead behind. Arthur Wellesley was impatient with the slow progress, and indignant at the size of the huge column and its supplies (it had with it 120,000 bullocks, with numerous horses, and many elephants). He, of course, had not campaigned in India before. Harris had been on the previous march to Seringapatam. Arthur said of the stores: 'Absolutely useless except as lumber.'

Tipu had expected a similar campaign to that of Cornwallis seven years previously. But Harris by-passed Bangalore, where Tipu had prepared a defence. Tipu, meanwhile, had attacked the more modest column of Stuart – it is said having been encouraged to do so by favourable omens. It was a fatal mistake, for Harris's advance was going so satisfactorily, despite its slowness and some loss of supplies, that even the defeat of Stuart would hardly have prevented the invasion. As it was, Stuart successfully beat off nearly twice as many of the enemy in what he described, in his despatch, with more accuracy than modesty, as a 'decisive, brilliant success'.

* J. W. Fortescue, *History of the British Army*.

Tipu made his stand against Harris at Malavalli, about twenty-five miles east of Seringapatam. He deployed his infantry on two ridges and made the mistake of attacking the 33rd Foot while the British square advanced. The Sultan's unwilling infantry were driven on by his own cavalry. The attack was routed and the Mysore infantry were easily brushed off the first ridge, and abandoned the second before it could be assaulted. The Company's losses at the Battle of Malavalli were only 7 killed, 53 wounded.

After two months on the march, the great column at last looked down on Seringapatam from the heights surrounding the town. The British closed in, to mount a siege. A British officer wrote:

> The Sultaun had a full view of the whole of our line as it passed. Although his horse had appeared in front, and on our right, we were suffered to pass without the least molestation. At this time the Sultaun appeared to feel the difficulties of his situation. By reports from his camp, we learnt that he was extremely dejected and undetermined; that plans of defence had been suddenly formed, and as suddenly abandoned.

The city was protected by a number of strong points, and these had to be cleared before the army could move in. Arthur Wellesley was given the task of taking the most important of these. He was not without experience of battle, having already fought in Holland against the French. He decided on Clive's favourite ploy – the night attack, in which neither he nor his troops had any experience. Arthur Wellesley, unlike Clive, was not an invariably lucky commander. He ordered no reconnaissance, and his force got hopelessly lost in the dark, and finally lost all sense of direction. There was total chaos. The troops entered a wood, in which they became even more confused, and then came under enemy fire. Attempting to reply, Arthur Wellesley's men merely succeeded in shooting at each other. Arthur Wellesley himself lost both his troops and his way. It was a humiliating failure for the vain young colonel. At daylight he regrouped his disgruntled troops and, quite unabashed, launched them at the strongpoint once more. In a rather remarkable feat of leadership, considering the circumstances, he got his regiment to follow him and the position was taken with brilliant dash. Another officer's career might have been finished; he had restored it within hours. Arthur Wellesley made a mental note of his earlier failure. He early promised his elder brother that he would never again launch 'an attack to be made by night upon an enemy who is prepared and strongly posted, and whose posts have not been reconnoitred by daylight'.

As the preparations for siege continued, a letter for Harris arrived from Tipu. '...In this matter what is your pleasure? Inform me, that a conference may take place. What can I say more?' Harris replied with a long list of demands, previously prepared by the Governor-General, including the loss of half Tipu's lands, a large sum of money, the extradition of all Frenchmen from Mysore, and four of his sons to be taken hostage. Harris finished his letter: 'What need I say more?'

There was no immediate answer. The British artillery bombarded the fortress. Tipu said he would send some envoys, but Harris refused to receive them unless accompanied by the hostages. The barrage continued for several days and one of the Mysore powder magazines was hit ('occasioned a dreadful explosion'). The fortress was stormed after fierce fighting in which twenty-five British officers were killed or wounded. A highland regiment was present, and the pipes played as troops poured through a breach in the ramparts. One of the first to enter was Harris's own son, a junior officer in the infantry.

After some confusion, Tipu's body was found near one of the gates. He had been shot dead by one of the last volleys of musketry. After less than a month, the siege was over; during it the British had lost 322 killed and 1,078 wounded. About 120 French were found in the fort, and their tricolour was personally captured by Harris's son, who was sent home with it, and who presented it to George III.

The Governor-General was delighted, for he had been apprehensive as to the outcome owing to Harris's enormous supply problems. He told the army that their successes had 'surpassed even the sanguine expectations of the Governor-General in council, have raised the reputation of the British arms in India, to a degree of splendour and glory unrivalled in the military history of this quarter of the globe, and seldom approached in any part of the world'. As soon as he heard of the victory, he wrote off to Lord Grenville:

To you I shall use no disguise, but inform you plainly that the manner in which I have conducted this war has been received with exultations, and even with the most unqualified admiration in India; and...you will gain much credit by conferring some high and brilliant honour upon me immediately. The Garter would be much more acceptable to me than any additional title, nor would any title be an object which should not raise me to the same rank which was given to Lord Cornwallis [i.e. a marquessate]. Tipu Sultan fought better and had a much more efficient army than in the last war.

It seems that Wellesley was after a dukedom. Grenville was displeased at this openness of seeking after honours. Wellesley got an Irish marquessate, which was inferior to an English title. Wellesley was quite distraught with fury. 'I cannot describe my anguish of mind...my bitter disappointment,' he told Pitt. The Company, however, awarded him a pension of £5,000 a year. Harris was also offered an Irish peerage, but he contemptuously turned it down. (Justice was not done till fifteen years later, when he was made Lord Harris of Seringapatam and Mysore; the third Lord Harris, his grandson, was Governor of Madras at the time of the mutiny.)

Harris organised an imposing state funeral for Tipu, something which amazed the local inhabitants. The bier passed through crowded streets, preceded and followed by four companies of grenadiers. The cortège passed into the great mausoleum of Haidar Ali as an avenue of troops presented arms. Tipu was buried beside his father. That night there was 'a most dreadful storm' in which two British officers were killed by lightning.

The Mysore Army was disbanded. Tipu's four sons were sent down to the Carnatic and the descendant of the original Rajas of Mysore placed on the throne. This was Wellesley's personal decision, as there were some who preferred to continue Haidar Ali's dynasty. Wellesley also supervised the dissection of Tipu's territory between the Company, the Nizam, the Marathas, who had to receive something because the Nizam did, and Mysore itself. A treaty was drawn up between Mysore and the East India Company which gave Mysore 'protection' in return for an annual subsidy of £280,000. Wellesley received the right of unlimited intervention in the internal affairs of the country. Mysore, in fact, was to be a vassal state.

To ensure the superiority of the Company, Wellesley appointed Arthur as the 'Governor' of Seringapatam. Lieutenant-General David Baird, who had commanded the assault and had once been a prisoner in Seringapatam, had expected the appointment. He was far senior to Arthur Wellesley. There was an explosive scene at breakfast in the mess, but Arthur was not in the least disturbed at charges of nepotism. For two years, during which he rose to the rank of major-general although still in his thirties — and in which he found time to fall in love with the wife of a humble captain in the Madras Artillery — he was a just ruler of Mysore.

The East India Company ruled all the territory between the Coromandel and Malabar coasts, virtually all of India beneath the fifteenth parallel, as well as Bengal and the lower Ganges, and Bombay. There was no doubt at all that it was the major power in India; anyone who had seen its vast army moving remorselessly into Mysore would not have doubted it. The French had lost their last vestige of influence. Only the old enemy, the Marathas, with the Afghans lurking to the north, stood between the East India Company and complete command of the Mughal legacy itself.

❦

After the defeat of Tipu, much of the rest of India seemed to fall into Wellesley's hands. The Governor-General collected territory with an insatiable, unabashed, almost frenetic lust, while the men of Leadenhall Street wrung their hands in horror. He devoted himself to a persistent and ruthless diplomacy. The East India Company would provide security for almost any ruler through the presence of British troops in or near the seat of power; but this military presence would have to be paid for. Thus Wellesley was increasing what he now termed 'the empire' in India and making sure the Company was paid for doing so. No sooner were the troops ensconced than Wellesley made various demands, and the Company became ruler in all but name. First to go was Tanjore (Thanjavur) in the south Carnatic. The Nawab of the Carnatic himself, who had been friendly with Tipu, died; Wellesley made sure his successor was a puppet, and the entire administration of the territory came to the Company. Oudh, over which the Company had dithered for so long, ceded part of its territory after negotiations conducted by Henry Wellesley, who became the Lieutenant-Governor of the ceded territory. This appointment caused an uproar among the directors in London because Henry Wellesley was not in the Company's employ, but was the Governor-General's personal assistant. The directors were overruled by Dundas and the Board of Control.

All this was happening with such speed that the directors in London had difficulty in keeping up with it. When they did gather what was happening, they were outraged. The old controversy about the East India Company's responsibilities blazed as never before. The directors (except some of the Nabobs) insisted the Company was in India for trade, not for territory. They wanted riches, not power. Above all, they thought Wellesley was too high-handed and was usurping their power, such as it was. Henry Wellesley was sent home on a mission to explain his brother's policy, and he wisely concentrated on Westminster rather than on the already committed East India House. The directors were represented in Parliament and did have friends there, particularly Sheridan (Burke had died), and powerful friends outside, including the Prince of Wales. But the Government was now in a more imperialist mood and Addington, the new prime minister, Pitt, Grenville, Dundas (and most of the Board of Control), and for a time Cornwallis, supported Wellesley's expansionist policy.

The directors had other enemies to contend with — those who had brought up the old monopoly question again. It was said that potential exports from India were now so great that the East India Company simply did not have the ships to carry them. The Company, they said, existed only for the purpose of making a close, exclusive circle rich. The directors replied that far from getting rich, the Company considered India a bottomless pool which seemed to have an inexhaustible need for money.

The main cause of financial difficulty was the vast army which Wellesley's expansionist policy required to be kept under arms. The Governor-General received from the court of directors 'a peremptory order to reduce the military strength of the empire, which had been made under my express authority, after the fullest deliberation, and after consulting all the most experienced officers in India'. He threatened to resign. But he was obliged to remain because of a new crisis — according to Wellesley, the Marathas were threatening the Company's position.

The Maratha confederacy claimed all central India, south-to-north, from near Goa to Delhi; west-to-east, from Kutch to the border of Orissa. Whereas the East India Company had south India and Bengal, and Muslim rulers held the north and east, the Marathas had nearly all the middle. But for years the five major groups of Marathas had been split and arguing, mainly over the succession to their nominal head, the Peshwa of Poona. The Peshwa had become isolated from the most powerful chiefs, Daulat Rao Sindhia of Gwalior and Holkar of Indore. The Peshwa had fled to Bombay from Poona.

The Maratha troubles had traditionally been a matter for the Bombay Presidency, but now Wellesley, exercising the power of the Governor-Generalship, himself decided to take control. Clear instructions from London arrived ordering him not 'to involve us in the endless and turbulent distractions of the Marathas'. But Wellesley had already decided to pursue a policy of backing the Peshwa against Sindhia and Holkar, providing he ceded certain lands around Bombay; the Peshwa had agreed. Sindhia feared this intrusion of the East India Company into the affairs of the confederacy. He impetuously allied himself with Bhonsla of Berar, a Maratha ruler who claimed *he* was the rightful Peshwa. The usual unhelpful correspondence was a prologue to war.* Holkar remained aloof for the time being.

Wellesley decided to conquer the Marathas in two simultaneous blows: one from Bombay, under Arthur Wellesley, was to defeat Sindhia and Berar in the field; the other, under the very experienced and able General G. Lake, was to rush to Delhi, where the descendant of the Mughals had for years been a captive puppet of the Marathas. Sindhia and Berar faced Wellesley. Another force, owing allegiance to them but commanded by a Frenchman, faced Lake.

Sindhia had over 40,000 men. Against him, Arthur Wellesley had less than 5,000, of whom about 2,000 were British troops, and including contingents from Mysore and the Peshwa. Arthur found he was chasing a wily enemy. But during his governorship of Mysore he had gained invaluable experience when dealing with a large and elusive bandit column. He marched with less of the incumbrances usual in Indian warfare, and he was a strict disciplinarian.

* Second Anglo-Maratha War, 1803–5.

150

At length the two armies came face to face, near Assaye. A river separated them. Every available boat had been destroyed by the enemy, and the guides assured Arthur Wellesley that only one ford was practicable; this was heavily covered by Sindhia's troops. Wellesley rode along the bank, ignoring all advice. He noticed that at one point there was a cluster of huts at each side of the river. He got his army across, as he said, 'By the common sense of guessing that men did not build villages on opposite sides of a stream without some means of communication between them.' The battle that followed was remarkable for its steady courage on behalf of the regular British Army regiments which continued in India because of a supposed French threat, made much of by Wellesley, and of the Company's own battalions of sepoys. In later life, Arthur Wellesley considered it 'the bloodiest for the number engaged that I ever saw', which meant it was very bloody indeed.

The British infantry moved steadily forward under a hail of round-shot and grape from Sindhia's French-commanded artillery. Support from their own artillery was ineffective. It was a murderous thing to ask any troops to do, but the Company and royal regiments marched steadily forward in perfect order, Arthur Wellesley and his staff well to the fore on their horses. As the Governor-General commented, 'the execution was terrible'. As they neared one flank of the Maratha line, Arthur Wellesley sent his cavalry charging at the other. The enemy, 'overawed by the steady advance of the British troops', according to Wellesley, began to give way. But the Marathas' fierce and war-like reputation was not based on nothing. Victory was not yet won, for in the concentration of their advance the British had failed to notice that many of the bodies over which they stepped were not dead at all, but only feigning death; these brave men now leapt to their feet and began firing muskets and artillery into the rear of the British, who nevertheless continued their advance in good order. Arthur Wellesley himself dashed about, at the head of two regiments, annihilating the groups behind the British line; he had his horse shot from under him. The Marathas withdrew, not in rout but reluctantly, and still fighting here and there. They left 1,200 dead behind, and 'the whole country covered with their wounded'. The British lost 951 killed and nearly 1,800 wounded. The Battle of Assaye had taken less than three hours. It had hardly been a brilliantly conducted battle by young Wellesley, as is so often claimed; it had been won by the new spirit and efficiency of the army in India, begun under Warren Hastings, improved under Cornwallis, and completed by the Wellesleys. The Governor-General, however, wrote of his brother: 'It is impossible to bestow any commendation superior to the skill, magnanimity, promptitude and judgment displayed by Major-General Wellesley on this memorable occasion.' Arthur Wellesley, realising his debt to his steady troops, said in his despatch:

> This victory, which was certainly complete, has however cost us dear...I cannot write in too strong terms of the conduct of the troops; they advanced in the best order, and with the greatest steadiness, under most destructive fire, against a body of infantry far superior in numbers, who appeared determined to contend with them to the last, and who were driven from their guns only by the bayonet; and notwithstanding the numbers of the enemy's cavalry, and the repeated demonstrations they made of an intention to charge, they were kept at a distance by our infantry.

After the battle, an envoy was received asking for terms. Arthur Wellesley rejected him as he did not seem to have Sindhia's authority. The chase dragged on for another two months, as Wellesley's army followed Sindhia and Berar through difficult terrain, hauling the guns and supply trains after it, covering little over ten miles a day. Another victory followed, at Arguam.

Almost simultaneously to Assaye, Lake's army had clashed with Sindhia's other army outside Delhi. The battle was fought within view of the minarets of the city. It was well conducted by Lake, the French commander of the Marathas having previously deserted. The Maratha army was entrenched in an extremely strong position. The British cavalry mounted a charge, but withdrew prematurely. The enemy accepted this feint and rushed from their positions, believing the British were on the point of turning. The cavalry withdrew to the rear, when it suddenly parted to each side, allowing the infantry to pass through and advance on the over-confident enemy. It was a consummate move, and the infantry – with Lake personally leading one of the regiments – continued advancing steadily, finally breaking into a bayonet charge. The Marathas broke. The victory was completed by the infantry forming into companies, allowing the cavalry to charge through the gaps. It was one of the finest set-piece battles ever fought by a British general in India.

Lake sent a message into Delhi, congratulating the Mughal 'on his emancipation from the control of the French faction which had so long oppressed and degraded him'. The British saw French influence everywhere, but there had been little indeed in Delhi. Wellesley, basing his report on Lake and 'private sources of intelligence', continues the story:

His Majesty was graciously pleased to direct his eldest son and heir apparent, the Prince Mirza Akbar Shah, to conduct the Commander-in-Chief to his royal presence. The Prince was to have arrived at the Commander-in-Chief's tent at twelve o'clock, but did not reach the British camp until half-past three o'clock p.m. By the time His Royal Highness had been received, remounted on his elephant, and the whole cavalcade formed, it was half-past four o'clock. The distance being five miles, the Commander-in-Chief did not reach the palace of Delhi until sunset. The crowd in the city was extraordinary, and it was with some difficulty that the cavalcade could make its way to the palace. The courts of the palace were full of people anxious to witness the deliverance of their Sovereign from a state of degradation and bondage. At length the Commander-in-Chief was ushered into the royal presence, and found the unfortunate and venerable Emperor, oppressed by the accumulated calamities of old age, degraded authority, extreme poverty, and loss of sight, seated under a small tattered canopy, the remnant of his royal state, with every external appearance of the misery of his condition.

The British, insisting to themselves and everyone else that they were liberators, settled into Delhi, and showed no signs of leaving. Unlike his previous liberators, they treated the Mughal 'emperor' with the greatest possible personal respect. The Emperor, the great-great-grandson of Aurangzib and direct descendant of Akbar himself, was gratified. Wellesley was glad to offer him 'protection'.

Lake went south and captured Agra, and again routed his enemy at Laswari. The campaign, which had lasted less than three months, ended in November 1803 when Wellesley followed Sindhia to Gawilgarh and stormed the formidable fortress there, driving Sindhia's remaining forces from the field. The Peshwa was escorted back to Poona, where he reclaimed his throne.

Only the ferocious Holkar of the once-dreaded Maratha chieftains remained independent of the Company. Four months after the treaty with Sindhia, negotiated by Arthur Wellesley, in which the East India Company gained more territory, the inevitable clash between the Governor-General and the last of the Marathas began. Holkar had followed the recent campaign closely; he had learnt some lessons from it. He had decided not to rely on infantry and artillery, as Sindhia, aping European methods, had done. He would rely on the traditional Maratha tactics of the mobility of large numbers of horsemen. Lake followed him, but could not bring him to a decisive battle. One of his columns was defeated by the Marathas and was compelled to retreat two hundred and fifty miles, leaving all its guns and most of its baggage strewn behind it. It was the first defeat for British forces since Wellesley's aggressive policy had begun. Holkar menaced Agra and actually besieged Delhi. Lake made a dash to Delhi, where the garrison of 2,500 had been defending the city against a force ten times that number, just in time. While the infantry dealt with the enemy at Agra, the cavalry followed Holkar. Believing the British to be well behind, Holkar paused for a rest, but the British, covering seventy miles in twenty-four hours, burst into his camp at dawn and almost annihilated the Maratha force. Holkar himself was one of the few who escaped. He collected his remaining troops, now barely 8,000 men, and retreated towards the Sutlej river. He crossed into the Punjab, hoping to find support there. By this time the Company directors had reached Wellesley with instructions to discontinue the war immediately.

By the end of 1805 the East India Company's influence, and its influence amounted to indirect rule, had reached to Northern India – to the borders of the Punjab, a mysterious, little-known state – an almost unthinkable situation only a decade before. The authority of the Mughal emperors had passed from the Maratha chiefs to the men of Leadenhall Street, many of whom had been no nearer India than Brighton. As Arthur Wellesley said, the Company and Government were 'in a most glorious situation, as the sovereigns of a great part of India; the protectors of the principal powers and the mediators, by treaty, of the disputes of all'. It did seem an amazing achievement for the proud people from the comparatively small island off the coast of Europe. There were few people, even the most bitter critics of Wellesley's policy, who were not excited by the prospects. No one was to know that the Marathas were not done for yet, that the Punjab was to be no easy neighbour, that defending its new dominions under the name of protecting the Mughal was to stretch Britain to unimagined limits in India.

It seemed to be all over. Lake became Viscount Lake of Delhi and Laswari (when he died in England, in 1808, he was in near penury). Of the three brothers, Henry Wellesley had been the first to go home; he had again become his brother's agent in London. He had a cool reception and did not receive a peerage until 1828; he eventually became ambassador in Paris (as was his son for many years after him). Arthur Wellesley left in March 1805. He returned with an established military reputation, received a knighthood and the thanks of both houses of Parliament. He was a cold, hard man of thirty-five, matured beyond his years. He became MP for Rye, but soon returned to his military career; nine years later he was created the Duke of Wellington; ten years after leaving India he defeated Napoleon at Waterloo; twenty-three years after leaving India he was prime minister.

Richard Wellesley, by now virtually an uncontrollable despot as far as the appalled directors of the Company were concerned, believed his work in India was complete. They censured him for his disobedience of their orders, for illegalities, for not protecting their monopoly, for encouraging shipbuilding in India (some directors had shipping interests), and above all, for profligate over-expenditure. He resigned at once and sailed for home five months after Arthur. He had left home an ambitious, little-known politician. He returned having tasted greater power over human beings than any Englishman had ever done before him. An early biographer, W. M. Torrens, described the home-coming of the Governor-General:

Lady Wellesley and her children awaited him on landing, and several private friends pressed round him with kind welcomes. The Port Admiral was also there, and certain military officials eager to see the little man of whom they had heard so much... But he had been playing king until the rarefied atmosphere of kingship had become so habitual that the murk of common-place in the best inn in a half-lighted seaport town almost stifled him. Had the successor of Aurangzib come to this? There he was, with wife and children, and two or three friends from town, after all his impersonation of paramount power and impersonation of Oriental magnificence, made much of by vulgar waiters just like any other Irish marquess on his travels. He did his best to look pleased and be gracious, but his mortification was unspeakable; and ere dinner-time was half over he broke out into expletives of impatience that made the circle stare. Hyacinth [his wife]...said, with an unlucky laugh: 'Ah, you must not think you are in India still, where everybody ran to obey you. They mind nobody here.' The disenchantment was complete. He rose early from table and withdrew, saying he was ill and must be left alone.

Wellesley had to face charges in the House of Commons, backed by Fox and the Prince of Wales, for the abuse of his office. A vote of censure was defeated by 182 votes to 31, a great victory for Wellesley and his empire-minded friends. He became ambassador to Spain, was Foreign Secretary for three years, and later Lord-Lieutenant of Ireland. Like most of the family, he lived to a very old age, and died in 1842.

The Wellesleys had gone to India as obscure personalities. They had returned famous, and became one of the greatest and most powerful of English families. They had used India as none had done since Clive, and as no one was ever to do again. They represented a new type of Englishman (Wellington scorned his Irish birth). The old notion of the Englishman as a gay and ruffianly buccaneer had gone for ever. European rivals were becoming aware of an Englishman typified by the Wellesleys: autocratic men of action with a laconic style and a disdain for foreigners. The heady opportunities, and the extraordinary demands, of service in India had not a little to do with this transition.

India was British, from Trivandrum to the Sutlej. Since Clive, men had tried to gain India for the Company, others had tried to withdraw, and the lands of the East India Company had fluctuated. Before the arrival of the Wellesleys these territories had shown every sign of soon contracting to the original presidencies of Bombay, Madras, and Calcutta. It had taken three single-minded, energetic, haughty Anglo-Irish brothers, who had no interest in Indians at all, and who were deaf to the commands and directions of men far away, to found British India beyond all recall. They had achieved it because of the political instability and fragmentation of the land,

156

through military superiority backed by Britain's growing wealth. They had found the East India Company a ramshackle concern trading in tea and opium, with territorial interests in Bengal and the Carnatic: they left it as the ruler of India. And they had done it in only seven years. Where the force of their unyielding diplomacy had failed, they had not hesitated to resort to the force of arms. It had been a bloody business.

Part Two RULE
OF INDIA

10 THE AGE OF RAFFLES

Richard Wellesley had left behind him the foundations of an empire greater even than that of Akbar himself. Territory actually belonging to the Company included Bombay Island, Bengal and Behar, the Carnatic, the Northern Circors, Malabar; as well as these, it controlled by subsidiary treaties Mysore, Hyderabad, Oudh, Travancore, and Jaipur. The subjection of the Marathas had brought nearly all the remainder of southern and central India under its control. Virtually all India south of Delhi was under the domination of the East India Company. At the same time, the Company had been expanding elsewhere; although the trade with Persia was almost dead,* the China tea trade continued profitably; by 1799 the Canton factory had a Company staff of sixteen, including the President. There had been a renewed interest in the East Indies. During the war the French had taken control of the Spice Islands from their vassal state Holland, and had thus threatened the route to China. The Company had acquired the almost uninhabited island of Penang, off the Malayan coast, from the local ruler, and was developing it as a trading station. After Ceylon, most of which had been under the commercial control of Holland for a hundred and fifty years, had been invaded during the war, it had come under East India Company rule, from Madras. Efforts to install the Company system of raising taxes in Ceylon,

* But successors to the defence treaties made by the East India Company with the 'Trucial States' lasted to present times.

however, had led to fighting, and in 1798 the island had come under the dual control of the East India Company and the Government, with a Governor appointed by the Crown, but under the direction of the Governor-General in Calcutta and the directors in London. The first Governor was Frederick North, son of the prime minister, who was able to get on with neither the local inhabitants nor the Company officials seconded from Madras. The first three paymasters-general of the new government of Ceylon were all accused of falsifying accounts, and there were many resignations in the civil service. In 1802 the system of dual control was abandoned and Ceylon was taken out of the East India Company sphere and made a Crown colony, although the Company retained a monopoly of trade there till 1821.

The Company was having the greatest difficulty in digesting its new acquisitions. As always, its finances were mostly chaotic. Although there were large new taxable areas, revenue from which could help satisfy the China coast merchants and Peking, and also the Company's creditors, most especially the Government, there had also been a great increase of expenditure. Dundas, sick and exhausted, had resigned, after seventeen years. He had been succeeded, as President of the Board, by Castlereagh. A group of irate directors complained, in a special report:

> Mr Dundas, on retiring from office, has represented India and the affairs of the Company in the most prosperous situation… yet, Mr Dundas was mistaken as to the real situation of the Company's affairs in India. The India debt on 30 April, 1800, was £14,433,717. When, in 1784, Mr Dundas took upon himself the administration of Indian affairs, the Indian debt was £4,521,685.

During three years of Wellesley's Governor-Generalship the Company had sent out to India £4,200,000 in bullion. The Board of Control's policies, and Wellesley's actions, had become such a scandal that the directors had managed to regain some of their lost power vis-à-vis the Board. Henry Wellesley had told his brother Richard: 'Both Addington and Castlereagh see the importance of your staying in India but they are not strong enough to contest the point with the Directors.' The leading director was Charles Grant, who combined his business activities with an association with the evangelical Clapham Sect; it was his wish that all the Company's subjects should be converted to Christianity without delay.

It was believed in London that only one man could save the Company from financial ruin, settle India, and satisfy Parliament — Cornwallis. During Cornwallis's first Governor-Generalship the net profits of the Company had frequently doubled that of a typical Warren Hastings' year. Although he was now sixty-six, and in poor health, he accepted the office of Governor-General for the third time. He actually arrived at Calcutta two weeks before Richard Wellesley had sailed for home. It was a difficult situation, for Cornwallis had been sent to undo much of what were considered Wellesley's wrongs. His object was to restore the confidence of Indian rulers in British justice and moderation. Although he had supported Wellesley early on, he was convinced that the British reputation had suffered during Wellesley's bullying, and it was the reputation of his country that Cornwallis cared for above all else. He made a treaty with Holkar in which the astonished Maratha chief was given back nearly all his lands. Sindhia also retrieved much of what he had lost. This meant that the Company withdrew its boundary from the north, retaining only Delhi, the upper Ganges, and the Jumna. The territory thus abandoned immediately became the scene of warfare and near-anarchy, as has often been pointed out, but no worse than it had been before the Maratha War; the Company had not had time to set up an efficient administration. Although the Marathas, having lost the war, had recovered much of what they had lost, the Company still controlled about half of India and was indisputably the major power.

Cornwallis, arranging this retrenchment, went up the Ganges from lower Bengal. For nearly two months his impressive barge was towed upstream, ploughing a steady course against the mighty river. He became increasingly ill and, because his secretaries began writing his letters, it was said he had lost his mind. He died at Ghazipore. A great mausoleum was erected over his grave, as was suited to so important a ruler in a country where signs of importance had to be unmistakable.

On Cornwallis's death, the power of government fell to the senior member of the council in Calcutta. This was Sir George Barlow, who had long been in the service of the Company. Barlow, as an old employee, was much to the directors' liking. The Board of Control agreed to Barlow's being the next Governor-General, but on a temporary basis. The Board, naturally, felt safer with its own nomination, who would be someone less close to the Company than Barlow. It was the old story: could the East India Company be trusted to bear such vast responsibilities over millions of people without outside control? As far as Parliament was concerned, the answer was No. A compromise was reached in the person of Lord Minto, a cultivated politician who had succeeded Castlereagh as President of the Board of Control. Barlow's short regime was chiefly noteworthy for the trouble he had with the military; the sepoys in the Carnatic mutinied when presented with reforms. The sepoys had been expected to wear hats instead of turbans and had been forbidden to appear on parade wearing forehead marks – as the diarist William Hickey said: 'A very mistaken and ill-judged order.' This had not only infuriated the sepoys, it had filled them with fear, for they believed these were the first moves in attempts to force them to become Christians – as, in an unconscious way, they no doubt were. The sepoys signalled their distaste by murdering their English officers. A British column, under Robert Rollo Gillespie, met the mutineers at Vellore, fourteen miles from Arcot, and killed 400 of them. That seemed to have settled the matter...no one thought much more about the question of the sepoys' sensitivity in religious matters.

On his supersession, Barlow became Governor of Madras, and there he fell foul of the army, this time with the British officers, whom he tried to discipline. From the time of Clive there had been clashes between royal officers sent to India and the Company's own officers, and the question of authority was always a source of discontent.

Minto arrived in Calcutta exactly two years after Cornwallis had done. He had been a friend of Burke, and thus could be relied upon to follow a non-aggressive policy with the independent states. He was one of six great men in India during the early years of the century: Thomas Munro (Madras), Mountstuart Elphinstone (the Marathas, Madras, and Bombay), John Malcolm (Bombay and the Deccan), Charles Metcalfe (Delhi and the North), Lord Moira, and Minto himself. These men, a new generation of Company servants and Governors-General, improved on the basis of good government founded by Warren Hastings and Cornwallis. They strove to make a career in India something of which an Indiaman could be proud. It is unusual in history to find men whose reputations are faultless, but these men are such.* Munro, who became Governor of Madras and at last brought some order to that notorious and turbulent place, believed that 'the good government of the people is the great end'. He warned the directors: 'Your rule is alien, and it can never be popular.' Nevertheless, he had no doubt as to the duration of the British stay in India, and its purpose:

> Our sovereignty should be prolonged to the remotest possible period…Whenever we are obliged to resign it, we should leave the natives so far improved from their connection with us as to be capable of maintaining a free, or at least a regular, government amongst themselves.

Before 1756 the Governor and Council of Fort William had required only one civil department to manage all their business. Despatches from home had been laid before them by the chief secretary, who then received their instructions for any action to be taken. But the pressure of business after the acquisition of Bengal made a larger organisation necessary. The Central Secretariat at Calcutta was in four main branches: General, Revenue, Commercial, and Judicial. The General branch was subdivided into Civil, Military, and Marine. This system lasted till 1834, when the Commercial department was wound up. These were all under the ultimate control of the Governor-General, the Council having become virtually powerless since Cornwallis, but the Civil department of the General branch was under his direct control. The secretaries who ran these departments were senior figures in the Company hierarchy, such men as William Kirkpatrick, Charles Metcalfe, N. B. Edmonstone, Lionell Hook, Charles Ricketts, Charles Lushington, and William Butterworth Bailey. Minto gave a good description of the working of the Council and the civil service, or Central Secretariat:

> The routine is this: the Secretaries in the different departments send in circulation to me and the members of Council the

---

* Lord Attlee once told of his stay with a modern Indian Governor, once a nationalist agitator: 'He told me how an Indonesian visitor to Government House admired pictures of notable Indian national leaders, but on finding a picture of a great British Governor, Sir Thomas Munro, said: "Do you keep pictures of your tyrants?" The Governor replied: "Yes, we are proud of him."'

despatches they have received since the last Council, and the documents relating to all business which arises in the interval. These are extremely voluminous, and would require pretty nearly the whole interval for mere perusal. The number and variety of affairs is also immense; for everything, small as well as great, must have the sanction of government...A declaration of war, and an estimate for an addition to a barrack a thousand miles off, may come next to each other in the Secretaries' bundle...The Secretaries attend at Council, each department in turn with its mountains of bundles. The Secretary reads or often only states shortly the substance of each paper, and the order is given on the spot. We are enabled to do this by having read these bundles at home. The Secretaries reduce all our orders into minutes of Council, letters, instructions, etc... We hold two Councils a week – Monday and Friday. We meet at ten and sit till three or four.

It is clear that there was some opportunity for the Secretaries to be the real power at the Company's capital at Calcutta, but by and large most of the Governors-General resisted this possibility and made their own decisions, not even heeding the advice of Council.

Minto's Governor-Generalship was dominated by the ambitions of Napoleon.* The British had an obsessive interest in protecting their newly won domains in India, despite the guilt-ridden attitude in London to Wellesley's conquests. Minto saw a danger of Napoleon coming down from Russia or through Persia. He decided to establish buffer states between the Company's territory and the threat from Europe. For this reason he sent off three of the Company's most able young men as special envoys: Malcolm to Persia, Metcalfe to the Punjab, and Elphinstone to the Afghans.

Malcolm had already visited Persia. He was now instructed to dissuade Persia from forming an alliance with the French and to prevent French depots being set up in that area. At Tehran, he found that the Persians were more impressed with the French than they were with the British, but a treaty with the Shah was eventually and reluctantly signed.

The Punjab, ruled by Ranjit Singh, Maharajah of Lahore, was peopled by the proud and independent Sikhs, who had broken free of the Hindu-Muslim-dominated society of India. Ranjit Singh

* Anglo-French War, 1804–15.

was known to be anti-British, and the Sikhs frequently raided Company territory across the Sutlej. Minto entrusted the mission to the Punjab to Charles Metcalfe, who had been born in Calcutta only twenty-three years previously. It took Metcalfe two months to reach Ranjit Singh after leaving Delhi. The Rajah sent an escort of 2,000 cavalry to meet him. Ranjit Singh was wily, mischievous, and untrustworthy; his objects in life were the security of his own throne and the independence of his people. After lengthy and difficult negotiations, he agreed to an alliance with the East India Company provided the Company turned aside while he conquered neighbouring Sikh territory. This condition Metcalfe refused, but Ranjit Singh began his conquests anyway. Ranjit Singh crossed the Sutlej and advanced his territory towards the British boundary, while Metcalfe could do nothing. The Sikh ruler was warned that the Company would protect its frontier with force. Metcalfe succeeded in persuading the Maharajah that the Company was in deadly earnest. Ranjit agreed to confine his activities north of the Sutlej, and the Company agreed not to interfere as long as he did so. He ceded all his newly acquired land south of the Sutlej to the Company in return for military protection. It was a great success for young Metcalfe.

Metcalfe had been a protégé of Lake, whose political adviser he had been. Elphinstone had acted in a similar capacity, during the Maratha War, for Arthur Wellesley, who had furthered his career. He had studied Oriental languages, and Minto chose him for the important mission to the Afghans. It was a dangerous mission, for the Afghans disliked all contact with Europeans. It was decided that it would be best if the Company's envoy went in style. He left with 400 troops, 600 camels, elephants, and boxes filled with his personal library. It took him four months from Delhi to reach Peshawar, where the ruler of the Afghans, Shah Shuja, met him, having come south from Kabul. Elphinstone was received in the greatest splendour by a ruler who to all appearances must have been one of the richest in Asia. But appearances were deceptive. The Shah responded to Elphinstone's suggestions by asking for an immediate loan to save his throne. Elphinstone agreed that he should receive an annual sum while he worked against a Franco-Persian alliance and kept Frenchmen out of his territory. 'A very unfavourable turn has taken place in the King of Kabul's affairs,'

Elphinstone reported to Minto. It had indeed. Within months the Shah fled his country, and was replaced by Dost Muhammad Khan.

Only in the Punjab, therefore, did Minto's diplomacy show much likelihood of success. He had serious troubles nearer home. Threatened with a cut in their allowances, the army officers in the Carnatic and Madras rose in revolt. For those who had worked so long to improve the standard and morale of the Company's army, it was a heartbreaking business. Minto rushed to Madras and saved the situation. 'No man of honour at the head of a government will compromise with revolt,' he declared. Senior officers, and those who had taken a particularly active part, were court-martialled or dismissed from the service. But most were granted an amnesty.

Minto attempted to restore the Persian trade by sending an armed expedition to the Persian Gulf, where pirates had made trade almost impossible for many decades. He also seized the French island of Mauritius, in 1810, which gave added protection to the route from England. In the previous year cargoes to a value of over £1,000,000 had been lost because of French raiders and pirates from Mauritius. These islands came under the direct sovereignty of the Crown, not the East India Company, but the government in Calcutta helped with the administration. At the same time the Company was looking towards the east again. Minto sent for one of the Company's representatives in the Spice Islands to report to him in Calcutta. His name was Thomas Stamford Raffles.

Raffles was a dark, good-looking young man whose short career was destined to be one of the most dramatic and tragic in the East India Company's history. He was the son of a hard-up ship's master and had joined the Company's service as a boy of fourteen at the East India House in London, in 1795. He had been an industrious and able clerk, but it was not until 1805, when he was twenty-three, that Raffles was sent east. In that year Penang became the fourth presidency. Dundas's son, Philip, was made the first governor. And young Raffles was sent out as the assistant to the Governor's chief secretary. It meant an increase in salary from £70 to £1,500. He hastily married – a handsome Company widow ten years older than himself – bought some clothes and embarked with Dundas and his staff. Penang was a bustling entrepôt of some 30,000 Asians and

168

just over a hundred Europeans. It was considered the least favourable of all the Company's stations, a dull spot compared to the style of Calcutta or the excitements of Madras. Young Raffles studied Oriental languages and customs. He worked hard. Within two years he was the chief secretary, the most powerful man in the presidency after the Governor. By the standards of the East India Company his rise from clerk to chief secretary had been meteoric. It did not make him many friends.

Raffles was sent to Malacca, farther down the Malayan coast (not to be confused with the Moluccas spice islands). It was of strategic importance, dominating the straits of that name, through which the Company's ships passed on the China route. It had formerly belonged to the Dutch, but had been occupied by the British during the Napoleonic War. Raffles submitted a report for the Governor of Penang suggesting that the place should be retained. He had a friend at Calcutta who urged him to go there and see the Governor-General in person. This Raffles did. Minto and Raffles struck up an immediate mutual admiration. 'His lordship cast a look of such scrutiny, anticipation and kindness upon me as I shall never forget,' Raffles said. Minto, for his part, considered Raffles 'a very clever, able, active and judicious man'. Minto also was interested in the old Dutch territories in the East Indies. He had his eye on Java, which the Company had coveted two centuries before. It was agreed that Raffles should go to Malacca as Minto's personal agent, dealing direct with him instead of through the Governor of Penang, who was not enthusiastic about territorial acquisitions. Raffles would attempt to make contact with the Javanese princes, to see if they would support an invasion by the East India Company.

This special position put Raffles in a difficult position vis-à-vis the authorities in Penang. There was also some jealousy in Calcutta. Raffles was seen as a pushing, maniacally ambitious young man who had flattered Minto in order to further himself. 'Insatiable in ambition', as one who had known him in London put it. In fact, among Company officials in the east, of his age, he was unusually selfless; but he was a dedicated imperialist. Raffles advised that a force of about 10,000 troops would be enough to take Java, and that the princes would support the invasion.

Minto had already begun his preparations. He went to Malacca to supervise the operation himself. He was the first Governor-

General ever to leave India during his tour of duty. Raffles became his chief adviser, and virtually his deputy. The invasion fleet of some ninety ships left Malacca on 18 June 1811. It was six weeks before it arrived off the selected landing place on the Java coast, ten miles from Batavia, the Javanese capital. Not a ship or a man had been lost *en route*. The invasion itself was a brilliant success. There was no opposition to the landing. Native inhabitants were assured that the expedition was not one of conquest but of deliverance from the French. The Dutch were invited to join with the British. Looting was forbidden. Batavia surrendered without a fight and the Java-Dutch army was defeated six miles away; the Dutch troops tore off their French cockades and trampled on them.

Only twenty-five days after the landing, Minto declared Franco-Dutch rule at an end and claimed Java for the East India Company. In this he was going against the directors at home, who, predictably, had only wanted the defeat of the French and had no desire for sovereignty; they had suggested the place be left to native rule. Minto, however, insisted that such a policy would lead to anarchy and the slaughter of the remaining Dutch population.

Minto was delighted with the success of the invasion; a disaster could have finished his career. He left for Calcutta, leaving Raffles as Lieutenant-Governor of Java and its five million inhabitants. Raffles was to report direct to Minto, and his appointment, unratified by London, amounted to a fifth presidency.

Raffles remained in Java for four and a half years. It was not an easy post, for the Company could not be certain whether their rule would survive the ending of the war in Europe; a peace treaty might well restore it to the Dutch. There seemed, therefore, little point in developing the territory. But Raffles, dealing with a recalcitrant prince in firm manner, completed the conquest of the island and set up an administration, reforming many Dutch methods. His administration claimed all the Dutch East Indies, including Sumatra, Borneo, the Moluccas, the Celebes, as well as Java. He himself lived in the style of a great sultan. His enemies multiplied.

❧❦❧

Minto's Governor-Generalship was coming to an end. The directors and board did not consider him a success. The expenses of the Company had kept up with the increase in revenue, and this was seen largely as a result of the aggressive policy in Mauritius and the East Indies with which Minto was associated, although the Government had been behind both policies in the interest of the war with Napoleon.

In 1813 the Company asked Parliament for an extension of its privileges for another twenty years, but only lost more power to the Crown, and at last the old monopoly was beginning to crack; the India trade was opened to other merchants by a new system of licensing ships of a certain tonnage with the permission of the court of directors. This ended the Company's monopoly, and its trade with India disappeared. The Board of Control gained a more complete supervision of the Company's finances. The offices of Governor-General, Governor, and Commander-in-Chief were now to be made subject to the approval of the Crown (in practice of the Government). The work of Christian missionaries was encouraged. A Bishop was appointed, with his seat at Calcutta, with three archdeacons; the ecclesiastical establishment was to be paid for by the Company. Most important of all, perhaps, the territories of the East India Company were to be held 'in trust for His Majesty, his heirs and successors'. With this charter, it was recognised not only that the rule of most of India was too vital a matter to be left to a company of traders, as the India Act of 1784 had already made clear, it was now recognised that the Government was interested in a new empire in the east even if the directors of the East India Company were not.

Minto resigned. He was, almost unique among Governors-General, coolly received by all factions, directors, Board, and Parliament, despite formal acknowledgements and an earldom. He spent a few weeks in London and then set out on the last lap of the journey home and the reunion with his wife, of which he had dreamed for seven years. He died at Stevenage, on the Great North Road, only a few hours before reaching his destination.*

The first Governor-General under the new arrangement was a soldier: Francis Rawdon-Hastings, Earl of Moira, no relation of Warren Hastings, in the impeachment of whom, like Minto, he had been prominent. The new system had made the choice difficult. At one time Wellington had been suggested. But the Prince Regent was not without his say, and Hastings, an Irish

* Minto's great-grandson, the fourth earl, was Viceroy of India, 1905–10.

gambling crony of his – heavily in debt – was appointed.* Thirty-eight years earlier Hastings had made a name for himself by great gallantry at the Battle of Bunker's Hill. A professional soldier nearly all his life, he had considerable experience both in North America and in Europe, and had become a general in 1803.

Hastings's instructions were to observe the strictest economy in India and to avoid all extension of territory; India was to produce wealth, not wars. Hastings was hardly the man for such peaceful activities. But he immediately realised that Raffles's administration in the East Indies was one of the largest drains on the Company. 'Prodigious sums,' he complained; in efforts to increase trade, Raffles had abolished or reduced various taxes. Hastings also listened to all the gossip about Raffles; the charge was the usual one brought against the Company's servants by their enemies: corruption. Raffles was also accused of failing to make Java pay, through his own incompetence. The laborious process of litigation was begun. Raffles was acquitted of dishonesty, but not of mismanagement. A few months before their old colony was due to be restored to the Dutch, Raffles was dismissed. He returned home. In London, he did much to restore his reputation, cultivated powerful friends, was knighted, remarried (his first wife had died in Java), and wrote a *History of Java*. He was still only thirty-five.

After only two years, Raffles was back in the East Indies. He had submitted a memorandum urging that a new station at the strategic exit of the Straits of Malacca should be established. The directors had not been much impressed by the idea, but Raffles was sent back to the East Indies, although since the Dutch restoration in the area his theoretical responsibilities were limited to a small Company post, Fort Marlborough, at Bencoolen in Sumatra. He was the East India Company's fifty-first chief representative at this place, since the Company had become established there a hundred and thirty-three years previously. Lord Hastings soon invited Raffles to see him and, like Minto before him, seems to have been impressed by the forceful personality of the man. He agreed to Raffles's pet scheme of a station in the Straits, and empowered him to find and establish a settlement.

* Rawdon-Hastings, Earl of Moira, did not become Lord Hastings till 1817, but he will be referred to as Hastings to avoid confusion.

Raffles picked a place: a small island off the southern extremity of the Malayan peninsular. He anchored there at 4 p.m. on 28 January 1819. It was Singhapura, or Singapore: a sparsely populated, desolate place, belonging to the Sultan of Johore. The Sultan came to the island and a conference was held in a tent near the island's village of huts. The Sultan agreed to a sum of 5,000 Spanish dollars annually, the local chief to a sum of 3,000 dollars; the Company would build and administer a settlement on the island. The Union Jack was hoisted. A salute was fired by the sepoys who had accompanied Raffles. After only a week, Raffles left, leaving a small party behind. In six months he returned for three weeks and helped with the laying out and planning of streets for the community. He anticipated a rapid growth. European and Calcutta merchants were showing interest in sites. Europeans, Chinese, Malays, and Indians were all to have separate quarters; but the local Malay chief was made a member of the Council (all Company establishments had a council to 'advise' the Governor). By 1825 the population was over 10,000.

The Board of Control made its displeasure known to Hastings and discussed the possibility of removing Raffles once more. George Canning had now become President of the Board, and he told Hastings of his 'decided disapprobation of the extension in any degree to the Eastern Islands of that system of subsidiary alliance which has prevailed perhaps too widely in India'. He described the acquisition of Singapore as 'not a little embarrassing'. The Dutch, hoping to close access to the Far East, were incensed at what appeared to be blatant disregard of a treaty which had accepted their ascendancy in the East Indies. The Colonial Secretary described Raffles in the House of Lords as a nonentity and his new station as unimportant. But Lord Hastings stood by him, and some directors, concerned about the Company's China trade, supported him. Raffles wrote: 'I learn with much regret the prejudice and malignity by which I am attacked at home for the desperate struggle I have maintained against the Dutch...[But] the great blow has been struck...the nation must be benefited.' In 1826 the rapidly growing town joined with Malacca and Penang to form the three Straits Settlements. Six years later Singapore replaced Penang as the chief town. The Dutch had finally renounced all claims two years before, in exchange for the Company posts in Sumatra, notably Bencoolen, to which they added a consideration of £100,000 — one of the East India Company's better deals.

Raffles continued in the backwater of his Sumatra post. He fought to abolish slavery, and freed the Company's slaves at the Fort Marlborough spice plantations, although not entitled to do so. One after the other, his children died of disease. He himself was often down with fever. He began to suffer from excruciating headaches. He left for England on 10 April 1824. He had lost all his possessions, and nearly his life, in a fire four weeks before. Only one of his five children, upon whom he had doted, survived. Back in London, Raffles was in almost continual ill health, after thirty years in the East India Company's service since the age of fourteen, apart from the short gap of his only previous return home. Like so many before him, he was the object of much discussion and controversy in informed circles, although the public knew little of it; the vast majority of the British population had never heard of him or of the obscure island on which he had founded a settlement. Some directors had never forgotten the old charges of ill-administration. Of all the Nabobs in England, Sir Stamford Raffles was unique; he was poor. The court of directors refused him a pension; on the contrary, it demanded £22,000 which it claimed Raffles owed, partly due to his drawing salary while in England on his last visit home (which Raffles, on Minto's advice, had considered paid leave). Three months after receiving a written demand from the Company, Raffles died as the result of a brain tumour, aged forty-four. He was buried so obscurely that his resting place was not discovered till 1914.

The Company accepted £10,000 from his widow 'in satisfaction of all claims of the East India Company'. If it had not been for Raffles, it is improbable the modern state of Singapore, of two million people, would exist.*

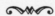

Having been sent out to maintain peace, Lord Hastings's Governor-Generalship was largely characterised by war. There were two important wars during his rule: the Gurkha War and the Third Maratha War. These wars had the effect of completing Wellesley's

---

* By the end of the East India Company administration the total trade of Singapore had reached £10,062,187, in 1857. The Straits Settlements remained under the Indian Government at Calcutta until the end of E.I.C. rule. The Malayan peninsula was under Malay or Thai rule.

work in tidying up the Company's rule south of Delhi, which had not been done under Barlow and Minto.

One of the most important powers beyond the Company's borders in India was that of the Gurkhas of Nepal. They had spread in recent decades from the foothills of the Himalayas and were threatening central India. They were known to be a formidable fighting people, although they had experienced little contact with the west. British frontier posts were being attacked and the garrisons killed or made captive. Hastings saw a real threat to the Company raj, and he ordered the Gurkhas to withdraw to their original boundaries in the hills. The Gurkhas showed no signs of obeying, and Hastings, disregarding blandly all the instructions he had received in London, prepared an expedition to defeat them.* He assembled a force of 34,000 men in four columns; one of them was under Sir Robert Rollo Gillespie, an Ulsterman, who had achieved as much fame by killing a tiger in the open of Bangalore racecourse as by defeating the mutineers at Vellore; he had commanded the invasion of Java and thought Raffles had received too much of the credit for that operation. The Gurkhas had only 12,000 men, but they knew the terrain and were capable of rapid movement. Hastings's plan was unnecessarily sophisticated and involved. The clumsy British columns marched off into land which few Europeans had ever seen. Three of them were soon checked. Gillespie was killed in an unsuccessful attack on a hill fort. Only one of the columns, under General David Ochterlony, pursued the Gurkhas and defeated them at a fierce engagement. The Gurkhas asked for terms, but did not accept those given. Ochterlony followed the Gurkha Army into Nepal by the only known pass, and made for the capital, Khatmandu. The Gurkhas built stockades and fortifications across the path of the British column, but each one was taken. When Ochterlony, after a great campaign, reached thirty miles from Khatmandu, the Gurkhas once more sued for peace. The treaty which followed brought the Company large tracts of land in the foothills, which included the village of Simla, and which would increase the Company's revenue; it was also agreed that the Company would have a resident representative at Khatmandu, and that all foreigners, except authorised British, were to be excluded from Nepal.

Lord Hastings's other conquest was in Central India. Here

* Anglo-Nepalese War, 1814–16.

increasing lawlessness had become anarchy, possibly as a result of the reduction of the Marathas by the Wellesleys. The mercenaries of the old Maratha armies had split up into small groups who roamed the country at will, pillaging and massacring; known as the Pindaris, plunder was their livelihood. They penetrated Company territory, reaching even into the Carnatic and threatening Bombay. The Company had firmly told Hastings, 'We are unwilling to incur the risk of a general war for the uncertain purpose of extirpating the Pindaris.' Nevertheless, relying as usual on his friendship with the Prince Regent, Hastings decided to deal with this menace.* But to do so he had to rouse the Maratha chiefs once more, for the Pindaris could not be defeated unless followed into the remaining Maratha lands. To beat the brigands and intimidate the Marathas, he assembled the largest British force yet seen in India: 113,000 men with over 300 guns. Included in the force were 3,000 men under James Skinner, known as Skinner's Horse, based on its depot at Hansi; Skinner was an Anglo-Indian, said to have had fourteen wives, by whom he had an enormous family; he had formerly been a mercenary of the Marathas (his regiment remained in the Company's service till his death in 1841). The force was split in two, the strategy being to sweep the bands into a net between the two armies. As the Pindaris withdrew towards Maratha territory, the Maratha chiefs were forced to take action, fearing a further British advance into their territories. It was a wearisome business. One officer wrote of 'this vile war, in which I nearly lost my life, in fact was given over by the physicians, owing to incessant marching, frequently from three in the morning to nine at night, and the thermometer an hour after sunset 110°. Enough to broil a devil.' Sindhia capitulated and Holkar was defeated. The Peshwa abandoned Poona and was captured after a long chase. Sir John Malcolm received his surrender. Asigarh was the last Maratha fortress to fall. The Pindaris were eventually destroyed by small columns, the two main armies having broken up and returned to their numerous military stations, which now scattered the Company raj and its boundaries. It had been perhaps the most difficult campaign ever conducted by the British in India, a matter of supply, organisation, and patience more than of battle tactics, and it had been a success.

* Pindari and Maratha Wars, 1816–18.

The Treaty of Poona, in June 1817, marked almost the end of Maratha power in India. The Peshwa was pensioned off and his lands went to Bombay. The house of Sindhia, humbled and lonely, kept its independence, but was defeated, at the battles of Maharaj-pore and Punniar, during a succession dispute twenty-six years later, which ended Maratha independence for ever. Hastings's operation had been one of tidying up the ragged frontier and scattered gaps in the East India Company's Indian territory. He had dubiously gained lands from rulers whose sovereignty, like that of the Gurkhas in the plains and of the Marathas, had themselves been dubious. His policy had not made him popular in London.

Hastings's last days in India were clouded by the customary charges of corruption. He had attempted to carry out the Board's wishes, but had been ruled by his own military intuition. Nevertheless, the receipts of his last year of administration were nearly £6,000,000 above those of his first; but expenditure had increased even more. He was worried about his responsibilities. He tried to improve administration and judiciary. A new note was sounded in his interest in education. He said:

This Government will never be influenced by the erroneous position that to spread information among men is to render them less tractable and less submissive to authority...It would be treason against British sentiment to imagine that it ever could be the principle of this Government to perpetuate ignorance in order to secure paltry and dishonest advantages over the blindness of the multitude.

Dismayed by the unfounded accusations against him, Lord Hastings resigned in 1821, although he remained till New Year's Day, 1823. The mature, wise, and compassionate man that India had made him during nine years was almost unrecognisable from the gay, gambling general of the Prince Regent's set. Exhausted and in poor health, he was granted a small annuity by the Company, but within a few months he was obliged to accept the comparatively humble post of Governor of Malta owing to his financial need. He died two years later, leaving little money, but with the curious bequest that his right hand be cut off and buried with his wife on her death.

Hastings had been a realist in India. He had once written home:

It was by preponderance of power that those mines of wealth [in India] had been acquired for the Company's treasure, and by preponderance of power alone could they be retained. The supposition that the British power could discard the means of strength and yet enjoy the fruits of it, was one that would certainly be speedily dissipated.

11 SERVANTS OF THE COMPANY

One of the great sights of the late eighteenth and early nineteenth centuries was the outward-bound East India fleet passing down the Channel; twenty or more great three-masters in double line, protected by watchful frigates of the Royal Navy busily flagging signals. The East Indiamen themselves were heavily armed, carrying between twenty and thirty guns, sometimes on two decks. They looked more impressive than they really were, for their fighting decks were cluttered with passengers' baggage and merchandise, and, on the other hand, the space taken by their batteries interfered with their commercial viability. But on at least one occasion the returning China fleet, some fifteen of the Company's ships, so intimidated a French fleet of four warships by running up naval ensigns and forming into line of battle that the French vessels made off (the commodore received a reward from the Company of £50,000 to share between himself and his captains). But with the ending of the French wars, and increasing agreement with the Dutch, the convoy system and the heavy armour became less important than speed and capacity. 'Blackwall Frigates' succeeded the old East Indiamen, and a fast journey at the beginning of the century was under five months to India, another two to China, to collect the all-important tea. The East India Docks and dockyard at Blackwall belonged to a different company, but there the Company ships were built (except for the naval vessels, increasingly built at Bombay), and there they docked, although heavily laden ships unloaded some cargo at Woolwich. Before its commercial operations ceased, the Company had several thousand employees at its warehouses, all in the City within half a mile of the East India House; India trade at St Helens, Lime Street, New Street, Billiter Lane, and Leadenhall Street; China trade at Fenchurch Street, Whitechapel, Crutched Friars, and Tower Hill.

Steamships were starting to appear on the oceans; in 1825 one made the journey to India in under four months. By the eighteen-thirties the passenger express route, via the Mediterranean and over-land across Egypt to the Red Sea, was increasingly in use, taking under two months; the sixty-hour journey across Egypt was partly done in horse-drawn stage coaches at bone-shaking speed, with the cargo going on camels. Passenger traffic was heavy, as the Company's staff was increasing all the time. Most found the old Atlantic passage an exceedingly unpleasant experience. Living conditions were cramped, the ships verminous, and food supplies dependent to some extent on the calls at St Helena and the Cape not being delayed by bad weather. One young lady in 1831, on board the *Alfred* to Madras, wrote of breakfast: 'You may see on the table two great dishes of hot rolls, bread baskets of biscuits, mashed and roast potatoes, boiled rice, cold fowl and ham, pork or anything that may be left from the previous dinner, which it resembled more than a breakfast, coffee, green and black tea, and butter running away.' Lunch, on a hot day on the same passage, consisted of 'hot plum pudding, biscuits, jam and port wine'. Much of the food – cows, sheep, and pigs – were carried 'on the hoof'. Early in the century a sight of, sometimes even a chat with, Napoleon (by arrangement with the East India Company, in exile on the Company's island of St Helena) was the proud boast of many a returning Company official. St Helena had belonged to the Company since 1661, being held in fee simple like Bombay. About twenty Company servants were stationed there. Passengers to the east provided their own cabin furniture. The diarist William Hickey took with him 'a bureau with writing desk and apparatus attached to it, a capital cot for sleeping on, a table and a few other articles of furniture' and 'an immense stock of linen of every description'. Some took pianos; a few took bath-tubs. Tempers were frayed, and not a few violent deaths occurred. The crew were sullen, and sentences of three lashes of the cat for minor offences were frequent; there was nearly always someone confined in irons. For the passengers there were dances in the evening, the endless playing of cards, and the excitement of sighting dolphins, flying-fish, and albatross. But the Atlantic was seldom kind. One young officer, on his first journey out, recorded in his diary: 'Ports all down. Ship labouring much. Exercise small arms...Sea very rough. Ports shut. A great scrambling at dinner, puddings, ducks and a large round of beef tumbling about, not able to save them, being so much occupied with seats... Unwell.'

With the introduction of steam vessels plying between Bombay and Suez, on the short route, the need for a coaling station and base between Red Sea and Arabian Sea was clear. The small Arab port of Aden, at which Sir Henry Middleton had dropped anchor in 1610, was recommended by Commander Stafford Haines of the Company's navy (Bombay Marine), who had been sent to find a site.* It consisted, Haines reported, of 'not more than ninety dilapidated stone buildings...a mere miserable village without trade'. It had, however, two excellent harbours. Haines made arrangements to purchase Aden for the Company, but the local Sultan then thought better of it. The Governor of Bombay agreed to a military expedition if necessary, without consulting Calcutta. But he reminded Haines of 'the importance of our obtaining a footing peaceably, or at all events without loss of life of anyone...in regard to the feeling with which our afterwards occupying the place would be viewed'. Haines stormed the place and took it, with the loss of fifteen casualties. Haines was given 'temporary' political and military command of Aden; he remained there for fifteen years, building the place from a village of 600 inhabitants to a port of 20,000, although his wish to make it a great entrepôt for Anglo-Arabian trade was not realised. The 'overland' route from home became increasingly popular, and the Atlantic route, despite sharp decreases in fares (down to £120) dropped away. By the end of the Company raj the Peninsular and Orient line had a regular service between Marseilles and Alexandria, and Suez and Bombay. Haines was to Aden what Raffles had been to Singapore; and he got similar treatment from the Company. Accused of financial irregularities, he was sent back to Bombay in 1854, where, although he was acquitted

* The Bombay Marine was styled the Indian Navy from 1830. By 1857 the East India Company had 43 warships, and 273 European officers and under-officers.

of embezzlement, he languished in debtors' prison for six years, having been made responsible 'for the whole amount of the public money deficient in the Aden Treasury'. He was treated with a vindictiveness of which only the East India Company among great corporations was capable. A civil action was commenced against him 'for the recovery of the unexplained deficiency'. As litigation proceeded, he was kept in gaol despite repeated protests from his doctor. Haines was released after the Company's rule ended. He died on the ship in Bombay harbour that was to take him home, penniless, aged fifty-four.

❧

Arriving in India, the new recruit to the Company's service, military or civil, found himself in a remarkable situation. The Company's territories, and those of the states subservient to it by treaty, were not dissimilar to that of modern contemporary India, less Kashmir and the Punjab. In this territory lived over one-sixth of the world's population. And its rulers, behind a thin façade of Indian princes, were less than 10,000 British who could be annihilated within hours. At any moment they could be overwhelmed.

There was a deep feeling of isolation among the Company's servants in this vast mass of foreign humanity, whose customs some of them, particularly in the army, neither cared for nor understood. Border stations were lonely and tense in the extreme; it took two months to travel from Calcutta to the border with the Punjab. Men faced this situation in different ways; some became, while still young men, among the finest administrators the British have ever produced; others spent a career facing the demands of India in an alcoholic stupor or in an opium haze.

The early nineteenth century saw a great increase in activity. New posts were set up, new laws and regulations established, the administration of whole states overhauled. A great new trade was being built up, supplying stores for the British administration, which could find little in India to its taste and which insisted on living in the style to which it was accustomed; the quantities of claret sent to India was proverbial. The industrial revolution at home had led to a new search for markets, and there were high hopes of selling cotton garments and other manufactures to the Indian millions.

A career in the Company's service was sought after increasingly by a more responsible type of young man; the old adventurers and fortune-hunters were already becoming legends. Rewards and promotion were on a sounder footing (the Company's army officers were by now among the best paid in the world). After ten years' service, three years' home leave could be claimed, and there was 'leave of absence on medical certificate to any civil servant to any place in India, in Europe, or elsewhere, as he may consider most conducive to the restoration of his health without any restrictions whatever as to the place to which he may resort'; pay up to £1,000 per annum was granted for such sick leave for at least fifteen months.*

As the Company servants' numbers and responsibilities increased, so their contact with the governed decreased. Even the traditional social contact with the Muslim aristocracy was on the wane. It had begun with Cornwallis's removal of Indians from senior Company positions, and had increased with the arrival of more and more English women, who apparently felt safer if they could keep their men to the conventional mores and customs of England rather than seeing them become involved with people they did not understand. This gap was finally and consciously dug by the Wellesleys, who had believed that the British were a superior people anyway, who could rule best by keeping to themselves. Many of the men now in high positions in India had been the young men under the Wellesleys, and Richard Wellesley was their hero. It was, perhaps, this new self-confidence, even arrogance, that enabled many to face the dangers and isolation of their position. With the arrogance went a profound sense of duty – often, it seemed, in straight proportion. New ideas of evangelism and, later, utilitarianism, that were sweeping across Britain, did not leave the Company's servants unaffected. There was a feeling that the Indians were an un-civilised people and that the British would soon have to take on the burden of civilising them. No one thought of consulting the Indians about this, but some of the religious practices were certainly barbarous, and it was obvious that the British would feel they would have to put a stop to them as soon as they felt powerful enough to do so. The judicial system was already heavily angli-cised, and it was not a great success. The more privileged Indian was

* These were the privileges in existence by the end of the Company's administration.

becoming adept at litigation, and he found ways and means of using the system to his advantage; but to most Indians the new legal system was an incomprehensible affair, the main object of which seemed to be to undermine traditional Indian life. Attempts to wipe out corruption had as much chance of success as attempts to wipe out the crafty house lizards. Charles Metcalfe wrote, in 1820: 'Our courts are scenes of great corruption. The European judge is the only part of them that is untainted. He sits on a bench in the midst of a general conspiracy, and knows that he cannot trust any one of the officers of the court.' Policing, with an overwhelming problem of lawlessness, was also no more impressive. An army officer wrote, in 1849:*

> The British rule is most defective in the prevention and detection of crime; and while supremely powerful in military means, the government is comparatively valueless as the guardian of the private property of its citizens. Thus a feeling of insecurity arises, which gives birth to a want of confidence, and will finally lead to an active desire for a change of masters. England has identified herself so little with the people of India that she leans solely on hireling agency, and trusts the preservation of internal order to men who fear her, indeed, but who hate her at the same time, and can deceive her with ease and impunity.

The Company's employees lived mostly in single-storey houses, often with thatched roofs, and always with a large veranda. The furnishings inside were as much like home as possible, with no concessions to tropical and sub-tropical conditions. Servants were cheap, plentiful, and trained in European domestic duties (at one time William Hickey had 63). Public buildings were classical, impressive and evidence of the Company's vast resources. Those of the Company's servants not wallowing in drink, or dazed with opium, began to study the society in which they lived. Anglo-Indian literature, in the form of memoirs and histories, was growing rapidly. Lady Impey, wife of the Chief Justice in Warren Hastings's time, Richard Wellesley, and Raffles had all sent back notable collections of flower paintings or flora and fauna. As early as 1787 the Company itself had founded a Botanic Garden outside Calcutta, and others were being established in all the major

* J. D. Cunningham, *A History of the Sikhs*.

centres.* Scientific surveys were made of such detail that they are still consulted today. So much material was collected, both officially and unofficially, that the Company felt obliged to set up a library and museum at their headquarters in Leadenhall Street, London; it became the chief institution in its field in Europe.

Social and sporting life was active in the extreme. Calcutta and Madras were still notorious; Bombay was considered more stuffy. Best of all was Simla, in the cool foothills, gained after the Gurkha War, which became a summer resort for the Governor-General, a train of some 15,000 men accompanying him there. Hunting for wild animals was popular and accompanied with much liquid refreshment. Receptions and balls were held at the slightest excuse. The numbers of English women were increasing (as late as 1770 there had only been 39 British women in Bombay). They had little to do but ride, keep themselves cool, bear children, and write innumerable brave letters home. Unattached women did not stay unattached long; many, finding themselves widows, married several times. Life expectancy had not improved much over the years (of 30 ensigns who had received their commissions in 1775, only 14 had still been alive by 1780). Doctors advised 'a change of air' where possible, preferably to Ceylon, or applied their remedies of blooding, purging, and blistering (in early days cholera had been treated by the application of hot irons to the feet). The cemeteries expanded relentlessly. Lady Emily Eden, sister of a Governor-General, Lord Auckland, wrote: 'How the ranks close in the very next day after death. The most intimate friends never stay at home above two days and they see everybody again directly. Dr —— had more warm friends than anybody, and there was not one who stayed away from the races after his death.' A few years later she wrote: 'It is melancholy to think how almost all the people we have known at all intimately have in two years died off. None of them turned fifty.' It was beginning to be accepted that India was a useful area for those ladies in search of a young husband with a promising career and a pension at the end of it; sisters, governesses, nieces, were starting to visit the three old presidencies. Fashionable artists, like John Zoffany and George Chinnery, made prolonged stays. Newspapers began to appear to report the goings-on; the earliest in regular circulation was the *Bengal Gazette*, founded in 1786.

* Few of these survive.

Officials were becoming split between interventionists and non-interventionists; those who believed the Indians should be instructed in European ways and those who thought they were better off if left to develop in their own way, with the Company's encouragement. The former, supported from home, were the most vociferous. The Charter of 1813 had required the Company to establish a bishop in Calcutta whose see was to be the whole of British India, to encourage missionaries and to provide education. There was considerable argument as to how the money put aside for education should be spent, and the operation of any education policy remained in abeyance for some time. Lord Hastings had suggested that the Company should 'furnish the village schoolmasters with little manuals of religious sentiments and ethic maxims'. The Company had its own medical staff; hospitals had been established in the presidencies as long ago as 1664. These hospitals were joined by others for Indians at the three main centres at the turn of the century, and about ten more were established throughout India in the first half of the century. The establishment of new industries in India was looked upon with as much displeasure as the building of ships there had once been; nothing was to be done to disturb the potential market for British manufactures (the first cotton mill was built by an American near the end of the Company's rule).

A typical garrison consisted of a 'cantonment', apart from an Indian town or city, forming a kind of military suburb. Beside the barracks would be the 'maidan' or open ground on which the troops drilled and exercised, around which were the offices, chapel, and bungalows of the officers and civil servants. Inside the bungalows were the dining-room, usually sparsely furnished without matting, the drawing-room, for the ladies, furnished as much like home as possible with chintz-covered chairs, piano, and portraits, and the bedrooms; all these opened directly on to the veranda around the building, on which, in fact, the family and servants spent most of the day, the cane chairs being gradually moved round to follow the shade.

It was now accepted that regiments of the royal army served in India alongside the Company's own troops. Life in the ranks for British troops was inhuman and harsh; the troops in royal regiments were known as 'bloody-backs' because of the ceaseless floggings (flogging in the Company's forces was abolished in 1835);

drunkenness in the ranks was even more habitual than in the officers' mess. Few had European wives; most married Indians and lived in varying degrees of squalor. As Private Waterfield of the 32nd Foot confided to his diary: 'The Pte. Soldier is not half cared for. In time of War they are thought much of, in time of peace – a pariah dog.'

The old rivalries were still keen, and in 1818 the sense of injustice and inferiority harboured for so long by the Company's officers, who ran one of the world's largest armies, was not even soothed when they were made eligible for honours and knighthoods in the same way as were the royal officers (Ochterlony was among the first to receive a knighthood). In the royal army, purchase of commissions was prevalent, and a posting to India was not sought after; officers, on being posted to India, often exchanged or sold their commissions. In the Company's army, promotion was more usually based on merit, although the directors had considerable influence on the acceptance of young officers. A large proportion of the Company's British soldiers were officers in the sepoy regiments, and they lived in lavish style, although Arthur Wellesley had done something to cut down luxuries among royal and Company officers. When at a posting, the officers lived hard. Many took refuge in opium. Others drank; in 1849 Calcutta boasted twenty-five wine merchants as compared to twelve 'general shopkeepers'. The diarist William Hickey, a formidable guzzler of wine, described one dinner at a regimental mess as the most demanding debauch of his full life; toasts were drunk of 'two and twenty bumpers in glasses of considerable magnitude', then the serious drinking began and continued till two in the morning; 'eight as strong-headed fellows as could be found in Hindustan', commented the impressed Hickey. Even Arthur Wellesley admitted that 'no blame ought to be attached to a cursory debauch'. Work, such as it was, ceased by midday, and all efforts were devoted to keeping person and wine cool; the former by servants with fans, the latter by use of wet towels in which the bottles were wrapped and hung in the breeze. Life was a sapping battle against debt, gout, and the heat, with the prospect of the English counties and a pension far ahead. Obliging Indian ladies helped the bachelors, and some of the husbands, pass a few hours, although such relationships were considered 'unnatural'. As one captain put it: 'Allowances are to be made for the ungovernable passions...which absolutely must have vent in this stimulating climate.'

On the march, officers still contrived to live well. The transportation of the personal effects of a senior officer could require fifty or even more camels, and he would have two dozen servants with him. His tent would contain bed, table, and chairs, and half a dozen large boxes containing his table requirements, his liquor, and his valuables. The tents themselves were often elaborate affairs; if the stay was for any length of time, they would have glass or wooden doors, and brick chimneys, 'by which means', as one of them put it, 'they were enabled to enjoy the pleasure of an English fireside with their wives and families'. Back in the presidency capitals, the social whirl continued. The *Bombay Courier*:

> On Thursday last, Major-General Bellasis gave an elegant entertainment to his friends at Randall lodge; on which occasion the extensive and beautiful gardens of this Mansion were displayed and illuminated in a style of varied magnificence which reflected the highest credit upon the taste and fancy of the projector. Notice having unexpectedly circulated that Masks would be admitted this evening, those who could prepare themselves on the short notice appeared in Masks accordingly...so much good humour and vivacity was evinced, and the novelty of the scene gave so much satisfaction that we trust it will prove only a prelude to other similar entertainments, at which Masks should be generally encouraged — the company did not separate till four the following morning.

By the eighteen-twenties the complement of the army of the Honourable East India Company was well over a quarter of a million, greater than that of any European power. It also had a considerable navy, with its own naval service, which patrolled Indian and East Indian waters, and which maintained a squadron in the Persian Gulf.

To fill the posts vacant in India, the East India Company had found it necessary to establish two colleges in England. At Addiscombe, near Croydon, young men were trained for military service in India. The Company's military seminary gained a high reputation. It opened in 1809, at the former mansion of Lord Liverpool, in fifty-eight acres of grounds. Fees for the first pupils were £30 per annum and the course lasted two years, including military subjects, mathematics, mechanics, and Hindustani. Of the first year's cost of £4,395, only £58 was spent on books. During the fifty-two years of its existence, 3,600 cadets passed out into the armies of Bengal, Madras, and Bombay. On passing the final examinations, cadets were posted to the Company's Engineers, Artillery, and Infantry (in that order of seniority). Engineers and gunners went on for further training to the British Army establishments at Chatham and Woolwich respectively. For the cavalry, however, no training was thought necessary; directors nominated candidates, who were given commissions direct to cavalry units. The seminary's most famous graduates were that Victorian hero Field-Marshal Lord Napier of Magdala, who served with the Bengal Engineers to the end of the Company's army, when he, like many others, was transferred to the royal army, Field-Marshal Earl Roberts of Kandahar, who was in the Bengal Artillery (both were to be prominent in the suppression of the revolt of 1857), and three of the Lawrence brothers.

Richard Wellesley had established a college at Calcutta, the College of Fort William, to which he sent all newly arrived young 'writers' in Bengal. There they were to receive a comprehensive education in suitable subjects, including Indian history, languages, and law; when educated, he hoped to send them all over India. The directors were indignant at his initiative – the college was fully operative before they even heard of it – and, pleading lack of funds, they ordered the college to be confined to a modest language school.

However, a college for their civil service was long overdue, and now the directors were not slow to establish one in England, where they could keep a close watch on it and also nominate its students. Having decided on a civil college in 1804, the directors agreed, on 22 October 1806, to make an offer for a house near Hertford, called Hailey Bury, which had formerly belonged to one of the directors. That same day they instructed a surveyor, who reported to them the following morning, not long before the auction was to take place. Their bid (£5,900) was successful, and in less than forty-eight hours the Company had found and bought itself the site for a civil college. An architect and principal were appointed with similar alacrity, and Hailey Bury house was in use as a school less than four months later (although the senior students were temporarily housed at Hertford Castle near by). The architect, a young man still in his twenties,* produced a collegiate masterpiece that must have delighted the directors; while providing the sort of dignity for which the Company longed, particularly in an imposing, classical terrace, he had elsewhere in his massive quadrangle clearly kept the Company's sensitive purse in mind. A remarkably distinguished academic staff was gathered together, mostly from Oxford and Cambridge. Very few of them were lured back and, as at Addiscombe, several remained for twenty years and more (one lecturer at Addiscombe, Jonathan Cape, was on the staff for almost forty years). Nearly every man on the East India College's staff during the half century of its existence wrote an important work. Among them was Thomas Robert Malthus, professor of economics and modern history, who remained at Haileybury, as the college was generally known, until his death nearly thirty years later; he wrote his most famous work on population while at the college. The intellectual tone was unique in Britain, being compounded of a strange mixture of some of the leading economists of the day and of linguists who thought nothing of speaking a dozen languages, together with a few Indians and Persians. Leading academics would visit the place to lecture and dine at high table. The four principals of the college, Samuel Henley, J. H. Batten, Charles Le Bas, and Henry Melvill, were all men of quality and achievement. The course, divided into two compulsory disciplines, 'Orientals' and 'Europeans', lasted two years and was open to youths between fifteen (later changed to seventeen) and twenty-two. A pass-out examination was instituted for Orientals in 1813, and for Europeas in 1820. The standards were not low — proficiency in at least three Oriental languages was demanded — and about one fifth failed to pass out (upon which many were nominated for the undemanding cavalry).

Haileybury was continually under attack, and a consequence of this was that it long suffered from a lack of funds. It was said to be wasteful and inefficient, and was criticised as a nest of privilege (without the nomination of a director it was virtually impossible to get in). But most of all it was attacked as a den of iniquity.

* William Wilkins, whose later work included the National Gallery, in Trafalgar Square, and Downing College, Cambridge.

In Oxford, Cambridge, and London, Haileybury students were notorious for their riotous behaviour. Drunkenness, lack of discipline, and wild local wenching were the main charges. On several occasions the students walked out; once they were sent down to London to appear *en masse* before the court of directors. A former student recorded a typical day at Haileybury:

Breakfast parties were a favourite thing, and at these there were all sorts of luxuries provided by the students, and generally tankards of beer or claret. Then those whose rooms did not look on to the Quad descended, pipe in mouth, and lounged about. At this hour a swarm of tradesmen from Hertford made its appearance. Two tailors, a hairdresser and some others walked round the Quad with pattern books and bags... As soon as lectures were over there was a rush to our rooms... A crowd then gathered at 'trap', which is the same as the buttery at an Oxford College, and had bread and cheese and beer, served by two very pretty girls, nieces of the College purveyor. This, like all other ceremonies at Haileybury, was accompanied by a ceaseless flow of foul talk and coarse jesting, with occasional horse-play...Dinner was served in Hall at six and evening chapel was eight, after which everyone went to the 'trap' again...amidst an indescribable hub-bub and uproar of oaths, songs, indecent jokes and horse-play as before...After this the steady men retired to their rooms and read far into the night. The noisy ones assembled by tens and dozens in someone's rooms where they held what was elegantly termed a lush; drinking, smoking and singing till two or three in the morning ...A bell was indeed rung at eleven and was, theoretically, the signal for everyone to go to bed, but I do not remember that any attention was ever paid to it...Towards two in the morning, those who sat up late working, heard faint sounds of distant voices singing very much out of tune...snatches of various ribald songs...Sometimes, one more drunk than the rest would have been brought home lying in the straw at the bottom of the cart...After about half an hour's screaming and fighting, the inebriates would somehow be got to their rooms and silence would at last descend upon the Quad.

Twice a year the court of directors clattered up the avenue in their coaches to distribute awards. George Canning, a director and one-time President of the Board, once had to go down to quell a riot.

'I have faced bitter opposition in the House of Commons,' he said, 'I have encountered turbulent riots at Liverpool...but I was never floored and daunted till now, and that by a lot of Haileybury boys.' Although the Haileybury students were an independent lot, the standard of scholarship demanded was high; the staff, many of whom were retiring scholars and gentle clergymen, would not have remained as long as they did if there had been unrelieved anarchy, as some rumours claimed. At Old Haileybury, it was work hard, play hard. Sons followed fathers at the college, and family links, as well as traditions, were built up. India was soon being ruled by men who had known each other at college, who could reminisce about football matches in Hertfordshire winters of long ago.

At Haileybury it was considered bad form to talk about India, but most of its ex-pupils became fine administrators of the Company's Indian empire, and administrators who, for the first time in the Company's history, were at last unquestioned in integrity. They had a responsibility to live up to each other, to maintain a certain standard, not to let down the Haileybury reputation. The patronage which had got them their places at college at least had one good effect in that it brought about a system of family connections with India with which at least two generations were connected in the Company's time, but in the case of Haileybury was to persist long after the end of the Company's rule. The Haileybury and Addiscombe men ran India not just for themselves and their own careers, as their predecessors had mainly done, but for the Company, and with a sense of duty towards the Crown, and often towards India as well.

❧

The civil servants of the Company in London were also often appointed by patronage. Considering the vast scope of its operations and the number of its civilian and military dependants (some 300,000 by the end), the Company's home staff was by no means overweight by modern standards of bureaucracy. By 1857 there were still under 120 permanent staff at the East India House, together with the small staffs at Haileybury and Addiscombe, nine officers at the military depot, and seven recruiting officers (three of them in Ireland). The Company offered security, hard work, a week's holiday, and a good pension after a life's labour. The staff of the East India House laboured away at their desks and committees in dedicated attempts to influence the raj itself as much as the Haileybury men on the spot. There were four departments: the Secretary's, the Chief Examiner's, the Military, and the Statistical. The first looked after the Company's finances, pay, and shipping, but the second was quite as important, if not more so, being responsible for the correspondence to India. From clerk, they rose to senior clerk and then to assistant, and a few could aspire to becoming chief examiner after more than a quarter of a century's service. The heads of the East India House were more distinguished than those at any department of the Government. The Secretary of the Company was on equal footing to the chief examiner, but usually less distinguished, as the latter were chosen particularly for their literary ability, but among the secretaries were James Cobb, a playwright, and Peter Auber, the historian. The list of examiners is decorated with many famous names. Charles Lamb, appointed in 1792, worked for the Company in the East India House for thirty-three years, but still found time for his hundred folios of essays and other literary work, most of them written at the Company's desk. He saw his connection with India as a form of 'slavery'. For his first three years as writer he received no pay at all, and then moved on to £40 per annum. Over a quarter of a century later, he wrote:

> Thirty years I have served the Phillistines, and my neck is not subdued to the yoke. You don't know how wearisome it is to breathe the air of pent walls without relief day after day, all the golden hours of the day between 10 and 4 without ease or interposition...I dare not whisper to myself a Pension on this side of eventual incapacitation and infirmity, till years have sucked me dry...I sit like Philomel all day (but not singing) with my breast against this thorn of a desk, with the only hope that some pulmonary affliction may relieve me.

Three years later he received a generous pension of £441.* James Mill, historian and philosopher, was there for nearly eighteen years, having been appointed on the strength of his *History of India*, despite, or maybe because of, its criticisms of the Company. On his death in office, he was succeeded by the important novelist Thomas

* This was the same as a Company servant, civil or military, received after the same length of service in India. Only Company surgeons received much more (£700 after thirty-five years' service). In 1858 John Stuart Mill received a special pension of £1,500.

Peacock as chief examiner. Peacock spent thirty-nine years in Leadenhall Street; among his many services was the introduction of iron steamers.

In policy, the most important of the civil servants in London was probably James Mill's son, John Stuart Mill, who followed his father into the East India House in 1823, at the age of seventeen. Thirty-four years later he also became chief examiner. The younger Mill propagated the philosophy of utilitarianism, which said that all moral, social, or political action should be directed towards achieving the greatest good for the greatest number of people. This obviously had a relevance to the arguments about what should be the Company's attitude towards the millions of Indians it ruled. It became a prevalent philosophy at Haileybury and spread throughout the administration in India. The controversy was furious, but it was exciting, too. The East India Company was now in its third century. Whatever it was going to do with the empire it had so reluctantly received from its soldiers and administrators, it would surely have many generations in which to do it.

12 ⸓ THE AGE OF REFORM ⸓

The next Governor-General cannot be said to have been dominated by the ideas of utilitarianism — rather he was dominated by his wife and by the determination to go down in history as a ruler of the Wellesley class. But Lord Amherst, nearly fifty years old, was no Wellesley.

The interim period, between the departure of Lord Hastings and the arrival of Amherst, had not been auspicious for those holding the new liberal ideas. The interim Governor-General had been John Adam, a member of the Calcutta council. The only notable event of his regime was the tightening of the already strict censorship of the press. Officials and directors alike, conscious of what they saw as the Company's insecurity in India, had for long supported censorship, although action under the regulations had rarely had to be taken. It was understood that the Company and senior officials were not to be lampooned. John Adam, however, deported an editor who had ridiculed the administration.

The arrival of a new Governor-General at Calcutta was the greatest event in Anglo-Indian society. The river was crowded with vessels. Guns pounded out a salute. Troops were drawn up on the bank. Behind them the shore was crowded with thousands of spectators trying to get a glimpse of the new ruler of the East India Company's empire. The members of the council, lined up at the steps, received the Governor-General with a few words of welcome, and then walked up to Government House, where the Governor-

General was taken to the great Council Chamber where he took the oath of office. The style of Calcutta often surprised the newcomers. 'Surprised we were,' wrote Lady Amherst, 'at the well-fashioned dress and manners of most of the ladies.'

Lord Amherst was almost immediately embroiled in difficulties over the Company's difficult neighbour, Burma. He saw a chance of adding his name to the great captains of India. But although he came from a military family, he had no military experience; his career had, in fact, been as a diplomat, and an unsuccessful one. From early in its history the East India Company had set up depots on the Burma coast in attempts to trade, but they had never met with any success. Relations with the Burmese had seldom been good. The new Burma state had only been in existence for about seventy-five years, but had spread its influence and power from Siam to Assam. It was now said to be threatening Bengal itself. Burmese sorties, and exiles from Burmese expansion, were violating the frontier. The Burmese king was either unable or unwilling to comply with the demands from Calcutta to observe the frontier. The king and the Burmese military hierarchy were, it was frequently said, people of extreme 'arrogance'. The new type of Englishman in India took such flouting of the Company's demands as arrogance of an extreme type, and as a direct challenge to themselves. Lord Amherst declared war on Burma on 15 March 1824.*

The main part of the operations was to be an expedition up the Irrawaddy from Rangoon, penetrating the hinterland. The army underrated the natural difficulties to be encountered and also the Burmese army. They had been expecting another Indian-style campaign, and were extremely confident. In command was Colonel Sir Archibald Campbell, who had campaigned in India since the days of Tipu thirty-four years before. He had 10,000 men, nearly all from Madras, and a small naval force (with which was Commander Frederick Marryat, later the author of *Mr Midshipman Easy* and other novels).

The Bengal sepoys proved most reluctant to join the campaign; there was unrest about pay, and many protested that they were unable to travel overseas because of the caste system. A mutiny at the depot of Barrackpore, outside Calcutta, was only put down at great cost of life. His handling of the mutiny nearly cost Amherst

* First Anglo-Burmese War, 1824–6.

his post, and he was only saved by the intervention of the Duke of Wellington.

Rangoon was occupied without resistance, but progress up the Irrawaddy seemed almost impossible. The Burmese were surprisingly well-armed, with good artillery, and were skilled in defensive operations. The British force languished in Rangoon, nearly invested by the enemy, being whittled away by disease and lack of supplies. In a few weeks less than a third of the force was fit for duty. But an attempt to take Rangoon by 60,000 Burmese was beaten off and the slow advance began; 4,700 troops delved into swamp and jungle, some by boat, but most on foot. Meanwhile an overland force from Bengal attempted to cross the mountains into Burma, but was forced back after being decimated by malaria.

Campbell's advance was a military nightmare; the Burmese destroyed all supplies as they retreated, and the British troops were half starved as well as disease-ridden. More than once the Burmese taunted with talk of peace negotiations which evidently they had no intention of concluding. The Burmese court capitulated, a year after the British force had left Rangoon, when Campbell was within sixty miles of their capital at Amarapura. The campaign, probably the most miserable that the Company's troops were ever asked to fight, had been a considerable achievement of leadership by Campbell.

By the peace treaty, the East India Company gained Tenasserim, Arakan, Assam (and protectorates over the adjoining principalities of Jaintia and Manipur), as well as ten million rupees (about £1,000,000), and the right to keep a Company agent at the Burmese capital. By the treaty the Burmese coast was shortened, Arakan adjoining Company possessions in the north, and Tenasserim, in the far south of the former Burmese possessions, was less than five hundred miles north of Penang. The Company had increased its control of the coastline of the Bay of Bengal from Tenasserim on the Malayan peninsula to Comorin. Amherst, who at one time had had to consider the whole war being a disaster, was delighted. So was his wife, who had noted in her diary: 'We may fairly say that our foes have been beaten into sueing for peace, their insolent language and high pretensions have vanished.' Campbell claimed that his victory 'has had the effect (I trust sufficiently) to humble that haughty and arrogant court to a submission which will, no doubt...not again wantonly disturb the peace of the British Government in India'. Said Lord Amherst:

> His Lordship declares his persuasion that the result of the contest, by teaching the Burman nation to know and respect the power which it had for a series of years insulted by its haughty demands and unprovoked aggressions, will prevent the interruption in future of those friendly relations which it is the interest of both states to maintain.

The revealing word was 'teaching'. Burma, in fact, was to behave. Only since the Wellesleys had the Governor-General spoken in such terms of the 'native states'. The end of the war was celebrated in Calcutta by a magnificent banquet at Government House, while fireworks blazed over the water and the guns of the warships anchored in the river fired off salutes.

Amherst may have been popular among the British in India, but in the East India House in London his name was anathema, although the Government were quite pleased with him. The war had cost £13,000,000, to say nothing of the lives of 20,000 soldiers. For twelve months the directors had greeted news of the war with icy silence. Lady Amherst complained to her diary: 'To this day...Lord Amherst has not received a line from these gentlemen, notwithstanding all the great and glorious events which have occurred.' The careful work of Lord Hastings in restoring the Indian finances had all been wasted.

Lord Amherst had also involved the Company in a war in Central India, where the famous fortress of Bharatpur had been besieged and overcome, after a succession dispute. Some 20,000 men and 100 guns had been sent to Bharatpur, and one of the first to enter a breach in the walls had been Amherst's son, a captain in the army: 'No words can describe the tremendous scene of noise and confusion. The town appeared one mass of dust from the mud walls and smoke; the shouts of the besiegers in triumph and the cries of the poor sufferers were heard many miles distant.' About 5,000 Indians were killed inside the walls. Lady Amherst wrote: 'The conviction of the impregnability of Bharatpur was held far and wide, and even in Calcutta was so rooted in the minds of its principal native inhabitants as to render them incredulous for a time to the account of its fall. It formed a kind of *point d'appui* for the hopes of all who were hostile to British rule.'

Amherst, bitter about the directors, had just time to make a tour of the northern area of the Company's territory before returning home. It was a stately progress. When one carefully prepared Nawab was informed that the Governor-General's party would be a fortnight late in meeting him —

> He flew into such a violent rage that it resembled frenzy. He tore off a fine turban with jewels and threw it into the river. Two rings off his fingers shared the same fate; some valuable filigree work — in short every valuable he could lay his hands on — was thrown overboard. He stamped and raved like a madman, and no one could pacify him. He threatened to cut off his beard and eyebrows, and make a fakir of himself.

Amherst returned to England after five years in office. He never again held an important position, but was patronised by the royal family. He lived to a good age, and almost survived the Company raj itself.

◦◦◦◦

The age of utilitarianism in India really began with the Governor-Generalship of Lord William Bentinck. He was the son of a Whig prime minister and had previously been Governor of Madras, in which post he had succeeded Clive's son. He had been recalled — the height of ignominy for a Governor — after the mutiny at Vellore in 1806. But the Bentincks, originally a Dutch family, were not without power, and two years later the court of directors issued a statement attempting to rehabilitate his reputation and tacitly promising to employ him again. Now his chance had come. His mission was clear: to cut expenditure. The President of the Board of Control, Lord Ellenborough, wrote that he had told 'the Governor-General practically that if he should not be economical one will be found who is'.

Bentinck was Governor-General for nearly eight years, and for all that time the Company was at peace — a novel situation in India. But he was well aware of the dangers. He wrote:

> One hundred millions of people in India are under the control of a government which has no hold whatever on their affections. British India may be assailed from the north by the Gurkhas; from the east by the Burmese; from the north by the Sikhs and Afghans, and the hordes of Central Asia in

co-operation or otherwise with Persia and Russia; from the sea on all sides of the territory. In the native army, which lacks physical strength and moral vigour, rests our internal danger, and this danger may involve our complete submission.

Bentinck believed that India should be governed for the Indians. He was much under the influence of the Mills, and he endeavoured to improve the lot of the Indians. He knew no other way of doing so except by westernisation. The 'interventionists', it seemed, had won. First of all, he had to gain favour with the authorities at home. He made drastic cuts in expenditure, and made sure Bombay and Madras followed the edicts of Calcutta; this brought him much unpopularity, especially among the officers of the army, who suffered a cut in their allowances. He travelled about the Company's domains, as far as Malacca and Singapore, ordering economies wherever he went. He revised the taxes on opium – a Company monopoly. Before long the India deficit was a surplus.

Bentinck now turned to the humanitarian reforms which he was determined to put through. The education policy of the Company had been shelved for many years: Bentinck said 'general education is my panacea for the regeneration of India'. He was convinced that the English language was 'the key to all improvements'. The Company began setting up schools and colleges to teach English, and there was much encouragement to westernise Indian society. English replaced Persian (the formal language of the Mughals) as the official language, and became the medium of the higher courts of law. Attempts were made to diminish slavery, sacrifice, child marriage, and female infanticide, all long established in India.

Bentinck now felt strong enough – as Amherst had not – to tackle some of the most deeply embedded aspects of Hinduism, which had long horrified officials in India and the public at home. The practice of suttee, or the burning of Hindu widows on the funeral pyres of their dead husbands, was widely performed. It was a holy, but horrible, rite. The superintendent of police in Lower Bengal had reported, in 1818, 'There are very many reasons for thinking that such an event as voluntary suttee rarely occurs; few widows would think of sacrificing themselves unless over-powered by force'. There were authenticated instances of widows escaping from the pyre, only to be hauled back by the excited crowd of on-lookers. It was this which gave Bentinck his opportunity. His intention was to make anyone using such violence, leading to suttee, chargeable with homicide. There was a good deal of apprehension about the effects of this, but in the event there was no uprising or violent demonstration, and suttee passed quickly away, with only isolated cases occurring from time to time. Charles Metcalfe predicted that 'it will be universally acknowledged by the people of India as the best act performed by the British Government'.

At this point it was thought politic, for reasons of security, to delay further reforms touching on Indian traditions. But one other matter, more a problem of policing, had to be done: the abolition of the incredible secret society of 'Thugs'. This was a murder organisation which befriended travellers, throttled them with a cloth, and secretly buried them. They roamed the country in the guise of merchants or pilgrims, and belonged to a fanatical sect which gave religious backing to their activities – although they were not above making a profit out of the proceedings. Sometimes they were protected by petty local rulers who shared their gains. They had existed at least since the fourteenth century, but the British did not become aware of their existence till near the end of the eighteenth century. In India life had always been tenuous, and the loss of a traveller could be put down to a tiger or some other misfortune. The British, however, were more persistent in their enquiries when some of their own were lost on journeys in the interior. Gradually the amazing secret society came to light, although so skilled and careful were its members that at first the greatest difficulty was found in bringing them before the law. Bentinck appointed a special Commissioner for the Suppression of Thuggee and Dacoity, William Sleeman. At last informers began to talk. Between 1831 and 1837 over 3,000 Thugs were convicted (more than a third of them in one year), some expressing regret that they had not been able to complete their targets; many owned to several hundred victims. Thuggee was virtually wiped out, and disappeared altogether in the second half of the century. It was one of the most extraordinary and difficult acts the East India Company had to do in all its history.

❦

Bentinck's reforms had been supported in London, and in 1833 the renewal of the Company's charter strengthened this policy. Indian reformers such as Raja Ram Mohun Roy, the great philosopher who rejected Hinduism and Christianity, and Dwarkanath Tagore, who founded the first great western-style capitalist family in India, put pressure on London to authorise reforms, particularly those concerning Hinduism. The charter required the Company to make further restrictions on slavery (which was finally abolished in 1843).* But the Indian reformers, seeking Indian representation on the councils of the presidencies, had been disappointed; Roy had also advocated positions for Indians in the executive, complete Indianisation of the army, and trial by jury. Ironically, the main social reform was one which affected expatriates only; the abolition of the death penalty for British subjects born in Europe, and their children.

A simultaneous act to the charter of 1833 abolished the Company's China trade monopoly, which had long been called for by the English provincial merchants – despite the disastrous history of free trade in India since the Company's monopoly had been abolished there. This was bound to upset the balance of the Company's finances, for the China trade profit had averaged over £1,000,000 a year since 1814 and helped to pay off the India deficit.† The Company's factory at Canton had been told nothing of this until the last moment. The first despatch mentioning the possible closure was not sent till 4 April 1833: '...a great change which is contemplated in the present mode of conducting the Trade between this Country and China, and the possibility of the Company consenting to place in obeyance the Right to carry on commercial operations...abstain from entering into any new contracts whatever ...we are your loving friends, etc.'‡

When the act for the new charter came before Parliament it was presented by the secretary of the Board of Control, the President being ill. The secretary to the board was Thomas Babington Macaulay, later to be one of the greatest Whig historians. Since the age of Burke and Warren Hastings, public and Parliament had lost

* The slave trade overseas had long been forbidden, in the case of the small trade to St Helena, as early as 11.11.1757, after five slaves from India had hanged themselves there.
† The total China profit for 1815 to 1829 was £15,414,000, the overall profit for the same period being £20,488,000.
‡ India Office Records: Court Letters to China, Vol. XXX.

much interest in Indian affairs, and the Company's fate received little attention. What, in fact, happened was that it was granted the administration of India for another twenty years, but it was no longer to trade. A rule based on trade, it was held, was unseemly, unethical, and open to distraction and abuse. 'The said Company shall, with all convenient speed after April 22, 1834, close their commercial business, and make sale of all their merchandize, Stores, and Effects at Home and Abroad.' This decision had mainly come about because no one could think of a better solution to the problem of running India. The Government had enough on its hands; it said that the Company's assets* could cover any losses resulting from the China trade, but it was at the same time convinced that good administration could make India pay for itself. The East India Company was, in fact, to be the Government's agent for the administration of India, for a term of twenty years. Macaulay's speech could hardly have been bettered:

Three things I take as proved – that the Crown must have a certain authority over India, that there must be an efficient check on the authority of the Crown, and that the House of Commons is not an efficient check. We must then find some other body to perform that important office. We have such a body – the Company. Shall we discard it?...It is true that the power of the Company is an anomaly in politics. It is strange, very strange, that a joint stock company of traders; a society, the shares of which are daily passed from hand to hand; a society, the component parts of which are perpetually changing; a society which, judging *a priori* from its constitution, we should have said was as little fitted for imperial functions as the Merchant Taylors' Company or the New River Company, should be entrusted with the sovereignty of a large population, the disposal of a larger clear revenue, the command of a larger army than are under the direct management of the Executive Government of the United Kingdom. But what constitution can we give to our Indian Empire which shall not be strange – which shall not be anomalous? That Empire is itself the strangest of all political anomalies. That a handful of adventurers from an island in the Atlantic should have subjugated a vast country divided from the place of their birth by half the

* Declared by the East India Company, to have been over £21,000,000 on 1 May 1829.

globe; a country which at no very distant period was merely the subject of fable to the nations of Europe; a country never before violated by the most renowned of Western conquerers ...that we should govern a territory 10,000 miles from us, a territory larger and more populous than France, Spain, Italy and Germany put together; a territory the present clear revenue of which exceeds the present clear revenue of any state in the world, France excepted; a territory inhabited by men differing from us in race, colour, language, manners, morals, religion: there are prodigies to which the world has seen nothing similar. We interrogate the past in vain. The Company is an anomaly: but it is part of a system where everything is anomaly. It is the strangest of all governments, but it is designed for the strangest of all empires.

Arthur Wellesley, Duke of Wellington, defended the Bill in the House of Lords. After saying he would not enter the controversy about whether a company was the right institution to govern a country, he continued:

But whenever I hear a discussion like this, I recall to my memory what I have seen in that country. I recall to my memory the history of British India for the last fifty or sixty years. I remember its days of misfortune and its days of glory, and call to my mind the proud situation in which it now stands. I remember that the Indian government has conducted the affairs of – I will not pretend to say how many millions of people, for they have been variously calculated at seventy, eighty, ninety and even one hundred millions, but certainly of an immense population – a population returning an annual revenue of £22,000,000 sterling; and that, notwithstanding all the wars in which that Empire has been engaged, its debt at this moment amounts only to £40,000,000, being not more than two years' revenue. I do not say that such a debt is desirable, but I do contend that it is a delusion on the people of this country to tell them it is a body unfit for government and unfit for trade which has administered the affairs of India with so much success for so many years.

The directors and friends of the Company, mainly Tory, faced with the loss of their precious trade, were overwhelmed in both Houses of Parliament. On 16 August 1833 they passed a resolution declaring:

204

They cannot contemplate without apprehension and alarm the great and important change about to be introduced in the system which has been so long and so advantageously acted upon. [But they] assure His Majesty's Government and the country that they will to the utmost extent of the functions with which they are about to be invested, contribute to give effect to the bill when it shall become law, and promote, to the best of their ability, the happiness of India and the honour and prosperity of the East India Company.

The directors managed to preserve for themselves one important privilege: the right to dismiss the Governor-General. Proprietors were to receive ten guineas dividend on £100 stock for another forty years. St Helena was to pass to the Crown, but the careers of the Company staff there and in Canton were to be safeguarded and employment found for them in India and the India possessions.

The new charter became law in 1834, and enabled Bentinck to carry out some of the reforms already mentioned. The position of the Governor-General, already strong, was strengthened. A fourth member was added to the new supreme council in Calcutta in order to disentangle the laws and regulations of British India. It was decided to send out Macaulay to fill this post, at a salary of £10,000 a year. He busied himself with many other affairs, particularly education and a clause in the new charter which reversed the policy begun by Cornwallis of keeping Indians out of high office in the Company's service. (The clause read: 'No native of the said territories, nor any natural-born subject of His Majesty resident therein, shall, by reason only of his religion, place of birth, descent, colour or any of them lie disabled from holding any place, office or employment under the Company.') There was no sudden change in employment, however; for many years Indians were as scarce in judicial and high executive posts as ever. The reason for this was stated to be that first they had to be educated in western techniques in order to administer such techniques. Macaulay, an 'Anglicist' as opposed to the 'Orientalists', was a great believer in the benefits of westernisation. He spoke of the 'uselessness' of oriental studies 'for practical purposes'. He admitted the impossibility of teaching English to the entire population, but he wanted to form a 'class of persons, Indian in blood and colour, but English in taste, in opinions, in morals, and in intellect', as 'interpreters between us and the millions'. This he and his successors largely succeeded in doing, until a hundred years later the only English Pukkha sahibs left in the world were Indian or Pakistani. The establishment of English schools to produce Indian civil servants for the Company was speeded up. Macaulay was only in India for less than four years, but his influence on the form and style of administration, for better or worse, was great. Some historians were to claim his policies as disastrous, but the English language was to help India weld in a way that Persian had never done.

The Company's loss of the China tea monopoly seemed at first a terrible, perhaps even fatal, blow. Trade had been profitable, despite the inability to get on with the Emperor and his court. Although the industrial revolution, and in particular Manchester cotton, had struck for a time at exports from India to England, it had not curtailed the demand for tea; rather the contrary. And a profitable trade exporting Indian cotton to China had been built up. The East India Company had sent missions to China in 1792, in 1805, and, under Amherst, in 1816. None of them had met with much success, and Amherst's mission, when he had returned after an argument about bowing, had brought the Company into ridicule. The main difficulty had always been the trading of opium from India to China, encouraged by the Company, which had enjoyed a monopoly of the opium trade in India since 1773, and whose merchants and agents had for years flouted the regulations of the Chinese authorities, which forbade the use of the drug. The profits of the opium trade with China had financed many a campaign in India. But the Company soon found that it could survive without this unsavoury source of revenue, although the trade continued in private hands.* Bentinck set up a committee to investigate the possibility of tea production in India, indigenous tea having been discovered in Assam in 1823 by Major Robert Bruce; it was the start of what was to become the world's greatest tea trade.

A year after the new charter, Bentinck, broken in health, resigned, to almost universal regret. The court of directors passed a resolution paying tribute to 'the distinguished ability, energy, zeal and integrity with which his lordship has discharged the ardu-

* The Company's monopoly of granting licences for the growing and selling of opium, however, flourished. The revenue from this source was £728,517 in 1834/5; it had become £3,309,637 by 1849/50.

ous duties of his exalted position'. He died five years later. This Anglo-Dutchman is not remembered today as are other great figures of the Company's rule in India, but in many respects he was the best Governor-General India ever had.

The age of reform continued with the brief administration of Bentinck's successor, that old Company servant Sir Charles Metcalfe, who was appointed interim Governor-General. He was the only Governor-General to have been born in India, his father having been a servant (and later director) of the Company. He had spent thirty-five years in India, having been the first student at Wellesley's college in Calcutta, and had now achieved the height of his ambitions, but rather too late. He was tired of India and Indians, and he longed for home. Greatly to the alarm of the directors, Metcalfe completely freed the press. When the new Governor-General arrived, Metcalfe was offered a lower post and resigned. But he was favoured in Parliament, and later became Governor-General of Canada and received a peerage. The age of reform cannot be said to have ended with Metcalfe's departure, for many of the reforms started in Bentinck's time were slow in operation and continued under sympathetic Governors-General to follow, although they were the background to more martial events.

When the new Governor-General arrived it was already evident that the peaceful era was ending. There were rumblings on the North-West Frontier, in the Punjab, and in Sind. The East India Company was about to return to its more usual state – one of war.

13 BEYOND THE SUTLEJ

One of Metcalfe's acts was to sign a further treaty with Ranjit Singh, still ruler of the Punjab and supposedly an ally to the Company. This enhanced the power and position of the Sikhs, whose lands were now pressing on those of the Afghans themselves. The Sikh power in the Punjab, squashed between the aggressive Afghans and the suspicious British, was clearly flammable. To the west of the Sikhs was the territory of Sind, also independent of the East India Company. Through it ran the Indus, of which the Sutlej was the major tributary. The Indus was to the north-west what the Ganges was to the east, and it was the cause of constant power struggles. Sind acted as a buffer state between Persia and the Company's territory, and the Punjab as a buffer between Afghanistan and the Company. The Afghan and the Sikh had no love for each other, and were now face to face at each end of the Khyber Pass, one of the two main gateways to Afghanistan. It was in this part of India that the Company was now to become deeply and unsatisfactorily involved.

The new Governor-General was Lord Auckland, an ambitious Whig politician, son of a colleague of Pitt, and a relative of Minto. He was the first Governor-General under Queen Victoria, who came to the throne in June 1837. Like every other Governor-General, he had high hopes of doing good in India. He furthered Macaulay's education policy and took more interest in the appalling economic problems of India than had many of his predecessors.

After the ending of the Company's trading, there was an increase in Anglo-Indian trade; India was becoming a good market for British manufactures, especially Lancashire cotton; jute, tea, and silk were all growing exports before the end of the Company rule; but the benefits did not sink down to the population. Trade demands security. Auckland's whole time in India was harassed by the problem of the north-west, as was that of his successors. The Foreign Secretary was Lord Palmerston, and Lord Palmerston had an interest in Russia and Russian ambitions that might well be called an obsession. He had been advised, particularly by a nervous and alarmist envoy in Persia, John McNeill, that Russia intended to use the confrontation between Afghans and Sikhs to its own advantage and to advance Russian influence right up to the Indus; this would be regarded as a hostile act in London and Calcutta, leading almost inevitably to war. There was a lot of alarmist talk, and Auckland was impressed.

The ruler of Afghanistan was the able Dost Muhammad Khan, who had deposed Lord Minto's nominee, Shah Shuja. Dost Muhammad tried to make an alliance with Auckland to embarrass Ranjit Singh, but Auckland was understandably suspicious. The idea of an expedition to Kabul, the capital of Afghanistan, or to Persia, to warn off the Russians began to be discussed both in London and Calcutta. Russian envoys were reported in Kabul. Palmerston was for a march to Kabul ('the proceedings of Russians in Afghanistan are certainly as direct an approach to British India as it is at present in her power to make'). The final decision was left to Auckland. He was not a man of strong character. The army in India was brought back, by heavy recruiting, to over 200,000. Preparations proceeded with apparent inevitability. Policy was agreed — there was to be no question of 'territorial aggrandisement'. Shah Shuja was to be restored.

In March 1838, 13,000 Company and royal troops began the long march to Kabul, first through the Sind, the rulers of which were somewhat indignant, by the Bolan and Khyber Passes, supported by their Sikh allies and by Shah Shuja's own troops.* There was the usual rivalry between Company and royal officers, which even the great improvements in the conditions of the Company's service had not entirely abolished. Some of the royal

* First Anglo-Afghan War, 1839–42.

troops, convinced that India should be government-run, ignored the connection with the Company and pointedly referred to 'British India' in their writings; there was in some quarters in India a distinct feeling of embarrassment, even shame, about India being ruled by a group of shareholders.

The march began well, with an average of three camp-followers for every soldier. Messes travelled with their regimental silver, and at least one with its pack of fox-hounds. One of the generals wrote that 'many young officers would as soon have thought of leaving behind their swords and double-barrelled pistols as march without their dressing cases, their perfumes, Windsor soap, and eau de cologne'. But as the weary trek continued, luxuries were shed on the way or simply left behind for delighted local inhabitants. The army rested at Quetta; then marched to Dost Muhammad's second city, Kandahar, which gave itself up to Shah Shuja with apparent pleasure. It was not until Ghanzi was reached, only seventy-five miles from Kabul, that the main column was obliged to do any fighting. But the great column, exhausted as it was, brushed aside the opposition. On 7 August 1839 Shah Shuja entered Kabul unopposed, with a triumphant cavalcade.

The policy seemed to have enjoyed reasonable success. The Russians showed no signs of interfering. Dost Muhammad fled into the wilds, but was later captured. Auckland was made an earl; he had kept the peace with Burma and Nepal; he had, it seemed, successfully shown the mailed fist to Sind; he had strengthened the alliance with the Punjab; he had kept Russia at bay, and he had warned off Egypt from the Persian Gulf. He was supported by some Tories as well as Whigs. But there was still some unease about the march to Kabul, with its evident bullying and interfering in the affairs of a distant, minor nation. Besides, it had become evident that Shah Shuja could only keep his throne while British troops remained in Kabul. For this purpose a force had been left in the capital, under Major-General William Elphinstone, a cousin of Mountstuart Elphinstone, who had been Minto's envoy to Shah Shuja when the Shah had previously been on the throne. The fact that the Company, so anxious not to be imperialist, could not withdraw was an embarrassment to both itself and to the Government. The prime minister, who had given somewhat half-hearted support to the venture, was Lord Melbourne. He said of the situation that 'he was in the habit of thinking nothing settled until completely finished'.

◦◦✕◦◦

One of Auckland's many weaknesses was his inability to pick good men. There were good men in the army, but there were many elderly generals who had lost any intellectual vigour they may have had through the combined effects of gout, climate, and drink. Such a man was Elphinstone. According to a contemporary account, he 'had almost lost the use of his limbs. He could not walk; he could hardly ride. The gout had crippled him in a manner that was painful to contemplate.' His mind had deteriorated to childishness, sometimes almost imbecility. He was, however, universally liked, despite the fact that he was a royal officer. The garrison at Kabul looked upon him as a kind of amiable mascot.

The main British force in Afghanistan was in camp outside Kabul; it had moved there from the citadel after the arrival from India of Shah Shuja's numerous harem of several hundred women. There was also a small force in the city, and the Shah was heavily guarded by his own men in the citadel. There were, as well, British garrisons guarding the route to India, at Jalalabad, Kandahar, and Ghazni, and one across the mountains at Peshawar. All this was a colossal expense on the Company, and after nearly two years a brigade that had been attempting to pacify the country, under General Sir Robert Sale, was ordered to return. No sooner was it on the road to India than Kabul rose in revolt.

The British Resident, two other British, and the detachment of sepoys kept in the city were murdered to the last man. Shah Shuja was confined to his fortress. Threatening crowds left the city and neared the camp. The situation demanded immediate action to quell the revolt before it grew out of control. Elphinstone did nothing. 'We must see what the morning brings,' he said, 'and then think what can be done.' What he did was to close his lines, thereby abandoning his stores, which, incredibly enough, lay outside the encampment. After two days the garrison was virtually invested, exposed on the open plain to the fiercest warriors in Asia and probably the most accurate shots in the world.

Elphinstone was fatalistic from the start. Only three days after the murder of the British Resident, he declared: 'It behoves us to look to the consequences of failure: in this case I know not how we are to subsist or, from want of provisions, to retreat.' The senior political officer with Elphinstone was Sir William Macnaghten, the son of a former senior Company servant and himself in the Company's service from the age of sixteen. He had been a confirmed advocate of the expedition, and Auckland had sent him from Calcutta to look after the political side. He began sending messages after Sale suggesting he turned back; when these had no result, he resorted to open begging and pleading. But Sale marched on, to Jalalabad. Sale's wife and daughter were in the camp at Kabul, his personal courage was legendary throughout British India; he had every reason to turn back. But he marched on. He felt unable to take the responsibility of going against his instructions.

Elphinstone pondered and argued over what should be done at long councils of war. His authority had so weakened that his second-in-command took his bed-roll to the conferences, lay down, and snored. One sortie from the camp, urged by Macnaghten, ended in chaos as the disgusted troops fled to their own lines after being made to stand for hours on a hill-top in full view of the Afghan marksmen. There were a number of efficient young officers, like Lieutenant Vincent Eyre and Captain George Lawrence, who had implored Elphinstone to go into Kabul at the start of the revolt. Eyre now commented: 'A general gloom hung over the cantonment; the most sanguine now began to despond; the troops had not only lost all heart – they had lost all discipline.'

Supplies were running desperately short and the animals were being eaten. Macnaghten began to consider negotiations – 'or, rather, capitulation, for such it would be' – as Elphinstone had suggested from the start. He continued to send out messages to Sale's column: 'Dozens of letters have been written from this, urging your immediate return to Kabul; and if you have not started by the time you receive this, I earnestly beg that you will do so immediately.' But Sale would not return. Macnaghten decided to open negotiations. Although he and Elphinstone were in tents only a few yards apart, they corresponded in writing, no doubt with an eye to the future. Macnaghten was careful to get Elphinstone's agreement in writing. Talks dragged on with the Afghan leaders, but Macnaghten would not meet their demands, which included the surrender of arms.

It was winter. Sleet and snow fell almost daily. At night the temperatures were well below freezing. The Indian sepoys were in a wretched condition and morale throughout the camp was low. Macnaghten continued to refuse to surrender. 'The consequences,' he said, 'would be terrific as regards the safety of our Indian Empire and our interests in Europe.' But at least he realised that a negotiated retreat was the only hope; for soon the troops would be too starved and weak to offer any resistance. Elphinstone was only too keen to concur: 'No time ought to be lost in entering into negotiations for a safe retreat from the country.' One of the main reasons for the delay in this decision had been the fate of Shah Shuja, who had been put on his throne by the British, and whom it was a matter of honour not to desert. But desert him they were now about to do. It is not at all clear that the Afghans would have resisted an evacuation long before; their only wish was for the British force to pack up its camp and to go away for ever. Some of the rebel leaders seem to have been well aware that the more bloodshed caused to the British the greater the likelihood of retribution from India. But they did not have control over their own people, and Macnaghten had made the likelihood of a successful retreat less by waiting until the troops were demoralised and half starved. He drafted a treaty agreeing to the evacuation of the four garrisons in Afghanistan and to the return of Dost Muhammad.

But supplies were not sent into the camp, as promised by the Afghans, and Macnaghten went out for further talks. In order to salvage something from the political disaster, and presumably of his career, he had involved himself in local intrigues, evidently hoping to benefit from the chaotic disorder among the Afghans themselves. It did him no good, for he was grabbed before the discussions started, was hacked to death, and his headless trunk displayed at the city bazaar. Elphinstone heard the news with resignation and appointed Major Eldred Pottinger, an imperturbable Ulsterman, to continue the negotiations as if nothing had happened. Talks took place on Christmas Day. Said Eyre: 'A more cheerless Christmas Day perhaps never dawned upon British soldiers in a strange land; and the few whom force of habit urged to exchange the customary greetings of the season did so with countenances and in tones indicative of anything but merriment.' The treaty was completed on New Year's Day and authorised by eighteen Afghan chiefs. They expressed goodwill and promised to care for any left behind 'with all respect and consideration', and assured a safe withdrawal for the British. Whether the chiefs had the power to carry out their promises was another matter, but Elphinstone was in no position to delay.

The retreat from Kabul began on 6 January 1842. As the crow flew, Jalalabad was some seventy miles away; as men marched, it was nearly a hundred miles across rugged, mountainous country. Without opposition it would have been a difficult operation; but Elphinstone knew he was at the mercy of the hordes of tribesmen. He had about 4,500 troops, including one royal regiment, the 44th Foot (Essex), of over 600 British soldiers, three battalions of Company sepoys with British Officers, nine guns, about 1,000 cavalry (including Skinner's Horse), and sundry engineers and irregulars. But with the military there were also some 12,000 wretched camp-followers, who had come from India with the original victorious expedition. There were about a dozen British wives and twelve children, who were carried in litters.

The march had hardly begun before the Afghans, realising the weak and vulnerable state of the column, began harassing the rear, picking off stragglers and slaughtering those who, after only a few miles, sat down and could go no farther. That night the column lay in the snow and waited impatiently for dawn. 'The confusion was fearful – nearly every man paralysed with cold. Many frozen corpses lay on the ground,' wrote Lady Sale in her diary. 'All scraped away the snow as best they could to make a place to lie down on. The evening and night were intensely cold. No food for man or beast procurable.'

The retreat continued in bitter cold, the great column becoming more and more bedraggled, men and women collapsing, to lie beside the way when groups of Afghans thundered up to them and cut them to bloody messes, staining the snow. Frost-bite became commonplace. Food was almost non-existent. The cavalry were so paralysed with cold they had to be lifted on to the remaining mounts. Nevertheless, when a party of Afghans blocked the way, Lawrence was able to launch a successful bayonet charge – a 'very spunky, active man', said Lady Sale. When the accompanying Afghans demanded hostages to guarantee the evacuation of Jalalabad, it was Lawrence who volunteered, with Pottinger and another officer. It was a decision at least as wise as it was noble, for soon afterwards the column was decimated as it struggled through a pass. Those who emerged at the other end of the pass included Elphinstone, most of the troops, some of the British wives (one staggered into camp carrying her baby), but many of the camp-followers had been massacred or, in the case of women and children, taken into slavery. The wounded lay where they were, and many perished during the night. Eyre wrote: 'Groans of misery and distress assailed the ear from all quarters.'

Next day the Afghans suggested the British women and children should be given up for their own safety (there was no mention of the Indian women and children). Elphinstone agreed and the women left to join the hostages, and in several instances their husbands accompanied them, claiming that their first duty was to their families. The next obstacle was a narrow gorge, only fifty yards long, but less than six yards wide. The Afghans fired ceaselessly into the column as it was massed below, struggling to escape. The sepoys, in their rush to get away, threw down their arms, upon which the Afghans descended and slew them with their swords. By the end of the day, the fourth since the retreat had begun, Elphinstone had with him less than half the 44th, about 200 horsemen, and some 3,000 camp-followers. The road back to Kabul was littered with over 15,000 corpses. For the next two days it was a running fight nearly all the way, with the survivors fighting desperately for their lives, until there were only small, isolated parties left. The last stand of the 44th was made on 13 January only a few miles from Jalalabad. Eyre wrote:

To avoid the vigorous assaults that were now made by their confident foe, they were compelled to leave the road and take up a defensive position on the height to the left of it, where they made a resolute stand, determined to sell their lives at the dearest possible price. At this time they could only muster about twenty muskets. Several Afghans now ascended the height and assumed a friendly tone towards the little party there assembled; but the calm was of short duration, for the soldiers, getting provoked at several attempts being made to snatch away their arms, resumed a hostile attitude and drove the intruders fiercely down. The die was now cast, and their fate sealed; for the enemy, taking up a post on the opposite hill, worked off man after man, officer after officer, with unerring aim. Parties of Afghans rushed up at intervals to complete the work of extermination, but were as often driven back by the still dauntless handful of invincibles. At length, nearly all being wounded more or less, a final onset of the enemy, sword in hand, terminated the unequal struggle and completed the dismal tragedy.

A few prisoners were taken, one being a captain who saved the regimental colours by tying them round his waist. With the end of the only British regiment, the retreat disintegrated into a fleeing rabble. Elphinstone had already gone to a conference with the Afghans, where he was no doubt relieved to find himself a hostage or prisoner. By midday only six British, riding hard, of Elphinstone's force of 4,500, were alive or free. Of them only one, a Company surgeon, survived.

At Jalalabad, Sale was waiting for news of the column, having decided to remain despite a letter from Elphinstone and Pottinger urging him to evacuate in accordance with the treaty they had signed. That evening, 13 January, Major Henry Havelock was watching the horizon from a roof-top. He wrote:

> One of us espied a single horseman riding towards our walls. As he got nearer, it was distinctly seen that he wore European clothes...a signal was made to him by someone on the walls, which he answered by waving a private soldier's forage cap over his head. The Kabul gate was then thrown open and several officers, rushing out, received and recognised in the traveller the first, and it is to be feared the last, fugitive of the ill-fated force at Kabul.

In the following days a few camp-followers staggered into Jalalabad, but no more British. Elphinstone's column had been annihilated. It was an almost unthinkable blow to East India Company pride, which was considerable, in India. There was to be nothing quite like it again till 1942, exactly a hundred years later.

Auckland was broken. 'I have been much and deeply affected by what has passed, more so than I can well describe,' he wrote. He had already received notice of recall, and he was bound to return in disgrace. His regime has customarily been considered a disaster, but he has taken the blame in history where it should have been more widely spread, particularly in the direction of Palmerston. His Governor-Generalship was important in that during his time the security of India became more important in British policy than ever before, even than in the Napoleonic period. The loss of Kabul had been seen in London, not as the minor frontier setback that it was but as a major incident in the context of European power.

Before Auckland left India he ordered a relief column in order to conduct a more honourable withdrawal from Afghanistan, which the East India Company and Board of Control had decided to leave to its devices. Some retribution would have to be enacted, and the prisoners brought home, for the sake of prestige. Then the Afghans could do what they wished.

The commander-in-chief of the punitive expedition was General George Pollock, commander of the garrison at Agra. He was a Company general and, while no genius, he was an able professional soldier who, unlike Elphinstone, owed nothing to nepotism and favouritism (his brother became a High Court judge in Bombay). One aspect of his task – what to do about Shah Shuja – was solved when the Shah was assassinated. And another problem was solved when the garrison at Ghazni capitulated to the Afghans. That left the garrisons at Kandahar and Jalalabad to be brought away, some retribution taken, and the release of some sixty British prisoners. The expedition began badly. The leading brigade was routed at the Khyber Pass, and returned to Peshawar. The column could not advance until Pollock had taken the heights dominating the Khyber. A few days later the sound of regimental bands in the distance told Sale and the garrison of Jalalabad that they were rescued.

By now a new Governor-General had arrived in India.* Lord Ellenborough was the son of a famous lawyer who had defended Warren Hastings at his impeachment. He had twice been President of the Board of Control and, as such, was considered one of the leading authorities on Indian affairs.† He had an excellent brain and

---

* Auckland was dead within seven years, but not before recovering something of his prestige and becoming First Lord of the Admiralty. His nephew became Lieutenant-Governor of Bengal.
† Ellenborough had a distant relationship with George Washington. His uncle, Thomas Law, who had been in the Company's civil service for eighteen years, later went to America to meet his hero, Washington. This he not only did, but married the granddaughter of Washington's wife (who had been married before). Law's daughter was mentioned in Washington's will. He remained in America, and became active in US affairs.

was widely acknowledged to be able, none acknowledging it with less reluctance than himself. He has been described as 'bombastic, masterful, vain and extremely ambitious'. While President of the Board, he had turned the East India House inside out, ignoring all opposition. Most of his contemporaries loathed him, and at least one (Robert Vernon Smith) believed him mad. His assignment was to restore peace. Ellenborough was an autocratic man, but he was exceedingly sensitive about the liberal views which he claimed. He was not a friend of the East India Company, and was among those who believed that the Crown should take over the government of India.

Soon after his arrival at Calcutta, Ellenborough left for Allahabad, in the north, to oversee military operations, although he admitted he was no soldier (he was on his own, his remarkable wife had deserted him and was living in a Bedouin harem). Learning of the setback at the Khyber and nervous of another disaster, he ordered a retirement, but when Pollock showed extreme reluctance to retire, he made the compromise that the withdrawal could go via Kabul (which lay in the opposite direction to India), and that General William Nott, commanding the garrison at Kandahar, could join with Pollock for this purpose. He told Nott: 'I would endeavour to inspire you with the necessary caution, and make you feel that, great as are the objects to be attained by success, the risk is great also.' But Pollock and Nott conducted their advances with care, with repeated bayonet charges, and with due respect for the formidable Afghan warriors. Pollock's column marched the same route as that taken by Elphinstone on the fatal retreat; rotted corpses and skeletons littered every mile of the way. One of Pollock's captains wrote: 'The sight of the remains of the unfortunate Kabul force was fearfully heartrending. They lay in heaps of fifties and hundreds, our gun-wheels passing over and crushing the skulls and other bones of our late comrades at almost every yard.' At one point there was a heap of some 1,500 corpses.

The army entered Kabul without opposition. The prisoners were released; Elphinstone was not among them – he had died of dysentery a few weeks before and his remains had been carefully sent by the Afghan chiefs to Sale at Jalalabad. (Pottinger died of disease on his way to England; both his brothers died in India in the Company's service at about the same time.) Pollock chose the magnificent great bazaar of Kabul, where Macnaghten's bloody hulk had been displayed to the mob, as the place for British retribution. The city shuddered and echoed as the engineers demolished it with gunpowder. With no delay, the combined force of Pollock and Nott marched through the Khyber, to a chorus of snipers' bullets, and out of Afghanistan. It marched on through the Punjab and reached the Sutlej, across which all British troops were brought once more on a specially constructed bridge of boats. Ellenborough ordered a vast parade on the south banks of the river, apparently as a display of power. It was the source of embarrassment to commentators at the time, and to British writers since, who have noted that the rows of elephants refused to salaam as instructed. In any event, Indian rulers were not impressed. Since the annihilation of a British column in Afghanistan, things were not the same. Ranjit Singh's successor, ruler of the Sikhs, did not even attend.

Ellenborough, hoping that the whole affair was now at an end, wrote huffily: 'The Governor-General will leave it to the Afghans themselves to create a government amidst the anarchy which is the consequence of their crimes.' He added a shaft for Auckland: 'To force a sovereign upon a reluctant people would be as inconsistent with the policy as it is with the principles of the British Government.' It was a statement of which Ellenborough's enemies were to remind him later. Meanwhile the incredulous Dost Muhammad was returned to Afghanistan from Calcutta, where he had been well looked after at Company expense. He renewed his interrupted reign, which lasted another twenty years, and lived to become a firm ally of the Company. 'I do not understand,' he said.

✺

Ellenborough's intentions were peaceful, or so he always insisted, but his actions were war-like. No sooner had he extricated the Company from the fiasco of Afghanistan than the question of Sind became pressing. This was the territory through which the original invasion of Afghanistan had made its way. The local amirs, or chiefs, were despotic and cruel, but they cared for their independence. They controlled the Indus, which was the main artery of the Punjab, and the lower Sind was a rich, fertile area. They were also Muslims, and Ellenborough believed that the Hindus were the natural allies of the British in India and the Muslims the natural foes. Major James Outram, of the Company's army, had been sent to negotiate with them, but his superior, General Charles Napier, an opinionated royal officer, believed a quick military conquest would be more efficient.* He was one of the most convinced advocates of the benefits of westernisation, and believed that this could only be achieved by direct and firm rule. He was not an optimist about the East India Company's rule: 'The system will not last fifty years. The moment those brave and able natives know how to combine, they will rush on us simultaneously and the game is up.' Outram, on the other hand, was heir to the old non-interventionists, but he could do nothing against the desire for revenue, security, and perhaps, most of all, for some easy-to-get glory after the recent military humiliation. Napier marched into the territory, and when Outram was threatened in the Sind capital he took it as an excuse to conquer the whole of Sind. Although heavily outnumbered, the Company's sepoys fought superbly in several fierce engagements, and Napier conducted the operations with confidence and flair. He is reputed to have sent a one-word despatch: 'Peccavi' (I have sinned). The conquest was just what many British had wanted. Napier became a national hero at once, and was knighted. The controversy was furious; 'most tyrannical – positive robbery', said Outram. Sind was annexed to the East India Company's dominions, under the direct rule of Sir Charles Napier. He turned out to be a rough military despot, but not inhumane, as his soldiers could have foreseen (he was always to the fore in battles, and after the conquest of Sind he was the first British commander ever to name in despatches humble private soldiers as well as officers). The civil administrators of India were horrified by his methods, but they worked; anarchy was subjected to some law and some order. But Napier had the ability to make enemies as few men even in India had ever done, and he was the constant target of the directors in London as well as of the authorities in Calcutta, and after four years he was replaced.

Ellenborough's hopes of a peaceful, Whiggish policy had ended in Pollock's campaign in Afghanistan, the military subjugation of an ally, and yet another conflict with the Marathas at Gwalior. Ellenborough was confused. Somehow the liberal patrician had become a notorious conquerer. Although the Company no longer traded itself, the directors still mostly represented Anglo-Indian trade

* Sind War, 1843.

interests. They sought economy and peaceful conditions. Ellenborough had continued Bentinck's liberal domestic politics, but the wars had been expensive. Having no respect for the directors, and little for the East India Company, he addressed them in his despatches with haughty disdain and took little or no notice of their strictures. In the Charter of 1833, when the Company had given away so much, it had retained the right to dismiss the Governor-General. And much to the astonishment of London, Calcutta, and Lord Ellenborough, the Governor-General was now dismissed. It was legal and there was nothing anyone could do about it. Ellenborough left for home. The Queen granted him an earldom. Parliament honoured him with a vote of thanks. He was made first Lord of the Admiralty.

The men of the East India Company in Leadenhall Street had wielded their power, as of old.

Between the Sutlej and the Indus, up to three hundred miles across, lay the great arid, dusty plains and hill-lands of the Punjab and the mountains of Kashmir. This was the territory in which the Sikhs had emerged as rulers. But since Ranjit Singh's death there had been confusion and disorder, the real power lying with the army which Ranjit had built up. The Company's troops hovered about south of the Sutlej, essential for security but an obvious threat to the Punjab. Up to 1838 the northern frontier garrison had amounted to about 2,500 men; Auckland had brought the total up to about 8,000, and had established the Ferozepore station; Ellenborough had increased it to 14,000; among his new garrisons was Simla. Major George Broadfoot, the Company's agent in charge of Sikh affairs, agitated matters by his arrogant diplomacy. The Sikhs, seeking unity and fearing British intentions, crossed the Sutlej on 11 December 1845 with an army of up to 40,000 men and up to 40 guns.*

The new Governor-General was Sir Henry Hardinge, Ellenborough's brother-in-law. He was a professional soldier who had lost a hand in battle two days before Waterloo. He was a stolid,

* Much higher figures (evidently based on the Governor-General's report) are sometimes given, but the whole Punjabi Army was only 42,000. 'Sikhs' are referred to here, although there were Muslim and Hindu units in the army of Lahore.

competent public servant, and a pleasing contrast to the vain Ellenborough. He was not unprepared for the Sikh invasion, and he had already gone north, anticipating trouble. He placed himself under Sir Hugh Gough as second-in-command (but reversed Gough's orders at least once). Gough was commander-in-chief in India, a racy and hardy old veteran and member of what was to be a famous military family.

The Company's troops advanced on the insurgents. The Sikh Army was not highly regarded – except by Henry Lawrence, who considered it equal to the Marathas – but it had the support of French advisers and officers, and its artillery was considerable. Within a week of the Sikh crossing of the Sutlej, Gough defeated the enemy at Mudki and then again at Ferozepore, where the British garrison of 7,000 had been besieged. Ferozepore was a costly and bloody engagement, and Gough was not without his luck to win it. Sale and Broadfoot were both killed (Broadfoot was one of three brothers, all of whom died in the Company's service in this period). The Sikhs streamed back across the Sutlej. Gough decided not to follow, thus giving the Sikh Army time to recoup and cross the river once more. The decisive battle was fought at Sobraon on 10 February 1846, when 15,000 British troops stormed the Sikh trenches held by 20,000 men; the cavalry poured through the broken line, a rout followed, and many Sikhs were drowned fleeing across the river. Hardinge and Gough crossed the Sutlej and marched to Lahore.

Hardinge did not covet the Punjab, but the Company's claimant for the throne was a young boy, Duleep Singh, whose legitimacy was extremely doubtful owing to Ranjit Singh's age and debility at the time of his birth. His mother was ambitious, and so was her lover, who was also violently anti-British. It was clear that the regime could only survive if supported by a Company military presence. A financial arrangement split the country in two; Kashmir, with its strong Sikh and Muslim population, was maladroitly sold by the Company to a Hindu Raja.

Sir Henry Lawrence, younger brother of the George Lawrence prominent in the Kabul campaign, was appointed the Company's Resident in Lahore, and he restored order and some law in extremely difficult circumstances, not having the real power to enforce his will, despite a great reduction in the Sikh Army. Lawrence was one of four remarkable brothers from Ulster, sons of an obscure colonel, who had spent many years in India and had fought at Seringapatam, of whom two others, George and John, were also to achieve fame. (The fourth, Richard, became a colonel in the Company's army.) They made a contribution equal to that of the three Wellesleys, although in a much greater period of time. Henry had already been Resident in Nepal, and was also considered one of the Company's experts on the Punjab. He was president of the regency council which ruled the state, in theory, on behalf of Duleep Singh, but in reality for the East India Company. He was aided by a new generation of able young men, like Herbert Edwardes, John Nicholson, and his brother John, who had previously been collector of taxes for Delhi.

Hardinge's remaining time as Governor-General was spent in desperate attempts to economise and put the Company's affairs on a better financial footing after the costs of the recent wars. Educational reforms proceeded extremely slowly while Hardinge struggled to balance the books. The army was drastically cut. But Hardinge's economies did not produce a regular surplus till after his departure. The East India Company's possessions were enlarged by the purchase of the few Danish stations in India and by the acquisition by treaty of the island of Labuan from the Sultan of Borneo. The adventurer, Sir James Brooke, in and out of the Company's service for thirty years, became Governor of Labuan; he was already 'The White Raja' of Sarawak, a title conferred on him by the Sultan of Borneo, for his help in putting down insurgents.

Exhausted, but confident of stability in the all-important north, Hardinge and Henry Lawrence decided to go home in January 1848, Hardinge proclaiming, 'It will not be necessary to fire a gun in India for seven years to come';* Henry Lawrence declaring, 'The Sikhs have come to terms and have settled down, because they have been well-treated by us.' For half a century the cry had always been 'as far as the Sutlej and no farther'. But the Company had crossed it once more, and until the end of its time it was never to return.

* Hardinge's grandson was Viceroy of India, 1910–16.

14 THE LAWRENCES

The East India Company had approached the summit of its rule. All that was necessary was to tighten the British embrace around the vast complex and to turn it towards Europe and the west. Amazingly enough, a man was found with sufficient energy and drive to be capable of directing this immense task. And he did it in just seven years. Lord Dalhousie was the busiest and most productive of all the Governors-General. He was able to get through an incredible amount of work, on numerous subjects, ranging from the mechanical details of railway engineering to aspects of foreign policy. Day after day he dedicated himself to the despatch boxes which surrounded him. Even his enemies, and after the revolt he was to have many, were never able to quite hide some admiration for the man. He possessed a cool, clear, uncluttered intelligence, spotless integrity, and a pleasing personality and disposition. One who knew him described Dalhousie well: 'If at first sight he gave an impression of smallness, that impression disappeared when he had anything particular to say or to do. Then his frame seemed to dilate...The voice had a good timbre, rich, resonant and somewhat deep. His manner in general was quiet, reserved and masterly.' He was the son of a former commander-in-chief in India, one of Wellington's old generals, and Wellington had acted as patron of his colleague's son. Dalhousie had become President of the Board of Trade while still a young man, and had been outstandingly successful; his main task had been to tackle the railway boom, a mania so widespread in

England in the late eighteen-forties that, in despair, he had been reduced to suggesting nationalisation. Although a fervent Tory and one who despised the Whigs, Dalhousie had been offered the Governor-Generalship of India by a Whig prime minister, Lord John Russell, and he had accepted providing he was allowed to retain his 'personal independence with reference to party politics'. It had been an appointment which brought great credit to the Whigs and Dalhousie at a time when party politics were peculiarly bitter. It had been at the suggestion of Wellington. But the most remarkable thing about it was that Dalhousie was only thirty-five.

Dalhousie reached Calcutta in exactly two months, having taken the short route via Suez. Climbing the steps from the river, he had become lost in the welcoming crowd. 'Where is he?' asked Hardinge. 'Here I am,' shouted Dalhousie. For the first six nights there were magnificent state banquets. Then the two men shook hands on the steps and Hardinge embarked. Young Dalhousie was alone. And within four months the Sikhs had risen.

An outbreak at Multan, in the far west of the Sikh area, had resulted in the death of two British officers. News of this reverberated across the Punjab. The Company's Punjab administration, tenuous and ambiguous, with small groups of British officers isolated across hundreds of miles of territory among millions of suspicious people, suddenly did not appear as reliable as Henry Lawrence had said. Many of the officers were young men in their twenties, with vast responsibilities; such a one was Herbert Edwardes (later Major-General Sir Herbert Edwardes), who took the initiative on his own responsibility, defeated a rebel force and, with the help of a friendly chief, besieged the rebels in Multan.* There he waited for assistance. But the Sikh Army at Lahore could not be relied on to follow its new British masters. Should a British force be sent back across the Sutlej immediately, risking defeat in a second Sikh war? Dalhousie and Gough delayed. There was a shortage of troops immediately available. The Governor-General cursed his predecessor, Hardinge, who had cut the army after the earlier war with the Punjab. Henry Lawrence, in London, advised the Government that the result should be nipped in the bud straight away, before it had time to spread. Gough, on the other hand, wanted time to make his preparations. Dalhousie took the decision

* Second Anglo-Sikh War, 1848–9.

not to go to Multan. 'Delay giving temporary immunity to a rebel was one evil,' he said. 'Action involving frightful loss of life, and the possible failure for a time of our enterprise, was another evil.' In London, he was roundly condemned, but modern military commanders would be likely to agree with him. By the time Gough had collected an army of 16,000 at Ferozepore, the Punjab was ablaze. The siege of Multan was abandoned. A British garrison was itself invested at Attock. Bannu, south of the Khyber, was in revolt. The troops at Peshawar mutinied, and George Lawrence, with two other officers, barely escaped with his life; 'Trust that it will be considered that I held my position as long as was practicable,' he noted in his report.

The Sikh rebels, led by one of their senior military commanders, son of a rebel chief, assembled near the Chenab river and Gough attacked them there, at Chillianwala, before further rebel forces could join them. Gough had first been in battle fifty-three years before. At this battle, on 13 January 1849, the Sikh military reputation was thoroughly restored. Gough was not a great admirer of artillery, believing in the invincibility of British-trained infantry. The guns could not be got up, and Gough decided to attack with no barrage. The infantry, going forward in thick scrub, were unsettled to find the enemy advancing to meet them; the cavalry were hindered by the undergrowth. There was a slight hesitation, and then the British cavalry turned and was quickly in total rout. The infantry staggered on and eventually took the enemy position, with very heavy losses, and then withdrew. The Sikh Army remained in the field. The irascible Gough was unrepentant. He told one of his brigadiers: 'I had not intended to attack today, but the impudent rascals fired on me. They put my Irish blood up, and I attacked them.'

Dalhousie did his best to claim a victory. But the public at home were not deceived. There was a widespread demand for Gough's recall; after the heavy casualties in the First Sikh War, and now at Chillianwala, he was being spoken of as a butcher, the worst British general for generations. Dalhousie wrote to Wellington: 'I treat it as a great victory. But writing confidentially to you, I do not hesitate to say that I consider my position grave. I have put into the field in the Punjab a force fit to match all India. In the hands of the Commander-in-Chief I do not now consider that force safe, or free from the risk of disaster. There is not a man in that Army, from his Generals of Division to the Sepoys, who does not proclaim the same thing.' Dalhousie, however, took a different attitude with Gough personally; he was as yet inexperienced and took a somewhat two-faced position, which he certainly was not to do with the Lawrences later. Within forty-eight hours of the arrival of the news of Chillianwala in London, it had been decided to replace Gough with Sir Charles Napier. The President of the Board of Control, Hob-house, told Dalhousie: 'The impression made upon the public mind is stronger than that caused by the Kabul massacre.' But within a few years the battle in which the Sikhs had held a British army, which astounded all Britain, was totally forgotten.

Hugh Gough, still insisting it had been a victory, was highly indignant. Napier, whose return to India was greeted with mixed feelings there, said of Gough: 'Were his military genius as great as his heart, the Duke would be nowhere by comparison.' Before Napier could arrive, Gough seized the chance to restore his reputation. Both the armies were reinforced after Chillianwala; they met again at Gujerat on 13 February. This time Gough ordered a long and careful bombardment. Gough, outnumbered by at least two to one, relied on the staunchness of the Company's famous sepoys once more, strengthened by British battalions. One of Gough's senior commanders was Brigadier-General Henry Dundas, Dundas's grandson. In one of the British Army battalions, the 32 of Foot (Duke of Cornwall's Light Infantry), Corporal John Ryder gave a good account of what happened:

The whole army was now formed for battle, in a line fronting the enemy, who appeared to be watching us very closely, for we could see them upon every rising ground, and on the tops of the houses at the village. We could discern a great stir in their camp, as if they were preparing to receive us. Horsemen were riding about at full speed, as if to carry orders to the different parts of their position...The morning was fine and clear, and as the sun rose it cast forth its golden rays in great splendour upon the two opposing armies, as they stood with glistening accoutrements, waiting to commence the deadly strife. It was about six o'clock a.m. when the line advanced...On our side, the shots were thrown in a masterly manner, and shell was pitched very skilfully, killing every man at their guns...The artillery had been in ploy about two hours when the enemy's guns began to slacken. We had most of this time been lying down upon the ground, and the enemy's shot had been flying thick about us, and two anxious hours they were...We advanced, and did not discharge a shot till within 150 yards or less, when we opened such a murderous and well-directed fire that they fell by hundreds...By this time the fight had become general along the whole line; roll after roll of musketry rent the air, and clouds of smoke rose high and thick, while death was dealt out without mercy...With levelled bayonets we charged; but they could not stand the shock of cold steel. They gave way in all directions; although some of their officers showed the most daring courage...but their artillery fought desperately: they stood and defended their guns to the last. They threw their arms around them, kissed them, and died. Others would spit at us, when the bayonet was through their bodies. Some of the guns and carriages were streaming with blood...On we went, charging and cheering, bearing all down before us; and the black flag fell into our hands, which we bore from the field in triumph. Everything was carried before us, and the dead and dying lay strewed all over the ground, in heaps...nothing could daunt the courage of the British soldiers, nor resist the shock of the levelled bayonets.

The fleeing army was hotly pursued, and eventually laid down its arms. The Afghans, who had come through the Khyber to aid the Punjabis in pushing the British back across the Sutlej, were forced back into their own territory. It was total victory; Gough and his faithful troops at Gujerat had brought it about. Gough was made a Viscount; hearing the news, he said, 'Well, now, I forgive them everything.' But nothing could save Gough from public opinion, which was totally prejudiced against him; his reputation as a blundering incompetent remained. He lived another twenty years, dying shortly after his ninetieth birthday.

Henry Lawrence had already got back to India, somewhat to the chagrin of Lord Dalhousie, who couldn't abide him. Dalhousie had decided that the only way to avoid further disturbance in the Punjab was to annex it to the Company, instead of trying to rule it from behind the scenes. Henry Lawrence was against this. He told

Dalhousie: 'I did think it unjust; I now think it impolitic.' Dalhousie got his way and the Punjab, right up to the Khyber, was proclaimed East India Company territory on 29 March 1849. Henry Lawrence had a great reputation at home, and Dalhousie could not get rid of him. He reduced his power in the Punjab by forming a 'board of administration', with Henry Lawrence as president of the board, claiming that Henry Lawrence was 'not, in my eyes, sufficient for the task' alone. Another member was Henry's younger brother John. These two men had strong and forceful personalities; the board was doomed, as Dalhousie later admitted he fully 'suspected' it would be. The unfortunate third member described himself as 'a regular buffer between two high-pressure engines'. But at first the administration was a success. One important modern historian has written that this period in the Punjab was 'the highest point of British rule in India'.

The first matter to be dealt with, in traditional East India Company fashion, was that of 'reimbursement' and 'monies owing'. Dalhousie claimed that Lahore should provide for the cost of the late war, and as part of the settlement the famous Koh-i-Nor diamond, which had once belonged to the Mughal emperors and had since passed through several royal hands, was 'confiscated'. The East India Company, which had borne the cost of the war, naturally conceived that the diamond would come to it. But Dalhousie, ignoring logic, thought differently. He declared that it should 'find its final and fitting resting-place in the crown of Britain...For there is not one of those who have held it since its original possessor who can boast so just a title to its possession.' The diamond was entrusted to the safe keeping of John Lawrence, a man more unaccustomed to the keeping of jewellery than most. He promptly lost it. 'This is the worst trouble I have ever got into,' he said. Fortunately, his servant found it in Lawrence's waistcoat pocket. Dalhousie took charge of the magnificent diamond on his first visit to Lahore. A naval ship was waiting to receive it at Bombay. The Governor-General travelled with the diamond sewn, by Lady Dalhousie, into a belt which he wore night and day; at night two fierce dogs were chained to his camp-bed. With some relief Dalhousie handed over the diamond to the ship's captain at Bombay, and the Koh-i-Nor diamond was safely presented to Queen Victoria, who was greatly pleased.

The rule of the Punjab was soon being fought for by the two remarkable brothers on the board of administration. Henry, idealistic, romantic, passionate, was an unlikely product of Addiscombe. John, conscientious, practical, compassionate, was in many ways a typical product of Haileybury. The excuses of earlier administrators that corruption in India was too inherent, too insidious, to be avoided, were ruthlessly repudiated; both men were utterly and totally above corruption. Both were thoroughly versed in Indian affairs; no servants of the Company ever tried harder to understand India and gain its sympathy than Henry and John Lawrence. They had lived among Indians nearly all their lives; Henry, born in Ceylon, was more at home with Indian princes than he was among his friends in England; he was against the prevailing ideas of westernisation. Both men spoke Indian languages fluently. They were hardy, tough, caring little for the luxuries and conceits of Anglo-Indian life in the south. They travelled over the Punjab endlessly. John spent sixteen years in northern India with only two brief visits to Calcutta. Henry spent thirty-four years of his life in India, twenty of them in the north, with only two home leaves in all that time. Their brother George was forty-three years in India, with only one visit home.

The brothers' different characters were at the bottom of their political differences. John, as a civilian administrator, was ruled by practicalities as much as by higher motives, although he certainly was not without the latter; he told the Sikhs, 'What is your injury I consider mine: what is gain to you I consider my gain,' but he added, 'I have ruled this district three years by the sole agency of the pen, and if necessary I will rule it by the sword.' He was a gnarled man, normally of few words, although he could call on fine rhetoric when it was needed, who made crisp decisions and stuck to them. He was, as he said, an old bullock for work, and he expected the same of his subordinates (some of whom objected to being 'turned into homeless vagrant governing-machines'). He told Dalhousie: 'We have agreed not to recommend any leave except when men are sick. There is still so much to do. Every day is of value.' After years of work without break, leave was restored. One of John Lawrence's young men wrote: 'There was a glow of work and duty around us in the Punjab such as I have never felt before or since. I well remember the reaction of feeling when I went on furlough to

England: the want of pressure of any kind, the self-seeking, the dulling and dwarfing lack of high aims.' John Lawrence felt for the common people. 'Our true policy,' he wrote, 'is to give up every restriction that we can possibly do without and retain the land-tax. By this means we conciliate the masses, and especially the industrial classes. Customs levies are harassing in all countries; in this country they are intolerable.'

Henry, also, was not without his compassion: 'Until we treat natives, and especially native soldiers, as having much the same feelings, the same ambition, the same perception of ability, and imbecility, as ourselves, we shall never be safe.' It was a point worth making, and John would not have disagreed. On another occasion, Henry said: 'In a new country, especially a wild one, promptness, accessibility, brevity and kindliness are the best engines of government.' They were words which many future Imperial administrators could have recalled with profit. But Henry, proud and touchy, felt also for his friends, the princes and military chiefs, who had lost their power to the Company, while John had little or no sympathy for men whom he believed deserved none. It was this which sparked off the row that ended in Henry's removal from Lahore, although if it had not something else would have; for Henry was impatient of his brother's obstruction on the board and of his influence with Dalhousie. After nearly four years of nagging disagreements, a final clash became inevitable; Henry was not a man to compromise on even the smallest points. At length both men offered to resign, Henry fully expecting that John's offer would be accepted rather than his own. Dalhousie was delighted at the opportunity to be rid of Henry. He wrote, with some glee, 'I opine he had not the least intention that he should be the one to go.' He added, 'I shall not be sorry when he goes, although he has many fine qualities...I think his brother John is a better man...Antagonism of opinion has, as I suspected, brought the brothers into violent collision.' Dalhousie answered Henry's resignation letter coolly, and exaggerated the fraternal differences:

You are aware that by the unreserved communications of yourself and your brother for several years past I have been made fully cognizant of your differences of opinion and of the partial estrangement they had created. On every occasion I have spoken frankly to each of you…I am bound to say that during the present year I have felt some doubt whether your estrangement was not beginning to be injurious. From the letters of both of you I have received the impression that differences of opinion were becoming more frequent and more acrid…

He went on to offer Henry the Company's representation at the protected Hindu state of Rajputana (Rajasthan), south-west of the Punjab, although Henry had asked for the more important Sind. Henry sadly accepted the rebuff, writing to his brother: 'I hope you will believe that, if you preserve the peace of the country, and make the people, high and low, happy, I shall have no regrets that I vacated the field for you.' Before he left Lahore, he and his wife knelt in prayer for John's success in the Punjab. The older brother, George, who had been in the far north of the Punjab, at Peshawar, preceded Henry to Rajputana as his deputy.

The board of administration for the Punjab was abolished, as Dalhousie saw no more use for it now that Henry had gone. John, forty-two years old, was left in supreme control, the most powerful man in the Punjab since Ranjit Singh. 'I desire earnestly to show what a man bred and educated as a civilian can do in a new country,' he wrote. He showed that such a man could do much. The Punjab, under John Lawrence and the 'Punjab School' of administrators, enjoyed the best rule it had ever known.

15 THE AGE OF DALHOUSIE

Although he had given up its immediate control to John Lawrence, Dalhousie always had a special interest in the Punjab. But his visits there, and his correspondence with the Lawrences at Lahore, Rajputana, and Peshawar did not detract him in the least from the remainder of his vast responsibilities. He travelled India, as no Governor-General had done before, in stately Grand Tours. By now the Company's territories in India were administered as follows: (i) Bengal and the subordinate presidency of the North-West Provinces, with its capital at Agra, both with Lieutenant-Governors from 1854, the Punjab, and Assam; (ii) Madras; (iii) Bombay, including its possessions at Aden, in the Persian Gulf, and Sind. The Straits Settlements were administered from Calcutta and Singapore.

The Company also had its own foreign missions, especially that at Baghdad, where a succession of remarkable men represented the Company, including Claudius James Rich. Rich joined the Company's service in 1803, when he was described as 'A most extraordinary young man'. During his teens he had mastered Hebrew, Chaldee, Persian, Arabic, and Chinese. The Company quickly realised his potential. After travels over the Middle East, often in disguise, he went to Baghdad in 1808, where he wrote an important book on the country, and collected some nine hundred rare manuscripts. He died of cholera aged thirty-three. A successor of his, Sir Henry Creswicke Rawlinson, also led an adventurous life on behalf of the Company. Fluent in Persian, he was sent to Persia to help reorganise that country's army, at the time of a Russian scare. He once rode 750 miles in 150 hours, a fantastic feat, to warn the British minister at Tehran of the presence of a Russian agent at Herat. Like Rich, he did important local research, and made himself a philologist of Assyrian, a previously little-known and undeciphered language. He became the Company's representative at Baghdad, from 1844 to 1849.

Dalhousie studied India and pondered on how best to 'civilise' it, by which he meant Europeanise it. Inevitably railways figured largely in his plans for the future, admittedly not only for economic reasons but also for military ones. The first section of line, from Howrah to Hooghli, was opened in 1854. Other lines were prepared at Bombay, Madras, and Karachi. By the time Dalhousie left India there were three hundred miles of line completed or under construction; half a century later there were 26,500 miles of what was widely recognised as the most magnificent rail network in the world. Dalhousie's plan was largely adhered to, but not his suggested methods. He wrote in 1850:

> I trust that the East India Company will ever avoid the error of viewing railways merely as private undertakings, and will regard them as national works over which the Government may justly exercise, and is called upon to exercise, a stringent and salutory control. This control should not be an arbitrary right of interference, but a regulated authority, declared and defined by law.

The construction of a telegraph system was also put under way, and this brought with it great benefits to the administrative machine. Four thousand miles of telegraph were completed by the time of Dalhousie's departure, from Madras in the south to Peshawar in the north, and across India from Calcutta to Bombay. In 1853 it took nearly a month for the Governor-General in Calcutta to communicate with Bombay. By April 1854 it took him under two hours. The grip of the Company was tightening.

An office of public works was established in each presidency and engineering colleges set up. Road building was undertaken, and the Grand Trunk Road, begun in Bentinck's time, was cut across India, with an extension as far north as Peshawar. The Ganges canal, considered an engineering marvel at the time, was opened. Irrigation

234

schemes were completed to combat famine (although taking a poor second place to railways). Bridges were built. Post offices were established throughout India, and postage stamps introduced. Dalhousie encouraged the cultivation of tea; brought in measures to protect the forests. All these schemes were directly due to Dalhousie's influence and energy. But he took as close an interest in moral welfare as in material. The gaols were put under a regular system of inspection, and the more brutal practices in them abolished. He saw to the preservation of ancient and historic monuments. He improved the legislative and judicial arrangements. Although he closed Wellesley's old college in Fort William, he set up others for civil servants around the country and instituted a system of examinations. A pattern for the system of government-aided elementary and secondary schools was laid down. Dalhousie improved the standards of the civil service by severely punishing all those engaging in trade, and by a careful watch on patronage.

One of Dalhousie's main worries was the state of the East India Company's army. The number of troops had been decreased by Hardinge, in the interests of economy. Dalhousie was more conscious than most of the dangers inherent in the Company's position, and particularly its dependence on such a large proportion of Indian sepoys. He called the attention of the Company to the dangers of the British population, whom he graphically described as 'a handful of scattered strangers'. On arrival in India he had available an army of 273,360 men, of whom only 26,096 were from the royal army, all European, the remainder being the Company's army, nearly all Indian.* There was a limit on the number of royal troops that could be sent to India without the consent of the court of directors of the Company, and this the directors had no wish to increase, as the Company had to pay for all royal troops in India. There was also a law setting a limit to the number of the Company's own European troops, which it needed particularly for its artillery and engineering units. The limit, which had been fixed at 12,200 in 1781, was increased to 20,000 in 1853, but this figure was exceedingly difficult to raise. Even this was considered too low by Lord Dalhousie, although he completed the establishment of three new European infantry regiments. Because of the needs of security, particularly in

---

* Or 348,000, including 'local' and irregular troops. These figures include the three East India Company armies: Bengal, Madras, Bombay.

the north, and because of these restrictions on European troops, both in the royal and Company's armies, Dalhousie reluctantly felt obliged to increase the number of sepoys. The 'scattered strangers', therefore, were as vulnerable as ever. At the same time, Dalhousie insisted on the civil government having ultimate authority over military affairs, and his insistence eventually led to the resignation of the controversial and fiery General Charles Napier. Napier left, remarking that mutiny in the Company's army was 'one of the greatest, if not the greatest, danger threatening India – a danger that may come unexpectedly, and if the first symptoms be not carefully treated, with a power to shake Leadenhall'.

Apart from the Second Sikh War, the other major campaign of Dalhousie's time was the Second Burmese War.* The Burmese had been proving as intractable as ever and, despite their early defeat, were evidently not impressed by the East India Company's power. British traders in Rangoon complained of ill-treatment, and the East India Company's envoys at Ava, the Burmese capital, had withdrawn because of insults, real or imagined. The commander of a frigate sent to investigate and admonish handled matters so crudely that his ship was fired upon. Dalhousie sent an ultimatum demanding satisfactory conditions at Rangoon, 'holding to the wisdom of Lord Wellesley's maxim, that an insult offered to the British flag at the mouth of the Ganges should be resented as promptly and as fully as an insult offered at the mouth of the Thames', as he said. No answer was received to this communication; Dalhousie himself had admitted earlier the near impossibility of making contact with the Governor of Pegu, the province of Burma in which was Rangoon. Preparations for war were already under way. 'I have done my very best,' Dalhousie wrote to the chairman of the Company, 'to avoid war – some people will think *too* much; and I am not to blame for its occurrence.' Lord Dalhousie hoped that an expedition to Rangoon would be enough 'to bring them to reason' and obviate an invasion into the interior. He supervised the preparations himself. He preferred a small but well-equipped force compared to that of the previous war. The expedition of 5,700 men, under General H. T. Godwin, from Madras and Calcutta, successfully took Rangoon after a brisk, well-conducted engagement. But the Burmese showed no signs of being brought to 'reason'. Godwin

* Second Anglo-Burmese War, 1852–3.

had been a member of the previous expedition and he was more than reluctant to delve up the Irrawaddy until all preparations were completed to his satisfaction, including the accumulation of a large amount of supplies. Dalhousie had to go to Rangoon himself and activate the force to move inland. Pegu was captured, only to be invested by the Burmese; the British garrison was relieved and the campaign ended in minor engagements. Dalhousie insisted in the cession of all Pegu province; the Burmese court refused; Dalhousie annexed it. The whole of the Burmese coast was thus under control of the East India Company, which was one way of ensuring a place, if not a welcome, for British merchants on it. Dalhousie was well pleased, and the directors were relieved to learn that the war had cost them less than £1,000,000, whereas the First Burmese War had cost over £12,000,000. Godwin, as so many successful commanders in the Company's history, was severely criticised for his tardiness and great care with supplies. Clive and Wellington will always be remembered; but Coote, Lake, Godwin, Napier, Pollock, and others...they have become lost to British memory although they fought in India at least as well.

❧

In his foreign policy Lord Dalhousie was a less attractive figure than in his domestic policies. One of the most controversial of these policies was in his use of the 'doctrine of lapse'. By this he declared that any Hindu state under the Company's protection, which meant practically all the Hindu states in India not already under direct Company rule, would come under direct Company rule if the prince or ruler should die without a direct heir. In the past the custom had been for a ruler without heir to adopt one – a blatant ploy to preserve such independence as existed. Dalhousie used his 'doctrine of lapse' just as blatantly to enlarge the Company's direct rule. He was not, however, the first Governor-General to practise it, as Auckland had already created a precedent at least once. Although some of the authorities at home spoke against Dalhousie's policy later, at the time they were often sympathetic. The President of the Board, Sir Charles Wood,* agreed to the measures, but later wilted when Dalhousie came under strong criticism in the House of Commons. Dalhousie spelt out his policy as follows:

* Later Viscount Halifax, grandfather of Lord Irwin (1st Earl of Halifax), Viceroy of India 1926–31.

There are three chief classes of Hindu States in India.

    1st. Hindu sovereignties which are not tributory, and which are not and never have been subordinate to a paramount power;

    2nd. Hindu sovereignties and chiefships which are tributory, and which owe subordination to the British Government as their paramount, in the place of the Emperor of Delhi, the Peshwa, etc.; [i.e. former Mughal and Maratha possessions]

    3rd. Hindu sovereignties and chiefships created or revived by the sanad [authority] of the British Government.

    Over principalities of the first class I contend that we have no power whatever, and have no right, except that of might, over their adoptions.

    Principalities of the second class require our assent to adoption, which we have a right to refuse, but which policy may usually lead us to concede.

    In the principalities of the third class I hold that succession should never be allowed to go by adoption.

Historians have not always agreed with Dalhousie's classification from a legal point of view, but nevertheless on the strength of it he annexed seven states to the East India Company during his Governor-Generalship: Satara, Jaipur, Jhansi, Sambalpur, Baghat, Udaipur, Nagpur. Of these, Nagpur was by far the most important. It was a territory of some 80,000 square miles, larger than Pegu and the occupied Punjab together, with a potential revenue of £4,000,000. The President of the Board told Dalhousie: 'I encourage your annexation of Nagpur, to which I have heard no objection, even from John Mill, who is the great supporter of Indian independence in the East India House.' The chairman of the Company, Sir James Hogg, told Dalhousie:* 'There never was, and could not be, a clearer case. Still Sulivan, at his dinner to Lord Harris, selected that occasion as appropriate for declaring his opinion that the annexation of Nagpur exceeded in iniquity the Russian aggression [in eastern Europe].' Dalhousie himself had no doubts: 'The possession of Nagpur would combine our military strength, would enlarge our commercial resources, and would materially tend to consolidate our power.' The state was taken over and the royal family placed on a generous pension – after much of

* Hogg had made a fortune at the bar in Calcutta; from 1839–57, he was one of the East India Company's main spokesmen in the House of Commons. Great-grandfather of the present Lord Chancellor, Lord Hailsham.

its jewellery had been confiscated by the Company's representatives. For over a century it had been Company policy that the valuables of the royal families of states were not private properties but, as Dalhousie said, 'public revenues hoarded by the raja which ought to have been applied to the payment of arrears due, and should now be applied to the purpose of which it ought to have been expended.' Such phraseology did not impress in India, where looting had long been common and easily recognisable.

In contrast to his ruthless application of the 'doctrine of lapse', Dalhousie refused to march into the protected state of Hyderabad, where the Nizam was conducting a medieval rule, his throne propped up by East India Company troops; such an invasion was continually pressed on him from London. Hyderabad was notoriously difficult campaigning country; its military conquest had never been attempted by the British or the French. The Muslim state of Oudh, however, was another matter, and there was also pressure for its annexation. Oudh lay to the east of the Ganges, between that river and Nepal. It had been a protected state for many years. There were rumours of atrocities and ill-rule from it, such as the mid-Victorians were more than ready to hear from many parts of Asia and Africa. In 1854 Dalhousie sent the dashing Brigadier James Outram, who had succeeded Haines at Aden, to be resident at Lucknow, capital of Oudh, and to report on the situation there.

Outram's report left no room for doubt. The worst suspicions were confirmed. 'The lamentable condition of the kingdom has been caused by the very culpable apathy and gross misrule of the sovereign …his days and nights are passed in the female apartments, and he appears wholly to have resigned himself to debauchery, dissipation and low pursuits.' A large part of the male population were either sepoys or former sepoys in the Company's army; this was not only for economic reasons but also because such service entitled them to the protection of the British Resident, which in a corrupt society racked by tax iniquities was more than desirable. This large proportion of sepoys from Oudh in the Company's army was to be of the greatest relevance to coming events.

The former President of the Board, Hobhouse, now Lord Broughton, had supported Dalhousie. He had already declared: 'I shall be most happy if the putting an end to the rickety systems both at Hyderabad and Oudh should be reserved for you. It is impossible to allow either of the states to remain in their present condition much longer.' When Dalhousie had asked him whether he would support him, Broughton wrote: 'To be sure I will...Of course, do what you will, or omit to do anything, and some fault is sure to be found with you. That is one of the inevitable consequences of your high place.' The new President of the Board, Wood, was more cautious:

> I am not at all averse to the operation, and only am anxious that it should be skilfully performed – skilfully, I mean, in reference to public opinion here...One cannot nowadays disregard public opinion.

At last Dalhousie got clear authority to annex Oudh, the last great Muslim-ruled state in India. Troops were moved up and Outram took over the administration peacefully. But the ruler refused to oblige and would not sign the treaty surrendering his country that was put before him. Dalhousie therefore blandly declared the Company's sovereignty by proclamation. Millions of Muslims were offended. The ruler was given an estate at Calcutta and a generous pension. Dalhousie wrote to a friend: 'So our gracious Queen has 5,000,000 more subjects and £1,300,000 more revenue than she had yesterday. It would have been better that a treaty had been signed, for an amicable agreement would have looked best.' This was the man who could also write: 'It is not by the extension of our empire that its permanence is to be secured, but by the character of British rule in the territories already committed to our care; and by practically demonstrating that we are as willing to respect the rights of others as we are capable of maintaining our own.'

The Company's charter of 1833 ran out during Dalhousie's Governor-Generalship, in 1853. For a year or two before its expiry, there had been the usual activity in London from pressure groups, and also in India. The British Indian Association was founded in Calcutta to influence both Indian and British liberal opinion; its secretary was Debhendranath Tagore, son of Dwarkanath Tagore; branches were set up in Madras and Oudh. A sister association was established in Bombay which indicted the Company's administration. The Hindu College in Calcutta, which was

240

very westernised in its approach (Tom Paine was a favourite author), was seething with Bengali nationalism. But, typically of India, nationalists, Hindu reformers, and political theorists, were all divided among themselves. But for the first time some Indians were beginning to see themselves as Indians rather than as solely members of a particular race or religion...

At Westminster, it was decided to continue the Company raj, but with still further restrictions to satisfy the numerous critics. Criticism had now taken the form, not so much of attacking the East India Company, as attacking the Government for not facing its responsibilities and taking over India in the name of the Crown. On 3 June 1853 Sir Charles Wood presented the East India Company Bill in a speech which lasted five hours. The new provisions had been decided by the coalition cabinet of Whigs and Peel Tories, largely on Dalhousie's advice. Dalhousie had come to detest the aloof, critical men of Leadenhall Street, as had so many of his predecessors; 'I owe them nothing – not even civility.' The Company did not only have to contend with its traditional enemies from the liberal and provincial lobbies, the major critics of continuing the Company were now Tories, particularly Benjamin Disraeli. Disraeli made a vigorous attack in the House and took 140 Tories with him into the division lobby. Once again the entrenched position of the East India Company proved too strong for the bitter and vociferous arguments of its many critics, whether based on envy, logic, patriotism, or, mostly, prejudice; it was a victory which gave many of the Company's servants in India a quiet feeling of satisfaction, for there was strong loyalty to 'John Company', and which brought many a middle-class critic at home to near apoplexy of indignation at the thought that the Indian empire was to remain in the hands of a public company.

Disraeli cultivated a keen interest in Indian affairs; he had been a member of the select committee which had preceded the new Act. He was a firm opponent of the Whig westernisation policy of Bentinck and Macaulay, now being carried on so energetically by the Peelite Dalhousie. He later denounced bitterly the doctrine of lapse and the annexation of Oudh.

The act was passed. The court of directors lost much of the power it had retained; a third were now to be nominated by the Government. The patronage at Haileybury and Addiscombe was ended; they were now to be opened to competition. The 1833 order against racial discrimination in the Company's service was repeated. The nomination of members of the councils at Calcutta, Bombay, and Madras were to be approved by the Government. The Governor-General was to be relieved of his duties as Governor of Bengal, for whom a Lieutenant-Governor was to be appointed. It was a tidying-up of the East India Company's rule for what seemed a further long period.*

❧❧❧

Dalhousie was ready to go home. He had already extended his period of office at cabinet request. He was in wretched health. He had worked himself close to death at the most demanding employment that British society had to offer, and very probably the most demanding job in the world. He had no time for those officials who did not accept the challenges of India. He described a typical Governor of Madras: 'Then the Governor comes from England. He sits down upon his chair and grows to it for the next five years. Then he returns to England. No district is ever visited, no officers are ever seen, unless they come to the presidency.'

Dalhousie left India in March 1856. The Governor-Generalship had made him almost as haughty as it had Ellenborough. The storm was about to break, but Dalhousie had not seen the approaching clouds. He has been blamed for much. He tried to change India, and he tried to change it quickly. Many of his westernising measures, taken at a time when Christian missionaries were more active than ever, had a disturbing effect, as they were bound to. What he saw as a victory for civilisation many Indians saw as a defeat.

Lord Dalhousie wrote his last letter from India on board ship on the Hooghly:

> *Opus exegi* — my work is done. I have laid down my sceptre, and taking leave of those over whom I ruled, have departed...I am so exhausted with fatigue, agitation and pain that I can write a very little only...We had a sad leave taking in the Council on Thursday, and it was not much better in the Legislative Council on Friday. The deputation which brought me up the address from the community were unmistakably sorry. And I myself was miserable. Today at the Government House, and

* *The Oxford History of India* confuses the act of 1833 with this act.

on the ghat where I embarked, there was a silence like a funeral chamber. Half could not speak.

Silence can be elequent of many thoughts. Within five years Lord Dalhousie, second to last Governor-General of India for the East India Company, was dead, aged forty-eight.

16 THE
STORM CLOUDS

The next Governor-General, the last of a line that had started seventy years before with Warren Hastings, was nothing if not well-connected. Although Charles Canning's grandfather had been the penurious scion of an obscure Anglo-Irish family, his father, George Canning, had risen through the House of Commons and his marriage to Henry Dundas's niece, to be President of the Board of Control; George Canning had been about to take up the Governor-Generalship as successor to Hastings when Castlereagh, the Foreign Secretary, had cut his own throat, and Canning had remained in London as Foreign Secretary, and as Prime Minister for a few months before he died in office. His son Charles was connected, through his mother, not only with the famous Anglo-Indian family of Dundas but also with Lord William Bentinck. Charles Canning became Postmaster-General, an unglamorous but important position, as the postal services were being drastically reorganised as 'the penny post'. But his main claim to fame was that, while out shooting at Windsor, he had narrowly missed the Prince of Wales, then an infant: a disaster so near and so appalling that Canning had fainted in horror. This incident had not endeared him to Queen Victoria; when she heard that Palmerston, prime minister, had suggested to the East India Company Canning's appointment as Governor-General in India she expressed herself 'quite ignorant as to the reasons and motives which led to his selection'. The surprise was not confined to the Queen. Dalhousie, when he heard the choice, wrote home: 'Everybody in India will be surprised, for his name is not known at all here.'

It was indeed an unlikely, even curious, choice, apart from the family connections. Canning, in his forty-third year, gave the appearance of being a cold, aloof man; his manner was exceedingly courtly and unforthcoming. He had few close friends. He was an awkward, stiff public speaker. He seemed to have a rather gloomy, pessimistic character. But his private correspondence reveals a witty and warmer personality beneath the reserve. He may have been one of those men who find social intercourse difficult and hide behind a negative personality. He was certainly able. Perhaps Palmerston believed this Peelite dark horse was the man to continue his fellow-Peelite, Dalhousie's, reforming zeal in a more frugal fashion; perhaps he believed the haughty manner was the perfect equipment for this great imperial task. Dalhousie commented, cuttingly: 'His manners will please here, and he will do the externals of the office exceedingly well.' One of the few who knew Charles Canning well was the future foreign secretary, Lord Granville; he recorded for posterity this pen-portrait of his friend:

A great gentleman, in character and demeanour. He was handsome, with singularly fine eyes...He paid much attention to whatever he did, and generally succeeded in it. He had extraordinary powers of continuous work for months and years, when the occasion arose, together with a facility for being perfectly idle for long periods...He was of temperate habits, but on one solitary occasion he rather exceeded at a dinner at The Angel, and I found him in his rooms kneeling before his candle, praying it to light itself...One great characteristic of Canning was his truthfulness.

This was the man whom the Company and cabinet had entrusted (at £24,000 a year) with the highest office in the Empire, and who was now going to have to face the greatest ordeal of any Governor-General in the history of the East India Company. Most believed him to be a dull, pompous, capable lightweight.

Thirty-three years after his father had been obliged to forgo the Governor-Generalship, Charles Canning attended the East India House to formally accept the office. The customary banquet given by the directors took place that evening. With a knowledge from hindsight, the speech that night of Canning, who had never seen India and had had little to do with it, was remarkable:

> I wish for a peaceful time of office, but I cannot forget that, in our Indian Empire, the greatest of all blessings depends upon a greater variety of chances and a more precarious tenure than in any other quarter of the globe. We must not forget that in the sky of India, serene as it is, a cloud may arise, at first no bigger than a man's hand, but which growing bigger and bigger may at last threaten to overwhelm us with ruin.

Canning and his wife left London in November 1855. By 12 January they were at Suez, embarked on an Indian ship, moving out into Indian waters, towards a strange new world of which they knew little. Canning did his best to familiarise himself with the country and its problems on the formal calls around the coast to Bengal. A proud letter arrived from Dalhousie:

> I...heartily rejoiced to hear that this Government is to pass into your hands. It is a noble charge, worthy of the sacrifice which with all its advantages it must always impose on any man who undertakes it. It is in fair progress towards lasting prosperity at present, and I sincerely hope you may fall on times which will be favourable to a continuance of peace and improvement.

Dalhousie added, in a later, more jocular, letter: 'You must both submit to large dinners and a ball as an essential portion of the Constitution of India. The constitutional forms observed, I collapse into privacy and leave you in full-blown despotism. I propose to remain till the day week after your arrival, and then bid you farewell.' Canning went through the rigmarole and pomp of the arrival of a new Governor-General, but was not impressed by the amenities of life in the east. 'No such thing as a WC in the house,' he recorded in dismay, 'nor in all Calcutta.' His nephew, who shortly afterwards arrived to join his staff, noted a further disconcerting feature of oriental life: 'The free and easy way which the natives have of coming into one's rooms at all times is rather a bore; the more so as they glide in so noiselessly that one never really knows whether there is really one hovering about or not...In fact, as Uncle C observes, one never knows how one may have committed oneself before being aware of the arrival.' Canning immediately immersed himself in work – from which he seldom emerged in the next six years. The job had become, as Macaulay had predicted it probably would, too much for any one man. Canning wrote: 'The pressure of business in these first days has been, and is so great, that I have only had time for one look out of doors since we arrived.'

Canning felt no more loyalty towards the East India Company than most of his predecessors had done. Nevertheless, the proprietors of East India Company stock still expected dividends, and for this it was essential to have a peaceful and economical administration. The old East India House had long since become a great administrative office rather than a great trading one. During the eighteen-forties there had been a Company deficit averaging just under £1,500,000 per annum, chiefly due to the troubles in the north. Dalhousie had brought a small profit in his first years, but in 1853–4 there had been a deficit of £2,000,000, and in 1854–5 there had been an even worse deficit of £2,500,000. Altogether during the eighteen-forties and fifties, up to Canning's arrival, the Company's debt had increased by almost £14,000,000.

Canning's start as a skinflint was inauspicious. He promptly mounted a war – the least known and least necessary of the Company's wars, which is saying a great deal: the Anglo-Persian War of 1856–7.

The Government, particularly now that Palmerston was in power, was as obsessed by Russian motives as ever. Persia had taken a pro-Russian stance during the Crimean War. This had infuriated the Company's officials, who had sought so fruitlessly to bring riches to the Company's coffers from Persia for so many generations. They had filled the governments in London and Calcutta with fears for India's security. The Persians had occupied the province of Herat, in the far north, two hundred miles north-west of Kandahar; the Afghans considered the territory theirs. 'It really makes me sick to think of having to waste time, money and useful men upon a quarrel with these scurvy brutes,' said Canning; there was very little reason, if any, why he should have done. But, to warn off Russia from supporting Persian intentions, the Secret Committee authorised the East India Company to wage war with a foreign power – for the last time.

A force from Bombay, under Major-General Foster Stalker, occupied Bushire after a bombardment; there it prepared for an expedition inland. Meanwhile, the fiery Outram, back in London after his exploits in Oudh, on hearing of the war, dashed back to India hoping for a command. Canning, however, wanted him back in Oudh; but the Government at home, where Outram was wildly popular, insisted that he should be given command in Persia. Taking reinforcements with him, Outram arrived in Bushire and probed inland with two columns, under Stalker and Colonel Henry Havelock, already a legendary figure for his active service in the north (Lady Canning wrote, 'the quantity of medals he has, like five shilling pieces, looks almost ridiculous, as if he carried his money tied up in a bunch on his shoulders'). The Persian army was defeated at Kushab, but the East India Company force, with the usual supply problems, could only return to the coast. Moving farther up the Gulf, Havelock attacked and took Muhammerah, and the retreating Persian Army was defeated by a following force of 300 men. Peace had already been concluded in Paris. The Shah agreed to evacuate Herat and to maintain a peaceful relationship with Afghanistan. All was over in time for Canning to attend the Old Etonian dinner in Calcutta with an easy mind as far as Persia was concerned. The most notable casualty was Stalker, who shot himself through distress at being superseded by Outram; somewhat curiously, the naval second-in-command took his own life two days later.

The Company's old enemy, Dost Muhammad, had watched these proceedings with pleasure and, perhaps, with his usual bewilderment. Herat was restored to him. A treaty was signed with the Company, after negotiations, by the understanding Herbert Edwardes (of whom Canning, referring to Edwardes's humanitarianism, said: 'is exactly what Mahomed would have been if born at Clapham instead of Mecca'). Dost Muhammad, impressed, said: 'I have made an alliance with the British Government and, come what may, I will keep it till death.'

All this had further depleted the finances of the East India Company. But Canning, well aware of Dalhousie's great reputation, followed in his steps faithfully, putting into law many of the measures that had been prepared by Dalhousie and adding a few confident ones of his own. In Oudh, still a source of worry, he installed Henry Lawrence; Henry's position at Rajasthan was taken by George Lawrence.* Henry Lawrence was an awkward choice, for

* George Lawrence returned to England in 1857 and survived to 1884.

he considered that the annexation of Oudh had been 'the most unrighteous act that ever was committed'.

In Oudh, there was some discontent; it concerned that state's thousands of mercenaries in the East India Company's service.

❧

The sepoys were discontented. There was nothing new in this; many authorities had known about it for years. Charles Napier, Henry Lawrence, Thomas Munro, and Mountstuart Elphinstone had all publicised the possibility of mutiny. But nothing had been done to alleviate the fears and suspicions of the sepoys. As far back as 1838 the Hindu sepoys had been restless during the Afghanistan campaign, when they could not frequently bathe as demanded by their religion, and when the cold had obliged them to accept the issue of sheepskin jackets. Despite the unease felt by some military authorities, Canning decided to alter the terms of enlistment among the major part of the troops in Bengal; in future they would be ordered to go overseas if necessary, as the Bombay and Madras troops and a few 'general service' Bengal regiments were already obliged to do. Canning was particularly concerned about Pegu, the occupied province of Burma, which needed regular changes of garrison; the transport of troops by sea took five days: by land it took six weeks. It was a demand for overseas service in Burma that had caused the mutiny of Barrackpore in 1824, and a threat of one in 1852. Canning was adamant:

> It is marvellous that this should have continued so long, and that the Gov't of India should have tolerated again and again having to beg for volunteers when any other Gov't — including those of Madras and Bombay — would have ordered its soldiers on their duty. It is the more surprising because no one can allege any reason for conceding this unreasonable immunity to the Bengal Sepoy. The difficulties of caste furnish none whatever; for the Bombay army is recruited in great part from the same classes and districts as that of Bengal.*

Canning adopted a similarly inflexible attitude towards the question of the Mughal emperor, now a mere pensioner of the Company

---

* The Bengal infantry were, in fact, mostly from Oudh, and high-caste Hindus; the Bombay infantry was less recruited locally than the Madras army, but Canning was grossly exaggerating.

with no power. Dalhousie had already made it clear that the pretence of Mughal rule was at an end, even suggesting the Mughal should leave Delhi. Canning confirmed that on the present Emperor's death the title would become extinct and his heir would have to live away from Delhi. To many Indians this was a final break with an old order, which some did not wish to see replaced. The favourite wife of the Emperor, and her son, were naturally displeased, and they may have been in contact with the Maulavi of Faizabad, an anti-British scholar and agitator from Oudh, who was travelling widely throughout the north. In 1838 Charles Trevelyan, later Governor of Madras, had said: 'As long as the natives are left to brood over their former independence, their sole specific for improving their condition is the immediate and total expulsion of the English…the existing connection between two such distant countries as England and India cannot, in the nature of things, be permanent.'*

Measures which Canning inherited from Dalhousie were the removal of all legal obstacles from the remarriage of Hindu widows, and the reorganisation of land tenure; both were humanitarian westernisation measures and, although these and others were not without their supporters among Indian intellectuals, both were widely resented. Conversion from Hinduism was encouraged by another act, which recognised the civil rights of such converts. Land alienation had already caused an outbreak in 1855, when swarms of impoverished peasants had reached to within a hundred miles of Calcutta, burning and killing. Added to the measures of recent years, starting with Bentinck, the whole of Indian society was groaning under the enforcement of unwanted and strange reforms. The flow of the great Ganges, holiness itself, which descended from heaven, had been tampered with in order to make a canal. Above all, the old privileges of caste were threatened. In India the class system and religion were closely entwined. In trains Brahmins had to jostle among people of inferior castes, which was extremely unpleasant and extremely worrying for them; in the courts, any peasant could accuse a man of the highest caste and respectability; in the gaols,

* Trevelyan was the prototype late East India Company man at his best. Macaulay, his brother-in-law, said of him: 'He has no small talk. His mind is full of schemes of moral and political improvement…His topics, even in courtship, are steam navigation, the education of the natives, the equalisation of the sugar duties…'

the castes were forced to mess together. Christian missionaries, the ill-effects of whom has not been overrated by historians, were more active than ever, and some colonels ruled their regiments with a sword in one hand and the bible in the other. There was every encouragement at home for a proselytising attitude in India. A chairman of the court of directors said, in the House of Commons: 'Providence has entrusted the extensive empire of Hindustan to England in order that the banner of Christ should wave triumphant from one end of India to the other. Everyone must exert all his strength that there may be no dilatoriness on any account in continuing the grand work of making all Indians Christians.'* The Company had its own 'Ecclesiastical Establishment', paid for out of Company revenue, all Church of England except for two ministers of the Church of Scotland. There was a bishop at the three presidency capitals, the senior of which, the Bishop of Calcutta, dated from the India Act of 1813. In the East India Company's seniority list, they took precedence over the commander-in-chief.

There was no widespread movement for national independence. As one Indian historian, Rustom Pestonji Masani, has written: 'To describe the revolt as a national war for freedom and independence, waged by a populace groaning under a sense of injustice and aggression, is nothing short of a travesty of history.' What had happened was that the East India Company, unlike the Mughals, had used its power to try to change society, utterly confident of the superiority of European systems, and in so doing had angered or frightened many sectors of that society for numerous individual reasons. The importance of discontent among ruling families had not been recognised in Calcutta or London, despite the fact that several had gone to the trouble and expense of sending personal envoys to London to state their grievances – such as the Raja of Satara, the Ranee of Jhansi, the former Peshwa's heir, and even the Emperor himself, all traditional rulers with great followings.

All this might have passed over peacefully, although it is unlikely, if it had not been for the fact that one of the most resentful sectors was that of the sepoys, who – and it is important to realise – were not as mercenaries in Europe but were mostly of a high class in society, many of them Brahmins. Their dignity, their self-respect, had been threatened. The sepoy was a mercenary, but he

* R. O. Mangles. His son was awarded the VC in the revolt.

expected to be treated with respect by men whose customs, such as eating meat, were disgusting to him, whose very shadow could contaminate his own food. The success of such an army required great tact and understanding. Half a century before, under Barlow, sepoys had mutinied at Vellore when they had been ordered to give up caste marks. Now there was a rumour spreading through India that the British were determined to forcibly convert all to Christianity, and thus to destroy the complicated and delicate system of Indian society, and that for this purpose a great army was on the way from England; in India it was easy to start a rumour, easy to multiply it, and almost impossible to stop it.

The many new discontents had brought about an explosive situation all over India; only a spark was needed to set it off. Canning, cocooned in a welter of advice and by the panoplies of power at Government House, the most impressive modern building in Asia, forged ahead with the westernising policies. There was a vague feeling of unease. There was said to be an old prediction that the Company raj would last a hundred years, and it was now a hundred years since Clive had conquered Bengal; Outram was 'convinced that the true course of the revolt may be traced to that prophecy'. There was one thing in particular, which seemed to illustrate something mysterious and sinister about the ways of India, which Europeans could not understand; in the north of India flat biscuits — chapatis — were circulating from hand to hand in considerable numbers. It was something which could not be explained and could not be controlled, and so it was vaguely alarming. Lady Canning wrote:

> There is an odd mysterious thing going on, still unexplained. It is this. In one part of the country the native police have been making little cakes — chuppaties — and sending them on from place to place...no one can discover any meaning in it.

Canning had predicted, in London, about a cloud 'at first no bigger than a man's hand', which could grow to such a size it could threaten and destroy all British India. It was in the early weeks of 1857 that he must have first seen the small but growing cloud.

༺◈༻

The Indian infantry of the East India Company's army had been armed with muskets known as the 'Brown Bess'. These were obsolete and were now to be replaced by the Enfield rifle. New cartridges for the rifles were being introduced, and it was rumoured that, in order that these could be rammed into the rifle more easily, the cartridges had been smeared with grease made of animal fats that were exceedingly offensive to both Hindus and Muslims. Canning himself, alarmed, admitted that the rumour 'turned out to be well-founded'. It appears that this had, incredibly enough, been the intention of the ordnance; but now instructions were issued forbidding the use of such fats. It was too late. No one believed the protestations of the military authorities, which began to take on an air of desperation. The sepoys at the encampment at Dum-Dum protested about the grease in the cartridges. What was being required of them, and of sepoys all over India, was instruction in a new form of drill for loading, which the new rifles would demand. Additional orders were given that sepoys were not required to bite open the ends of the cartridges, as they were being taught in the drill. Too late again. The sepoys were unconvinced. Their Indian under-officers, subadurs, who felt untrusted and discriminated against, in defiance of the India Acts of 1833 and 1853, had grievances of their own; they did little to calm the fears of the sepoys, and their influence, sympathy or, at best, indifference, may have been decisive.

The first regiment to demonstrate because of the 'greased cartridges' was the 2nd Native Infantry; it was ominous that it did so simultaneously while stationed at two places over a hundred miles apart. The affair, which involved the burning of officers' quarters, seemed to blow over. On 26 February the 19th Native Infantry at Berhampore refused to receive the new cartridges; the delicate task of disbanding the regiment was successfully accomplished. Canning sensibly ordered that the men should be spared unnecessary ignominy. But elsewhere he was not handling the discontent with similar speed, tact, and firmness. Most of the men returned to their homeland, which was Oudh, where Henry Lawrence was having trouble about the cartridges with his own local troops. The 19th had recently been in contact with the 34th Native Infantry, which was commanded by a religious fanatic, Colonel S. G. Wheler. The 34th was restless, but Canning and the Government did nothing. The commander-in-chief, General George Anson, was famous for being the finest whist player in India, but for little else. He thought the 34th should be disbanded, and so did the brigade commander, Major-General J. B. Hearsey, at Barrackpore, who had himself tried to reassure the 19th and 34th at a combined parade. Anson went off to Simla and suggested Canning should join him. Canning, as he said, was 'rather glad' to have Anson out of the way. There were further acts of arson at military centres. On 9 April Canning was able to write: 'It has been a much more anxious time than Persia, ten times over; for a false step might have set the Indian army in a blaze. As it is, I am rather pleased with the way in which it has been dealt with.' At last, on 30 April, Canning agreed to have the still troublesome 34th Native Infantry disbanded; the order was carried out on 6 May. All seemed to be quiet. Major-General Hearsey reported tranquillity.

Charles Napier had said: 'If ever mischief comes in India, it will come like a thunderbolt.' It came to Calcutta on the afternoon of 12 May 1857, when a private telegram from one of the East India Company's most important garrison towns, Meerut, only forty miles from Delhi, was received at the post office. The sender was the sister of a civil servant there, and her domestic message was the first definite communication of disaster that the Government received:

> The cavalry have risen setting fire to their own houses and several officers' houses, besides having killed and wounded all European officers and soldiers they could find near the lines. If aunt intends starting tomorrow evening, please detain her from doing so, as the van has been prevented from leaving the station.

After that — nothing. The telegraph line from Meerut was dead. And then silence from Delhi.

17 THE GREAT REVOLT

On Saturday, 9 May 1857, the entire garrison at Meerut was paraded before the divisional commander, Major-General William H. Hewitt, known as Bloody Bill. Hewitt had at Meerut one European infantry regiment, a European cavalry regiment and batteries of horse and foot artillery; of Indian troops there were two regiments of Native Infantry, the 11th and 20th, and the 3rd Cavalry. The purpose of the parade was to humiliate eighty-five Indian cavalry who had refused to use cartridges which were not even of the offensive kind. While the ranks of sepoys watched, the men were each stripped of their uniforms and fastened with leg-irons by smiths. The fitting of the irons was a lengthy business; the task took several hours. The offenders were then marched off to ten years' imprisonment. The General and the brigade commander, Brigadier Archdale Wilson, believed such measures would break any further indiscipline.

The following day, while most of the British officers and their families were preparing for evensong, the three outraged Indian regiments mutinied and released the condemned men. They slew as many British as they could find, set fire to a number of buildings, and marched off down the road to Delhi. They must have been in fear of their lives, for behind them they left a force of Europeans about equal to themselves in number and far better armed (the sepoys were still equipped with the Brown Bess musket). But, to the dismay of several officers, Meerut HQ did nothing. As the mutineers

255

marched on towards Delhi, Hewitt pondered on the situation. He had under his direct command the largest force of British troops at that time assembled together in India, about 1,500 strong; but he did nothing. Some rioters remained in Meerut, and the British also had the fires to contend with, and the safety of the women and children had to be considered. One officer begged to be allowed to ride to Delhi to warn of the advancing mutineers, but his request was refused. Hewitt's clumsy handling of the cartridge affair, and now his over-caution in the face of local mutiny, made a widespread outbreak virtually inevitable. It was Bloody Bill who provided the spark.

The mutinous cavalry made for Delhi with relentless and significant speed; some of the infantry followed in small groups, others, frightened at their temerity, left their families and disappeared into the surrounding countryside. In Delhi there were no European troops, only a few officers and Company civilians. There were three regiments of Native Infantry. And there was the old Mughal 'emperor' himself, the King of Delhi, Bahadur Shah, wandering about powerless in the courts of his palace; a man before whom the British grovelled in a careful pretence of respect for his sovereignty – which did not exist; with him were his princes, who knew that under Company rule they were to be deprived of their inheritance, such as it was.

The first horsemen from Meerut arrived within sight of the walls of Delhi on Monday morning, after a ride conducted at furious speed through the night, in small groups. The East India Company's commissioner at Delhi was still in bed when he heard of the rebels' arrival; the chief tax collector arrived at the commissioner's bungalow soon afterwards. Both men rode to the Calcutta gate, which was already closed. They went to the palace. Orders were given to close the other gates. Meanwhile, an excited crowd had gathered outside the palace. Bahadur Shah, bewildered and alarmed, asked them to go away. The Rajghat gate was thrown open. The mutinous cavalry surged into the city.

Immediately knives and swords began to work at Europeans and at Indian Christians. The rumour spread through Delhi that the sepoys had revolted for the sake of their faith. All Europeans at the palace were slaughtered. Officers at the encampment outside the city were cut down while attempting to command their men. Leaders of the mutineers pleaded with Bahadur Shah to take up

256

their cause. He was not a strong-willed man, as some of his ancestors, and he was evidently appalled by the lack of authority engulfing the city. He sent off a messenger to Agra, informing the Lieutenant-Governor of the North-West Provinces, John Russell Colvin, member of an extensive Anglo-Indian family (who later got himself into great trouble from Canning and the British public for offering a free pardon to all who laid down their arms). Having told Colvin the situation, Bahadur Shah capitulated to the rebel demands; he assured the sepoys that he had no means of paying them, but they protested that pay did not concern them. At midnight, twenty-one salvoes were fired to announce that the Emperor of India, a descendant of his famous ancestors Babar, Akbar, and Jahangir, more direct than the Queen of the British was of hers, had claimed his throne.

The survivors of the massacre in Delhi and at the military camp slipped away into the country, or concealed themselves as best they could till they had an opportunity to escape. Many were killed on the road by robbers and outlaws unconnected with the rising. Among the survivors were five British soldiers who had blown up the magazine before their departure, killing some of their comrades and many sepoys in the colossal explosion (all five were eventually awarded the Victoria Cross, an award which had been instituted the previous year).

Before the telegraph wire was cut, two Anglo-Indian youths managed to flash a message north to the Punjab: 'The sepoys have come in from Meerut and are burning everything – Mr Todd is dead, and we hear several Europeans – we must shut up.'

It was May. The long, burning, stifling heat of summer in India had begun.

❧❦❧

First intimations of the rising in Delhi reached Calcutta on the Tuesday; by Thursday the full scale of the catastrophe was known. Canning considered his resources, and his map. Between Bengal and Delhi lay the restless Oudh, which might be expected to join the revolt at any moment. There were seventy-four regiments of Native Infantry in the East India Company's Bengal army and twenty-eight regiments of cavalry, all of which were now liable to mutiny (in the event, only five NI remained intact during the mutiny). To face these in Bengal itself Canning had precious few white troops. The demands of the war in the Crimea and of the garrison at Pegu had brought the European troops in India to their lowest number for years. Only the previous month he had told London: 'I wish to have more European troops.' Between Calcutta and Delhi he had only five royal army regiments: two near Calcutta, one at Dinapore, one with Henry Lawrence at Lucknow, and one at Agra. This meant that in lower Bengal and Bihar there were some 3,000 European troops scattered among a potentially hostile population of over 40,000,000. The commander-in-chief had some white troops in the north, and he was now preparing to assemble with the force at Meerut. John Lawrence had some in the Punjab. There were five British regiments in the Bombay presidency. Altogether, in India and Burma, Canning had twenty-six royal regiments and the statutory nine European regiments allowed to the Company – some 45,000 men.*

Now that his worst fears had come true, Canning acted with a decisiveness and speed that astonished those who had known him, and restored some confidence in a panicky Calcutta. The remaining telegraph wires hummed as he sent off message after message. Elphinstone, at Bombay, was told to rush the return of the troops from Persia. Lord Harris, at Madras, was ordered to prepare his two regiments for immediate embarkation. A regiment in Ceylon was sent for. A steamship was sent to Rangoon to get the European regiment stationed there. Vessels were sent to Ceylon and Singapore to intercept a British expedition on its way to the China coast; Canning told Lord Elgin, the government representative with the expedition: 'I am willing and anxious to bear the whole responsibility of all the consequences of turning aside the troops from China to India.' Letters were sent home to the President of the Board and to the Chairman of the court of directors, urging the despatch of reinforcements for India 'immediately'. But it would be October before troops could arrive from England, and another two months before they could be got up-country.

A message arrived from Henry Lawrence, holding the vital link in Oudh: 'Give me plenary military power in Oudh: I will not use it unnecessarily.' Canning replied: 'You have full military powers. The Governor-General will support you in everything that you think necessary.' A few hours later he telegraphed John Lawrence at

* Fortescue's *History of the British Army*, Vol. XIII, underestimates the number of regiments.

Lahore: 'You will be supported in every measure that you think necessary for safety.' The Lawrences were the two men upon whom, in the immediate days ahead, he would have to rely more than any others.

There was nothing more Canning could do. He ordered that life in Calcutta should continue as usual. He decided not to change his Indian guard at Government House for a British one. On 25 May carriages drew up at Government House for a magnificent State Ball in honour of the Queen's birthday.

Everyone waited for news from the north.

Anson collected 2,500 troops at Ambala, on the road from Simla to Delhi, and began the long march to the capital. The rest of the country, tense and nervous, waited on the brink. Would the whole sepoy army rise in support of their comrades at Delhi? For two weeks nothing much happened. British in isolated positions busied themselves with defensive preparations as inconspicuously as they could. Only at Ferozepore and Aligarh were there minor supporting mutinies. Two days after leaving Ambala, Anson died of cholera. The delay in marching on Delhi was already causing anxiety in Calcutta and elsewhere; it was felt that time was running out. Anson passed on his command on his death-bed to General Sir Henry Barnard. The column, joined by the Meerut brigade, moved slowly on. Twice the rebels tried to stop it, and twice they were defeated. A month later, outside Delhi, Barnard also died of cholera. He was succeeded, in turn, by Major-General T. Reed, who was also sick and 'fit for little more than lying on his bed all day'. The Delhi Field Force camped on a ridge facing the north side of the city: too weak to storm the walls, or even to invest the city, too strong to be dislodged by the rebels, despite the reinforcements they had now received. In the British camp, conditions were bad; food, candles, and other essentials changed hands at exorbitant prices. Reed's health deteriorated, and he was succeeded by Archdale Wilson, who had behaved with such lack of distinction after the original rising at Meerut.

In Calcutta, Canning had appointed General Sir Patrick Grant, commander-in-chief Madras, to take Anson's place as commander-in-chief, India, a post normally appointed by the authorities in London. Grant went at once to Calcutta. British troops coming into

Calcutta began to move north. It was a desperately slow business. From Calcutta the railway north had only been constructed for less than fifty miles; after that the way was by river or bullock train. The military transport had been abolished three years previously, and all transport had to be hired from private contractors. It was the hot season, an appalling time for long marches. The river was at its lowest, making navigation difficult.

The sepoys of eastern India had waited for the rebels at Delhi to be punished. But Delhi remained independent of the Company under the descendant of the great Mughals. At the end of May and in the first two weeks of June the garrisons at other stations rose one after the other. There were risings of sepoys at Bareilly, Sitapor Jallandar, Faizabad, Sultanpore, Nowgong, Shahjehanpore, Allahabad, and Jhansi, names once almost as familiar to Englishmen as Cheltenham or Eastbourne only a century ago. At Jhansi the Ranee, who had objected fruitlessly and energetically against Dalhousie's 'doctrine of lapse', which had disinherited her son, seized the opportunity to stake her claim; she busily fortified her capital and raised an army. At Benares the sepoys were disarmed by the recently arrived Madras Fusiliers in disorder and confusion; the British troops gave vent to their fears and frustrations by firing on the assembled sepoys with artillery. They then proceeded to Allahabad, where there was a further orgy of retribution. At Agra, Colvin managed to disarm his sepoys peacefully.

At Cawnpore, fifty miles south-west of Lucknow, General Sir Hugh Wheeler was in command of a division of sepoys and about 300 white troops. He was seventy years old and had served thirty-eight years in India with 'but three months general leave, and was never absent on medical certificate'. He had prepared a defensive position, with a trench dug round two of the barracks. It was away from the river, and the magazine lay outside it. When, after several weeks of unbearable tension, the four sepoy regiments mutinied, they sought support from a man who also had no reason to love the British — Nana Sahib, the adopted son and heir of the last of the Maratha Peshwas, who had been living near by. Since the start of the year Nana Sahib had visited Delhi and Lucknow and had corresponded with Russia.*

* The suggestion that he visited London, in G. M. Trevelyan's *British History in the Nineteenth Century and After*, is incorrect. It was Nana Sahib's envoy who went

About a thousand persons crowded into the prepared perimeter at Cawnpore: 210 European soldiers, about 100 European officers, 125 regimental musicians and non-combatants, over 100 loyal Indians, and the remainder women and children. The mutineers almost immediately began an artillery barrage with guns and ammunition obtained from the magazine. Under two flags, one Muslim, one Hindu, the sepoys settled down to harass and starve the defending British.

Inevitably the mutiny came to Lucknow, capital of the deposed ruler of Oudh. Henry Lawrence was at dinner. He acted with almost histrionic calmness, remarking that the mutineers, whom he had been expecting, were unpunctual. His house was one of the few which was not robbed or burned that night. Lawrence fortified the Residency, stocked it with supplies, and withdrew all British troops and civilians inside. He wrote, 'Every outpost, I fear, has fallen, and we daily expect to be besieged by the confederated mutineers and their allies.' As the regiments mutinied, more and more of the sepoys streamed home to Oudh. Lawrence made a sortie but was defeated. 'Very critical,' he wrote; 'unless we are relieved quickly, say in 15 or 20 days, we shall hardly be able to maintain our position.' Crowded in the fort were soldiers, civil servants, merchants, not all of them British (there were at least two Frenchmen, and an Italian), and the women and children. One of them wrote: 'The Residency was one scene of confusion. Women and children were flying to the Resident's house from all the outposts, leaving their property unprotected. Everyone thought of his life only; men were seen running to the trenches with arms in their hands.' Soon up to a dozen native regiments besieged the Residency. The nearest help was at Allahabad – but was it strong enough to raise the siege at Lucknow?

There was now a whole strip of India, including most of Oudh, in rebel hands. Even with the vital Allahabad and Agra in British hands the connection with the north was tenuous in the extreme. No help could be sent to Company agents and magistrates, who found themselves alone in outlying stations to face rebellious mobs. Some were murdered, but in most places the Indian populace con-

to London, a former table waiter to an Anglo-Indian family; the only achievement of this ambassador in London had been the conquest of a remarkable number of English ladies.

tinued to cultivate the earth undisturbed by the rumours and news spreading across the land. Canning's early despatch of the available troops north had solved nothing; it seemed he would have to wait for the troops from Europe. Meanwhile he enrolled volunteers in Calcutta, clamped a censorship on the press, and detained the ex-king of Oudh (who was in his bath). By now Havelock had arrived in Calcutta from Persia; and he was given command of the column at Allahabad, which it was hoped might restore Oudh. Grant told Canning: 'Your Excellency, I have brought you the man.' With two more British regiments, Havelock dashed north.

'The rebellion has lost all distinctive character,' Canning said. 'It is not more Mussulman than Hindoo. The ranks of the rebels are swelled from day to day by mutineers and deserters...My belief is that it will collapse as soon as Delhi is entered and the European Force proceeds to move southward from there. But I do not disguise my fears.'

John Lawrence had some 10,000 British troops in the Punjab, and it was on him that Canning had to rely to take Delhi. For the Delhi Field Force was still languishing on the ridge facing the town, and was now itself in danger of being surrounded. It was also in danger of being annihilated through disease (in one week a regiment lost nearly two-thirds of its strength to the field hospitals). John Lawrence had been obliged to delay until he could satisfy himself that the Punjabis would not rise, and until he could concentrate a column to send over the Sutlej from his scattered force. He wrote: 'No precaution was omitted to prevent the spread of the treasonable infection. A system of passports was introduced; guards at the ferries were doubled, with orders to prevent the passage of suspicious characters...letters addressed to mutinous regiments were opened; the Native Press was put under censorship.' The Punjab remained quiet – a tribute to 'the Punjab System' of wise administration under the Lawrences. But how many troops could be spared? Lawrence suggested giving up some territory in the Punjab in order to send men south, but Canning forbade it: 'If we were now to abandon territory, no matter how distant, it would be impossible that faith in the permanency of our Rule should not be shaken.' Lawrence, therefore, was typically cautious in the numbers of men he sent down to Delhi. But troops, including Sikhs, began to cross the Sutlej. John Lawrence told Canning: 'We have sent every man we could spare, perhaps more.' In command of the Punjab column on its way to Delhi was 'Brigadier' John Nicholson, a fierce, reckless, courageous substantive Captain of only thirty-five. Nicholson did not much care for Indians, but he was usually utterly tolerant and fair in the Punjab System tradition. He had previously been in service under an Indian prince (seconded from the Company's service, like many of his contemporaries), where he had learnt not to be squeamish; the prince in question had disciplined his chiefs by flaying them alive. Nicholson suggested a 'Bill for flaying alive, impalement, or burning, of the murderers of the women and children at Delhi'. He was longing to reach Delhi and hurl his force against its great walls.

⟨❦⟩

At Cawnpore, where the British were huddled into the ill-chosen enclosure, the situation was appalling. W. J. Shepherd, a Company clerk, wrote of the conditions of those who had 'never ventured out in the hot winds, except in a covered conveyance, thus pitilessly exposed a whole day to the powerful heat of the sun — some covering their heads with cloth dipped in water and others putting up a temporary shelter of empty boxes, sheets, etc.'. There was little hope of being able to hold out. Only three days after the rising, one of the besieged wrote: 'We are so hemmed in by overpowering numbers that there seems no hope of escape. Only about forty European soldiers are left out of 120 men – a sad number to hold out against such an awful enemy…The walls are going. This is an awful hour, my darling.' As the barrage continued, the women and children had to take cover in the trenches, for not everyone could obtain entry to the more sheltered rooms in the barracks, which were zealously kept for themselves by some of the officers. Wheeler's son, a lieutenant and his father's aide-de-camp, was hit in a trench, brought back to his mother and sisters in a room, where he was decapitated by a shell. The bombardment and musketry were not the only worries. Food was getting seriously scarce. After the first week 'all were reduced to the monotonous and scanty allowance of one meal a day, consisting of a handful of split peas and a handful of flour'. Water was also in short supply. There was only one well inside the perimeter, and as it was the height of summer the water had sunk to the bottom of the well. It was in an exposed position and all who used it risked their lives. One of the officers, Mowbray

Thomson, wrote: 'I have seen children of my brother officers sucking the pieces of old water-bags, putting scraps of canvas and leather straps into the mouth to try and get a single drop of moisture upon their parched lips.' Disease was rampant. In three weeks 250 of the besieged were buried. The air was foul. Vultures fluttered about above. Mowbray Thomson wrote: 'Often we imagined that we heard the sound of distant cannonading. At all hours of the day and night my men have asked me to listen. Their faces would gladden with the delusive hope of a relieving force close at hand, but only to sink back again presently into the old careworn aspect.'

It was on 23 June, exactly a hundred years after the Battle of Plassey, that the mutineers made their most determined effort to storm Wheeler's defences, but they were hurled back. Nana Sahib, who had expected the siege to succeed after only a few days, was disturbed, for there was news of a relief column assembling at Allahabad, a hundred and twenty-five miles away. Two days after the failure to break the defences, he sent an Englishman's wife whom he had found in Cawnpore to the barricade with a message. It was addressed to 'The subjects of Her Most Gracious Majesty Queen Victoria', and it read: 'All those who are in no way connected with the acts of Lord Dalhousie, and are willing to lay down their arms, shall receive a safe passage to Allahabad.' As a victim of Dalhousie's doctrine of lapse, Nana Sahib's particular grievance wasa gainst Dalhousie; none of the besieged was in any way directly associated with that law. Old Wheeler, who had far more experience of India than any of the others, was suspicious. But because of the lack of supplies and the approach of the monsoon, which would destroy the entrenchments, he agreed to accept the offer, providing arms could be retained. Nana Sahib was to provide a fleet of about forty boats to take the besieged down-river to Allahabad. At about 7 a.m., with women and children first, the British trooped out of the defences and made for the steps of the ghat on the river bank. The siege of Cawnpore had lasted three weeks.

To the watching Indians, who lined the way and who had gathered in thousands at the river, it was an amazing sight. The emaciated troops, civilians, women, and children, filthy, stinking, and in rags, riding in carts, on the backs of animals, or tottering on their feet, took two hours to evacuate and congregate at the ghat.

The last officer to leave had his baggage carried for him by a mutineer sepoy. The boats, on the muddy banks of the low river, were boarded and everything was ready for departure.

What followed was not, alas, an accident sparked off by the accidental discharge of rifle or musket, as some modern British historians claim. Most of the boats had native crews, and these suddenly jumped overboard, in several cases setting light to the thatched roofs of the boats before they did so. Immediately a hot fire was levelled at the passengers from sepoys who had been concealed along the banks and from cavalry at the ghat. Men frantically tried to push their boats out into the river, but few succeeded in doing so; only four men (including Mowbray Thomson) survived the escape down-river, ending with a six-mile swim to safety.

The survivors of the massacre were herded together and nearly all the men were shot. The terrified women and children were herded into a house built round an open courtyard; about three of the women, including one of Wheeler's daughters, may have been carried away by sepoys. Nana Sahib, whose written order for a massacre exists, later protested to the British: 'By means of entreaties I restrained my soldiers and saved the lives of 200 English women and children.'

Ten days later Havelock began the march from Allahabad to Cawnpore. Henry Havelock, in his early sixties, had been plucked from near-retirement by the revolt. He did not come from a military family — his father was a self-made north of England industrialist — but he had entered the royal army in 1815 and had spent nearly all his career in India. It had taken him twenty-three years of service to rise to the rank of captain. The authorities had seemed not to appreciate the seriousness with which he had devoted himself to soldiering. He had learnt Hindustani and Persian before leaving England (for a time he had been Elphinstone's interpreter at Kabul). Of all the religious officers in the Army in India, few were more pious than Havelock. His religious fervour dated from his first journey out to India, when he had been influenced by a fellow-officer on the ship, Lieutenant James Gardner, 'a humble, unpretending man', according to Havelock, who changed his life. 'I owe you more than I owe any man living,' he told Gardner. Before Outram had picked Havelock for the Persian campaign, he had seemed fated to end his career as a 'desk-wallah' in Calcutta. His appointment to the command of the relief column had been bitterly attacked by the Calcutta press, who had described him as 'a worn-out red-tapist'. His view of the suppression of the mutiny was that it was by 'the blessing of Almighty God on a most righteous cause – the cause of justice, humanity, truth and good government in India'.

Havelock's orders were to relieve Cawnpore and Lucknow, settle Oudh and reopen the way north. For this purpose he had 1,000 British troops, a few Sikhs, and six guns. The monsoon was imminent. Havelock's advance party, under a fanatical officer, remorselessly burnt villages and killed Indians indiscriminately as it advanced, and Havelock seems to have been powerless to stop it. He was a good leader, but there was a growing mood of uncontrolled anger among British troops all over India.

Nana Sahib attempted to turn back the column, but his troops were thrust aside. Havelock reached Cawnpore in ten days, his troops having marched the hundred and twenty-five miles in extreme heat, many of them in winter issue, and having fought much of the way. Seven miles from Cawnpore they fought the first major battle of the revolt, against 5,000 sepoys, and they won it when the 78th Highlanders charged with their bayonets to the sound of the pipes. Havelock issued a typical order of the day: 'Your General is satisfied and more than satisfied with you.' To Calcutta he sent a typical despatch. 'By the blessing of God, I recaptured this place yesterday, and totally defeated Nana Sahib in person.'

But Havelock and his column were too late. As the column had approached, the British prisoners, nearly 200 of them, had been slaughtered, and for once the word is used literally. The sepoys instructed to murder them had fired wildly, into the ceiling and walls, in an effort to avoid the task. A number of butchers were thereupon called from the bazaar. They entered the house with their swords and knives. Most of the women and children were huddled together in the centre of the courtyard. The butchers did their work. The corpses were then dragged down to the Ganges or thrust down a well. It had been the day before Havelock's entry to Cawnpore, and the evidence was still all too fresh. One of Havelock's officers wrote that the 'whole of the pavement was thickly caked with blood'. Another wrote: the 'floor of the yard and the verandah and some of the rooms were bespattered with blood and bore bloodmarks of children's hands and feet; women's dresses, hats, Bibles, marriage certificates, etc., lay scattered about the place.' These were the two most restrained accounts.

The flag of the United Kingdom fluttered once more over Cawnpore. It flew over terrible retribution. Havelock, anxious to hurry on to Lucknow as soon as possible, left Brigadier-General James Neill in charge at Cawnpore. From the Indians' point of view, he could not have chosen anyone worse. Neill, who had come from the Madras presidency, had already permitted his troops the excesses at the retaking of Benares and Allahabad. Havelock had given orders that any British troops found plundering should be hanged. But an orgy of looting took place.

Neill gave some thought to the treatment which those responsible for the massacre of the women and children should receive. Although it was far from easy to establish who were the guilty, he at length decided on the punishment to be meted out:

> I wish to show the Natives of India that the punishment inflicted by us for such deeds will be the heaviest, the most revolting to their feelings and what they must ever remember …The well…will be filled up, and neatly and decently covered over to form their grave…The house in which they were butchered, and which is stained with their blood, will not be washed or cleaned by their countrymen [but by] such of the miscreants as may hereafter be apprehended, who took an active part in the Mutiny, to be selected according to their rank, caste and degree of guilt. Each miscreant, after sentence of death is pronounced upon him, will be taken down to the house in question under a guard and will be forced into cleaning up a small portion of the blood-stains; the task will be made as revolting to his feelings as possible, and the Provost Marshal will use the lash in forcing anyone objecting to complete his task. After properly cleaning up his portion, the culprit is to be immediately hanged.

As the British officers were more than reluctant to admit each man's task completed, this wretched building now became in effect a place of prolonged torture. One Indian under-officer of the 6th Native Infantry, 'a very high Brahmin', had to clean a portion of bloodied floor under the whip, after which he was hanged and buried in the highway. A Muslim civil servant was made to lick a bloodstain away with his tongue. 'No doubt this is a strange law,' Neill commented, adding, 'but it suits the occasion well and I hope I shall not be interfered with until the room is thoroughly cleansed this way.' As a final, and most terrible, blow Neill ordered that 'all the Brahmins will be buried, all the Mohammedans burned'.

While Neill and his soldiers were thus engaged, Havelock was pushing forward to Lucknow, fighting Nana Sahib's troops and also sepoys from Oudh. The opposition was worse than had been expected. One of Havelock's officers wrote: 'The entire population of Oudh is against us.' Havelock was realising that his troops and his supplies were not enough. The monsoon had begun and the whole country was under a deluge of rain. Dysentery and cholera were diminishing the column every day. He could expect no help for months. Lucknow was only forty miles from Cawnpore, the most difficult barrier being the crossing of the Ganges, which he had already done, but Havelock, who spent hours at prayer, was not over-confident of success.

In India, the atrocities committed by the British were accepted with a kind of resignation; the British had merely proved themselves much the same as other military conquerors in a land where the terrors of war had never been far away. But in Britain the news of Cawnpore, to which were added other atrocities wildly exaggerated, did much to turn the British public against Indians for half a century. As for the British Army, Cawnpore had a terrible influence. The Army's own historian, Fortescue, put it well: 'The geographical situation of Cawnpore ensured that the greater number of British soldiers should pass through it, and not a man left the blood-stained scene of the massacre without blind fury in his heart.' What had begun as a mutiny to be suppressed had become a war of as much hatred as any in human history, with all the terror and horror that holy wars induce.

⧼⟡⧽

At Lucknow, the defenders had been waiting for news of Havelock's column. In the area of the Residency, Henry Lawrence had about 3,100 people, of whom some 1,600 were combatants, including loyal Hindu and Sikh sepoys. An early message from the relief column had assured Lucknow that 'we have ample force to destroy all who oppose us'. Owing to lack of leadership among the mutineers, the siege had been badly conducted at first. But now the situation was becoming exceedingly serious and there was doubt as to

269

whether the defenders would be able to hold out. Lawrence's arrangements for the defence, although more sensible than those of Wheeler at Cawnpore, were far from perfect. The Residency itself offered little protection because of its wide windows and porches, and eventually part of it collapsed after ceaseless bombardment. All other buildings were pounded to ruins. The compound was almost everywhere vulnerable to musketry fire owing to Lawrence's refusal to have overlooking mosques and houses of prominent citizens destroyed before the siege began. 'Spare the holy places,' he had ordered, to the dismay of his staff and engineers.

Henry Lawrence himself was among the first to be hit. His nephew, young George Lawrence, on his personal staff, was present, and wrote:

> About 8 o'clock, just before breakfast, when Uncle and I were lying on our beds, side by side, having just come in from our usual morning walk and inspection, and while Wilson, the Deputy Adjutant-General, was standing between our beds, reading some orders to Uncle, an eight-inch shell thrown from a howitzer came in at the wall, exactly in front of my bed, and at the same time burst. There was an instant darkness, and a kind of red glare, and for a second or two no one spoke. Finding myself uninjured, though covered with bricks from top to toe, I jumped up; at the same time Uncle cried out that he was killed. Assistance came, and we found that Sir Henry's left leg had been almost taken off, high up by the thigh.

The doctor pronounced his condition terminal (amputations during the siege were almost certain to prove fatal because of the poor facilities). Lawrence gave detailed instructions for conduct of the defence, and passed on the command to Major J. S. Banks, as Chief Commissioner, with Brigadier John Inglis, an Anglo-Canadian, in military command. Lawrence was then heavily drugged, and within two days he was dead. His last instructions were: 'Put on my grave only this – "Here lies Henry Lawrence who tried to do his duty. May God have mercy on him." '

The news of Henry Lawrence's death did not get out of Lucknow, and then down to Calcutta, for several weeks. When it did so, Canning wrote to John: 'I have felt towards him something more than mere respect for his high qualities and admiration of his honourable simple character...My own sincere opinion is that there is not a man in India who could have been less well spared at the present moment.' It had also been the view in London that Henry Lawrence, with his deep sympathy for India and Indians, had been the man for the hour, and eighteen days after his death (which was, of course, unknown in London) he had been appointed temporary Governor-General designate, in the event of Canning's death.*

Lawrence's transference of command was not satisfactory. Banks was shot through the head not long after and Inglis took over sole command, but not without difficulty from the civilians. His wife, Julia, and their three children were with him. Julia kept a diary, in which she described the anxieties of the siege with admirable fortitude:

> In a few minutes the cannonading and musketry fire were most terrific. We felt sure the enemy must get in, when the most terrible death awaited us. We sat trembling, hardly able to breathe, when Mrs Case proposed reading the Litany...Poor Mrs Palmer had her leg taken off by a round today, she, with some other ladies, having remained in the second storey of the Residency house, though warned that it was not safe...John said that he had made up his mind that every man should die at his post, but what were the sick and wounded, the women and helpless children to do? The contemplation seemed too dreadful. At one time he talked of blowing us up at the last minute, but I have since heard this would have been impracticable. It was strange how calmly we talked on these subjects.

These subjects were much on the minds of the men as well as of the women. Martin Gubbins, senior civil servant remaining in Lucknow, and a man who made difficulties for Inglis, wrote:

> Several of the men contemplated the destruction of their females if the enemy should overpower us. I was, during those terrible days, one evening taken aside by a military man, who was one of my garrison. He had, he told me, agreed with his wife that if the enemy should force his way in, he should destroy her. She had expressed herself content to die by a pistol ball from his hand. He was, he told me, prepared, if I should fall, to do the same deed of despair to my own wife.

* His brother John, however, did become Viceroy and Governor-General, 1864–9.

Both Inglis and his wife had to hold down personal servants while they were operated on for wounds without chloroform. Rations, tempers, patience, and health were running out. The shortage of opium was quite as trying for some addicted officers as was the shortage of food; at least one committed suicide.

Havelock was making poor progress. His column was diminishing daily through the ravages of disease and accurate musketry. He wrote back to Neill, at Cawnpore, asking for more guns and men. Neill, who considered Havelock an upstart as far as commanding operations in the field were concerned, was, with some reason, unimpressed at Havelock's efforts. He was concerned about his own exposed position. He could only offer a proportion of what Havelock had asked for, and replied: 'You ought not to remain a day where you are...You ought to advance again and not halt until you have rescued, if possible, the garrison at Lucknow. Return here sharp.' Havelock, when he got this, was incensed. 'I do not want [your suggestions] and will not receive any of them from an officer under my command, be his experience what it may. Understand this distinctly, and that a consideration of the obstruction that would arise to the public service at this moment alone prevents me from taking the stronger step of placing you under arrest.' Owing to the rising at Danapur, near Patna, as the result of a badly managed attempt to disarm three sepoy regiments, the reinforcements coming up were delayed. The mutineers from Danapur, about 3,000 strong, took the field under Kunwar Singh, one of the few capable rebel leaders.

Havelock's difficulties were increased by his lack of maps of the country between the Ganges at Cawnpore and Lucknow. The only one he had found in Calcutta was a ten-year-old sketch of the road. Although he made another attempt to get on, he had to withdraw several miles because of sickness. Cholera was his deadliest enemy. He sent a message to Inglis, 'When further defence becomes impossible, do not negotiate or capitulate. Cut your way out to Cawnpore.' This got through to Inglis, but he replied that he did not think a break-out was possible. 'If you hope to save this force, no time must be lost in pushing forward.' Then Neill told Havelock: 'I cannot stand this; they will enter the town, and our communications are gone; if I am not supported I can only hold out here.' The situation at Lucknow was becoming more desperate every day, but

Havelock decided to return to Cawnpore. He was then directed to Bithur, where some 4,000 mutineers were gathering, and his sick, exhausted column won a magnificent victory, the Highlanders once more being to the fore. Then he waited at Cawnpore for reinforcements.

Havelock read in a copy of the *Calcutta Gazette* that his command had been taken by Sir James Outram, who was on his way up to Cawnpore. Many people believed this was because of Havelock's failure to relieve Lucknow, but in fact Canning and Grant were well aware of Havelock's difficulties. Outram, back from Persia, had come from Bombay under his own initiative, and was determined to play a prominent role in the suppression of the rebellion. He left for Cawnpore after only five days in Calcutta, and joined Havelock five weeks later. Havelock, desperate for reinforcements, had been threatening to retire to Allahabad.

Twelve days after the arrival of Outram at Calcutta, the first reinforcements from England arrived in the formidable person of Sir Colin Campbell, who had been appointed commander-in-chief, India, with instructions to pacify the country. (His real name was Macliver; when this was discovered, he explained that Campbell was his *nom de guerre*.) Campbell was one of the most experienced and professional generals available to the home government. He had fought under Sir John Moore at Corunna, under Wellington, under Gough at Chillianwalla, and had commanded the Highland Brigade at Balaclava. He was in his fiftieth year of continuous military service, and he was so anxious to get to India that he had left London within twenty-four hours of receiving his command. The first Canning knew of the appointment was when Campbell arrived at Calcutta.

Outram made the curious and unwise decision of leaving Havelock in command of the relief of Lucknow, although Canning had clearly intended otherwise. Outram announced that, 'in gratitude for, and admiration of, the brilliant deed of arms achieved by Brigadier-General Havelock, and his gallant troops, [I] will cheerfully waive rank in favour of that officer on this occasion and will accompany the force to Lucknow in [my] civil capacity as chief commissioner of Oudh.' This was yet another in the remarkable series of incidents which marked the attempt to finally relieve Lucknow. It may have been that Outram had become impressed by the aura that had begun to surround Havelock's name. What happened was that Outram occasionally gave orders and that the vital clarity and responsibility of command was not present.

Havelock now had 2,388 European infantry and about 800 loyal sepoys, mostly Sikh, as well as a detachment of cavalry and three batteries of artillery. With this force, and with Outram at his side, Havelock successfully got to the outskirts of Lucknow in three days, having marched in heavy rain and having defeated a rebel force at Alambagh. Outram, having lived in Lucknow, knew the lie of the land and suggested a way into the town. As the troops advanced through the houses they were shot at from all sides; more than one man in four were killed or wounded. 'At length,' Havelock wrote, 'we found ourselves at the gates of the Residency and entered in the dark in triumph. Then came three cheers for the leaders, and the joy of the half-famished garrison, who, however, contrived to regale me, not only with beef cutlets, but with mock-turtle soup and champagne.'

After nearly three months of actual siege, Lucknow was relieved at last. The women, and even some of the men, believed now that the war for them was over, that British authority had returned once more to Oudh, and they shed tears of joy. But the amazing story of the Siege of Lucknow was not over yet.

⤜⧓⤝

The taking of Delhi, two hundred and fifty miles to the north-west, had reached its climax at almost exactly the same time. As the Company raj was being rent apart, these two small columns, one at Delhi, the other at Lucknow, numbering less than 10,000 men in all, were the only two British forces on the offensive across the whole vast areas of disaffection in the sub-continent; surrounded as they were by a potentially hostile population of over 200,000,000 strangers, they presented a not ignoble spectacle as they endeavoured to patch the cracks in the disintegrating framework of the East India Company's authority. But in terms of military efficiency they were only successful in contrast to the inadequacy of the leadership of the rebels. One of the few British commanders in the mutiny who acted with the kind of vigour and confidence that the situation demanded was John Nicholson; and he had now arrived on the ridge facing the walls of Delhi.

The vast walls of the imperial capital were nearly seven miles in length, and mounted on them were at least 174 guns and not less than 40,000 rebel sepoys who had come from all over central and eastern India. They had entered the city in good order, singing familiar British songs, and with regimental colours flying. But a force of well-disciplined British regulars, supported by an accurate artillery barrage, ought to have been able to outwit and outfight the enemy. And Nicholson knew it. And at least the weary months of inactivity on the ridge had helped the British in an unexpected way; it had given time for the hopeless confusion and argument within the walls to ripen into near-chaos.

The Emperor's main difficulties were the enforcement of law and order, and finance: in neither was he successful. In attempts to raise money for the war, the inhabitants of the city had been called upon to contribute to a levy, only the very poor being exempt. But the raising of the levy, done by several agencies, had brought confusion and dismay. The sepoys were impossible to control, billeted themselves where they wished, and plundered the shops for their supplies. Provisions and gunpowder were growing short.

With the arrival of a siege-train of heavy artillery, hauled by elephants, the British engineers constructed battery positions, under heavy enemy fire; many Indian pioneers were killed in this work. By now about half the British force on the ridge were natives of India. The bombardment of the walls began on the morning of 11 September, and by 13 September there were two breaches. Wilson, under pressure from his younger officers, decided to storm the city on the following morning.

The assault was undertaken by four columns, with one in reserve. Nicholson himself commanded one of the columns. Charging through a breach, his was the first column into the city. He led it through the streets to the Kabul gate, which was opened, letting in another column. But the sepoys began to rally, and the British were held at a fort farther along the wall. Nicholson sprang up to lead his men forward, but was shot down. With heavy casualties, the column withdrew to the Kabul gate. Other columns had penetrated into the heart of the city, but the sepoys were still resisting fiercely. As night fell, Wilson thought of evacuating the city, but the dying Nicholson persuaded him not to.

The British troops had been basking on the ridge for weeks. That night they went beserk. The city was searched for liquor and a large part of the army was drunk (some authorities say that the drink had been purposefully made available by the sepoys). It took some time for the troops to sober up, but after Wilson ordered all liquor to be poured away into the city conduits the mutineers were gradually pushed out of Delhi, although it took another five days of street fighting. The guards at the royal palace remained at their posts and stood to attention to face their doom. Everyone found in the palace was killed. But the royal family had joined the exodus. The remainder of the population cowered in their dwellings.

Wilson moved into the royal palace of the Mughals. The occupation of Delhi had cost 3,837 casualties (one Gurkha regiment losing 60 per cent of its strength). How many Indians had died and were to die will never be known, but it ran into many thousands. For now the retribution began, and it was as bad as at Cawnpore. Sepoys and civilians discovered in hiding were ruthlessly bayoneted without mercy; their bodies were strewed over every street. Houses were plundered with pitiless efficiency (when some of the regiments involved in the occupation of Delhi eventually returned to England, a great many of the men were able to buy themselves out from the proceeds of the plunder of Delhi; one particularly zealous officer was reported to have made 200,000 rupees). The Urdu poet Ghalib saw it all:

> Here there is a vast ocean of blood before me. God alone knows what more I have still to behold...Thousands of my friends died. Whom should I remember and to whom should I complain? Perhaps none is left even to shed tears on my death.

Evidently nothing could stop the soldiers, although several civil servants of the East India Company did complain as soon as they moved into the city. One such wrote: 'The policy of the military authorities has, it is too evident, occasioned a vast amount of misery and distress indiscriminately among the innocent; even those who suffered bitterly from the mutineer reign at Delhi.'

Not long before the sacking of Delhi, the news of the Cawnpore massacres had reached London. *The Times*, which had often been sympathetic to Indians, was appalled at the acts of the ungrateful 'natives'.

> Deeds of infamy which will set the blood of every Englishman boiling in his veins...We thought we were lifted above such a

dreadful risk, that our higher than Roman citizenship would shield us, that some Palladium would protect one of English blood from the last indignities, even in such terrible extremeties as these. It seems we are mistaken. Here are men who know us well, know our power, our superiority, our discipline, who have benefited by our kindness, who have actually been raised far above their native resources by us, and who can yet treat the persons of English people in this way.

Understanding of the problems had not improved since the start of the revolt. Then rumours began to get home of similar, or even worse, atrocities carried out by the British themselves. What could be said of these? The historian of British India, G. O. Trevelyan, son of Sir Charles, wrote:

The heat of the climate and the conflict, and scarcity of food and the constant presence of disease, the talk which they had heard at Calcutta, the deeds that they had been allowed and even enjoined to commit during their upward progress, had depraved the conscience and destroyed the self-command of our unhappy soldiers. Reckless as men who for many weeks had never known what it is to be certain of another hour's life — half starved, and more than half intoxicated — regarding carnage as a duty and rapine as a pleasure — they enacted a scene into the details of which an Englishman at least will not care to inquire.

Canning himself was more forthright. He told the Queen: 'There is a rabid and indiscriminate vindictiveness abroad, even amongst many who ought to set a better example, which it is impossible to contemplate without something like a feeling of shame for one's fellow-countrymen.' Queen Victoria was not among the many blood-thirsty propagandists at home. She replied to Canning: 'Lord Canning will easily believe how entirely the Queen shares *his* feelings of sorrow and indignation at the unchristian spirit shown — alas! also to a great extent here — by the public towards Indians in general and towards *sepoys without discrimination!*' Canning issued a series of instructions ordering moderation: '...the punishment of crimes should be regulated with discrimination.' Canning's instructions were based more on practical than humanitarian grounds. He pointed out the 'difficulties of settling the country hereafter' if animosity was increased, and that the burning of villages could lead to unsown lands and famine adding 'to the other difficulties with which the Government will have to contend'. Nevertheless, his instructions caused an uproar at home and in India, and he was dubbed 'Clemency Canning', a term of contempt rather than of praise. A petition for his recall was presented at East India House.

On the first day of Archdale Wilson's residence at the palace, Bahadur Shah was found outside Delhi and brought back to the city. On the following day three princes were brought back in a bullock cart, but as a mob gathered at the Delhi gate the officer in command ordered the princes to strip and then shot each one with his own hand; he later said he had feared a rescue attempt. Twenty-one princes of the royal family were hanged shortly afterwards. The Emperor himself lingered on in imprisonment in a modest house, an object of curious attraction for all Europen visitors to Delhi. One officer described him:

> Sitting cross-legged on a cushion placed on a common native *charpoy*, or bed, in the verandah of a courtyard, was the last representative of the Great Mughal dynasty. There was nothing imposing in his appearance save a long white beard which reached to his girdle. About middle height, and upwards of seventy years old, he was dressed in white, with a conical-shaped turban of the same colour and material, while at his back two attendants stood, waving over his head large fans of peacocks' feathers, the emblem of sovereignty – a pitiable farce in the case of one who was already shorn of his regal attributes, a prisoner in the hands of his enemies. Not a word came from his lips; in silence he sat day and night, with his eyes cast on the ground.

At Lucknow, Outram had taken over command, with Inglis and Havelock splitting the defence between them. Outram was alarmed at his position. The 'relief' had achieved nothing. He was neither strong enough to evacuate nor to hold the Residency indefinitely. He was cut off from Cawnpore and even from his base at the Alambagh, on the environs of the city, which was itself in a dangerous position. He was worried about food supplies, although there were in fact plenty, much of Lawrence's horde still being intact. The sepoys began mining the defences in sophisticated fashion. The British had to build counter-mines. 'I am aware,' wrote

278

Outram, 'of no parallel to our series of mines in modern war. Twenty-one shafts, aggregating 200 feet in depth and 3,291 feet of gallery, have been executed.' Messages were got out written in Greek (a ploy used widely by the British in other areas as well) and by semaphore (the instructions for which were found in the *Penny Cyclopaedia* of one of the civil servants). A clerk got out in disguise, to act as guide for the expected relief, for which feat he was awarded the Victoria Cross and £2,000 from the Company.

Colin Campbell, always cautious, had hoped to spend still longer on his preparations. But as the weeks passed his continued presence in Calcutta brought some unfavourable comment. At last he moved up to Cawnpore. He reached the Alambagh with little opposition. With nearly 5,000 men and 49 guns he burst through Lucknow, taking a different route from that which Havelock had followed. The rebels fought courageously and held various strongpoints, two of which fell to the 93rd Highlanders; a loyal regiment of Sikh sepoys was also conspicuous. The pipers 'struck up the Highland Charge' to such effect that Sir Colin later congratulated the pipe-major. Outram and Havelock unnecessarily risked their lives by running out under fire to meet the royal officer Campbell, who was suitably impressed.

The Residency was relieved once more, but now Campbell had the difficult task of getting the whole force away, with some 2,000 white civilians. The column streamed back to the Alambagh, but Havelock died on the way. He turned to his son, who was his aide-de-camp, and remarked: 'See how a Christian can die.' Despite having exposed himself to danger for months, Major-General Sir Henry Havelock expired from the debilitating effects of dysentery. He had done little to deserve the great reputation the revolt had brought him, but the public at home had been much impressed by his despatches larded with religious epithets, and a statue of him was erected in Trafalgar Square by public subscription.

Outram, with about 4,000 men, remained at the Alambagh while Campbell returned to Cawnpore, where the garrison was under severe pressure. On the march, Campbell was faced by a large force of rebels, many of which had just arrived from the Maharajah Sindhia's Gwalior, which had so far been inactive in the revolt. They were under the command of a civilian protégé of Nana Sahib, Tantya Tope. Sending his civilians down to Allahabad separately,

Campbell defeated this overwhelmingly superior force on 5 December 1858. With this victory, Colin Campbell secured the British position in the vital Allahabad and Cawnpore area. But much of the remainder of the Bengal presidency was still in open rebellion. Campbell could do little about this vast area of action before more reinforcements arrived. It had been decided that the regiments from England had to go via the Cape rather than take the overland route as it involved less complications (and more profit for the ship-owners). Campbell believed that Oudh could wait for the time being, but Canning insisted that he should return to Lucknow: 'Every eye is upon Oudh as it was upon Delhi. Oudh is not only the rallying point of the sepoys, the place to which they all look...but it represents a dynasty; there is a king of Oudh.' Campbell was back across the Ganges, marching through Oudh, in February, with fifteen battalions of British infantry. Joined by a strong force of Gurkhas from the friendly Nepal, he again penetrated the city, encountering fierce resistance. Pockets of rebel sepoys held out for days. The British troops were distracted by the needs of looting. William Howard Russell, *The Times* correspondent who had recently distinguished himself in the Crimea, witnessed the occasion:

> The scene of plunder was indescribable. The soldiers had broken up several of the store-rooms, and pitched the contents into the court, which was lumbered with cases, with embroidered cloths, gold and silver brocade, silver vessels...Through these moved the men, wild with excitement, 'drunk with plunder'. I had often heard the phrase but never saw the thing itself before.

While this was going on, the rebels were fleeing across the countryside, to congregate again at forts and castles, thus prolonging the campaign by many months. Among them was the Maulavi of Faizabad (only to be killed later by a loyal raja). Resistance was increased by a proclamation from 'Clemency' Canning which declared that all land owned by rebels was to be confiscated. For this, Canning found himself in a great deal of trouble, both in India and at home. Ellenborough, now President of the Board, wrote:

> To us it appears that, whenever open resistance shall have ceased, it would be prudent, in awarding punishment, rather to follow the practice which prevails after the conquest of a country which has defended itself to the last by desperate war

than that which may perhaps be lawfully adopted after the suppression of mutiny and rebellion.

This statement suggests that the cabinet were viewing the India disturbance as all-out war rather than as mutiny, as indeed Indian historians have since claimed it was. The controversy over the Oudh proclamation at home led to Ellenborough's resignation. The proclamation was toned down, but the damage was done.

Campbell now turned his attention to Rohilkhand, the neighbouring province, which had become a centre for the revolt. He approached the main city of Bareilly from several sides. Here the cause of the rebellion had been led by Khan Bahadur Khan, grandson and heir of the last independent ruler of Rohilkhand. He had proclaimed himself subject to the Emperor at Delhi and had been joined by many of the rebels from that place after its fall. After several engagements, the steadfast Campbell, who always kept his nerve despite many difficulties, succeeded in retaking the province.

⟨∽⟩

The revolt in central India, the old lands once claimed by the Marathas, remained to be subdued. The task was given to Major-General Sir Hugh Rose. The son of a diplomat, he had been born in Berlin, where he had been educated and where he had received his military training from Prussian officers and non-commissioned officers. The least known of the leading British commanders in the revolt, he was certainly the best. The land to be subdued was dotted with formidable fortresses where hereditary rajas had assumed independence with the backing of, or the insistence of, the mutineers. A successful campaign would demand patience, rapid movement, and doggedness. Hugh Rose, with his mixture of dash and perseverance, was able to supply them all.

Rose took several places without bringing the rebels to battle. Among those opposing him were the Raja of Banpur, the Nawab of Banda, and the Raja of Shahgurh. His main objective was the capture of Jhansi, a fortress which had assumed a symbolic as well as a strategic importance. Here the small British community had been massacred, after having been promised a safe passage, as at Cawnpore. The ruler was the Ranee of Jhansi, a beautiful and capable woman of about thirty. She was the widow of the last ruler of Jhansi, who had died without a direct heir. Jhansi had been taken over by the East India Company under Dalhousie's doctrine of lapse. The Ranee's marriage had been arranged by the last of the Peshwas, Nana Sahib's father. After the mutiny of the sepoys at Jhansi, she had been persuaded to proclaim herself ruler and the state independent. The yellow flag of the Marathas had been run up. From the start her regime had been remarkably democratic, by Indian standards, although she may have been obliged to seek and accept advice more through force of circumstance and the weakness of her position than some writers have been willing to admit, rather than by idealism. No distinctions were made on the grounds of caste or religion. New courts, public offices, and currency were established. All the arts were encouraged. It seemed a fine new idealistic regime, but it did not last long.

At first, the Ranee had tried the dangerous diplomacy of trying to keep in with the Company and retain her independence as well. To this effect she had contacted the British authorities. But the nearest British agent had heard from George Frederick Edmonstone,* Foreign Secretary to the Government of India, that such a compromise would not be considered: 'It appears that the Ranee did lend assistance to the mutineers and rebels and that she gave guns and men.' The Ranee hastily prepared for war. She raised and organised an army of 14,000 men, including 1,500 former Company sepoys. An unusual feature of the Jhansi army was the inclusion of women, who enlisted in some numbers.

Rose's column duly arrived within sight of the walls of Jhansi. A siege and bombardment were begun. The Ranee held a meeting of representatives of the city and military, asking whether she should attempt to negotiate. She herself was for fighting, and the meeting supported her. It is likely that the decision was swayed by the resolution of the rebel sepoys, who believed, with justification, that to surrender would mean certain death. The Ranee declared: 'We fight for independence. In the words of Lord Krishna, we will enjoy our freedom if we are victorious; if defeated and slain on the battlefield, we will earn eternal glory and salvation.'

After a week's bombardment, the light of fires in the distance announced the arrival of Nana Sahib's Maratha army of 20,000 rebel sepoys and Afghan mercenaries, under the command of Tantya

---

* Later Sir George Edmonstone, Lieutenant-Governor North-West Provinces, 1858–62.

Tope, hurrying to the relief of Jhansi. Rose's position seemed desperate, placed between the Ranee and Tantya Tope, hopelessly outnumbered, and running short of supplies. He was saved by the poor generalship of his enemies. Tantya Tope had made a name for himself, but as a clever commander in retreat rather than in attack. His assault on Rose's line, near the Betwa river, broke when the British attacked both his flanks; the mutineers 'retired in confusion', leaving behind most of their stores, equipment, guns, and 1,500 casualties.

Rose now ordered the storming of Jhansi fortress. The walls, like those of all Indian castles, were so vast and forbidding that it seemed an almost impossible task. The British approached with their scaling ladders under a frenzied fire, home-made bombs, wooden logs, and garbage. An eye-witness wrote of how 'the enemy fire waxed stronger, and amid the chaos of sounds, of volleys of musketry and roaring of cannon, and hissing and bursting of rockets, stink-pots, infernal machines, huge stones, blocks of wood, and trees – all hurled upon their devoted heads – the men wavered for a moment'. Many of the ladders were found to be too short. But one party got over, and they were soon joined by others. Fierce hand-to-hand fighting ensued. 'Every room was savagely contested. Fruitlessly, however. From chamber to chamber the enemy were driven at the point of the bayonet.' The worst fighting was in the palace itself: 'The wounded men came straggling out with the most terrible sword cuts I ever saw in my life.'

While the town was still being captured, the troops were wreaking their by now familiar and awful vengeance. Civilians were stabbed with the bayonet as mercilessly as the troops. 'No maudlin clemency was to mark the fall of this city,' wrote a British doctor present at the scene. 'The Jezebel of India was there – the young, energetic, proud, unheeding, uncompromising Ranee, and upon her head rested the blood of the slain, and a punishment as awful awaited her.' Vishnu Godse, one of the Ranee's own priests, described the sacking of Jhansi for the benefit of his family, who lived near Bombay:

I offered my evening prayers, ate a meal and went upstairs to see the condition of the city. And what a sight I saw: It looked like a vast burning ground [i.e. crematorium]. Fires were blazing everywhere and although it was night I could see far enough. In the lanes and streets people were crying pitifully, hugging the corpses of their dear ones; others were wandering, searching for food while the cattle were running mad with thirst...How cruel and ruthless were these white soldiers, I thought; they were killing people for crimes they had not committed...Not only did the English soldiers kill those who happened to come in their way, but they broke into houses and hunted out people hidden in barns, rafters and obscure, dark corners. They explored the inmost recesses of temples and filled them with dead bodies of priests and worshippers. They took the greatest toll in the weavers' locality, where they killed some women also. At the sight of white soldiers some people tried to hide in haystacks [in the courtyards] but the pitiless demons did not leave them alone there. They set the haystacks on fire and hundreds were burnt alive...If anybody jumped into a well the European soldiers hauled him out and then killed him, or they would shoot him through the head as soon as he bobbed out of the water for breath.

Fires raged for days as bodies were collected in great heaps and set alight. The Ranee herself only just managed to escape, dressed as a man. With a small bodyguard she fled across the country, chased by the British cavalry. The Ranee rode over twenty miles during the first night of her escape. The cavalry actually came within sight of her and her remaining escort of four horsemen, but were beaten back by the ferocity of the bodyguard's defence, the British officer to the fore being hit and forced to slacken his chase.

The rebel forces were reformed at Kalpi, on the road back to Cawnpore. With the Ranee at Kalpi were Rao Sahib, Nana Sahib's relative and personal representative, the Nawab of Banda, and Tantya Tope. The latter once more commanded the army, and lost to the remorselessly chasing Rose at Kunch, about half-way between Jhansi and Kalpi. Elaborate fortifications were prepared at Kalpi, which was not a fortress city, and Rose came very close to defeat there. But after another desperately fought battle the Union Jack was unfurled at Kalpi; it was Queen Victoria's birthday.

The defeated rebel army was uncertain of where to go. The sepoys naturally wished to cross the Ganges into Oudh, where pockets of their comrades were still fighting. But it was decided that a stand should be made at Gwalior, the most famous fortress in

India, and one of the former Maratha capitals. The Maharajah there, Sindhia, had remained loyal to the Company. Tantya Tope defeated Sindhia's army outside Gwalior and occupied the great fortress. He permitted no looting. A provisional government was established, and Nana Sahib was proclaimed Peshwa of the Marathas, with Rao Sahib as his ruler of Gwalior. Unwisely, the Maratha chiefs waited for Rose to arrive instead of going into the country to gain allies, for the taking of Gwalior and the proclamation had caused a sensation throughout central India.

It was high summer again and Rose's column marched in apalling heat through its own vast cloud of risen dust. Hugh Rose drove his men with incredible and relentless determination. He made them fight the rebel army outside Gwalior when they were exhausted after a long day's march. 'A prompt attack has always more effect on the rebels than a procrastinated one,' he commented firmly. 'I therefore countermanded the order for encamping and made…arrangements to attack.' The British infantry, supported by the 8th Hussars, broke the enemy, and Rose prepared to storm mighty Gwalior itself. The Ranee had died in the fighting. A British officer described her last moments: 'This Indian Joan of Arc was dressed in a red jacket and trousers and white turban. She wore Sindhia's celebrated pearl necklace which she had taken from his treasury. As she lay mortally wounded in her tent, she ordered these ornaments to be distributed among her troops. The whole rebel army mourned her loss.' Hugh Rose described her as 'the bravest and best military leader of the rebels'.

Most of the garrison had deserted, and Gwalior fort was taken. Several minor battles punctuated the chase. Rao Sahib and Tantya Tope fled, the former to live as an outlaw for four years, for some of the time with one of the Delhi royal princes, the latter to harass the British for many months until he was betrayed. Both men were hanged. The fate of Nana Sahib himself was as mysterious as had been his whereabouts and power throughout. The sepoys broke into bands, virtually brigands, and were pressed through Oudh towards Nepal, to which Nana Sahib had already escaped. For nearly forty years there were unconfirmed reports of 'the last of the Peshwas' appearing in various parts of India and Arabia. But nothing definite was ever discovered.

The 'Indian Mutiny', the most bitterly contested and terrible war in which the British had ever been engaged in their long history of wars, had come to an end. On both sides it had been conducted with ferocity, bungling, and muddle. Among the British, the civilian leaders had kept their heads better than the military, of whom only Rose, Nicholson, and Campbell had displayed much professionalism beyond sheer courage. That it was more than a mutiny was clear (although historians endeavoured to deny it, against overwhelming evidence to the contrary). What started as a mutiny became a war, a war not for independence but of protest. As Outram said at the time: 'It is absurd to call this a military rebellion.' There were clear elements of a general revolt against the British. Some of the peasants of east Bengal had already risen. The rebellious sepoys came from every caste, class, religion, and sector of the population. Their leaders were not just mutineers but men like the old emperor himself, like Nana Sahib, the would-be Pashwa, aristocrats like the Ranee of Jhansi, heirs to usurped thrones like Khan Bahadur Khan, landowners like Kunwar Singh, former civilians like Tantya Tope, and intellectuals like the Maulavi of Faizabad. The rising was, however, confined to the Bengal presidency. The Madras presidency, under Lord Harris, and the Bombay presidency, under Lord Elphinstone, remained virtually untouched. Sind, under Sir Henry Bartle Frere, and the Punjab under John Lawrence, also escaped. That the uprising had not spread farther had not a little to do with these men and the dedication of others, such as James Thomason, Colvin's predecessor as Lieutenant-Governor of the North-West Provinces, at Agra, of whom it was said 'there was hardly a place or a road in an area of 70,000 square miles, scarcely a clan or a tribe in a population of 30,000,000 with which he was not acquainted' (Thomason's son died in the revolt).

It was no accident that the revolt centred around the holiest places of India. Soon after the outbreak, *The Times* declared:

> The barbarities of the mutineers in India are so shocking, so atrocious, they almost amount to an argument that religion is not merely a pretext for this Indian mutiny. When men astonish you with their wickedness, when they are worse than the very worst that you expected, when malignity surpasses itself, when they lose everything human and behave like very demons, in nine cases out of ten in history it turns out that they

have been under the stimulus of what they choose to call religion.

The Times was referring, of course, to the religion and atrocities of the Indians. Its words could just as well have applied to the British, equally moved by religious conviction and equally guilty of atrocities. At the sacking of Lucknow one kilted Highlander was heard quoting the psalms as he thrust his bayonet in and out of his quailing victims.

Afterwards, neither side had gained much in understanding. The British realised that the Indians' reluctance to become Christian *en masse* was something not to be under-estimated, but one of Canning's first acts after the revolt was to announce a day of thanksgiving for all India: 'A Solemn Thanksgiving to Almighty God for His Signal Mercies and Protection.' He was not referring to Vishnu.

The Indian mutiny brought deep feelings of distrust and dislike by the British for the Indians that lasted for half a century. For the Indians it confirmed that the British were, as previous rulers, cruel, martial, and zealous of their conquests; and it brought themselves closer together than ever before. In the end this mutual convulsion, in which so many of both sides had lost their lives, was one of the factors which helped to bring a deeper understanding, and indeed bond, between the population and the imperialists than can be found in any other place in Asia colonised by the Europeans.

18 DEATH OF THE COMPANY

Few people doubted that the revolt in India would mean the end of the East India Company. For over a generation it had been the subject of widespread criticism. The ordinary public did not like the Company, seeing in it a stronghold of privilege (in 1857 there were about 1,700 stockholders). Its responsibilities had evidently outgrown its abilities. It now administered, directly or indirectly, some 250,000,000 people. Within living memory the Bengal presidency had grown from that state and Bihar alone to reach from the mouths of the Ganges to the Khyber: Bombay presidency from a few little islands and a strip of coast to nearly all west or north-west India. The nation had been forced to come to the Company's rescue; it was the Company's army, the largest army in the world, which had mutinied. The India debt had almost doubled during the revolt, standing now at an unprecedented £98,000,000, one-ninth of the entire British national debt. The Company was held to be not only inefficient but inert and an anachronism in a new age. Above all, the East India Company was a scapegoat. Although its charter had only been renewed five years previously, in 1853, it was obvious even to most of the directors that it could no longer survive. Queen Victoria noted, with satisfaction, that the country felt 'that India should belong to me'.

Lord Palmerston was prime minister. His government introduced a bill to the House of Commons, in February 1858, which sought to place Indian affairs under a President and a council of eight, the latter being composed of those who had served in India or were Company directors. The President and council, heading a new government department or ministry, were to take over all authority from the East India Company. '*All*...to be mine,' noted the Queen.

It was expected that the Company would put up a fight, although with not much hope of success. It did so in the form of eloquent plea and powerful argument from the pen of one of its chief civil servants, John Stuart Mill. The Mills, father or son, had been employed by the Company for forty years, partly for their literary ability, and it was fitting that this great epilogue to the Company's correspondence should have been written by its greatest and most famous servant in London. The gist of Mill's argument was that a government department would be a poor exchange for the personal experience and traditions of the Company; that the Company was the best method of keeping the rule of India out of party politics; and that the Company was not solely responsible for the revolt.

> The foundations of this Empire were laid by your petitioners at that time neither aided nor controlled by Parliament, at the same period at which a succession of administrations under the control of Parliament were losing to the Crown of Great Britain another great Empire on the opposite side of the Atlantic. During that period of about a century which has since elapsed, the Indian possessions of this country have been governed and defended, from the resources of those possessions, without the smallest cost to the British Exchequer, which, to the best of your petitioners' knowledge and belief, cannot be said of any other of the numerous foreign dependencies of the Crown...If the character of the East India Company were alone concerned, your petitioners might be willing to await the verdict of history. They are satisfied that posterity will do them justice.

Palmerston's government fell, over a matter unconnected with India, before the bill had got far. It was succeeded by a Tory government, under Derby and Disraeli. It was the latter half of that partnership which grasped the Indian nettle with glee. Disraeli introduced the second India Bill of 1857. It was the product of the powerful but untrustworthy mind of Lord Ellenborough, President of the Board of Trade for the fourth time, and the only active survivor among former Governors-General (Dalhousie was still alive but sick, and completely retired from public life). Ellenborough, of course, had been dismissed by the Company fourteen years previously, and was no friend to it. In Disraeli's bill the council assisting the President was to have ten more members than Palmerston's. The intriguing aspect of this plan was that five of the councillors were to be nominated by the cities of London, Manchester, Liverpool, Glasgow, and Belfast, thus recognising the centuries' old claim of the provincial ports against the dominance of London interests in India. Only four of the eighteen members were to have been associates of the Company. This scheme attracted opponents even from outside the Company, including the Queen. It got no further than Palmerston's bill, and Disraeli withdrew it. After a number of resolutions in the House of Commons, in which the Company was able to make its influence felt, a third bill was introduced on 24 June 1858. By this time Ellenborough had resigned because of Canning's 'Oudh Proclamation', which he had censured without Cabinet approval, but some of his ideas regarding the abolition of the Company's power – to which he looked forward with such relish – were incorporated in the new bill.*

Derby passed to his son the task of transferring the rule of India to the Government, and Lord Stanley thus became the last of the Presidents of the Board of Control for India. Parliament considered the third India bill of the year with some weariness. As it was said, if it was not a very good bill, it had ceased to be a very good joke. India was to be under a Secretary of State (i.e. a minister on a par with the Secretaries of State for Foreign or Home Affairs), who would be assisted by an advisory council of fifteen, of whom seven were to be nominated by the Company's last court of directors. This was, in effect, a compromise between Palmerston's and Ellenborough's bills, and seemingly an improvement for Company interests, although still in a minority in the new council. Members of the council would not be MPs as so many of the board of directors had been. The Secretary for State would not be able to overrule the council in financial matters. Canning was to remain as Governor-General, with the new title of Viceroy. The possessions of the Government of India, like Aden, Pegu, Penang, and Singapore, were also to pass out of Company control. Addiscombe was to

* Ellenborough never held office again, and died in 1871.

continue, but Haileybury, still hated by some though it had been open to competition since 1854, was to be closed down (a victory for a pressure group led by Macaulay and Benjamin Jowett).*

The debates which accompanied the passing of the India Act of 1858 were of a suitably high and responsible standard. Opposition was mostly confined to detail and a series of amendments from the House of Lords. It received the royal assent on 2 August 1858, to take effect on 1 September of that year.

> Whereas the territories in the possession or under the government of the East India Company were continued in trust for Her Majesty, until Parliament should otherwise provide... The government of the territories now in possession of the East India Company, and all powers exercised by the Company in trust for Her Majesty, shall cease to be vested in or exercised by the said Company; and shall become vested in Her Majesty as aforesaid and all territories which may become vested in Her Majesty and be exercised in her name.

On 1 September 1858, the last day of their authority, the Court of Directors of the Honourable East India Company held their final meeting at the East India House, Leadenhall Street. Throughout its long history, the East India Company had been nothing if not both elequent and proud. It now issued a statement of farewell to its many thousands of servants.

> The Company has the great privilege of transferring to the service of Her Majesty such a body of civil and military officers as the world has never seen before. A government cannot be base, cannot be feeble, cannot be wanting in wisdom, that has reared two such services as the civil and military services of the Company...Let Her Majesty appreciate the gift — let her take the vast country and the teeming millions of India under direct control; but let her not forget the great corporation from which she has received them.

So ended the Company raj, with more dignity than it had sometimes displayed during its life. In its former days it had been a rule sometimes corrupt, and often irresponsible, of rapacious looting, of

* Forty-one former pupils had lost their lives in the revolt. Haileybury reopened as a public school four years later; although the East India Company had nothing to do with the new school, East India Company families continued to send their boys there, and the tradition of service in India was maintained until recent times.

patronage and blatant nepotism; a rule during which the 'Honourable' Company had at times displayed the most outrageous disloyalty to its own best servants. A rule which had started for trade, had continued as a graveyard for British youth, and ended with the integrity of men such as the Lawrences and thousands like them. A rule arising from the original intention of bringing back great wealth from the east, it had ended by supervising the flow of great wealth from the west.

⌒⋙⋘⌒

It was thought that the teeming millions of India would be interested in the changeover, and great lengths were taken to announce the new raj in suitable style. 'It will be necessary to make some formal announcement of the transfer of authority from the Company to the Crown,' Stanley told Canning. Canning fixed on 1 November 1858 as the day on which the proclamation would be presented to the people of India. It was to be issued in eighteen languages and read out at suitable places, not only at the three presidency capitals but at Lahore, at Lucknow, at Peshawar in the far north, at Karachi on the mouth of the Indus, and at Rangoon in Burma. 'The proper salutes and parades have been ordered,' Canning assured Stanley, and a public holiday and firework displays were announced. Canning was at Allahabad, having gone there to be nearer the centre of the revolt. Allahabad, at the convergence of the Ganges and Jumna, was one of the most holy of Hindu cities, but also closely associated with the Muslim emperors, the great Akbar himself having often lived in the magnificent palace there.

The Governor-General, with Colin Campbell behind, rode in state through streets lined with British troops, behind which peered inquisitive crowds. He arrived at a raised dais near the fort and sat on a throne surrounded by high-ranking officers in formal dress, their ladies, prominent civil servants, and leaders of the Indian community. The Union Jack was raised above the platform, to the thuds of saluting guns. Lord Canning delivered the proclamation, but he was a poor orator and few could hear what he had to say:

> Victoria, by the Grace of God of the United Kingdom of Great Britain and Ireland, and of the Colonies and Dependencies thereof in Europe, Asia, Africa, America, and Australasia, Queen, Defender of the Faith. Whereas, for divers weighty reasons, we have resolved...to take upon ourselves the govern-

ment of the territories in India heretofore administered in trust for us by the Honourable East India Company...We desire no extension of our present territorial possessions, and while we will permit no aggression upon our domains or our rights to be attempted with impunity, we shall sanction no encroachment on those of others. We shall respect the rights, dignity and honour of native princes as our own*...We hold ourselves bound to the natives of our Indian territories by the same obligations of duty which bind us to all our other subjects, and those obligations, by the blessing of Almighty God, we shall faithfully and conscientiously fulfil...And it is our further will that, so far as may be, our subjects, of whatever race or creed, be freely and impartially admitted to office in our service...We will that generally, in framing and administering the law, due regard be paid to the ancient rights, usages, and customs of India.

Whether the majority of Indians ever heard of all this must have been doubtful. And whether they would have understood the expressions of 'duty', given by the Queen on behalf of the new rulers, would have been even more unlikely, but their descendants would surely know, and would recognise that the British kept faith with the promise made by their queen, and that when they finally departed from India they left behind the best record of their imperial history. But that was not to be for nearly a hundred years...

It seemed that little was to be done in the way of democracy for India, despite the warning of Sir Henry Bartle Frere, who had kept the peace in Sind during the revolt, that it was unwise 'to legislate for millions of people with few means of knowing, except by rebellion, whether the laws suit them or not'.†

The Queen's proclamation was well loaded with religious (i.e. Christian) references, and ended on a note of high religious fervour. The Governor-General hastened to assure the Queen of his satisfaction about this. 'I cannot tell you with what pleasure I have read the passages relating to Religion,' he told her. 'They are in every way admirable.'

~~~

* This assurance was a reflection of the importance attached to the disaffection of so many princes during the revolt.
† Indians were first admitted to the Governor-General's council, and to the High Court bench, by acts of 1861.

Two days later the new 'Council of India' in London had its first meeting in India House. But the new ministry did not have long in the magnificent premises it had inherited from the Company. It was felt that the city was no place for a government department, and new offices were built in Whitehall near the Foreign Office. After three years the East India House was bought by a group of property developers, demolished, and a block of offices built on the site. In 1923 this, in turn, was replaced by Lloyd's insurance building.*

The East India Company had been considered fusty, imbued with old-fashioned commercialism, by its critics. A new spirit of expertise and efficiency was claimed. The number of home civil servants concerned with India rapidly grew. The old intimacy and informality of the East India House, where generation had followed generation, did not survive the move to Westminster. The days were gone when letters from the East India House were written to the dependencies in the Company's exquisite, clear English, spiced with sarcasm, praise, or schoolmasterly remonstrances ('we are quite astonished...' or, more often, 'we desire that you will account for the purchase of...'), as the occasion seemed to demand: no longer the letters from the Court of Directors, meticulously signed by each director in turn, and always ending with the traditional 'We are your loving friends'.

In India, the accent now was on material change rather than spiritual; public works rather than public morals. It was felt that social change would come anyway, if slowly, without any forcing, as a natural successor to material improvement. After the Queen's proclamation, a more subtle approach to westernisation was required. It was typical of the Company's later days that its last great act was the establishment of the long-promised universities at the three presidency capitals, while the revolt was at its height. Under the new regime there were no serious social reforms for over half a century: all efforts went into improved communications, public services, and administration. The concept of service to the community, begun under the Company, was continued. But, perhaps not surprisingly, within a few years to be 'in trade' was almost as much a bar to joining a club in Calcutta as it was to be coloured.

* There is a memorial plaque, placed by the Corporation of the City of London, stating, simply: 'Site of East India House, 1726–1861.' There are also memorials concerning the East India Company in the nearby Church of St Andrew Undershaft.

When it was announced that the Company's 15,000 European troops automatically passed to the crown, there were rumblings of discontent throughout the cantonments of India. The officers and men objected to being passed to and fro without consultation, for their terms of service with the East India Company had been carefully worked out over the years and were not the same as those in the royal army; they were clearly contracted, for instance, to serve in India and its possessions only. There was a demand for financial compensation and for the opportunity of discharge. While legal arguments ensued, two regiments, the 4th European Light Cavalry and the 1st Madras Fusiliers, the latter one of the Company's crack units, showed signs of unusual discontent. The commander-in-chief in India, Campbell, now Lord Clyde, suggested the men should be offered re-enlistment or discharge. But Stanley and Canning refused. There were to be no major concessions to the former Company troops. The men, however, did not want to serve in the royal army. When unrest spread to Meerut, a shudder ran through the Indian administration. The 2nd European Cavalry there were reported to be restless. Slogans were appearing on walls: 'John Company is dead: we will not soldier for the Queen.' There was talk of disarming the 1st European Cavalry at Allahabad. The 5th European Infantry, at Berhampore, were officially reported to be 'in a state of positive mutiny'. The authorities backed down and every man and NCO was allowed discharge from the service if they wanted it, in which case they would be transported home free of charge. About two-thirds of them accepted the offer and returned to Britain to enjoy the proceeds of looting during the revolt (about a quarter of these re-enlisted later). Their bluff had been rewarded with success. It cost the nation over a quarter of a million pounds.

After this unhappy affair, the service in India settled down to Anglo-Indian life; the revolt, seeming a hideous nightmare, receded into the past. W. H. Russell, of *The Times*, reported on India 'in mourning':

> ...a handsome church, some large barracks; a few English children and soldiers playing and sauntering in the shade... English bungalows, with the names painted on the gateways, 'Laburnum Lodge', 'Prospect', 'The Elms', and such-like home reminiscences, and the clang of pianofortes, and streams of song rushed out through open windows...parties of ladies

and gentlemen on horseback…the mails from England and the formation of shooting parties…Our civilians, established in their country retreats, began to give dinners as the best evidence of the returned vigour of our administration and of the security of our power.

〰️

As a ghost of its former self, the East India Company lingered on in London. There were still financial affairs to be cleared up, pensions for the ever-dwindling number who proudly attached HEICS after their names to be haggled over with the Government (the Company had a high reputation in the matter of pensions), and remuneration and assets for the dogged proprietors and directors. But those who believed that the end of the Company would add to their fortunes were disappointed. After all, the Company had been hopelessly in debt. Rooms were found at No 1 Moorgate, at which one secretary and one clerk were employed. The court of directors continued to hold their meetings at this office, but less than half a dozen usually attended. The new India Office set aside £800 a year for the East India Company's expenses. The chairman, Colonel William Henry Sykes, MP, received a salary of £150 a year. The secretary received £120. Later more modest premises were found at 11 Pancras Lane. Sykes had become chairman in 1856; a veteran of the Company, he had joined its service as a cadet in 1803, later being seconded from the military to the civil service, where he had researched into natural history and population. After thirty years in the Company's employ, he had retired in 1833, becoming a director in 1840. He loved the Company and enjoyed the once mighty and influential title of Chairman of the Honourable East India Company. It was sad, for whatever else the Company had been, it had never been ridiculous. Apart from engaging in unrewarding correspondence with the India Office, with cranks, and with the inquisitive, there was very little for the Company to do. Maintaining the Company tradition for unabashed nepotism to the last, Sykes's son became secretary. Thus the East India Company, after a period of two and a half centuries, returned to its original frugal state.

Sykes died in 1872, aged 83; with him went the last hope of keeping up pretences. On 1 June 1874, the 1854 charter having run out, the public were surprised to learn that the East India Company, like a sigh from the past, had been finally dissolved. The Government rewarded the persistence and patience of the proprietors with £200 for every £100 of India stock, as had been agreed in the bill of 1854 in the event of the Company's being wound-up, although they were asked to accept government securities in lieu. Although it was generally held that the Company was being treated somewhat more than well, the directors, presenting a petition, fought for more money to the last.

Five years previously, on the coast between Karachi and Bombay, a boy had been born named Mohandas Karamchand Gandhi.

Here and there in India a memorial to the Company is to be seen. The most eloquent are the cemeteries, where tangled undergrowth, relentlessly creeping in, surrounds ornate tombs, with noble messages blithely ignored by posterity; names of 'writers', majors, children, inspectors, corporals, of brothers, sons and fathers, wives and daughters, all swept aside in the flow of time. Hardinge's statue no longer graces Calcutta — now it is in the English garden of his descendants — but outside Frere Hall in Karachi Queen Victoria stands on a pedestal and gazes down on a Muslim state where once all religions lived together. Across Sind, the desert, and the hills of Rajasthan, and down the mighty Ganges, in Calcutta, Tipu Sahib's throne, one of the Company's proudest trophies, still stands in Government House; not far away is Cornwallis Street, where one of Asia's greatest universities is situated. From Bombay, the Poona Express clangs and thunders through the canyons of Maharashtra to the capital of the Peshwas, on the line begun by the East India Company, the whirring fans, the slapping blinds, and the shrieking boys with soft drinks endeavouring to combat the stifling heat. The signs of an irrevocable contact with Britain and the west are everywhere visible and all too often uneasily incongruous. In a Delhi hotel, where the orchestra plays tunes from old London shows in the glittering restaurant, the staff treat insect life with loving and meticulous respect. At Benares, now Varanasi, hundreds of thousands still take the pilgrimage, pouring the holy waters of the Ganges before them at dawn, to receive through it the blessing of the rays of the sun; smoke rises from the funeral pyres lining the ghats; but above the hypnotic and age-old sounds of gongs and bells, and the rhythm of the chanting, comes the familiar wail of a factory hooter...

India may be a better or a worse place in which to live and die since the East India Company's first envoy, William Hawkins, arrived at Jahangir's court in April 1609, but it is certainly different. No small part of the change was due to the East India Company, the most remarkable institution of private enterprise and capitalism that the world has ever known. *The Times* made its tribute in 1873:

Now when it passes away, with the solemnities of Parliamentary sepulture, out of the land of the living, it is just as well, as becoming, to record that it accomplished a work such as in the whole history of the human race no other trading company ever attempted and such as none surely is likely to attempt in the years to come.

I   APPENDIX

PRESIDENTS OF THE BOARD OF CONTROL FOR AFFAIRS
OF INDIA

1790   William Grenville (Lord Grenville)
1793   Henry Dundas (Lord Melville)
1801   Lord Lewisham (Lord Dartmouth)
1802   Lord Castlereagh
1806   Lord Minto
1806   Thomas Grenville
1806   George Tierney
1807   Robert Dundas
1809   Lord Harrowby
1809   Robert Dundas (Lord Melville)
1812   Lord Buckinghamshire
1816   George Canning
1821   Charles Bathurst
1822   Charles W. W. Wynn
1828   Lord Melville
1828   Lord Ellenborough
1830   Charles Grant (Lord Glenelg)
1834   Lord Ellenborough
1835   Sir John Hobhouse
1841   Lord Ellenborough
1841   Lord Fitzgerald & Vesey
1843   Lord Ripon

1846	Sir John Hobhouse (Lord Broughton)
1852	Fox Maule
1852	John Herries
1852	Sir Charles Wood
1855	Robert Vernon Smith
1858	Lord Ellenborough
1858	Lord Stanley

GOVERNORS AND GOVERNORS-GENERAL 1758–1858, THE EAST INDIA COMPANY'S REPRESENTATIVES IN INDIA FROM PLASSEY TO THE MUTINY

Governors of the Presidency of Fort William

1758	Robert Clive
1760	John Holwell
1760	Henry Vansittart
1764	John Spencer
1765	Lord Clive
1767	Henry Verelst
1769	John Cartier
1772	Warren Hastings

Governors-General of Bengal, with authority over the Governors of Madras and Bombay

1773	Warren Hastings
1785	Sir John Macpherson
1786	Lord Cornwallis
1793	Sir John Shore
1798	Lord Mornington (Lord Wellesley)
1805	Lord Cornwallis
1805	Sir George Barlow
1807	Lord Minto
1813	Lord Moira (Lord Hastings)
1823	John Adam
1823	Lord Amherst
1828	Lord William Bentinck

Governors-General of India and Governors of Bengal

1833   Lord William Bentinck
1835   Sir Charles Metcalfe
1836   Lord Auckland
1842   Lord Ellenborough
1844   Sir Henry Hardinge (Lord Hardinge)
1848   Lord Dalhousie

Governors-General of India

1854   Lord Dalhousie
1856   Lord Canning

2 ⧘ APPENDIX ⧘

MUGHAL EMPERORS 1600–1857

Independent

1600 Akbar
1605 Jahangir
1628 Shah Jahan
1657 Murad
1657 Shah Shuja
1658 Aurangzib
1707 Azam Shah
1707 Bahadur Shah
1712 Jahandar Shah
1713 Farrukhsiyar
1719 Muhammad Shah

Under Afghan or Maratha domination

1748 Ahmad Shah
1754 Alamgir
1759 Shah Alam

Under East India Company domination

1806 Akbar Shah II
1837 Bahadur Shah II

3 APPENDIX

EXAMPLE OF EIC FINANCES: 1850–51

Taken from the Finance Letter of the Court of Directors to the Governor-General, 3 June 1852, and *The Administration of the East India Company*, J. W. Kaye (1853).

9 rupees = £1 approx.

RECEIPTS

	Rupees
Land Tax: Presidencies	
Bengal	3,56,25,000
North-West Provinces	4,97,50,000
Madras	3,52,89,200
Bombay	2,21,65,480
	14,28,29,680
Customs:	
Bengal	1,02,73,500
North-West Provinces	52,22,000
Madras	11,36,460
Bombay	31,13,600
	1,97,45,560

E.I.C. *Tobacco Monopoly*	6,04,980
E.I.C. *Opium Monopoly*	3,72,41,784
E.I.C. *Salt Monopoly*	1,72,44,980
Tax on Spirit-Vending	1,04,69,840
Total Revenues from Dependencies	
Lahore (the Punjab)	1,30,00,000
Sindh	28,00,000
Eastern Settlements	31,00,000
Burmese Territory	20,00,000
	1,91,00,000
Other Items	
Stamps	46,37,490
Post Office	20,44,170
Marine	18,00,000
Subsidies from Indian Princes	65,10,181
From Calcutta Mint	1,14,162

EXPENDITURE

Civil Expenditure	
Revenue charges (surveys, canals, etc.)	2,00,13,066
Judicial	1,95,82,604
Customs	20,27,739
Marine (E.I.C. Navy, pilots, etc.)	56,32,853
Military Expenditure	10,09,56,040
Interest on Debt	2,69,84,603
General Charges (allowances to princes, public works, education, church, etc.)	4,48,52,088

J. W. Kaye: 'The charges have reached the amount of $22\frac{1}{2}$ million (rupees). To these are to be added the Home charges, amounting to $2\frac{1}{2}$ million more, raising the total charges to 25 millions, and leaving a deficit of half a million. These statements are extracted from the last general review of the Company's finances, taken by the Court of Directors. But they are intended here rather to convey a general idea of the revenues of India, and the charges incurred in the government of the country, than to determine the financial results of a particular year with any precision. Indeed, nothing is more difficult than to secure, in any such statement, an amount of accuracy that will satisfy all financiers. The accounts are made up, by different authorities, so differently, that the inquirer is often staggered by the discrepancies which look him in the face, and bewilder the understanding.'

INDEX

316

THE
HUMAN
MACHINE

THE HUMAN MACHINE

A view of intelligent mechanisms

I. ALEKSANDER

With a foreword by J. G. Taylor

Georgi Publishing Company

ISBN 2-604-00023-7
© 1978 Georgi Publishing Company
CH-1813 St. Saphorin, Switzerland

Distributors:
UK : Global Book Resources Ltd.,
109 Great Russell Street,
London, WC1B 3ND
USA : Renouf, Inc.,
170 Fifth Avenue,
New York, NY 10010.
Canada : Renouf Ltd.,
2182 St. Catherine Street West,
Montreal, Que. H3H 1M7

Cover design by Allen Kilner
Composition by Le Book Production Unit
Printed in Great Britain by
Whitstable Litho Ltd.,
Whitstable, Kent.

78-301927

CONTENTS

3

FOREWORD

Workers in artificial intelligence have acquired a doubtful reputation for predicting enormous strides in their ability to create intelligent machines... then failing to achieve anything.

Decade after decade, we keep hearing that the super-intelligent machine is imminent. Only several weeks ago, I listened in amazement to a respected worker in artificial intelligence suggest that there are UFO's circling the earth for the express purpose of monitoring our activities. Apparently, when we are about to develop the super-intelligent machine, these extra-terrestrial spies will be ready to restrict our powers to endanger other civilizations in the galaxy.

If such caution is truly necessary, then perhaps we should take as much notice as our alien neighbours. However, computers still overcharge or overpay at an alarming rate to cause irate customers heart attacks and other unpleasant effects. This would seem to indicate that studies in machine intelligence have not progressed as far as has been claimed.

There is the very apposite story of the machine programmer who devised a computer programme so that his machine could play dominoes. He entered it in the World Dominoes Championship against the best players available, was remarkably successful and defeated all the other competitors. At this point, an emergency meeting was held to change the rules and exclude computers from future championships. Thus, even though computers have been programmed to play some simple games well — and others more complicated like chess, less well — they are still some way from achieving the level of guile often shown by human beings.

The problem of relating computers and similar machines — usually called automata — to human beings is not a new activity. It has been going on for decades and never fails to arouse interest as well as emotions.

Philosophers would claim that any argument about the nature of human experience is too short. It could only be achieved with some success after a great deal of analysis, using the various forms of experience that do arise. Those with a religious bent

5

would certainly add that it is not possible to provide a correct description of human experience without the nature of religious experience itself forming the basis.

I would include myself amongst those who, like Professor Aleksander, have attempted to analyse human experience from the point of view of mechanical activity. Yet I do not think we should apologize for such attempts. It would seem to me very difficult to attempt to understand our experience — especially of a mental sort — without first trying to come to grips with it in a scientific fashion. By science, we normally mean a quantitative analysis in which numbers are attached and this reduces to analysis of the mathematical features of mental processes.

The thesis presented in this book is that such features can be described in terms of state activity, i.e. the way the state of the system will change from one time to another. The description of the system in terms of how its state changes is a very broad one and allows a vast range of phenomena to be discussed in a rather unified fashion. As is pointed out in this book, one can not only discuss human thoughts and experiences in this way, but the same process can be applied to gene activity, human social interreactions and even society itself. I would argue very strongly with Professor Aleksander that it is only in this way that we can begin to describe the processes that are occurring in any detail.

The level of the book is such that it should be accessible to most. I can recommend it most highly as a salutary lesson in how to apply one's own thought to one's own thought and see it take sense in as precise manner as is possible at present. The insights to be gained from reading this book will, I am sure, be of great value in helping people to face up to the strange phenomena that seem to abound. "Things that go bump in the night" are occurring to more and more people, yet they seem to get used to the idea that the world itself is a strange and mysterious place. I can only recommend this book as an attempt to discuss in a very rational way the most important features of our experience, that is our own mental states. It does so successfully at the level at which it is aimed. It can undoubtedly be used as a spring-board to further self-searching and also to the deeper analyses that are going on at present.

We are in a state of transition from groping around in the dark about the brain and the mind to the emergence of an interpretation of it that will stand up to the searching probe of science. This book is part of the movement and will tell it successfully.

J.G. Taylor
Professor of Mathematics,
King's College, University of London

December 1976

PREFACE
AND
INTRODUCTION

At first sight, the title of this book may seem somewhat provocative. Indeed, whenever humans are described in mechanistic or machine-like terms one meets an endless series of taboos. The reason for this is probably due to the word "machine" which conjures a view of gears, pulleys, belts and levers. We *know* that human beings don't work like Swiss Clocks and any attempt to describe them as such can be rightly dismissed.

The salient aim of this book is to demonstrate that one's view of a machine has, in fact, changed within the last thirty years. Modern machines are no longer restricted to purely *mechanical* acts. They can work out formulae instead of lifting weights; recognize formalized languages instead of spinning cotton yarns; and even play chess instead of merely propelling themselves along the ground. Of course, I am referring to computers, but I must immediately dispel the notion that this book is *about* computers or that it supports the existence of any similarity between men and computers.

This book is primarily about *automata* which, as a first attempt, may be described as machines that process information. It is true that digital computers have been responsible for the study of *automata* becoming a respectable science, rather than a Frankenstein desire to build man-like robots, as the name might suggest. However, the computer is only one of a vast class of systems that fall under the heading of *automaton*. The inescapable fact is that most of the definitions of automata (like the one given above) include human beings. It is my express purpose therefore, to submit that very simple concepts in automata theory lead to a different way of looking at descriptions and explanations of human behaviour and other "natural" events. This way is essentially different to the traditional methods of philosophy and most of psychology : it relies on theoretical statements regarding what automata can and cannot do and then uses the methods of description as a language for describing the behaviour of naturally occurring automata.

7

Although automata theory is in some sense mechanistic it does not offend our common sense when applied to humans. This is largely due to the fact that it deals with the mechanics of informational structures (which, for the moment remain undefined) rather than palpable physical structures.

An early aim of this book is to make it as clear as possible to a reader with no knowledge of information processing machines what is meant by the abstract term "automaton". Chapter 1 is, therefore, devoted to a formal definition of this term, and to an introduction of the reader to the concept of an *internal state*. Such states are the bones of an automaton and the changes from state to state, a structure : a kind of automaton skeleton. It is this structure that is entirely responsible for the range and richness of behaviour of the automaton and this is illustrated by means of a simple example : a clockwork mouse.

In Chapter 2 one makes use of this newly found knowledge to tackle a rather over-rated automaton : the digital computer. The main aim is to clarify largely what is meant by "memory" in such a device and to dispel the notion that the organization of a computer is in any way similar to that of a mammalian brain. It is shown that the computer is rather poor on intelligence but very good on speed and is thus able to hide its stupidity. The point is taken further in Chapter 3 where work that goes under the heading of "machine intelligence" is examined. This describes the struggles of scientists to give the computer a semblance of intelligence in trying to make it behave as much as possible as a human being. In this chapter, what seems a more profitable approach to machine intelligence is also considered : a study of networks of models of brain cells that seeks to discover the laws which are at work. It is in this area that one sees the first twitches of an embryonic form of machine behaviour which could be termed as being "intelligent". It is here also that one begins to appreciate the sophistication and accuracy of the human brain automaton. This leads to the conclusion that technology-limited machines will have to wait a while before such an accomplished performance can be equalled.

In Chapter 4 one returns in greater detail to a study of state structures. The point is made that state structures of simple automata may be drawn as figures on a piece of paper. This not only helps to visualize the skeleton of automata but has also some aesthetic merit. Starting with the simple state structure of the clockwork mouse, more complex structures are developed mainly for automata consisting of simple networks of cells (such as introduced in Chapter 3). Two most important arguments are developed in this chapter. First, the state structure of an automaton is only tenuously related to its physical structure. Similar physical structures can have vastly different state structures and automata with very different physical structures can have identical state structures. The implications of this are far-reaching in the sense that it seems futile to devote a great deal of time to the study of physical structure. Careful charting of all the connections of the nerve cells in the brain will *not* reveal what the brain is doing.

The second important argument partly answers *how* one is going to discover the function of a complex automaton given that a physical investigation appears doomed to failure. It is shown that the cellular networks of Chapter 3 have a state structure that is closely related to the nature of the information impinging on the network. In human terms, the state structure of the brain is a kind of reflection of one's environment. Not an accurate reflection, but one which ignores unimportant details and, in a way, *makes sense* of the world to which it is exposed.

On this basis, in Chapter 5, one enters the discussion on the concept of *mind* and its relation to state structure. The classical philosophies of mind come under scrutiny in an argument which stresses that it is largely a result of the lack of a descriptive language that brings about highly opposing views, ranging from the Cartesian self-sustaining spiritual mind to Gilbert Ryle's body-integrated description.

Using the language of automata description, "thought" and "learning" are shown to be easily defined as characteristics of the state structure of the brain. In the same way as "thought" and "learning" are attributes of mind, other features such as emotion, self-knowledge, etc... are also seen to be characteristics of state structures. Since *mind* can only be defined in terms of its attributes it is argued that mind *is* a set of characteristics of the brain's structure. One hesitates to push the debate home by saying that mind *is state structure*, since the state structure must also be responsible for other functions which are *not* normally regarded as being attributes of mind. These are the self-supporting, or homeostatic, functions of the brain which keep the body alive : heart beat regulation, temperature control etc...

Questions of perception, awareness, attention, free will and emotions are considered more deeply in Chapter 6. Here one sees that it is a mistake to consider the brain as being one amorphous cellular automaton with one huge state structure. Questions of *free will* are best tackled by assuming that there are at least two automata interacting with one another, one acting as a controller of the other. It is seen that the state activity in the controlling automaton can cause the state activity or "thoughts" of the controlled automaton to be altered "at will". This is not meant to imply that the brain is partitioned into two sections, but is used as an argument for the likelihood of it consisting of a hierarchy of sections with the higher sections controlling those below them.

Two further aspects of mind that are the cause of debate in psychology, are tackled in Chapters 7 and 8 : the nature of dreams and the nature of the pathological mind. The nature of dreams is embedded in the premise that an automaton's state structure is not likely to alter simply because some of its perceptual inputs are "out of action". It is seen that this "out of action" situation is a part of state structure itself which causes the automaton to "reminisce", somewhat at random, the events in its past history. The possibility of strange juxtapositions of the memory of such events is also explained.

Two aspects of what one could call the "deep" properties of mind are considered in Chapter 8. The first deals with the Freudian concept of the "unconscious" and is related primarily to the normal mind. However, the existence of the unconscious is seen to follow directly from the arguments concerned with dreaming. Indeed, much of behaviour hinges around parts of state structure that cannot be "reached" during conscious periods and that are seen to form the "unconscious". In looking for the origins of such remote parts of state structure one finds that they are largely due to exposures to the environment early in the automaton's "life" and it is here that things can go wrong. There one sees the second facet of the "deep" nature of mind : the abnormal, or psychotic, mind. It is not difficult to explain that certain events in an automaton's "upbringing" cause the creation of "traps" in the state structure. These could be responsible for many types of psychotic behaviour.

In Chapter 9 a very specific type of automaton is considered in detail : that used to model a collection of genes and to predict cell behaviour. This has a most interesting property in the fact that it does not need to interact strongly with its environment in order to produce a stable and intelligent behaviour. Finally, Chapter 10 goes from the minute scale of the last chapter to the gigantic scale of societal systems. Here an individual is considered as the cell of a vast automaton and it is seen that certain grouping tendencies in society become predictable as a result of the automaton's natural tendencies towards stability. One hopes also to see a state structure relating to an "economy". However, the chapter concludes on a totally different note. It considers the possible effect of the creation of a society that has to make room for non-human automata such as digital computers. The results could be beneficial or otherwise. The fact that it is still possible to decide between favoured and unfavoured courses of action leads to a reasonably optimistic conclusion.

10

1

THE
ANATOMY
OF
AUTOMATA

A clock-work mouse is an automaton, so is a human being, and also a computer. A pencil is not an automaton. A piece of paper is not an automaton. What distinguishes an automaton from other things ? Having slipped into this question I have avoided justifying the rather gross statement that a human being is an automaton. I shall return to this question very often in this book.

A device which we call an *automaton* is largely recognized by the fact that it has an internal action which is not immediately obvious to the observer. In the case of the clock-work mouse, this internal activity is, for example, the state of the spring, which could be wound or unwound. An observer who approaches the mouse and releases its motor catch will see one of two possible results depending on this internal state. That is, the mouse will go into motion if the spring is wound or it will do very little if the spring is not wound. A pencil, on the other hand, holds no such surprises; if it is worthy of the name *pencil* it should write when acted upon to do so, but that is about all.

In describing the internal activity of the clock-work mouse, I have used the word "*state*", namely the "*state* of the spring". This is precisely the word which is used by automata theorists to describe the internal activity of any general automaton. Thus the first part of the necessary requirement of an automaton, which distinguishes it from other things, can now be defined as its set of internal states. Clearly, a human being or an animal possess such internal states. This is seen in the way we express common thoughts : "John is in a bad state this morning, he didn't even greet me when he saw me." This implies that there is something internally different about the man this morning. This is a rather naive usage of the word *state*. The state of a human being is an extremely complex thing and governs almost every form of his activity. As a further example, the fact that a person speaks and understands language — i.e. in a state of being able to communicate with people around him — indicates that there is something internal going on which enables him to perform this act. In an automaton there could be a complex

11

range of internal states; exactly how these interact and the way they are structured will be considered later.

At this point it is merely important to note that the nature and range of these states is somehow dependent on the structure of the automaton. In the clock-work mouse the internal states are there merely because someone built the spring into the mouse, whereas in the human being, the internal states are a result of some very complex interaction of the cells in the nervous system. Though complex, this action is clearly a result of the existence of the brain as, without a brain, a man would be very poorly off indeed, and his internal state activity would be greatly limited.

Having once acquired this set of states it is important to know how the state of the automaton changes from moment to moment. I will argue that these changes are largely influenced by the way that the external world or an external observer interacts with the automaton itself and that indeed, the state of an automaton is, in fact, a measure of its past history.

We can trace some of the history of the clock-work mouse. Presumably when its spring was inserted it was in a state of unwind. After being secured into place, someone must have wound the spring, that is, the person winding the spring changed its internal state through all its stages from a state of complete unwind to a state of being fully wound. Subsequently, someone releases the motor catch and allows the spring to unwind setting the mouse on its way. It is clear, therefore, that the state changes depend on the action of outside bodies on the device. However, if someone were to release the catch when the spring was unwound there would be no further state changes, that is, the spring would stay exactly where it was. In this way we see that the changes from moment to moment do not depend only on the action of the outside intervener but also on the state itself.

So far we have seen that an automaton characteristically contains internal states and that the changes in these depend on the states themselves and the action of the environment on the automaton. The only item which remains to be considered is the action of the automaton itself. Every automaton has at its disposal a range of possible actions. In the case of our simple mouse its actions are probably to move or not to move. Whether the mouse moves or not depends on (a) whether the spring has been wound and (b) whether the catch has been released. This is a characteristic of all automata; the action of the automaton depends on some combination of its internal state and incoming intervention. We are now in a position to give a much more rigorous definition of an automaton; one which concurs with that used by automata theorists.

There are three sets of messages associated with each automaton. The first is the set of interventions which is normally called the set of input messages (I). We then have the set of internal states (S) and the set of possible actions of the automaton which are commonly called outputs (P). In addition to these three sets, the automaton becomes completely specified if one provides two sets of rules. The first of these tells us how the state at the next moment depends on the value of the present input and the value of the state at the present moment*. We label this set of rules, f_s. The second set of rules, f_p, tells us how the output value at the present moment depends on the present value of the state and the present value of the input.

What is meant by present moment and next moment needs a little elaboration. It is assumed that time evolves in little jumps from moment to moment. It will be seen later that this helps us in our thinking and our explanations of the behaviour of automata. At this point suffice it to say that to approach a real-life situation one can think of these momentary jumps as being so small as to factually provide a continuum of action.

For our clock-work mouse (I) consists of four elements:

1) motor latch *on, no pressure* on winding spring;
2) motor latch *on, pressure* on winding spring;
3) motor latch *off, no pressure* on winding key;
4) motor latch *off, pressure* on winding key.

The set of outputs, (P), consists on two elements;

1) mouse moves;
2) mouse does not move.

The set of internal states, (S), may be very large indeed as it consists of all possible values of tension in the spring from zero to maximum. However, it would not destroy our understanding of the way in which the mouse works if we assumed that the spring tenses and releases its tension in little jumps. As in the case of the time jumps, the jumps in the spring state can be considered as infinitesimally small so as to almost give a continuum of action.

In the case of the clock-work mouse it is quite easy to formulate the rules for f_s and f_p. f_s may be stated as follows:

for input combination (1) there are no internal state changes, that is, the state the next moment is the same as it is at the present moment;

for input combination (2) the spring tension will be increased in its little jumps from moment to moment;

*By "value" I refer to one of the possible elements of either the set of states or set of inputs.

13

for input combination (3) the spring will unwind;

for input combination (4) one will have the same effect as input combination (2).

As far as the output function f_p is concerned this may be stated as follows : whenever the spring is unwinding and the motor catch is released the mouse will move, at all other times it will not move.

It now becomes possible to see that, under the simple definition of an automaton which we have considered, the human being appears to belong to the class of automata. However, making this kind of statement does not tell us a great deal about the human being. The key to the understanding of an automaton lies in the ability to specify completely the rules f_s and f_p. Even though it has been relatively easy to specify these rules in the case of the clock-work mouse, the same cannot be said for a human being. All that can be said is that a human being has certainly a large set of inputs (that is, combinations of messages from his five senses); a set of outputs (combinations of his muscular activity); and an absolutely vast set of states. We shall only be able to say that we understand a human being once we can give some information about the nature and origins of f_s and f_p.

2

THE
COMPUTER
AUTOMATON

The digital computer is an automaton of a very special kind. Its design stems largely from the work (around 1946) of John Von Neumann, a brilliant American mathematician of Hungarian origin. He sought to implement a machine which was capable of carrying out complex calculations and which would not only have a memory of the data involved in these calculations but would remember the procedure (or program) for the calculations themselves. Here I shall try to relate the digital computer to the general automaton discussed in the last Chapter.

In the general automaton it is seen that the internal states are in some way related to what one might term the *experience* or the *memory* of the device. Indeed, in the digital computer, the internal states reside mostly in its *memory*. It is important to note that in the last two sentences, I have used the word *memory* in two different ways. First, I used the term in its usual colloquial sense. Whereas second, I used it as a technical term which forms part of the language of the computer user or designer. I am therefore, trying to alert the reader to the fact that the word *memory* may be described and explained in terms of a conventional digital computer but that it also may have a meaning in automata which is much more akin to its conversational use.

The memory section of a digital computer is made up of a large number of primitive cells. Physically, these cells are either magnetic rings or little electronic switches. Each such cell may be described as an elemental automaton in itself. This avoids having to know anything about electronics, and I will show that the function of such a cell, and indeed the entire memory, can be described in terms of a general automaton. The only assumption that need be made is that the cell operates on the basis of pulses of electrical current.

Consider Figure 2.1. Each memory cell has only two internal states, the *zero* state and the *one* state. It is for this reason that such a cell is said to store one *binary unit* (which is abbreviated to "bit"), binary meaning "two-valued". The set of input messages to

Fig. 2.1. The primitive memory cell.

the cell is supplied on three wires. The first of these wires is known as the *address* wire and *selects* the cell among others if an impulse of current is applied to it. The second wire is called the *read/write* input which, in the absence of a pulse, causes the cell to output on a single wire the value of its state, whereas in the presence of a pulse it enables one to change the state of the cell. The third input wire, the *information* input, dictates the next desired value of the internal state. A pulse at this wire makes the state change to a 1 whereas in the absence of a pulse the state will change to a 0. There are 8 possible 0/1 combinations of input for this cell and these have the effect on the internal state and output as shown in Table 1 below. The "next state" part of the table completely specifies the next-state function, f_s, and the "output" part of the table specifies the output function, f_p. These functions may also be specified in simple words. Function f_s merely ensures that the internal state changes to 1 or to 0 according to whether the *information* line is pulsed or not pulsed provided that the address line is pulsed *and*

Table 1. 0 refers to "no pulse" 1 refers to "pulse" conditions.

Input*			State			Output
a	r	i	present		next	
0	—	—	←	no effect	→	0
1	0	0	0		0	0
1	0	0	1		1	1
1	0	1	0		0	0
1	0	1	1		1	1
1	1	0	0		0	0
1	1	0	1		0	0
1	1	1	0		1	1
1	1	1	1		1	1

*a = address, r = read/write, i = information

the read/write line is pulsed. The output function f_p on the other hand is such that the output line produces a pulse, if there is a pulse on the address line and if the internal state is a 1. Thus, when we say that the cell *stores* one binary unit of information we mean that it is equivalent to a little box in which we can choose to store or not store one object, say a coin. In terms of Shannon's theory of communication this represents the smallest amount of information that one can possibly store. Indeed, such stores of information may be found all around us. For example, the label outside my office can be made to read either "In" or "Out" and it conveys information. If we had a large number of such indicators outside the building in which I work, each one indicating the presence or absence of myself or one of my colleagues, this board would convey information regarding the total internal state of that building with respect to presences or absences of its occupants. Thus, if there were 8 persons occupying the building we would need 8 indicators and these would store a total of 8 binary units, 8 *bits* of information. Now if we do our sums correctly we find that this kind of indicator board could hold a total of 256 possible messages (2^8) which is precisely the number of combinations of presences and absences of myself and my colleagues. The complete memory unit of a digital computer is made of a large number of the cells I have described above and, in the same way as our indicator board, manages to store very many messages.

The way in which the cells of the memory are connected together is shown in Figure 2.2. Cells are connected in groups in such a way that each group has a common address wire. In other words all the address wires of the cells in a group are connected together to one address terminal. Such a group of cells is normally referred to as a *word* and contains somewhere between 12 and 40 cells. As an example, let us imagine that such a group contains 16 cells. In general, computers contain between 4,000 and 500,000 such words. The former figure applies to a small desk-top computer whereas the latter figure applies to very large scientific machines. The memory is arranged in such a way that, in use, an address, say one of the possible 4,000, is specified in order to select one specific word. Information can then be written into all 16 cells simultaneously or read from all the 16 cells simultaneously.

The entire memory can now be described in the framework of a general automaton. Let us assume that we are dealing with a 4,000 word memory. The total number of possible internal states is quite enormous ($2^{16 \times 4000} \cong 10^{21000}$). This calculation is not very helpful, and it is better to think of the memory as a collection of information boxes, one box for each word. Each word has 16 bits and can, therefore, be in one of $2^{16} = 65,536$ possible states. That

17

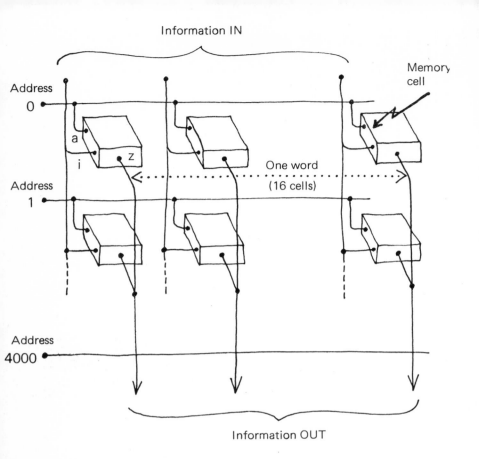

Fig. 2.2. Memory organization; read/write wires are not shown but are common to all cells.

is, each word can contain one of 65,536 possible messages. The whole memory has 3 sets of inputs. The first set receives the address number. The second set is told by a single pulse whether the memory must accept a message (i.e. be "written" into) or merely accept an address and output a message (i.e. be "read" from). The third set contains 16 wires and receives the message which is to be stored in a selected word when the memory is in a *write* mode. It may be educational for the reader to formulate the function f_s and f_p for the memory. However, in very simple language one can say that the memory is merely a large container which is divided up into small sections, one section for each word, into which the user can place information and then retrieve it.

At this point I ought to stress that even though an electronic computer has often be called an electronic brain, on looking at this very regular, compartmentalised and highly structured make-

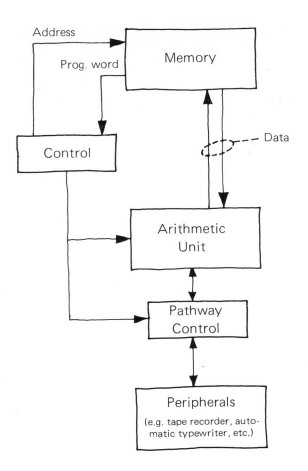

Fig. 2.3.

up of the memory, it is most unlikely that it should bear any resemblance to a mammalian brain.

We can now look at the way in which the rest of the computer is organised in order to make use of its memory. In order to do this let us consider a very simple programming task. The computer is required to read a number from punched paper tape and insert it in say, address 200 of its memory. It is then required to read a second number (which was previously placed following the first on punched paper tape). It is then asked to add the two numbers and to print out the result on an automatic electric typewriter.* There are two other automata besides the memory in the main frame of a computer: a control unit and an arithmetic unit as in Figure 2.3.

*This is often called a *teletype* machine.

19

The program which contains the necessary sequence of instructions is stored in consecutive addresses in the memory. How it gets there is not of immediate importance, we merely assume that it is resident starting, say, at address 10 in the memory and exists in the following form. Each word of the program is split into two parts (generally it is split into more parts, but two parts will suffice for the purposes of this explanation). The first part is a message regarding what has to be done with the data and the second part is a message regarding where the data must come from or go to. We call these two messages the *instruction* message and the routing message respectively. With a 16 bit word it is clear that if the word is split into two groups of 8 bits we can have as many as 256 (2^8) instructions as well as 256 routing messages. Our short programme would have to be put into the form shown in the table below :

Address location in memory	Instruction	Routing
10	TRANSMIT FROM	Paper tape reader
11	TRANSMIT TO	Address 200
12	TRANSMIT FROM	Paper tape reader
13	ADD FROM	Address 200
14	TRANSMIT TO	Teletype

We note that under the heading of INSTRUCTION we have listed the following :

TRANSMIT TO,
TRANSMIT FROM,
ADD FROM.

These three instructions could be coded 00000001, 00000010, 00000011, respectively. Under the heading of ROUTING we have listed the following :

various memory addresses,
the paper tape reader, and
the teletype machine.

We assume that the memory addresses are coded in binary code in the usual way (that is, 200 decimal = 11001000 binary). We also assume that only 256 addresses are available and that the last 10 numbers in the routing code (i.e. from 11110110 to 11111111) refer to location outside the memory such as the paper tape and teletype machine. For this example we assume that the paper tape machine is addressed by the digit 11111111, and the teletype is addressed by the digit 11111110. The programme can reside in the memory as shown in the table below :

Binary address	Program word	
	Instruction	Routing
00001010	00000010	11111111
00001011	00000001	11001000
00001100	00000010	11111111
00001101	00000011	11001000
00001110	00000001	11111110

The salient point seen here is that the entire program is stored merely as the internal state of address locations 10 to 14. It was the realization of this possibility that led to John Von Neumann's proposals for an automatic computing machine which is the basis of the computer as we know it today.

For the purposes of the above example the arithmetic unit is an automaton which functions only in one of two ways. It either receives and stores temporarily a 16 bit word or it adds an incoming 16 bit word to the word already stored within itself. Which of these two functions is performed is determined by a message transmitted to the arithmetic unit from the other automaton in the system, the control unit. The function of the control unit is to receive the program word at its input terminals, to store it, and to activate its outputs in such a way as to (a) put the arithmetic unit in its desired function mode, and (b) to open pathways from the various devices from which information can be entered into the arithmetic unit (the teletype, the paper tape and the memory in this case). When the control unit requires that information be transferred from the memory to the arithmetic unit it also supplies the desired address to the memory unit itself. It should be realised, of course, that even though only two functions have been named for the arithmetic unit and very few instructions have been mentioned in this simple example, a conventional computer can have a vast repertoire of instructions and operations in its arithmetic unit. For example, the arithmetic unit could add, subtract, shift its digits to the left or the right, and in some cases, even multiply and divide.

A large computer system does not only have a memory situated inside itself, as described above, but it has also other data banks known as *peripheral* memories. These consist either of long magnetic recording tapes similar to those used in common tape recorders, or magnetic discs which are not too dissimilar from gramophone records, except for the fact that they are magnetic rather than mechanical in action. Program words can be used which (via the control unit) can request information from any of these data banks and thus, place at the disposal of the computer, vast amounts of data. Whereas I have said that the memory inside the computer can, at most, have 500,000 or so words, the peripheral stores can store many millions of words. It is here that the great power of the conventional computer lies. The vast amounts of stored data can be manipulated in the arithmetic and control units at very great speeds. For example, a typical cycle of operation in these two units last only 30 millionths of a second. However, it is here too, that the stupidity of a conventional computer lies. It is only capable of manipulating vast amount of data and performing simple operations on it. It relies entirely on a very carefully selected, designed and chosen program to be resident in its memory before any operation can take place. In summary, it is my belief that the conventional computer is a total "flop" as an intelligent automaton, but its powers as a stupid machine are very great indeed, and it is precisely the latter property which has caused it to be one of mankind's great machines, at a par with the steam engine and the aeroplane.

3

MACHINE INTELLIGENCE

The term machine intelligence is very popular amongst computer scientists at present. The object of this exercise is to make a computer behave as much as possible as a human being. My purpose is not to describe how this is done, but to point out that whenever it is said that a computer is behaving intelligently there has been no fundamental change in the stupidity of the machine itself, but that it is a programmer who has behaved intelligently. Much of the philosophy of machine intelligence enthusiasts stems from the work of Turing, a British mathematician who stated that a machine is intelligent if, on working with it, it is difficult to discover whether one is working with a machine or a human being.

I personally support a diametrically opposite view and suggest that the Turing test has nothing to do with the degree of intelligence of a machine and that machines can be found which are inherently more or less intelligent depending on their makeup. On being tested they may or may not fail the Turing test, but this, I believe, is not an indication of their potential intelligence. To my mind, the Turing test is a bit like saying that a horse is a mammal which has four legs and moves along the ground. Therefore, any other object which has four legs and moves along the ground, is very much like a horse. Anyone who has tried to ride a mouse will know that it is not true.

Let us look at some of the so called machine intelligence applications of computers that are in existence at present. There are two areas in which intensive work is being carried out, the first of these is pattern recognition and the second is that of game playing and problem solving. Both these areas are topics in which man reigns supreme as an intelligent automaton. Pattern recognition is an activity which enters almost every walk of human life. When we are reading a book, we are recognising patterns, that is, the characters of the printed text. When we listen to someone speaking we are recognising speech patterns. When we drive a car we recognise patterns in the shape of the road and we take appropriate action. One could say that our entire ability to survive depends on our recognition of patterns. If we fail to tell the difference between mushrooms and toadstools this would be a fault of our pattern recognition abilities which could be fatal. If we were not able to recognise the characteristic patterns of specimens of the opposite sex, the entire procreative system of mankind might fail and lead to an extinction of the human race. The answer to the question of whether computers can recognise patterns is, "Yes, but with great difficulty". One of the great distinctions between automata and computers is that humans seem to learn to recognise patterns as one of their inherent natural properties, whereas, for a computer to learn to recognise patterns, is a most difficult and arduous task, as we will see.

Consider the patterns that can appear on the simplest form of an electronic eye; one that consists of a 100 photocells arranged as a 10x10 matrix. We assume that each pattern falling on this matrix causes the photocell to transmit or not transmit a pulse onto one of a 100 wires. This therefore, is a *binary* matrix. The total number of patterns that can occur on such a matrix is 2^{100} which is approximately equal to 10^{30}. Now, this is a very large number particularly if one realises that the total population of the world is not in excess of 10^9. If we had a Universe of as many worlds as there are people on this world and then took account of the entire population of this little Universe, there would still be a total of only 10^{18}. Therefore, the most obvious way of recognising patterns on this matrix that is, to store all the possible patterns with appropriate class labels for each, would be quite impossible, because we would have to store 10^{30} patterns. This would exceed by many orders the entire storage capacity of all the computers available in the world now and also those that are likely to be available in the next million years. Computer scientists have devised many ways of getting around this problem with varying degrees of success. I shall mention one or two of these techniques.

Let us say that photographs of written numbers could be projected onto our 100 photocell matrix and let us imagine that the computer were required to classify these numbers into their correct categories, that is, it should tell us whether a projected number is a 1, a 2, a 3, etc. A common and fundamental starting point for this type of recognition is for the programmer to store, in the memory of the computer, a few prototypes or average patterns of each class. When an unknown pattern is presented to the machine, the computer can compare it with these stored prototypes and calculate a measure of similarity between each of the stored prototypes and the unknown pattern. A simple and notoriously unsuccessful way of measuring this similarity is merely to count the number of points on the matrix in which the unknown and the stored patterns differ. The unknown pattern is then classified in the same way as the prototype with which it has the lowest count. Many computerised methods depend on similar, but perhaps more sophisticated methods of measuring this difference. Clearly, such methods require a number of prototypes to be stored which is very much less than the number of 10^{30} mentioned earlier. The failure of this method lies in the fact that it classifies as similar patterns that ought to be distinct. For example, in the recognition of hand-printed numerals an O and a Q might differ very little according to most measures causing confusion.

Methods similar to the above are called *adaptive* or rely on *learning* programs. When one says that a computer is being *taught* to recognise patterns, what one means is that the stored information regarding the prototype of a class is continuously modified as examples of such patterns are presented to the machine. However, even in the above two methods the amount of storage available in most computers for storing these average or prototype patterns, is highly restricted and leads to poor results.

Some scientists have sought a totally different approach to the recognition of patterns. They have tried to extract, from a set of patterns such as handwritten numerals, the essential features. For example, the essential features of a figure 8 are that it consists of two more or less circular shapes joined together one underneath the other. Or, a figure 7 may be described as two roughly straight lines, one horizontal and the other slightly oblique from the vertical, joined together in the top righthand corner. Elaborate computer programs have to be written in order to detect the presence of such features and it is on this detection that the eventual recognition is based.

At the department of machine intelligence and perception at the University of Edinburgh a computer has been successfully programmed to recognise simple shapes in its field of view again, by extracting the essential features of such shapes. For example, the shapes used are cups, pencils and eye-glasses each of which can be described in terms of their essential features in very simple ways. However, it is interesting to note that vast computing facilities and some rather erudite programs were needed to persuade the computer to accomplish this comparatively simple task.

The question bothering scientists who have managed to accomplish pattern recognition tasks with computers is whether or not the work throws any light at all on what is meant by "intelligence". Clearly, when human beings recognise patterns, this is thought of as being an intelligent task. Is it true therefore, that when a computer performs this task, by no matter what means, it is also being intelligent ? First, one must realise that no computer program is yet available which recognises patterns with the flexibility and adaptability of a human being. A human being who could only barely recognise the difference between cups and eyeglasses could not be considered as being very intelligent. There also appears to be little hope for saying that future technological advances in computers and increase in the ability of programmers and the speed of computers, is going to make much difference to this situation. The needed computing power increases tremendously as one tries to make the recognition a little more sophisticated and a little more human in nature. Second, one finds objection in the argument that if two systems perform similar tasks that the behaviour of the one system throws much light on the other. These are the same objections as one finds to the Turing test mentioned earlier in this Chapter. It is difficult to imagine that a human being has stored in his brain standard prototypes of patterns and that he calls upon some arithmetic unit, which performs the calculations necessary to compare the unknown incoming patterns with his stored prototypes. It is also difficult to imagine that a human brain will develop separate areas or activities which will be sensitive to well defined features of the patterns that it sees and that other parts of the brain will be able to collate these features and do a statistical analysis of whether a particular occurring set of features does, or does not, imply the presence of an object. Therefore, as far as the conventional computer is concerned, it appears that machine intelligence and human intelligence are two very different things.

I have said very little, so far, about the other area of machine intelligence : game playing and problem solving. In many ways, the concept of playing a game (say, chess) is also a pattern recognition activity. Patterns of piece positions on the board are recognised and translated into moves by the players. The solving of logical problems can also usually be reduced to the recognition of patterns where elements of a sequence of logical operations are recognised before an entire solution is pieced together. Needless to say, machine intelligence scientists have been applying techniques very similar to those used in pattern recognition in the area of game playing and problem solving. Therefore, to go over these techniques would merely be a repetition of what has been said and the final objections would still be the same : that the digital computer solves problems and plays games largely as a result of the existence of intelligent programmers whereas the human has a system which has built-in abilities that enable it to become "intelligent", by exposure to a seemingly ordered world.

I would now like to consider whether stepping away from the digital computer, automata have been devised which are endowed with abilities similar to those of a human being, in the sense that

26

they will inherently recognise patterns and try and piece together their experience from exposure to an environment.

There is a totally different school of thought in the field of machine intelligence which believes that one ought to study automata which have some inherent property that enables them to recognise patterns and to make "sense" of the environment to which they are exposed. Much work in this field is dominated by the early thoughts of McCulloch and Pitts who proposed that one could make an electronic model of a brain cell. Although significant in 1943, this work is not as important a step forward as that made by Caianiello in the 1960's who showed that for a network of electronic elements (somewhat resembling the nerve cells or neurons of the brain) one discovers inherent activities which seem to possess some of the intelligent properties that we are looking for. Indeed, it has been possible to discover this type of activity in very simple networks whose elements are not at all models of nerve cells and which I shall describe below. One most interesting feature about Caianiello's networks and indeed, the networks which I shall describe, is that the operation does not depend very heavily on the way in which the elements are connected. In fact, a great deal of work has been done with networks whose elements are connected totally at random.

Imagine an electronic box with two wires entering it (the inputs) and one wire coming from it (the output). Assume that these wires are binary, that is, they are activated by the presence (1) or absence (0) of electric current. Clearly, such a device is an elementary automaton. We assume that the automaton can be in one of 16 possible internal states.

Each of these states completely determines the relationship between the input and output of the element. To explain this, consider the table below.

Inputs	Output P																State No
x y	0	1	2	3	4	5	6	7	8	9	10	11	12	13	14	15	
0 0	0	0	0	0	0	0	0	0	1	1	1	1	1	1	1	1	
0 1	0	0	0	0	1	1	1	1	0	0	0	0	1	1	1	1	
1 0	0	0	1	1	0	0	1	1	0	0	1	1	0	0	1	1	
1 1	0	1	0	1	0	1	0	1	0	1	0	1	0	1	0	1	

In the above table the inputs to the element are labelled x and y. We see that there are 4 possible combinations of input activity at these inputs. We can express the relationship between the input and the output of this element by means of one of the output

27

columns, labelled p, which indeed, states specifically the output activity for any input combination. Since the entries in the p column are binary, that is, they are composed of 0's and 1's, and there are only four possible positions in which the entry can be made, it is possible to calculate that 0's and 1's can be entered in this column only in 16 (i.e. 2^4) ways. These are all shown in the table.

It is required that our little automaton should be able, in any one instance, to perform in any one of these 16 possible ways, it's specific behaviour being determined by its internal state. Since the device can have 16 possible internal states, it must have four bits of storage at least. Indeeed, in most practical cases, the contents of these four bits is identical to the entries in the p column of our truth table. It is not proposed here to go into the details of how the contents of the store interact with the input in order to produce the output, however, an interested reader can find out more about this elsewhere [1]. The way in which the little element (which incidentally is either called a RAM, Random Access Memory, or a SLAM, Stored Logic Adaptive Module) enters a particular internal state, is quite simple. The element has an additional input which we will call the "teach" input and this operates as follows. During a "teaching" time whenever an input is present on the x and y terminals the output will assume whatever value is "taught" to respond for a particular pattern at its inputs. What is actually happening inside it, is that the relevant storage element in the truth table is set or reset.

An interesting recent discovery has resulted from Stuart Kauffman's [2] simulation of large networks of the contents of above element. The elements were interconnected in a "higgledy-piggledy" manner and their storage content was set totally at random. If we consider this sort of network as an automaton and assume that the internal states of the elements are fixed, that is, they are no longer contributing to the variability of the internal state the new automaton, we see that this larger automaton has its own internal states due to the following reasons.

We have said that the network consists of many RAMs connected to each other at random. This means that the output of every element feeds on average the inputs of two other elements. If the system is started with some arbitrary set of 0 and 1 inputs and we assume that its outputs are generated at the arrival of a timing signal, (that is, once again time is assumed to be quantised as in Chapter 1), then the set of inputs will create a specific set of outputs. This set of outputs clearly becomes a new set of inputs for the system which at the arrival of the next timing signal will produce a new set of outputs. This *feedback* system therefore, will cause the network to go into a series of changes of output entirely autonomously without the intervention of an outside cause. It is, therefore, the total pattern at the output of the system which is indeed the internal state of the system itself at any one instant.

Kauffman's experiments showed that large networks of these elements would enter cycles of state changes that is, you would observe state changes in which, eventually, a state would repeat itself. These cycles were observed to be very short and even very large networks contained very few such cycles. It is interesting that Kauffman used this as a model of a biological cell where each of the elements was a model of a gene. The existence of very few and short state cycles indicates that this rather random and hazardous circuit is behaving in a stable and somewhat predictable manner, whereas as a first guess, one would think that the system would behave in a totally unpredictable and unstable way. That is, one would imagine that the system would enter long endless series of state changes. It is in this sort of stability that one sees the first signs of an internal inherent "*intelligence*" of a very random and hazardous electronic network.

In some of our own experiments [3] we have also discovered that these networks are capable of learning to enter into useful state cycles if the teach terminals are made active during certain periods and that this learning enables the network to recognise patterns and act with a certain degree of intelligence. It is not my purpose to go into details of these experiments, the interested reader can again find these details in published material. At this point I would merely like to stress that in addition to the conventional computer, in the future one is likely to find automata which do have inherent intelligence modes of activity. I shall certainly not ignore the existence of such automata in the rest of this book.

4

STATE STRUCTURES

Much of the rest of this book will be concerned with the use of *state structures*. I find it useful therefore, to devote a Chapter to the subject not only to introduce and explain the concept but also because they provide an element of aesthetic satisfaction.

We return to our clockwork mouse, but this time assume that it only has internal states:

Wound (W)
Unwound (U)
Half wound (H).

The inputs and outputs remain as before, and we are able to draw a diagram of the entire activity of the mouse (Fig. 4.1). The circles show the internal states. The arrows are called transitions, that is, changes from state to state. As we saw in an earlier Chapter, the transitions are caused by combinations of input conditions, and these are shown in the rectangular labels. Also, as seen previously, the output depends on the state and the input, that is, the same parameters on which depends the state transition. Thus, the output may also be associated with a state transition and this is shown in the triangular labels.

Inputs: 1. latch ON   key pressure OFF
         2. latch ON   key pressure ON
         3. latch OFF   key pressure OFF
         4. latch OFF   key pressure ON

Outputs: M indicates Movement

Fig. 4.1. State diagram for a clockwork mouse.

Let us now look at the state structures that can be obtained with simple memory cells (RAMs or SLAMs) as described in Chapter 3. A connection of three such elements is shown in Figure 4.2. Here the output of every element is connected to the input of the other two. This automaton has no inputs, only eight internal states, that is, the eight possible combinations of binary outputs of the system. We shall assume that for any one state diagram the internal states of the elements themselves do not change.

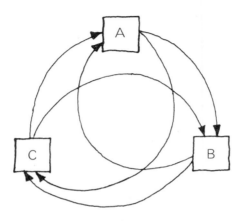

Fig. 4.2. A three RAM network.

First assume that each element has such an internal state that the element outputs a 1 only if both its inputs are 1. Again we assume that state changes can take place only at discrete intervals of time. The resulting state structure is shown in Figure 4.3. This diagram shows a number of important things. First, there are only two "final" states in which the system will be found two or more time steps after being started in any arbitrary state : 000 and 111.

Second, if the probability of starting in any state is the same (viz. 1/8), one has a 7/8 chance of finding the system in state 000 and a 1/8 chance of finding it in 111 after two or more timing steps. Besides giving the above information about the system we also see a certain pleasing design in the state structure.

Assume now that the elements in Figure 4.2 have totally different functions; that is, they have different internal states. Their functions are as follows :

A becomes 1 whenever B is 1;
B becomes 1 whenever C is 1;
C becomes 1 whenever A and B have the same value
(A = 0 & B = 0, or A = 1 & B = 1).

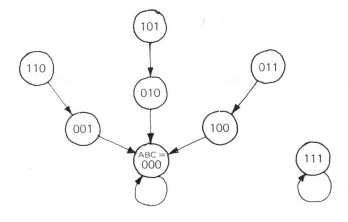

Fig. 4.3. State diagram for case where the output is 1 and both inputs are 1.

The resulting structure is shown in Figure 4.4. We see that here we have a totally different situation. The state of the system at any time is quite unpredictable and has a probability of 1/8 of being in any one of its values. In some arguments it might be said that due to this lack of predictability the state structure of Figure 4.3 is more *stable* than that of Figure 4.4. What we *have* established is that the *state* structure of an automaton with a given *physical* structure can vary greatly depending on the function of its elements. This is important since there is possibly a false idea implicit in many sciences and that is to endow unique properties to unique physical structures. Indeed, one has sought to explain the behaviour of some natural information processing systems such as the

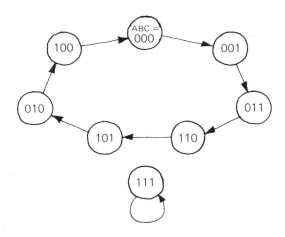

Fig. 4.4. State diagram for new RAM functions.

brain solely in terms of the physical connections of brain cells. "Behaviour" in this context does refer to the state structure of the system and even from what has been said so far it can be seen that a knowledge of physical structure does not suffice to explain this "behaviour".

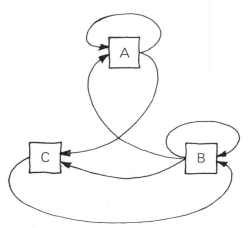

Fig. 4.5. Altered RAM connection.

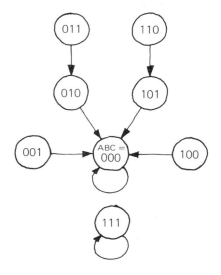

Fig. 4.6. State structure for Figure 4.5.

I will press the point further. Consider the physical structure in Figure 4.5. Even though this is considerably different to Figure 4.2 it can produce the state diagram in Figure 4.4 if the elements have the same functions as before for that state diagram. However, if we now let all the elements have the function that

34

their output becomes 1 only if both inputs are 1, (as was the case for Figure 4.3), then the state structure of Figure 4.6 is obtained. We see that this is somewhat different from the structure in Figure 4.3. The reader will notice however that the two have a comparable stability. This is not as important as the main point that is being made here and that is that the state structure is a function of *both* the physical structure *and* the function of the elements. To study the one without the other cannot lead to an understanding.

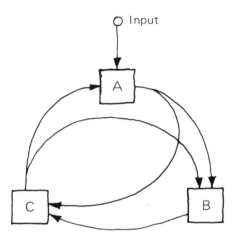

Fig. 4.7. Network with external input.

Let us now see the way in which such an automaton can interact with an environment. First, consider the effect of inputs. In Figure 4.7 an automaton similar to the one of Figure 4.2 is shown. The difference here is that A receives one of its inputs externally, rather than internally, from B as in Figure 4.2. Assume that the function of the elements is the same as in Figure 4.3. There are now two possible exits from each state, one for each binary value of the input. This is shown in Figure 4.8 a.

This is rather complex diagram which may be better understood if decomposed in the following way. The structure may be divided into two, one for an input of 0 as in Figure 4.8 b and the other for an input of 1 as in Figure 4.8 c. In a way these two structures can be thought of as "reactions" of the internal state changes to the particular inputs. In true fact, however, manipulations of the input will *always* lead this automaton to the 000 state (except from 111) where it will remain, indifferent to further input changes. Despite this characteristic, the reader may feel that he now understands the relationship between input and state structure.

Consider now the case where an automaton has an input as

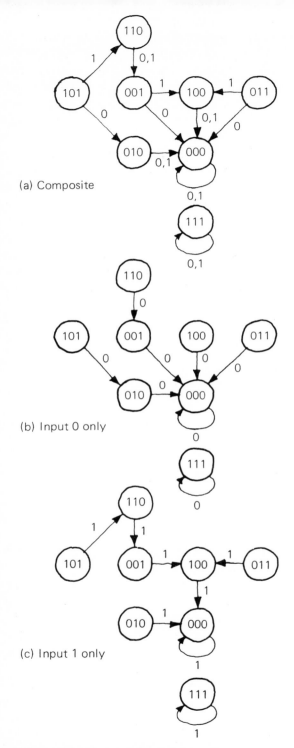

Fig. 4.8. Effect of input on state structure;

36

well as an output. For example, imagine that the automaton of Figure 4.7 has a binary output (z) issuing from element B. Such an automaton is now fully capable of interacting with what we may call its "environment" as shown in Figure 4.9. Clearly, the combination of automaton and environment creates another *autonomous* (inputless and outputless) automaton. The nature of this new automaton may be somewhat complex, depending on the degree of perversity of the environment (which in itself, may be considered to be an automaton). For example, the environment automaton may be probabilistic in the sense that one might only assign a probability with which i is a function of z. For example, the environment may have a 40% probability of making i 1 when z is 0 and 60% when z is 1. To conclude the consideration of this concept, assume an environment automaton in which i is made 1 when z is 0 and i is made 0 when z is 1. Then assuming that the state structure of the automaton is still that of figure 4.8a the structure of the automaton plus environment may be derived* as shown in Figure 4.10.

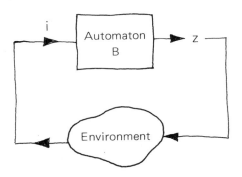

Fig. 4.9. The automaton in an environment.

Finally, it may be interesting to consider another way in which an automaton may interact with the environment. So far we have assumed that the elements of the automaton have unchanging functions. However, we shall now consider what happens if the environment can, in some way, change the element functions, that is, the environment will be responsible for changing the state structure of the automaton. We shall see that here the automaton may be said to be "learning" from the environment.

Consider the network in Figure 4.11. Here the "teach" terminals (T) (discussed in the last Chapter) come into play. The inputs

*To do this it is assumed that the internal states (A, B, C) can only change at discrete time intervals as before and that the reaction of the environment is instantaneous.

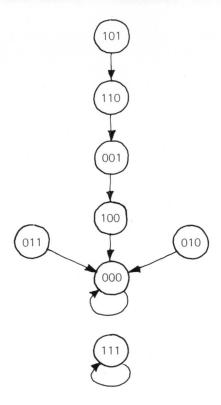

Fig. 4.10. State structure for Figure 4.9.

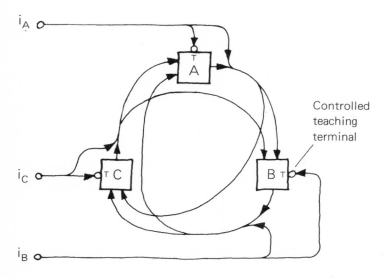

Fig. 4.11. A learning automaton.

38

i_A i_B i_C are there to *force* the automaton into a particular state and also to input information to the T terminals. The clocking arrangements which enable the internal states of the elements to change are not shown, but will be assumed to exist in our discussions. Assume first that the elements are all reset. This would bring about a state diagram in which all states (including 000) enter 000. Assume now that the pattern 0, 0, 1, is applied to i_A, i_B and i_C respectively, and that the same information at the T terminals is made to enter the elements. We stipulate that an input assumes a value of 1 if one or more of the lines leading to it have the value of 1 (for example, logically the top input of A is 1 if the output of C is 1 *or* i_C is 1).

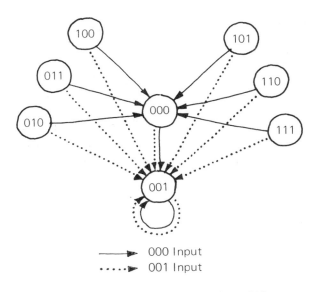

Fig. 4.12. State diagram after training on ABC = 001;

Thus, after the application of the teaching information we see that the system enters state 001. We note also that through this action one has ensured that the state 001 leads into itself. Indeed, the entire state structure is as shown in Figure 4.12, where it is interesting to note that 001 has become the final stable state of the system. Now assume that the system is additionally exposed (by energising the T terminals) to the pattern 110. The resulting state structure is shown in Figure 4.13. Here we see that a second stable state corresponding to the second exposure is created.

Some interesting properties of this state structure arising from the exposure to the environment can be stressed (now it is assumed that the T terminals are de-energised and do not enter the argument).

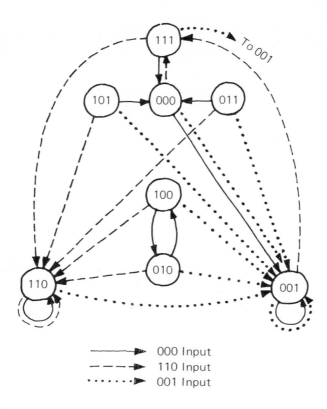

———————▶	000 Input
— — — ▶	110 Input
·······▶	001 Input

Fig. 4.13. State diagram after training on 001 and 110.

    1. If pattern 001 or 110 is applied to the input (while the automaton is in 000) the network will enter the corresponding internal state. This may be termed the automaton's "perception" of the input pattern.

    2. If the input pattern is then removed (i.e. the input is reduced to 000), the automaton will remain in the relevant stable state. This is the automaton's ability to *remember* a pattern.

    3. If input 110 is applied while the system is in state 001, the immediate result is that the automaton will enter state 111 and then 110. Then on reduction of the input to 000 the system will remain in 110. That is, the automaton's attention has been switched from remembering state 001 to remembering state 110, merely by "showing" it an input 110.

    4. The reverse process also applies. If the input is 000 and the system stable in 110, an application of 001 will cause an entry into 001. Since the automaton did not possess these properties before "exposure" to the two patterns, it may be said that they have been *learnt*.

Let us summarize what has been discussed in this Chapter. The concept of a state structure, in terms of a diagram drawn on a piece of paper, has been introduced. This was applied to a clockwork mouse, but it is my opinion that the exercise was not particularly fruitful. The reason for this is that a purely mechanical description of a clockwork mouse is sufficient to give us an "understanding" of the mouse. However, in the case of the 3-element network, the informational behaviour of the system is much more mysterious and the description in terms of the state structure leads to an explanation of the system's behaviour. It has also been possible to deduce some quite complex interactions between the system and an environment even going as far as providing a crude description of terms such as learning, perceiving, remembering and switching attention. These are usually part of the language of experimental psychology.

It is possible that had we not the concept of state structure at our disposal we would have been tempted to enter into discussions about whether our undeserving automaton, had a "mind" or was possibly "conscious".

5

MINDS
AND
AUTOMATA

The concept of *mind* has puzzled philosophers, psychologists, neurologists and mathematicians in some cases for over 2,000 years. In this Chapter, I would like to advance the idea that the concept of mind may be explained more simply than expected and that it is, in fact, closely related to what we have called *state structure*. This statement in itself may immediately raise some difficulties particularly as we have said that the state structures are associated with all automata and therefore, if one defines *mind* just as a state structure it means that even clockwork mice have minds. This would run counter to many arguments in which a definition of mind must be such as to distinguish not only between lower forms of life and humans, but certainly between rather simple mechanical toys and living things. It will be reasoned later that this is a matter of degree and therefore, the impatient reader is asked not to dismiss the idea at this stage, but to bear with the argument in order to see how some of these difficulties may be resolved.

I propose here to extract some salient characteristics of the way in which philosophers have come to grips with the concept of mind.*

The main stumbling blocks have been :

a) What "substance" constitutes *mind* ?

b) How is this substance, whatever it might be,
    related to the body ?

On the first of these points, Greek philosophers believed *mind* to be an *invisible* substance which certainly resides in the body during life but exits or stays (according to differing beliefs) with the body after death. It was not thought that this substance was different from other matter on Earth except for our inability to perceive it in individuals other than ourselves.

With Descartes (in circa 1641) the substance of mind became a little less clearly defined as an "animal spirit". It was distinguished

---

*The reader can obtain a full picture of this question by reading "*Body and Mind*", selected readings edited by G.N.A. Vesey, Unwin Books, 1964.

by having an existence of its own which was largely unrelated to the existence of the body. The two could impinge on each other in the same way as two communicating human beings without losing their autonomy or independence. In a curious way, Descartes decided that the mind (which is not distinguished from the soul) resides in a tiny "pineal gland" in the centre of the brain and that its influence on the body is exerted by little movements which *cause* the brain to act and transmit these movements to the nerve and hence, the limb. Also, perceptions of the body and the brain are transmitted to the mind by means of vibrations on the periphery of the pineal gland.

Spinoza (c.a. 1677) and Leibnitz (c.a. 1685) set a contrast to Descartes' division between body and mind by arguing that the two are aspects of the same substance (Spinoza), or part of a vast master plan by being facets of a whole harmonious set of substances which constitute the universe (Leibnitz). Both these philosophies are heavily couched in a belief in God and rely on this belief in order to remain credible.

More recently, the mind-body question seems to have evolved into an argument regarding "which - causes - which ?".

Bertrand Russell (1921) and A.J. Ayer (1950) argue that "private" (mind) and "public" (body) happenings are merely correlated (in the sense that elements of the one are observed to occur together with elements of the other) and that in such a situation the word "cause" loses its meaning. In this and the next Chapter it will be seen that it is indeed difficult to talk of "causes" relating the physical to the state structures of an automaton, but that it is also insufficient to dismiss the connection as a vague correlation. The two are intimately related to one another in a way that can be expressed mathematically.

A different emphasis is found in the philosophy of Gilbert Ryle (1949) who criticises most approaches to the Mind-Body problem for making the assumption that one *can* talk of any relationship between the two at all. He claims that such an assumption is a "category mistake" of the same nature as induced by the old joke :

"He came home in a taxi and a flood of tears"

To search for a relationship between a taxi and a flood of tears is the "category mistake" since *taxi* and *flood of tears* are just not the same sort of thing and they cannot be compared just as (in Ryles's view) "mind" and "body" cannot be compared.

It would be wrong for me to create the impression that no philosopher has tried to identify mental states with brain processes. Indeed, there exists a recent theory in philosophy known as the Identity theory which is rather succinctly discussed by Jerome

44

Shaffer (1961). This work claims that mental states *are* brain processes, but gets heavily bogged down in discussions regarding the precise location of states in the brain. In the previous chapter it has been seen that it is nonsense to try to locate a *state* in the physical structure of an automaton, since *state* is a description of events throughout the entire machine.

Of course, philosophers are not the only ones who have tried to explain the function of the brain and to provide a logical basis from which one could understand the meaning of the word "mind". Psychology is a relatively recent science and is based on providing an explanation of the internal mental processes of human beings by observing their external behaviour. Sigmund Freud stands out among the innovators in psychology for having distinguished between types of internal activity : consciousness and sub-consciousness. Physiologists and anatomists on the other hand, have looked at the physical structure of the brain in order to unravel some of the mysteries of its working. The most notable achievement in this type of work has been the discovery that different parts of the brain cope with different mental problems. For example, some parts of the brain are devoted to processing nerve impulses which come from and go to specific parts of the body. One area may be dealing with a hand, another one with a foot and so on. Beyond that, it is hardly surprising that such studies have not thrown light on the more sophisticated aspects of mental behaviour. I say that it is "hardly surprising" merely because if mental behaviour may be described in terms of state structures, we have seen, albeit in an elementary fashion, that such structures need not be closely related to the physical connections of the elements of an automaton.

The most recent contributors to theories on the function of the brain and the nature of the mind have been physicists, mathematicians and electrical engineers. I have previously referred to the work of Caianiello, but it may be worth mentioning again that his theory of the laws of thought is based largely on the state structure of brain-like machines. Also, the work of Zeeman [4] is based on describing "a thought" as a cyclic trajectory in some space of states of the brain. In the rest of this Chapter, I shall try to elaborate on this concept as simply as possible (and possibly as crudely, as a result) so as to relate to state structures those attributes of mental behaviour which we call the mind.

One can assert with confidence that the mammalian brain is an automaton with an implied state structure. A brain is composed of very many cells which, to the best of our knowledge, transmit information between one another by means of electrical impulses. It is not far from the truth if one states that each cell of the brain is either firing or not firing at any one time. This has a neat correspondence with the type of memory-cell automaton discussed in the last Chapter. At any instant of time the pattern of firing and not firing of all the cells of the brain constitutes a *state*. This pattern changes from moment to moment and therefore the claim that the brain is an automaton with an attendant state structure is easily satisfied.

There are a few characteristics of state structures that can be seen even at this stage of the argument. The cells of the brain are known to be variable in terms of their own internal states in a manner very similar to that of the memory element in the last Chapter. This means that whatever the state structure of the brain-automaton is at birth it will certainly change during its lifetime. It is very likely that these changes occur through exposures to the environment (as was the case for our simple 3-element automaton in the last Chapter). Besides these long term changes which are caused by exposures to the environment, the immediate trajectories of the brain automaton among its states are continuously controlled and influenced by the inputs to the brain, that is, channels that are eventually connected to the sensory organs of the human body.

So far, I have only argued that the brain is an automaton with an attendant state structure. The question which still remains unanswered is : where in this system does one find *mind* ? Is *mind* something that has already been described or is it something which is totally extraneous to the state description given so far ? *Mind* is concerned with thinking and it would not take much to convince ourselves that thinking cannot be unrelated to the state structure of the brain. Broadly, while this merely re-states the views of Zeeman and Caianiello, one can elaborate on the logic of the argument as follows. The sources of behaviour can be traced to the input/output (or perception/motor-output activity) relations of the brain. *Thought* is that which in combination with perception determines the motor-output activity of the brain. In *any* automaton the output is determined by the input and the resulting trajectories among its states. Thus, state trajectories and cycles are, in fact, thoughts.

However, the total number of states of the brain is very great and the state structures extraordinarily complex, therefore it would be wrong to believe that we have trivialized human thought by associating it with simple state structures. Indeed, one should be aware that the mere statement that thoughts are state trajectories does in itself *not* provide a deep explanation of the nature of thought.

The argument may now be continued as follows. The brain is an automaton with a state structure; the nature of this state structure represents the total thinking ability of the brain; *mind* is an aspect of the thinking power of the brain, therefore, *mind* is an aspect of state structure. To be more specific, the main attributes of *mind* can be summarised as being composed of will, emotions, self-knowledge (that is, awareness and conciousness), sensation, imagination and intellect. Thus, even though we have introduced in this Chapter a tenuous link between mind and state structure, the topics just mentioned are numerous and important and will therefore, be tackled in greater detail in the next Chapter.

All that remains to be done here is to satisfy a seemingly dubious point made earlier : the fact that *mind* is often said to be that which differentiates between man and animal. If *mind* is an aspect of state structure and we have seen that state structure belongs not only to man but also to animals and indeed, clockwork mice, one must question whether there exists a difference between *mind-like* state structure and state structure which cannot be called mind.

It is most likely that this is merely a question of degree. The size and complexity of state structure increases rapidly with the number of cells of a mechanism. Therefore, the difference between a human state structure and that of say, an ape, may be quite enormous even though the human has only a slightly larger brain than the ape. However, it is this small difference which could be all-important. To illustrate this effect consider first an automaton with 10 binary cells which will have 2^{10} (that is about 1000) states in its state structure and one which is only 20% larger, that is, one with 12 cells, whose number of states is 2^{12} that is, roughly, 4,000 states. We see that this 20% increase in physical complexity leads to a four-fold increase in state complexity. Indeed, this argument supports the suggestion that *mind* is an aspect of state structure because it predicts that the animal with the most developed cell structure will have intellectual powers which greatly exceed those of its nearest, less developed rival. Man just happens to be the animal with this greater degree of development.

6

THE
HUMAN
MIND-AUTOMATON

In the last chapter a close relationship between "thinking" and trajectories in the state structure of the brain was introduced. The reader was warned that this concept in itself did not dramatically reveal the constitution of a substance called *mind*, but merely provided a language with which *mind* could be described in a way that does not offend our common sense. This is sadly not the case with the more traditional philosophies.

The aim of this chapter is to use this language in order to discuss certain attributes of *mind* more closely. The first three such characteristics are :

perception : the influence of the environment through the senses;

awareness : the ability to distinguish between several perceptual events on the one hand, and between several internal events on the other;

and, *attention* : the ability of the mind to be selective among several percepts or thoughts.

The latter leads directly to a discussion of *free will* by searching for the agent which determines the selection of percepts or thoughts.

Another aspect of free will is then tackled, and that is the influence of the mind on *bodily actions*. Finally, the sensitive question regarding the nature of emotions is considered briefly.

I shall treat the concepts of perception, awareness and attention together. In order to make my point of view clear I find that I have to proceed by making hypotheses about a mind-automaton and treating myself as an external observer. Introspection can be misleading : it leads to circular arguments such as, "what happens when I am thinking about thinking about thinking ?" These are amusing but hardly lead to clarity. I shall, therefore, avoid basing arguments on introspection as much as possible.

Perception unequivocally involves the senses : sight, hearing, touch, taste, etc. These, without a doubt, are inputs to our mind-automaton. We have seen that the effect of inputs on an automaton is to cause it to enter specific regions of its state structure. Indeed, *which* state structures are entered may be *learnt* through exposure of the cells of the automaton to an environment. This has been seen in simple automata in earlier parts of this book and there is no reason to believe that it does not occur in more complex systems. I submit that if two perceptual inputs cause the automaton to enter the same path of its state structure then this automaton will not be *aware* that the two perceptual events are different. The opposite of this is also easily seen to be true, that is if two inputs result in two state paths the automaton will distinguish between the inputs.

Above I have had to use the word *"aware"* when describing the automaton's ability to distinguish between inputs. Indeed, I would find it very difficult to describe this behaviour without the use of this word or another word which means almost the same thing.

Therefore, *awareness* in automata concerning external events, is related to the entry into specific paths of the state structure. However, the concept of awareness must be explained with respect to internal events as well. Consider a brain automaton with all its sensory inputs more or less cut off. For example, this could be a human who is completely relaxed and unmoving in a dark and quiet room. This automaton will not cease to journey through its state structure. That is, it will continue to perform trajectories among its states. Thus, the internal activity of the automaton is no different in kind to that which it was during the perception of external events. Instead of being in a part of state structure controlled by external events, the automaton now explores parts of state structures which are related only to its past experience. Clearly it can be *aware* of as many different internal "ideas" as there are paths in the state structure. No two ideas can result from the same path. Therefore, internal awareness is again related to journeys through differing paths in the state structure.

As defined earlier, attention is the action of selecting between two percepts or thoughts. A typical example of the first is the ability of a person to select which of several conversations he wishes to follow in a crowded room where there are several speakers within earshot. Similarly, it is quite possible to switch one's meditations from one line of thought to another. This is evident in a person who "changes the subject" while one assumes he is quite at liberty not to do so.

Both these phenomena relate easily to our path-through-state-structure description of "thought" if we make the assumption that instead of the brain being just one, haphazardly connected set of cells (which we know it definitely is not) but at least two fairly distinct automata in which the one has some influence on the other. (It is likely that the brain is made up of a very large number of such independent areas, but two suffice to establish the present argument). We call one the P-automaton and assume that this has a structure which, through experience, contains the various paths from which one can be selected. The other is the C- automaton which is responsible for the *switching*. It is easily seen that in order to perform such switching the C-automaton has merely to be connected to the P-automaton providing inputs to the latter which can *change* the path in P as was done in the very simple automata in Chapter 4.

What determines *how* the selection is made in C leads to a discussion of *will*. To an automata theorist the concept of free will is not as mysterious as it might appear to a philosopher. To pinpoint an instance during which one might exercise free will, we can use the example of a mental journey. What happens if one *thinks* of following a road which comes to a fork ? Will may be exercised in deciding whether one shall *think* of continuing to the left or to the right. There is a general feeling that the choice can be *freely* made. One also *feels* free to think of continuing one way first and then the other, or even of making a completely arbitrary choice.

Referring to the P- and C-automaton defined above and taking the standpoint of an external investigator, the matter can easily be explained. The thoughts regarding the mental journey can be defined as state-structure paths in the P-automaton. Arriving at a fork requires a decision, that is, an input from the C-automaton. The C-automaton must be "aware" of the need for such decisions and must therefore *receive* inputs from P as well as having outputs to it as seen earlier.

The C-automaton can then act in several ways. It either has an aim, for example, it might try to ensure that the P-automaton eventually arrives at a destination or even its aim may be to explore both routes. It could also "know" the choice is arbitrary, in which case, it would let the P-automaton continue along either path without exercising control. In summary, we have defined three exemplary actions for the C-automaton :

    a) a desired end point,
    b) the exploration of both routes,
    c) an arbitrary choice.

I submit that these are internal state paths in the C-automaton, which in essence, are no different to the paths in the P-automaton. They (i) can be learnt and (ii) can be controlled by an external event.

There is no difficulty about (i), controlling actions can be learnt given that the C-automaton has an adaptable state structure. As far as (ii) is concerned, which of the three actions is performed *must* in the long run be related to the thinker's environment. In writing these pages, my mind-automaton has been forced to take several mental journeys of the kind described simply because I am writing this book. The fact that I am writing this book is a result of several years of education i.e., interaction with my environment.

Clearly, the matter of will has been oversimplified here, and has been related to the interaction of an individual with his environment, which poses far greater difficulties than the concept of will alone. The simple point that needs stressing is that, to an external observer, "will" in an individual merely appears as the effect of the state activity of one part of the mind-automaton on another, the former being on a higher level in a *controlling hierarchy*. As must be stressed again, the human brain probably possesses several such levels which are likely to be somewhat indistinct from one another giving a hierarchical connection of automata in which the higher controls the lower, but the action of each may be learnt from the environment and is controlled by the environment.

Will is also clearly involved in the control of some bodily actions and, indeed, is at the crux of the interaction between mind and body. I can think of picking up a pencil and then decide whether to do so or not. This involves the only concept that has not explicitly entered the arguments of this chapter that is, the notion of *output*. All bodily (i.e., muscular) actions are outputs of our mind-automaton. They are due to nerve impulses which originate in specific parts of the brain (the motor sections) and which, after transmission through long nerve cell endings (axons) to muscles, cause the muscles to contract and move the appropriate limb.

The function of *will* is to connect the thought of a limb movement to the actual initiation of pulses from the brain to the desired output. This again may be explained in terms of an interaction between a P- and a C-automaton. The *thought* of movement lies in the state paths of a P-automaton (which in this case has outputs connected to the motor section of the brain), while the decision of whether to move or not to move the limb is a path in a C-automaton. With this arrangement, appropriate states in C could cause transmission of information to P which releases the necessary impulses in P's output towards the parts of the body that have to be moved.

Finally, a brief word about those elusive properties of mind : emotions. Basic emotions are branches of two fundamental streams : fear and pleasure. For example, hate and love leave us in no doubt as to from which of the above branches they stem. There are also other, less basic emotions, which generally go under the heading of feelings [5].

The latter, being less deep-rooted, are discussed first. *Feelings* are the things that people refer to as "tickles", "twinges", "thrills" or "shocks". The common factor among these is that they are unquestionably related to *inputs*. This is obvious in the case of a *tickle*, and becomes obvious in, say, the case of a *thrill* if one examines the way that the word is commonly used. "I am thrilled at the thought of seeing her" is a typical example. Given all that has been said about state structure, expressions of feelings may be reworded as follows.

"I am tickled at the thought" may be expressed as "when part of my automaton (P) performs the state trajectory related to this thought, it forces another part (F) into a similar trajectory to that experienced when I am tickled". This is a much longer expression of the sentiment but one which underlines the possible existence of an automaton part F one of whose state trajectories is related to being tickled (and which, in fact, can control a "laughter" output). Several internal and external events can access this trajectory causing the internal ones (thoughts) to be related to previous external ones (physical tickles). The *thrill* feeling presents no additional problems it merely means that the F part of the automaton has a trajectory related to the experience of externally thrilling events, these being also accessible to internal ones such as "the thought of seeing her".

It is interesting that the deeper emotions bring the *output* into closer focus. Taking only fear and pleasure (rather than their ramifications) one sees that they are related respectively to *retracting* and *forward-going* attitudes. One learns that fire burns and one must retract from it rapidly requiring the mobilization of physical energy. Thus, the sight of fire causes a part (P) of the mind-automaton to enter the trajectory which would normally lead to retreat. However, a C-automaton is at work in deciding whether to activate the limbs or not. If C decides that there is no need to run, the limbs are not activated. Nevertheless, this does not affect the alarm trajectory in which P finds itself and the name we have given to this trajectory is *fear. Pleasure* may be understood in similar terms stemming from basic forward-going attitudes such as those of a child on seeing it's parent. If I say "I am pleased to see you", it means that the P-automaton is in a trajectory that would produce a forward-going movement which may or may not be held in check by a C-automaton.

Summarising what has been said in this chapter, one sees that most seemingly mysterious functions attributed to *mind* can be expressed in terms of state trajectories which are controlled by an input and which themselves control an output. The most difficult functions such as *will* and *emotions* merely require the postulate of an interaction between at least two automata.

I must stress that structures such as P- and C-automata are used merely to illustrate that rather abstruse philosophical concepts *could* be explained in terms of simple machinery. Again it is emphasized that one does *not* imply that such machinery actually exists in the brain. The brain is complex and as yet, unchartered, the point being made here is that one need not evolve mystical concepts to provide a basis for its function.

7

DO
AUTOMATA
HAVE
DREAMS?

Why is the whole subject of dreams so fascinating? Part of the answer must surely lie in their immense unpredictability and contrast with real experience. A dreaming experience can be pleasant or unpleasant, horrifying or blissful and yet one which, on waking, leaves us largely unscathed. We dream of flying, swimming, crashing and drowning : all these being experiences which we might not have encountered in our normal daytime existence. We do not control and choose our dreams : they happen. This unpredictability and the added twist on experienced events are the major attributes which distinguish the activity of the brain during dreaming with that experienced during waking. It will be argued that the cause of the unpredictability is simple : during sleep the mind-automaton becomes freed from the fetters of what we shall call a *chain of perceptual control*.

This gives us a basis for "explaining" the nature of dreams. That is, one tries to answer the question : "What happens to mind-like automata once the input and certain control loops are *frozen* ?". We shall discuss the lack of correlation with experienced events after having paid some attention to the perceptual control concept.

Clearly it is not sufficient to say that, during sleep, all that happens is that one's sensory channels are "switched off". It must be more than this, otherwise there would be no distinction between sleep and sitting in a darkened room (see Chapter 6 : Awareness). In the latter case the subject is in control of his thoughts. He can continue to think of a topic of his choice, come to logical conclusions and solve problems which occupy his mind. This is not a characteristic of dreaming. The implication is a simple one and may be explained by means of a diagram (Fig. 7.1). *

At first sight this looks somewhat complicated, so we shall proceed cautiously. Our aim is to demonstrate that the automaton

---

*Here one again adopts the principle of taking a simplified automaton and showing that it *can* have the attribute under discussion : dreaming, in this case. However, the proposed automaton is not intended as a comprehensive model for human dreaming.

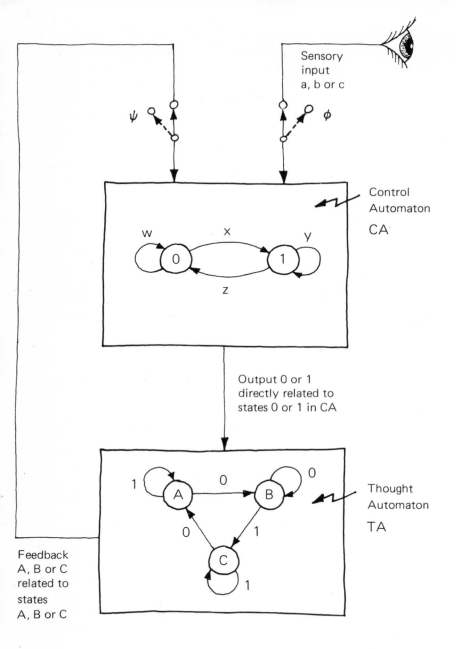

Fig. 7.1. Model for dreaming.

in Figure 7.1 has behaviour states which could be described as
"awake : senses *off*" and "dreaming". The two-automata structure
is not new, and was introduced in the last chapter under discussions
relating to free will. The "thought automaton" (*TA*) can reside in

56

three states : A, B, C. These have a correspondence to three possible sensory inputs : a, b and c respectively. In the way in which "perception" was previously defined, the "thought automaton" enters state A when a is present at the sensory input b for B, and c for C. The task of the "Control Automaton" is to ensure that this should happen. Ignoring, for the moment, the rôle of switches ϕ and ψ let us look at the way in which the "Control Automaton" might do this. (At this stage the reader may be wondering why there is a need for a control automaton at all, and why the "thought automaton" is not driven directly from the input. Suffice it to say that its presence is necessitated by the arguments put forward for "free will" as mentioned earlier).

The "control automaton" (CA) receives two inputs, one from the sensory channel (carrying one of the three messages a, b, or c) and the other from the "thought automaton" (carrying messages A, B, or C).

During its "upbringing" (see : the concept of "teaching" in Chapter 4), in order to achieve the desired perceptual tasks it must have learnt the following rôles for the state changes w, x, y and z :

For an input a, the automaton CA must enter :

State 1 if automaton TA is in state A,
State 0 if automaton TA is in state C, and
State 1 if automaton TA is in state B.

The last of the above is needed so as not to trap TA in state B. These allow us to start labelling w, x, y and z a little more precisely :

w and z must happen for input combination aC
x and y must happen for input combination aA or aB.

Similarly we can continue the labelling for inputs b and c, and the reader may verify that the complete labelling is :

w and z occur for (aC), b or (cA)
x and y occur for (aA), (aB), (cB) or (cC).

That takes care of "perception".

Now for switch ϕ. Assume this "switches off" the sensory input, that is information is lost regarding the a, b or c input. The major effect of this is that one must assign new rôles to w, z, y and z. Appealing again to the idea of an upbringing period, we can arbitrarily insist that the automaton under these conditions has learnt to systematically scan through states A, B and C. This means that, starting in A, say, automaton TA would first require a 0 input to enter B, followed by a 1 input to move on to C and finally a 0 input will take the system back to A where we first came in. In other words, one expects automaton CA to control its coupling with *TA* in such a way as to produce a cyclic behaviour which (starting as above) maintains a steady sequence at the input of *TA* : 0 1 0 0 1 0 ..... It will now be shown that the connection (feedback loop) from *TA* to *CA* is essential in order to obtain this behaviour. It may be seen that if A causes transition x, B causes transition z and C causes transition w the following behaviour will take place.

State of *TA**	State of *CA*	"Next" State of *TA*	"Next" State of *CA*
A (→ x)	0	B	1
B (→ z)	1	C	0
C (→ w)	0	A	0
A	0 → back where we started.		

This is precisely what was needed. The purist might wish to work out for himself what would have to be done if switch ϕ were thrown at some instant not included in the above conditions, for example at an instant of time during which *TA* is at A and *CA* at 1.

The point which is being stressed here is that automaton *CA* *needs* knowledge regarding the state of *TA* in order to take the right transition. Now assume that in addition to ϕ, switch ψ is activated, removing this vital information. Again one tries to re-examine the rôle of w, x, y and z.

Now *CA* no longer finds it possible to have two exits from each state, simply since it no longer receives variations in input. Hence one of either w or x will vanish and one of z or y will vanish.** There are only three resulting possibilities for this auto-maton: it might "stick" in the 0 state, it might "stick" in the 1 state, or it may oscillate between the two. This has three corre-sponding effects on the *TA*. In the first case the *TA* will always enter and remain in state B; in the second case it can either settle in C or in A, depending on the time at which ψ is closed; while in the third case it will eventually stagger around the state structure as

A A B C A A B C A A... etc.

We now have all the components needed to complete the implied analogy. Our automaton in Figure 7.1 has, first, a highly

---

*The implied transition is shown in brackets under this heading.

**Precisely which of these events takes place is unimportant: it depends on the detailed functioning of *CA*.

controlled "waking" state with both ψ and ϕ switches passing information. When ϕ is opened one loses control from the perceptual channel and yet one can maintain a desired, learnt, controlled activity functioning within the system : this is the "eyes-closed-but-awake" situation. Finally with ψ interrupted, the thought automaton can enter one of several somewhat erratic saunterings through a state structure. Even though this is related to what has been learnt during waking hours it is a bizarre version of it. For example, the continued sequence A B C A B C A B C... may be related to the thought of seeing a cat and observing its head, body and tail in turn. The "dreaming" sequence A A B C A A B C ... may be sensed as a vision of a cat with *two* heads, that is an experience which is a distorted version of reality due to a relaxation of control within the automaton.

At this stage, it may be appropriate to squeeze the analogy further and consider its relation to some physiological aspects of dreaming. That is, the question of *what controls* switches ψ and ϕ must be disposed of. First, ϕ is partly controlled by some other part of the automaton and partly merely by relaxation. Even though one's vision is entirely controlled from within (shutting and opening the eyelids through muscular effort) one cannot shut off hearing or touch. Nevertheless similar factors come into play. From within, attention mechanisms can effectively ignore or shut off sensory information, and through some kind of muscular effort one generally tries to sleep in a dark, quiet place. It appears, however, that the primary factor affecting switches such as ϕ is one of *relaxation*, and this is purely physiological. There is evidence that the "depth" of sleep varies in an up-down wavelike fashion during the night. It is likely that this depth is related to a state of physiological relaxation of the body. Therefore, it is also likely that switches such as ϕ and ψ are regulated by this process of relaxation in the sense that it would cause the switches to stop transmitting information.

In our model, ψ would be found to open in a deeper state of relaxation than ϕ. Indeed, one can think of a much longer chain of automata controlling each other, than the two-automaton structure of Figure 7.1. For example, the function of the *TA* itself implies the existence of feedback loops with the possibility of other relaxation switches at levels deeper than ψ. Such switches, if relaxed, would strongly impair the ability of automata such as the *TA* to function at all. The implication here is that the mechanisms of awareness itself (as in Chapter 6) would be severely curtailed. Again, this supports some known physiological facts : dreaming ceases at the deepest levels of sleep. Clearly if the awareness mechanism stops there would be no dreaming. In the rest of this chapter we shall refer to these chains of automata as being *hierarchically* controlled.

Having pursued possible mechanisms of dreaming this far, it is tempting to approach the question of whether dreaming performs a *useful* function. Well-documented experiments have been carried out [6] to show that artificial deprivation of dreaming causes an increase of dreaming periods when the subject is allowed to sleep without interruptions. This does not happen if the subject's sleep is interrupted outside dreaming periods. The effect of dreaming deprivation on waking behaviour is, however, not fully understood and is an area of intense research among psychologists. Therefore much of what is being said regarding the rôle of dreams is hypothetical. What follows is therefore yet another hypothesis, but may be of some interest since it concerns itself with the question of why *an automaton* (rather than a living being) might *need* to dream.

The automaton in question is the familiar one which underlies much of the work in this book, that is, the automaton which learns to perceive by creating stable areas of state activity in its state structure, these areas being related to perceived events. Take an automaton which is learning to perceive the letters of the alphabet. On day 1 it is shown the letter A. As soon as teaching is over some switch such as ϕ is operated to cut off the senses. After a night of sleep, on day 2, the automaton is shown B. The question that arises is "What was the state of the automaton just prior to being taught B ?". There are two possibilities : either the automaton remained the whole night in a state cycle corresponding to A, or it returned to some previous "neutral" state cycle. The former possibility would be disastrous for the simple reason that in subsequent interaction with the letters of the alphabet, the automaton would be unable to perceive B without having perceived A first. This is due to the fact that no transition from the "neutral" state to B would have been learnt. Therefore it is essential that some form of "resetting" action should take place between learning periods.

Fortunately, the postulated mechanism of relaxation of control loops provides just this : a kind of winding back through the state structure to some neutral point. It may be, therefore, that the erratic state trajectories during dreaming are merely those encountered on the way to some "reset" state which enables the system to learn to interact with its environment better after sleep. It appears that babies dream a lot, which would support this theory. When deep sleep without dreaming has been reached, this may be a sign that a "neutral" area has been entered. Naturally, several passes might be needed as there may be several "neutral" areas, the ones found later being better (in the sense of their predisposition to learning) than earlier ones.

So far, we have been content to treat the dream as a somewhat meaningless excursion through the states of an automaton. This type of argument would find disfavour among followers of Freud, and quite rightly so. Dreams are more than meaningless excursions as they often emanate from hidden and powerful modes of thinking. The lack of regard for the meaning of dreams was not caused by a lack of belief in or respect for Freud's theories of dreams. It was merely necessary so as not to get involved in arguments about *meaning* too early. Certainly not before some plausible mechanisms for dreaming had been discussed. This has now been done and it may be possible to deepen the discussion a little by seeing whether state-structure concepts allow us to discuss the *meaning* of dreams with greater clarity than would otherwise have been possible.

It is easily accepted that Freud's genius centers on his stipulation of the existence of the "unconscious". The unconscious is commonly defined as a collection of mental processes of which the subject is unaware. We recall that our definition of awareness is related to the "entry of certain paths among the states of an automaton". To translate the definition of the unconscious into these terms one must first clarify the phrase "... of which the subject is unaware... ". This does *not* refer to material of which the subject is not aware at any particular point in time, but rather to material of which the subject is unlikely to be aware at *any* time. For example the fact that while X is driving his car he is not thinking of his wife does not mean that thoughts of his wife belong to his unconscious. He would have no difficulties in thinking of his wife should the occasion demand it. In state-structure terms, therefore, the unconscious must be defined as those parts of state structure which even though present are not likely to be entered.

This directly brings to mind the question : "If such parts of state structure cannot be entered do they exist ?" Followed closely by : "If they do exist what possible effect can they have on behaviour since they cannot be entered ?" These are precisely the questions that were asked by skeptics about Freud's concept of the unconscious.

The reader who has followed the earlier description of dreaming as a loss of control in a chain of hierarchical controller-automata will by now have worked out that the only contact one can have with unconscious areas of state structure is in the process of dreaming. That is, it comes as no surprise at all that, as a result of loss of perceptual control, an automaton can deviate into areas of state structure which would normally *not* be available to it during waking hours. The real questions which remain to be answered are : how are these areas created and how do they affect behaviour ? There are two mechanisms in an automaton which can lead to the creation of state structure which is unlikely to be entered while all hierarchical controls are in operation. The first involves early interactions with the environment which, later during learning, are infrequently encountered. This corresponds to a type of *forgetting* in human behaviour. The second involves the recognition by the automaton itself that certain state trajectories are undesirable and a subsequent generation of control actions which avoids such areas. This corresponds to the Freudian concept of *repression*.

There are several ways in which one can view *forgetting* in an automaton. The first and simplest merely involves the wiping out of learnt transitions by forcing new transitions in their place. In such a case one cannot argue that the material of the transition has entered any form of unconscious. Indeed, no-one would argue that everything which humans forget enters their unconscious. A more interesting mechanism of forgetting is the following. This involves the assumption that hierarchically controlled automata develop their state structures in ascending order of depth : that is, the deepest first. There is sufficient evidence for this in human beings, that is, the fact that most modes of behaviour become refined with learning during childhood merely implies a development of control mechanisms at a time subsequent to that of more basic "thinking" centres of the brain. More rigorous evidence may be found in what is known about a specific part of the brain called the *cerebellum* which, in early life, is partly inactive and causes the output of "deeper" brain centers to reach human muscles directly producing rough limb movements. The rôle of the cerebellum seems to be to control such movements and to refine them : an ability which develops *after* the establishment of the deeper "thought" centers which are actually responsible for initiating the movements.

Returning to the mechanism of forgetting, one assumes that some primitive thought automaton has, at times, "seen" input event y immediately following input event x, and at other times input event z following input event x. The corresponding states in the thought automaton would be say X, Y and Z. It is possible that in a way similar to the "fork-in-the-road" scheme discussed in Chapter 6 (where an arbitrary choice of exit from a state is shown to take place), if started in state X with no input, (i.e. a ϕ switch cutting perception) the automaton could enter either state Y or state Z with, say, equal probability. Now one assumes that later the education of the automaton some *CA* (as in Fig. 7.1) learns that, in order to achieve a certain goal (which also has become important only later in the development of the automaton), state Y (rather than Z) must be entered after state X. The *CA* simply ensures this transition whenever the *TA* reaches X. It is under these conditions that I would submit that state Z has become part of the *unconscious* of our automaton. The scheme has the necessary qualification : Z *would not* be entered while the *CA* is in control but *could* be during "dreaming" periods when the ψ switch would put the *CA* out of action and the original tendency to enter Z or Y after X arbitrarily would be restored.

The repression concept may be explained in almost identical terms. The only difference lies in the "driving" information which causes the *CA* to learn to exert its control. More specifically, one assumes again that the *TA* has, early in its life, learnt to achieve both goal states Y and Z from a starting state X. Only later in its development does it learn that it may be "wrong" to achieve Z, and counteracts this by forcing the X → Y transition via the controller causing the X → Z transition to enter the "unconscious". Clearly the difference between forgetting and repression in our automaton lies only in the *reason* for which the *CA* is made to shun the X → Z transition : this being caused by a need for goal achievement in the former instance, and rule obeyance (moral, social, etc.) in the latter. When it comes to the complexity of human automata one can accept that concepts of "wish fulfilment" and "censorship" which are commonly used by Freud and his followers may be based on quantitative rather than qualitative elaborations of the above mechanisms.

Several other concepts stem from Freudian dream theories : namely, condensation (the novel combination of two thoughts into one), displacement (the replacement of one thought by another) and symbolization (the use of symbols to represent things). These all provide fodder for detailed explanations in terms of state structure, material which would be too repetitive to be included in this summary discussion. The common theme running throughout these arguments is, nevertheless, one in which the loss of control by *CA*s is the primary responsible factor.

Finally, we turn briefly to another question partly implied earlier in this chapter : "Does the unconscious have any effect on the conscious part of the human state structure ?" The answer according to modern psychology is "Yes" in the sense that aspects of behaviour are regulated by residues of what has entered into the unconscious. This often underlies *abnormal* behaviour for which the real cause has entered the unconscious and therefore cannot be explained by the subject. This is a deep and interesting question, to which a great deal of attention will be devoted in the next chapter.

Here, it may be worth summarizing what has been said about dreams and the unconscious so far. The unpredictable and bizarre nature and characteristic of dreams is typical of the type of behaviour one finds in a hierarchical control automaton as various levels of control are relaxed. The relaxation process is found in humans purely as a physiological result of sleep. During this bizarre activity an automaton can enter areas of state structure normally not available to it when the control connections are functioning properly. In humans such areas would be termed as the unconscious. To find a mechanism for the creation of an "unconscious" in an automaton, the only requirement is that during the learning process (i.e. formation of an environment-related state structure) the control functions are learnt chronologically later than the more basic perception functions. This is sufficient to explain the creation of an unconscious in humans both by means of forgetting and self-induced repression.

8
THE
PSYCHOTIC
AUTOMATON

When a student of psychology is first introduced to the extremely sensitive and complex question of mental illness, he is presented with a somewhat rationalized and simplified explanation [7]. It is this explanation which will be re-stated here to form a basis for expressing the question in terms of an automaton structure.

Much of mental illness which is not due to obvious physical causes (e.g. brain damage), is generally thought to occur as a result of an individual's inability to resolve conflicts. Life, seen as a human being's struggle with and eventual adaptation to his environment, could almost be said to consist of a series of conflicts which require decisions. Normal survival is a matter of weighing up the predicted results of each decision and then actually making what is thought to be the best decision. A conflict arises when these predicted results do not give a clear-cut lead as to how the decision should be made. For example a man with a weight problem has to resolve a conflict between his desire for food and the dangers of obesity. A woman may be torn between a husband and a lover. One goes for a swim bearing in mind the danger of drowning. A normal person will take decisions despite the uncertainty of possible lines of action, whereas a person whose behaviour may be described as "abnormal" could find his continuing existence seriously hampered by such conflicts.

The prime parameter which ensues here is what is described in humans as "anxiety". Anxiety is an emotion linked to the primary concept of fear and is present in every individual. It is the *amount* of anxiety arising in a subject which determines the "normality" of his or her behaviour when faced with a conflict. For example the prospect of swimming might cause such deep fear in an individual as to prevent him from approaching water. He would colloquially be described as being "a bit neurotic about swimming". Too low a level of anxiety would also be considered as abnormal as this is often found in habitual criminals whose low level of the fear of consequences does not prevent them from committing criminal acts. Individuals with high anxiety levels are normally classed as mentally abnormal (in a continuum of degrees) whereas low-anxiety abnormality leads to what is termed "social deviancy". It is the former concept which is primarily discussed in what follows, although an extension to the latter would not present problems of principle.

Before entering a discussion of different *kinds* of abnormal behaviour, let us *design* an automaton which possesses the property of *anxiety* discussed above (Fig 8.1). I purposefully use the word *design* so as to remind the reader that here one is not concerned with accurate models of behaviour. The salient aim of this discussion is to show that rather loose and wordy concepts in psychology *can* be described as state structures of automata. The structures thus produced are minimal in the sense that they are barely sufficient to possess the properties under discussion. To model *human* intelligence and behaviour, a great deal of additional elaboration would be required. Nevertheless, I submit that this elaboration would contain little change of *principle* over and above the automata structures appearing in these pages.

Once again, in Figure 8.1 we face a seemingly complex device and need to proceed cautiously. We assume the now-familiar fork-in-the-road situation. The whole automaton has reached a point in some activity, which requires it to move either to the left or to the right. This situation is represented in the thought automaton *TA* as a possible exit from some state A into either state L which (when the muscular activity automaton *MAA* permits) would cause an eventual movement to the left, or state R which would cause movement to the right. Long before the *MAA* permits any action at all, the *TA* would commence a search through the possible state transitions controlled by a supervisory automaton such as encountered in previous chapters. This control automaton has been labelled "Search Controller" in the diagram. Its task is to force the *TA* to enter the L and R states alternatively.

In order to take a sensible decision the result of entering L or R must be evaluated in terms of some goal. This is done by an "evaluation automaton" which is merely a deeper device in an hierarchical chain. It is a thought automaton which weighs up the consequences of entering L or R. That is, it runs further in the chain of learnt events (starting from an entry into L or R) and evaluates them with respect to one or more goals.

Returning to the concept of a conflict, we shall first show that, in order that a serious conflict might arise, the evaluation automaton must consider at least two goals. In psychology, one defines three primary types of conflict : approach-approach, avoidance-avoidance and approach-avoidance. Referring to the left-right alternatives in our automaton, the approach-approach conflict

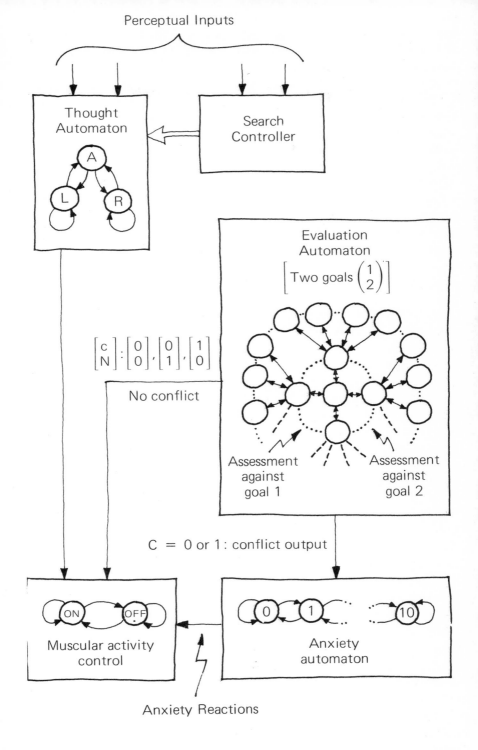

Fig. 8.1. The psychotic automaton.

would occur in a condition in which the evaluator finds that both alternatives meet a goal. This is not a serious conflict and is akin to the instance of the little boy who must decide whether to go swimming or fishing, both of which he finds pleasant. He can take either decision and end up feeling reasonably cheerful. The avoidance-avoidance conflict is the exact opposite, that is one in which both alternatives are unpalatable. For example the little boy may find himself confronted by the choice of going shopping with mother or helping father to paint the house, "duty" being the goal that needs to be met here. Again the conflict is not a serious one in the sense that the only result of taking either decision may merely be one of leaving the little boy somewhat disgruntled. It is the third type of conflict that causes the greatest difficulties. Taking the example of a little boy again, the approach-avoidance conflict may be illustrated by his having to decide whether to go to school or play truant and go fishing. Here taking the first choice (to satisfy the *duty* goal) might lead to frustration and the second (to satisfy the *pleasure* goal) to guilt, and this may leave the boy in a state of anxious vacillation. This is where anxiety may arise, and a normally adjusted individual will override his anxiety and forget whichever goal he chooses to leave unsatisfied. The salient point here is that in this third type of conflict, the conflict itself arises as a result of the fact that one is faced with *two* conflicting goals, both of which cannot be satisfied at once.

For simplicity we assume that in our automaton there are *always* two goals (1 and 2) and that these are either likely to be satisfied (S) or unsatisfied (U). The end product of a search between L and R must result in a pair of assessments taken from the table which defines the function of the automaton*.

		L			
		$\binom{S}{S}$	$\binom{S}{U}$	$\binom{U}{S}$	$\binom{U}{U}$
R	$\binom{S}{S}$	c	N	N	N
	$\binom{S}{U}$	N	c	C	N
	$\binom{U}{S}$	N	C	c	N
	$\binom{U}{U}$	N	N	N	c

*The decisions made by the evaluation automaton are listed as, say, $\binom{S}{U}$ which means that goal 1 is satisfied and goal 2 unsatisfied.

Here the major conflicts are labelled, C, the minor ones, c, and non-conflict situations are shown as N. It is re-emphasised that the major conflicts C are those in which it is difficult for the automaton to take a decision, whereas in the minor ones, the automaton "knows" that it does not matter which decision it takes.

How does the automaton *know* that Cs are difficult ? The answer lies in the fact that C and C only triggers off the *anxiety* automaton, whereas c and N allow normal behaviour of the automaton by a release of the muscular activity section. Before discussing the possible effects of triggering off the anxiety automaton we return briefly to the simple explanation of abnormality in terms of anxiety reactions.

First, one realizes that there are no clear dividing lines between different types of abnormality, and indeed, between normal and abnormal behaviour. There is a continuum of behaviour disorders which ranges from the occasional depression or outburst of temper to the utmost in violence or withdrawal from interaction with fellow beings. It is usual for the modern psychiatrist to measure the degree of abnormality by the amount by which the disorder prevents the subject from accomplishing everyday tasks. The milder forms of disorder usually go under the heading of *neuroses*, whereas more severe disabilities are called *psychoses*. It is generally said that the common factor among disorders is that they may be viewed as different forms of reactions to anxiety. The prime symptom of a neurosis is that the patient is overtaken by an uncontrollably high degree of anxiety, a feeling of paralyzing fear from which it is difficult to retract. This causes a reaction which is seen as an abnormality in the subject's behaviour. We shall look at known examples of this and discuss them in the light of our automaton of Figure 8.1. The only requirement is that one should first clarify the function of what has been labelled the anxiety automaton. This is simply a device which, when triggered off by a major conflict, will progress through states of fear of every increasing intensity (numbered from 0 to 10 in Figure 8.1). There are states which, as seen in Chapter 6, are related to a *retracting* muscular activity.

Thus the simplest form of anxiety reaction is one in which the subject merely reports a great feeling of fear. Typical is a case discussed in the previously cited text [7]. A young man developed a love-hate conflict for girls whom he was dating, and was overcome by feelings of wishing to kill the girl whom he was escorting. This triggered off acute anxiety attacks which he reported, but the source of which he could not explain. As implied, here one distinguishes two clear and opposing goals, the satisfaction of love and the satisfaction of destruction. The most interesting question, however, is where did the tendency to hate come from ? In a normal individual this conflict would not arise since the hate-goal would not be there. The answer is found as in the majority of cases in what follows, in the unconscious. In the above case it was known that the subject in his youth was very attached to an insecure and frustrated mother and built up the love-hate conflict in his interaction with her. What is interesting, however, is that the entire automaton mechanism including the trajectories of the thought-automaton and the evaluation automaton may have become part of subject's unconscious as discussed in the last chapter on dreams. It was sufficient for the subject to enter a state such as A (the thought of an imminent encounter with a girl, in the above case) for the anxiety automaton to be triggered off directly without the logical searches through the equivalent of L and R and their evaluation. This appears to be a characteristic of most mental illnesses, namely that the subject is unaware of the conflict which is at the root of the problem. It is the discovery of the residual traces of the unconscious state trajectories of such conflicts which is so much a part of the psychiatrist's professional activity.

In the above case, the connection leading from the anxiety automaton to the muscular activity (i.e. behaviour) automaton would have remained largely passive, since the subject did nothing to alleviate his anxiety attacks. A common form of behaviour which might result from this link is what is labelled as the "obsessive-compulsive" reaction. Cases have been reported in which, for example (op. cit.) a mother who suffered from a love-hate reaction towards her small daughter would alleviate her anxiety by compulsively making the sign of the cross and saying "God preserve my dearly beloved little daughter". Translated into the automata terms of Figure 8.1 this is the equivalent to the production of muscular activity controlled by the anxiety automaton which attempts to influence the environmental position of the *entire* automaton (i.e. its relation to God in this case) so as to effect an exit from the conflict situation in the *TA* and allow the anxiety automaton to return to the 0 state.

A somewhat different activity is seen in so-called *phobic reactions*. Typical of these are fears of enclosed spaces (claustrophobia), of heights (acrophobia) etc. For example, the person with an irrational fear of crowds is faced with the continuing conflict of, say, having to go into shops to buy his provisions and the possibility of such places being too crowded for his liking. The anxiety reaction may be such as to prevent the subject from even venturing out into the street which, if not given attention, might even lead to starvation.

The most direct activity of the anxiety reaction loop is found in what psychologists call *conversion reactions*. Typical of these is the case of the soldier whose conflict between extreme distaste for battle and guilt arising from thoughts of desertion triggers off the anxiety automaton which, as it starts climbing through its anxiety states automatically *blocks off* part of the muscular activity automaton causing (say) paralysis of the legs. Initially this may be triggered off only at high levels of anxiety, but adaptation can take place in the need to avoid the conflict, shifting this reaction to ever lower levels of anxiety until permanent paralysis takes place (even with the anxiety automaton cycling in the lowest state).

The reactions which have been described so far are generally labelled "neuroses". More severe are "psychotic" reactions to anxiety. Although there appears to be no clear distinguishing line between the two, the main difference between a neurotic and a psychotic is that the former alleviates his anxiety and copes with it, retaining some form of useful interaction with his surroundings, whereas the latter largely gives up and retrenches to an isolated world with a minimum of useful social interaction.

Several types of psychotic reaction may be identified, first there being two major classes: the *manic-depressive* reaction and the *schizophrenic* reaction. The latter may be subdivided further, as will be seen later. The manic-depressive psychosis* is particularly interesting because it highlights a possible mechanism of operation of a "mood-automaton": yet another device in our hierarchical chain. Moods are emotions again related to forward going and retractory activities in a way similar to fear and pleasure. However, they are not as closely related to environmental inputs. Fear and pleasure are felt, in most cases, as a direct result of seeing or hearing something. The cause of moods is deeper and more mysterious. They may be due to physical causes: lack of sleep can cause a bad mood as, indeed, can hunger. Sometimes moods are residues of emotions. For example depression can follow a distressing emotional experience or a period of elation can follow a pleasant encounter.

In a normal person, it is this weak link with external causes which keeps moods in check either by the sheer variety afforded by one's environment or by direct activity aimed at moulding one's environment. For example, one often hears statements such as: "When I am depressed I take a warm bath", or "When I get over-enthusiastic about a project, I talk it over with my wife : she brings me down to earth". In a manic-depressive subject, this

---

*The common symptoms of this disorder are that the subject enters long periods of deep depression or furiously elated activity, or possibly swings between the two. It is often cyclic in nature, that is, the disorder reappears fairly regularly after intervals of many months of normality.

control appears to have been lost, and the emotion automaton is able to drift among its states without any form of restraint. Contrary to modern beliefs in psychology, this leads me to submit that a manic-depressive reaction may not be of the same kind as a chronic anxiety reaction based on conflict. It has too much of the flavour of lack of control of the mood automaton through some twist of adaptation, rather than a blockage of the mood automaton. Clearly, in the long run, lack of control in a mood automaton must obviously affect the anxiety automaton as it is certain that a manic-depressive sufferer becomes anxious about his attacks. But this is due to a malfunctioning of the anxiety automaton and the sources of this malfunction might be that the subject was not surrounded by a favourable environmental situation during his upbringing and has consequently not learnt to "... take a warm bath..." when depressed or "talk it over with someone". In fact if a young child when seeking consolation on feeling sad finds rebuke instead, one can easily see that he could have the control of his mood seriously impaired for future life.

Schizophrenic reactions have mainly one factor in common : a split between internal thought and external behaviour (and not, as is sometimes thought, a split between two contrasting modes of thought or behaviour). We shall follow the six divisions of schizophrenic behaviour used by Hilgard et al. (op. cit.) which are summarised below for completeness.

1. *Disturbances of affect* : The link between outward behaviour and emotion is lost. For example the subject reacts to tragic events by smiling or without any show of emotion at all.

2. *Withdrawal from interchange* : This implies the subject's loss of interest in his surroundings which may lead to unbroken silences and immobility lasting several days, or longer in some cases.

3. *Autism* : This is an overabsorption in an inner fantasy world which results in a lack of awareness of a proper interaction with one's environment.

4. *Delusions and hallucinations* : The subject's inner thoughts lead him to interpret his surroundings wrongly. He hears or sees things that do not exist, or she believes untrue facts (such as that there may be a plot against her).

5. *"Bizarre" behaviour* : The inner fantasy world takes over control of the subject's behaviour so that his actions seem unrelated to environmental requirements.

6. *Disturbances of thought* : This implies a peculiar association of thoughts and deterioration in intellectual ability.

Again one must realise that the above effects do not have clear lines of distinction between them and that, in one subject, they can occur in conjunction with one another with different levels of intensity. It is interesting to view the above six divisions as effects in an adaptive automaton as, it will be seen, that they can stem from one prevalent cause : lack of control in a hierarchical chain.

It is not even necessary to postulate the complexity of the existence of evaluation and anxiety automata : a three-automaton structure will do. These are, (a) a perception automaton, PA, which, in the usual way, recognizes the environment by entering sympathetic state cycles; (b) a thought automaton, TA, which, again in the manner of this and the previous chapters, plans the activity of the entire automaton; and (c) the muscular activity automaton MAA. Again one recalls that the PA controls the TA which in turn controls the MAA. We assume that the emotion states occur in the TA. The common factor among all the six aspects of schizophrenic behaviour (and, indeed, manic-depressive effects) is that they imply a weakening of the chain of control. The first three all imply a lack of control of the TA on the MAA. There may be a vivid interchange between the PA and the TA in these three cases, but in each instance there appears to be a weak link between thought and behaviour. In disturbances of affect, the subject may indeed feel deeply sad in a tragic situation and yet this brings about a forward-going or smiling reaction from the MAA. Here, as in the manic-depressive situation, and in many of the other schizophrenic reactions, one could postulate that this lack of control is created during the automaton's up-bringing. For example, a child who is scolded too often for crying might force the wrong TA-MAA links to satisfy his environments (viz. parents, teachers, etc.) In withdrawal from interchange and autism it is not the *wrong* link that is made, but there appears to be no link at all and the MAA merely becomes dormant or autonomous. In early upbringing the main functional links between TA and MAA which have to be forged are those which enable the entire automaton to *manipulate* its environment (or, at least, to approach it in order to achieve certain goals). It is a lack of experience in this activity which may bring about the eventual malfunction. For example, autism may be caused very early in life by a child not being given enough opportunity to realize that activity in the MAA (initially perhaps random) can affect what is noted by the PA and hence TA. It is only by the completion of this loop *outside* the automaton that the correct control links can be forged[*]. Hence, early games, being allowed to thrash about and generally *explore* one's

---

[*]For a further discussion of this see : I. Aleksander and M.C. Fairhurst, "An Automaton with Brain-like Properties", *Kybernetes*, 1, 18, 1971, where this concept is used to explain speech production.

environment must be vital to the subsequent mental health of the individual.

In the latter three of the six groupings of schizophrenic reactions, it appears that the link between the PA and the TA has gone wrong. Hallucinatory effects are clear examples of an occurrence in which the TA is not properly linked to the PA and acts somewhat autonomously. When the subject's behaviour is described as "bizarre" this is due to the fact that autonomous activity in the TA *does* control the MAA and produces actions unrelated to proper interactions with the environment. Clearly such disturbances are regenerative in the sense that milder forms bring about a disengagement from the environment which further weakens the link between the PA and TA which, in turn, produces a further disengagement, etc.

As to the mechanism which causes this broken link, it is likely to be the same as that for the TA-MA link : a lack of sufficient self-exploration and interaction with the environment during early upbringing. It is sad to think that the PA-TA breakage is likely to occur in individuals with a higher-than-average intellectual ability. I refer to individuals whose TAs are highly active and demand environmental interaction in order to channel activity along proper lines. If this is not allowed the TA might break away and create that intangible inner world that is so characteristic of many schizophrenics.

Incidently, early upbringing cannot be the only factor to be blamed in sufferers of schizophrenia. It is known through statistical evidence that hereditary effects can come into play. This can be explained as follows. The automata one is considering here have, as all living automata, a certain randomness in the local interconnections of their network-like structure. This must bring about in some automata a certain predisposition towards instability if compared with the average. However, a normal exposure to the environment is likely to overcome this. Nevertheless, in confirmed sufferers of schizophrenia this predisposition may be due to more than just randomness and may, indeed, be inherited as part of the physical structure of one's neural automaton. Nevertheless it is my opinion that, despite the fact that environment is not the *only* factor, such predispositions play only a minor role in the creation of a veritable psychotic sufferer. The flexibility and adaptibility of neural automata must surely be such as to make early upbringing the dominating factor, even in the presence of hereditary predispositions.

To conclude this discussion and to flex the muscles of automata descriptions a bit further we shall comment briefly on some therapeutic methods used in combatting mental illness. The immediate difficulty is more than clear. We have been able to relate (albeit rather embryonically) various forms of mental illness to deviations from some norm in supposed state structures. We have learnt in the past that such state structures are almost unrelated to physical structure, hence any form of surgery in the case of non-organic mental illness is seen, at best, as being capable of only incidental changes. Indeed, this has been understood for some time and frontal lobotomies are happily relegated to history. The remaining "physical" treatments which are practiced at present center mainly around chemotherapy (the use of drugs) and, to a much lesser extent, shock therapy. They can both be described as being "global" in the sense that their effect is distributed through much of the brain. Looking at the effects of shock therapy on state structure they can, at best, be described as irrelevant. The likely effect of shock therapy is that it places the brain-automaton into some arbitrary state. Possibly, this could be a state which the patient would normally not reach during waking hours. However, it has been argued that most mental illnesses are due to disabled state structures, therefore merely placing the brain in some arbitrary state within such a structure is likely to be of little avail. Any changes in the logical functioning of the brain due to the possible physical causes of shock (e.g. the killing of certain neurons or the alteration of their logical function) are bound to remain arbitrary. The only justification for shock therapy may possibly be found in effects brought about by a patient's *belief* that something is being done for him or her. However, there are better ways of achieving this, as will be seen.

Despite its globality, chemotherapy makes more sense in some ways. It is likely that the major effect of drugs used on mental patients is to "dullen" the activity of the brain. In automata terms this is equivalent to increasing stability by a global "opening" or "blocking" of feedback paths. This can have a calming effect on runaway parts of an automaton such as an out-of-control anxiety automaton or an over-active emotion center. Again, the success or otherwise of this technique in *curing* patients will depend on whether other methods are being used at the same time; methods which aim more directly at correcting the disturbed parts of the state structure. The obvious drawback of chemo-therapy is that it dulls the patient's intellectual ability as a whole, and this could make it more difficult for him to recover through his own will. One thing is clear: a correction of maladjusted state structure must involve a process of re-education. This might require that the patient be as alert as possible and not hampered by drugs.

It is interesting to note that the remaining methods of psychotherapy do aim at interaction with state-structure. Psychoanalysis*, for example, aims at discovering *unconscious* causes of mental illness. This can be quite helpful in, say, a neurotic subject who does not understand why he has a fear of the dark. The discovery that he was severely frightened in the dark as a child might help him to understand the cause of his initial anxiety and to superimpose this thought on others when anxiety sets in, thus re-establishing a control over the anxiety itself. It may be equally true, however, that in more severe tendencies psychoanalysis may be a waste of time and may make things worse for the patient by increasing his or her frustration. The reason for this is in fact that the cause of the illness might *not* lie in the unconscious. The patient is therefore as aware of the causes of his discomfort as he will ever be and psychoanalysis becomes merely irritatingly ineffective.

More recent off-shoots of psychoanalysis make more sense in the automaton contexts. An example is client-centered psychotherapy where the patient is allowed to develop the discussion with his analyst along self-chosen lines. This may be most helpful particularly when the patient's self-confidence is at stake, but is unlikely to be of avail in severe cases where the patient is unable to satisfactorily interact with his analyst and where a fundamental re-education may be the only answer.

Behaviour therapy is a method which does involve a crude form of re-education. It is based on the principle that some neuroses must have been *learnt* and hence can be *unlearnt*. In automata terms this involves the creation of healthy state transitions to replace incorrect ones. For example a person with an intense fear of the dark may be brought to terms with his or her problem by gradually being forced to face dark rooms for ever-increasing periods. In this way one hopes that this fear at some stage no longer triggers off a mounting trajectory in the anxiety automaton. Again, this method is clearly useful in treating obvious and exaggerated phobias, but cannot be sought in the case of more severe psychoses.

Since schizophrenic reactions involve the cutting off of the subject from his surroundings (i.e. people), currently practiced methods of *group therapy* seem to hold some hope. Here the individual is brought into contact with other patients and, under the guidance of the therapist and in a series of meetings one tries to re-establish an intellectual intercourse.

It seems to me that the last method holds the greatest hope

---

*This may be roughly described as the practice of putting the patient into a relaxed state and seeking, by discussion, to discover associations (state structure links) that would normally not be evident in his or her behaviour.

for schizophrenics, but seems far too haphazard at present. It may be better to design a course of re-education for each patient, where initially, the encounters are highly staged (with, say, voluntary workers) and tailored to the therapist'a assessment of his patient. That is, a picture must be formed of the automaton links which have gone astray for *that* patient. After all one does not cure a broken leg by making the patient play football with other sufferers. This area requires a great deal of research and the scope for useful developments is tremendous.

By way of a summary, it may be worth asking whether anything has been gained by using the language of automata descriptions in the context of mental illness. If the only thing that has been gained is a way of describing mental disorders functionally, as deviations form some "normal" state structure, the objectives of the exercise will have been satisfied.

Initially, it was shown that anxiety-based neuroses could indeed be described in terms of an automaton in which the assessment of the consequences of a decision as evaluated against certain goals could trigger off an anxiety-instability. I feel that this may only be important as an introduction of the automata theorist to neuroses, but is almost derivative of what is known of such disorders anyway. More important seems the fact that, in going to more severe forms of disorder, a much simpler automaton structure could be used (again, it is stressed, purely as a *descriptive* tool). Here the issue has been focussed on the environment → subject → environment loop and things which could go wrong during an upbringing period. It is felt that a much deeper study of this concept is required, one in which the re-education of the patient was carefully tailored to a clearly diagnosed failure of part of the automaton.

9

THE
GENETIC
AUTOMATON

So far, in this book, the main automaton that has come under our scrutiny has been *mind* as the state-structure of the brain. There is however another automaton which is responsible for life itself: the behaviour of a biological cell — its division and replication to form human beings, animals and plants and, indeed, the brain itself. We shall devote this chapter to a description of some fascinating characteristics of the state structure of collections of genes as automata.

The foremost distinction between the automata we consider here, and those we encountered under discussions of *mind*, is that the former have a much more autonomous characteristic in their behaviour. That is, they do not depend on environmental interactions to the same extent, and it is the stability and predictability of their behaviour which will be central to our discussions.

The almost magical development of an organism relies on the process of cell division. Central to this process is a complex chemical reaction in which molecules of deoxiribonucleic acid (DNA) reproduce themselves. As is well known, particularly in humans, there are clear differences between members of one species. For example, some have blue eyes, some have brown eyes, some are short and some are tall. The biological element held responsible for such differences is the *gene*. A gene is a unit of DNA, that is, a small portion of the *chromosome* which is the carrier of DNA in a cell. It is known that the number of genes per cell is greater in complex organisms than in simple ones. For example, man has about 2,000,000 genes per cell, while bacteria have about 2,000.

The number of genes per cell must somehow be related to the number of different cell types that exist in their respective organisms. These numbers are surprisingly low, for example bacteria have only two types of cell, whereas in man one finds about 100. These low numbers are responsible for the distinctiveness of the organism and the similarity of one member to another in a particular species. This, in turn, guarantees the stability and survival of the species itself.

In modern biology, much thought has been given to the way in which genes affect one another. They are, after all, large molecules, and one is interested in the chemistry of what happens when they interact with one another. There are two important results on which biologists agree. First, a gene is often affected by only two or, possibly, three other genes. Second, the effect that a gene can have on another is often thought of as being binary: or "on-off" (e.g. represser and inducer in biological terms). Thus a system of interacting genes may be represented as shown in Figure 9.1. (This is a physical network and *not* a state diagram).

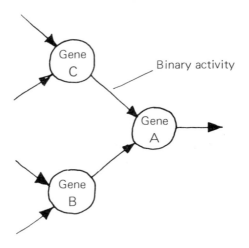

Fig. 9.1. Connections between genes.

An assembly of genes therefore acts as a binary network of two-input (say) elements in which every output leads to one or more inputs. Clearly such a net behaves as an autonomous automaton, that is, one which has no inputs from its surroundings. Thus at any instant of time the "next state" of the automaton can depend only on the "present state". If one starts such a device in an arbitrary state, and one follows the sequence of subsequent states, one must eventually return to a previously encountered state. At that point one has completed a *cycle* since all subsequent states have been previously encountered. The system remains in such a cycle until some outside disturbance occurs. In a collection of genes this cyclic activity must be related to cell division. As briefly mentioned in Chapter 3, Stuart Kauffman [2] has suggested that this relationship is, indeed, a close one and that the number of states in a cycle is equivalent to the number of chemical activity patterns that occur among the genes of a cell between one division and the next.

Continuing with this analogy, each cell type should correspond to one possible cycle. Going back to the behaviour of the autonomous automaton, one should realize that there is more than one cycle in the state structure. In fact, the entire set of states is "partitioned" into completely disconnected subsets, each of which contains only one cycle. The question that may be asked at this stage is : "How do the genes function in order to have few and relatively short cycles ?" One says "few" and "relatively short" because for some mechanisms of gene interaction there could be very many. For example, in a bacterium that has two cycles there may be, on average, 40 patterns per cycle, whereas in man there may be about 1000. Now, considering the fact that a bacterium has about 2,000 genes per cell, there is a total of 2^{2000}, that is, 10^{700} possible states. The fact that the entire cyclic activity is restricted to only about 80 of these states is quite remarkable. The figures for man are even more surprising.

It is as well to realize, however, that were these cycles not as short as they are, and were there not as few such cycles as there are, the entire scheme of biological growth would not work. An instability in cell division resulting from too much diversity among all types would lead to lack of distinctiveness in species, which would augur badly for its survival. Even more important is the length of the cycle in this respect, since one genetic state change takes about one minute. Any form of state instability resulting in long cycles would lengthen growth periods, since times for the development of organisms are directly proportional to these cycles times.

Therefore, the question asked earlier becomes even more burning and pertinent. One wonders not only about functions of the genes, but also about the way in which genetic nets are connected in order to produce this great degree of stability. Having discovered patterns in these functions and connections one is faced with an even greater problem : "How did these functions and connections come about : evolution ? God ? "

In his early research work, Kauffman decided to make the hypothesis that both the functions and the connections in a genetic net are totally random. He proposed to simulate, on a digital computer, nets containing up to 1000 genes per cell (this limitation being set largely by computing difficulties). Skeptics predicted a disastrous failure of this experiment for the following simple reason. Taking a statistician's standpoint, due to randomness all round, one guesses that the automaton takes a "random walk" among its 2^{1000} states. In order to complete one cycle, the statistician would predict that, to have a reasonable probability of encountering a state which has been encountered before in this "random walk", the sequence of states would have to be about $\sqrt{2^{1000}}$ (i.e. 10^{170}) states long. Even the most modern computer can change state only 10^6 times a second, which would require 10^{164} seconds (i.e. 10^{159} years !) to complete one cycle.

Undaunted, Kauffman proceeded with the simulation and discovered that, on average, only about 100 states were involved in the total cyclic activity of the system (i.e. the sum of all cycle lengths). This compared much more favourably with the situation found in nature than the statistically predicted result. Extrapolating from his simulation results he predicted that random nets of the size found in man would have about 0.5×10^5 states in their cyclic activity, which compares well with the number of about 10^5 generally accepted to be true. So, all this means is that the "random walk" theory is wrong. It also means that one need not appeal to concepts of "evolution" or "God" in this context. The rest of this chapter will be devoted to giving an automaton-based explanation of stability in totally random gene-like networks.

We restrict our discussion solely to the representation of a gene as two-input binary device with a well-defined reaction time of precisely one minute. This means that at some instant of time the inputs of the gene (say, A and B) have four possible patterns of acitivity (due to connection to two other genes). This activity, being binary, may be represented by either a 0 or a 1 at each input. Precisely one minute later the output of the gene (say Z) will become either 0 or 1 depending on the "function" of the gene. We can see in the table below that the gene can only perform one of sixteen possible functions.

Inputs A B																	
0 0	0	0	0	0	0	0	0	0	1	1	1	1	1	1	1	1
0 1	0	0	0	0	1	1	1	1	0	0	0	0	1	1	1	1
1 0	0	0	1	1	0	0	1	1	0	0	1	1	0	0	1	1
1 1	0	1	0	1	0	1	0	1	0	1	0	1	0	1	0	1
	f0	f1	f2	f3	f4	f5	f6	f7	f8	f9	f10	f11	f12	f13	f14	f15

— label for the 16 different functions.

For example, if the gene is performing function f1, the output will become a 1 only when both the inputs are at 1.

As an example we shall follow the behaviour of the network shown in Figure 9.2. This can be thought of as a small, randomly connected net of four genes : G1, G2, G3, G4. Our main aim is to discover the most likely cyclic state activity given that the func-

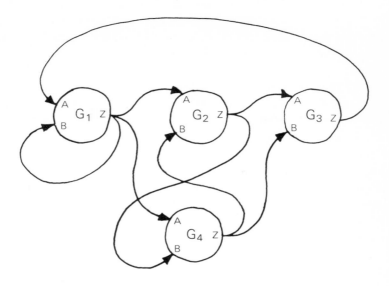

Fig. 9.2. A Genetic network.

tion of the genes are chosen at random from the list f0, f1... f15. First we pick four functions at random (actually done by tossing a coin).

G1 ⇒ f12; G2 ⇒ f3; G3 ⇒ f6; G4 ⇒ f2.
(⇒ reads : performs function.)

To show how cycles arise we shall follow through in some detail the way in which one finds the cyclic structure of the system. One first considers the complete set of state combinations Z (G1), Z(G2), Z(G3), Z(G4). There are sixteen of these. The "next" value of Z(Gj) for every gene may be computed using the truth table above and the randomly selected function values. All that one needs do is to realise which genes are connected to the A and B points of the gene one is considering. For example, for gene 1, and according to f12, Z(G1) will become 1 whenever its (A,B) inputs are (0,0) or (0,1). That is, whenever the A input is 0 irrespective of the B input. This means that Z(G1) will become 1 "next" whenever Z(G3), which is connected to A of G1, is 0 "now". The complete results may be summarised in the following table for all possible states.

This table may be interpreted as follows, referring only to the state labels. State a leads to state i, state i to state n, etc. In shorthand one can write this as

a → i → n → m → o → g → c → a

83

State label	Now				Next				State label
	$Z(G1)$	$Z(G2)$	$Z(G3)$	$Z(G4)$	$Z(G1)$	$Z(G2)$	$Z(G3)$	$Z(G4)$	
a	0	0	0	0	1	0	0	0	i
b	0	0	0	1	1	0	1	0	k
c	0	0	1	0	0	0	0	0	a
d	0	0	1	1	0	0	1	0	c
e	0	1	0	0	1	0	1	0	k
f	0	1	0	1	1	0	0	0	i
g	0	1	1	0	0	0	1	0	c
h	0	1	1	1	0	0	0	0	a
i	1	0	0	0	1	1	0	1	n
j	1	0	0	1	1	1	1	1	p
k	1	0	1	0	0	1	0	1	f
l	1	0	1	1	0	1	1	1	h
m	1	1	0	0	1	1	1	0	o
n	1	1	0	1	1	1	0	0	m
o	1	1	1	0	0	1	1	0	g
p	1	1	1	1	0	1	0	0	e

Here we have discovered a cycle since after c the system returns to state a. We note that state b does not feature in this cycle, so we once again follow the chain

$$b \rightarrow k \rightarrow f \rightarrow \underline{\underline{i}}$$

State i is in the previously found cycle, hence b leads eventually to that cycle as well.

State d has not been accounted for yet:

$d \rightarrow \underline{\underline{c}}$, again entering the cycle

Continuing,

	$e \rightarrow \underline{\underline{k}}$	which we have already accounted for,
then	$h \rightarrow \underline{\underline{a}}$	which we have already accounted for
then	$j \rightarrow b \rightarrow \underline{\underline{e}}$	which we have already accounted for,
then	$l \rightarrow \underline{\underline{h}}$	which we have already accounted for.

We have now accounted for all the states and found one cycle of length 7. One can now probe a little more deeply into the nature of such cycles.

The primary reason that cycles exist is due to the fact that changes of output from 1 to 0 and from 0 to 1 can be endlessly transmitted round and round some path in the circuit. In the above example there are several such paths and these will not be dwelled on. But consider a simpler situation.

Let the functions of the genes be the following :

$$G1 \Rightarrow f3, \quad G2 \Rightarrow f5, \quad G3 \Rightarrow f2, \quad G4 \Rightarrow f3.$$

We note that f3 merely acts as a delay function of input A. That is, whatever the present value of A, that will be the value of Z a minute later. Function f5, on the other hand, does the same with respect to input B. The scheme now looks as one ring transmitting changes from G1 to G4 to G2 to G3 and back to G1. So if the system is started in either the 0000 state (a) or the 1111 state (b), these will remain in single stage cycles. We write this as a $\circlearrowleft$, p $\circlearrowleft$. The rest of the states form cycles as follows :

$$i \to e \to c \to b \;\; ; \quad m \to g \to d \to j \;\; ; \quad h \to l \to n \to o \;\; ; \quad f \to k$$

One sees that *all* the states are in the cyclic activity, because we have chosen functions which allow transmission round a long loop. One only needs to change the function of G1 form f3 to f5 then all the cycles except a $\circlearrowleft$ and p $\circlearrowleft$ are destroyed. This is due to the fact that the only closed physical loop left is that leading from the Z terminal to the B terminal of G1 itself. If the function of G1 is now changed to f0, even that path is destroyed and the only remaining cycle is a $\circlearrowleft$.

Functions f0 and f15 are particularly powerful in the breaking up of closed paths. Their output is stuck at 0 or 1 respectively and is quite independent of either input. Next on the "destructive" list are f3, f5, f10 and f12. They are independent of one of their two inputs and therefore "break" any loop connected to this input. There are other functions which break loops conditionally, where the functions mentioned so far do so unconditionally. For example f1 breaks the loop between B and Z *if* its A input has become "stuck" at 0. That is, if its A input is connected to (say) a gene performing function f0. Functions f2, f4, f7, f8, f11, f13 and f14 fall into this category. The only functions which can *never* break a loop are f6 and f9. Therefore, in order to get a sustained and rich cyclic activity, it is seen that one must be somewhat fortunate in one's choice of functions and connections which are not broken by these functions.

In the circuit of Figure 9.2. it would not be unlikely that all the functions were of a type similar to f1 (that is, conditional loop breakers). In fact, we can compute what happens in such a case by assuming, without loss of generality, that all the functions in the circuit *are* f1. This is the logical AND function which requires that both inputs be 1 before Z becomes 1. In this case one notes that there are only two possible single-state cycles, one with all outputs stuck at 0 and the other with all outputs stuck at 1. One notes also that starting in any state other than the all-1 state, the system can only end in the all-0 state.

This gives the reader merely a flavour of the reason for the high probability of localization of cyclic activity in a random net and the resulting stability. Detailed calculations reveal the same situation : namely that instability is a low-probability event [8].

Kauffman's work goes a little further in ramming home the network analogy. He argues that genetic systems are continuously subjected to noise : that is, chemical perturbations resulting from incomplete reactions, etc. Subjecting the theoretical model, or its simulation, to noise shows that, although forced to leave a cycle temporarily, the system is very likely to fall back into the same cycle from which it was perturbed. Only rarely does the system jump into a new cycle. Translated into biology, this predicts that a genetic system will resist mutation, a cycle jump being just that : a mutation.

Finally, while on the subject of biology, the reader is reminded that the human machine contains several mechanisms which, when looked at as a state structure, exhibit interesting and sometimes beautiful patterns. Examples may be found in many autonomous activities of the body such as heartbeat, breathing and so on [9]. These all underlie the principle that mechanisms which work well are in some way beautiful. Indeed, the state structures of natural phenomena contain an artistry which is worth noting.

10

AUTOMATA
AND
SOCIETY

The title of this chapter was purposefully chosen to be somewhat vague. It enables me to explore two broad areas of thought. First, one wonders whether social behaviour and social interactions may be modelled as automata. Second, in the light of the development and proliferation of man-made automata (mainly in the guise of the digital computer) one can discuss social attitudes towards these machines.

The Social Interaction Automaton

The glib answer to the first of the above questions is "yes". Having established that a human being is an automaton (in the spirit expressed in the earlier parts of this book) it becomes clear that interacting numbers of human beings form automata. Examples of such groups are couples, families, communities, nations and races. Even in enumerating these we notice interesting interaction mechanisms, since most of these groups contain others. This gives rise to hierarchical systems such as have been encountered in several earlier parts of this book.

To take an example, we can consider a couple : man and wife, say. It is no accident of language that one sometimes hears phrases such as "... they live in a state of bliss... " or "... their marriage is in sorry state... ". In a two-person interaction some of the output of one acts as input to the other for both. Ignoring interactions with the rest of the world (just for the time being — this cannot be ignored for long) one notes that the closed system of interactions defines an autonomous automaton. Its state is the combination of the states of the two individuals. However, it may be of some interest that the state changes can only take place as a result of very restricted communication channels : the senses.

The well-known fact about autonomous automata is that they have a rather restricted life. One predicts that after a settling-in period (that is, a transient state trajectory) the system enters a cycle. This behaviour can, in fact, be observed in couples who lead rather isolated existences. After an initial period, perhaps of exhilaration, love, a series of ups and downs, and so on, the state of a relationship settles into a cyclic routine of some sort. The restricted channels mentioned earlier are responsible in a way for maintaining the stability of the cycle. This effect has been met before in the case of genetic nets where the fact that one gene only interacts with two others (i.e. a restricted communication) is a stabilizing factor. The lesson one learns here is that an uncommunicative couple will reach a more stable equilibrium than a highly communicative pair. One hastens to add that this word "stability" has somewhat of a false ring here. A stable cycle need not necessarily be a "good" way of existing. In fact, a highly stable cycle may be described by an external observer as being "dreary". Also, at the other end of the scale, an unstable relationship could have its drawbacks in the sense that the couple would be eternally chasing their figurative tails without ever encountering each other on the same plane. There is also the possibility that a stable cycle may be of a love-hate kind, where one partner wishes to upset the other and the other wishes to do the same to the first, causing the pair to enter into a see-saw relationship where each is winning only part of the time. In other words, the length of the cycle is no indication of its quality. The latter depends solely, in the autonomous case, on the nature of the two automata which make up the couple in the first place.

Clearly the above concept is somewhat artificial; a real couple-automaton would be strongly buffeted by its environment, and it would be difficult to discern endless cyclic activity. Quarrels are interesting phenomena which merit some attention. More often than not they are triggered off by the interaction of the couple with some aspect of their environment. Typical is the quarrel caused by the husband going to have a drink with "the boys" and neglecting his wife. Or the wife buying a new dress when the finances are tight. This sets one partner's automaton into a state in which he wishes to rebuke the other. The latter then retaliates, and so on, until both have reached individual states of anger which taken as a pair puts the couple into a state of quarrel. It is often the realization of having entered this state which brings about an exit from it. This is also often accompanied by a need to act and communicate differently. One of the pair might go for a walk after slamming the door. Once again it is the nature and make up of the individual automata which strongly determines the behaviour of the couple.

At this point it becomes compelling to turn to automata concepts in order to examine whether one can approach an explanation for the fact that people live best as pairs, that is, at their closest relationship level. The sexual interaction and its twosomeness is an obvious reason for the existence of couples. It may be, however, that this is not as important as it appears. A stronger reason may be that in a more-than-two-group, again due to restricted communication channels, there would be a localization of state activity as in genetic nets. Although there is only a very superficial similarity between the two types of system it is easy to imagine that long-routed loops of activity in human relationships seem unlikely. In other words, a contact from A to B requires an immediate reply. Should it be routed through a third party C the chances of keeping a chain $A \rightarrow B \rightarrow C \rightarrow A$ etc. alive become remote. Therefore it is only the *pair* which seems to have the property of being able to establish easily sustained relationships. One might argue that A could contact B some of the time and C the rest of the time. Presumably, this is precisely the type of relationship that occurs in communes. Nevertheless, at any one point in time, relationships are more likely to be going on between pairs within the group.

One strong difference between human relationships and genetic networks lies in the fact that the element of the human network (that is, the human himself) is an adaptive automaton with a much more complex structure than that assumed for the gene. The effect of this is that even though an interaction may become cyclic in the short term, the processing functions of the human network may adapt (in the longer term) to the cyclic activity and change, or even destroy, the cyclic activity itself. There is no doubt that divorces, for example, are often caused by a change in one or both partners' behaviours. Adaptation to a cycle may be found in the divorce court where the deserting husband merely says "I became tired of and depressed by my daily hum-drum routine". Therefore, the human group automaton looks rather like the brain-automaton in terms of short-term and long-term activity. The daily interaction between humans is equivalent to the moment to moment thinking process in the brain, whereas the evaluation of relationships over a long term is equivalent to the learning process.

It is of some interest that there appears to be a certain progression, briefly seen earlier in this chapter, in which a group of automata become a single unit when viewed from a higher plane. This unit becomes the element of a new interacting group. Reiterating, we have interacting neurons in the brain which form a brain-automaton; brain automata which form couple automata, couple automata which (on becoming family automata – an interesting concept, but left for someone else to explore) form community automata, and so on until we arrive at a world-population automaton at which the process abruptly stops. There are fascinating similarities in behaviour at all levels which makes it interesting for scientists (particularly social scientists) to get a better grasp of the automata theory which governs interactive systems. Here one finds the laws by which we seem to live, and they are the same laws from brain to nation.

Society and Automata : Partnership or War ?

The digital computer is the first example of an electronic automaton which has touched the everyday lives of most human beings in the Western world. Most of us have had contact with computerised banking or reservation systems such as used by airlines. Armies of people are employed in positions dependent on making or using computers in one way or another. Important aspects of defence, space exploration and communications depend on the computer. All this does not dispel the suspicion that computers may be a "bad thing" as they have mysterious "brainlike" powers which give them a potential for outsmarting their masters. On this topic there is little that can be added over and above the sound writings of many, among whom Norbert Wiener is probably the most notable [10]. As the man who coined the word "cybernetics", defining it as the study of control and information processing in man and machine, he was only too aware of the Frankensteinian characteristic that such an "electronic brain" could assume. He laid down two prime guiding principles which one should bear in mind when learning to live with automata. First, storage of information in a computer represents a concentration of power. Information has a dynamic power of its own and a monetary value. This means that easy access to a great deal of information may be as dangerous as easy access to high explosives. Fears of invasion of privacy in computers are quite common and, indeed, well founded. But, as in the control of arms and explosives, it is a process of agreed legislation which will control the machine. No machine can take off and start amassing data purely autonomously. It must be fed, and once fed it must be questioned. These are human activities and are as much open to abuse as other human action. There is little difference, in what regards social responsibility, between the man who controls a car on the public highway and the computer manager who controls data flows in his machine. Of course, in the eyes of the law the latter is less approachable than the former, but that is a result of ignorance for which no machine can be blamed. Also, too little access to information is as wrong as too much if the decrease of accessibility applies to the rightful owner of the

90

data. Cases of decreased efficiency in banks are only too common examples of this effect. Before computerization one could have immediate access to one's account merely through the mechanism of asking a teller, who would extract the account from a nearby file. It is now common practice for the teller to interrogate a distant computer through a terminal and only obtain the present balance. A request for the entire statement can be made, but this can only be posted on to the customer from the location of the distant computer.

Once again the cure to this ill lies in the willingness of the computer user to restore the service to its desired lines and not say in answer to a complaint : "Sorry sir ! It's the computer : it does not produce immediate local statements". The reply to that is surely a resounding : "Rubbish ! The computer is not at fault, it's the way in which it's run". It is well known that terminals exist which provide printed output. They just happen to be expensive.

The second of Wiener's foreseen areas of difficulty is that of endowing a computer with the power of judgement, which it clearly does not have. In Wiener's words: "...You can program a computer to give you victory, and victory it will give you even at the cost of the destruction of all your troops ..." This example is often said by computer enthusiasts to be exaggerated and unrealistic. This may be so, but the danger lurks even in less exaggerated examples. Say that a large chain of stores decides to optimize their stock-buying for maximum profit. This is a difficult operation, which might require a computer. Quite rightly the computer might decide that as a result of stocking a very small size of shoe the store will incur a lower profit than otherwise. Say that all shoe shops in a particular High Street belong to chains with similarly computerized stock-buying. It could easily happen that some small-footed person would have to go barefoot. No automaton can re-place an astute but human stock-buyer.

As seen, it is the existence of computer-like automata that has highlighted more than ever the value and economic force of in-formation. Clearly, this is nothing new, as is well known by anyone who owns copyright, patents or earns high wages as a spy. But with computers it has become possible and indeed necessary to take a much closer look at the nature of information in respect to its economic dynamics. A telephone network transmits information from one subscriber to another without altering it in any way. Computers are being introduced in communication networks. The fact that they *store* information brings about problems of security, protection and ownership of information as if it were as concrete a thing as a chair or a table. Information has both a kinetic and a potential force. By "kinetic" one refers to an economic force such as may be found in information that goes under the heading of "know-how". It is kinetic because it changes the state of knowledge which in itself has an economic value. Typically associated with computing automata is "software" : information with powerful kinetic properties. "Software" is the collection of programs which enables the computer to be used by means of predefined languages. Without this information firmly resident in one of the stores of the computer, the machine becomes a useless hulk of electronics. The development costs of software can exceed by several factors that of the hardware (machinery), and software is, without a doubt, a highly marketable item.

The *potential* force of information is best seen in things that generally go under the heading of "secrets". The blueprints of a newly invented aeroplane need not exist as white lines on a piece of blue paper. They could equally well be resident as strings of 0's and 1's in a computer. This means that in a widely developed, possibly international, computer network, protection routines will have to be developed, mimicking some of the laws of conventional protection as they are generally known. As a result, interesting questions arise. For example, will one have to develop programs that act as "software police" ? One of the main problems for society to come to terms with computer automata in this way is that old-fashioned laws will have to be revised and recast, taking into account the microcosm of societal interactions that can take place in an automatic data processing system.

What then are the principles which have emerged *since* the time of Wiener's writings ? One fact which has emerged rather painfully is that society has *overestimated* the effect of machines. The general feeling among some is that a computer can do anything provided that you pay enough for it. People are surprised to find that computers do certain things very badly. For example, they cannot recognize and easily generate speech or recognize handwriting. It is likely that considerable technological break-throughs are required to achieve these tasks. Even among computer-minded scientists there is a tendency to overestimate the computer automaton. For example, the attempts at "Machine Intelligence" mentioned in Chapter 3 have not achieved their designers' original predictions. The image of the computer as the all-powerful electronic brain looms large, despite its failure to live up to such expectations. One hopes that as time goes by, the computer automaton will be recognized ever increasingly for what it is : a rather moronic, but fast, storage and manipulation device for information.

Where does this leave the argument that computers herald an "information processing revolution" equivalent in importance to the Industrial Revolution ? One thing seems certain, and that is that some of the pessimistic implications of this notion have not happened. For example, automation by computers was thought to have a potential for making people jobless. Automation has created more job opportunities with a strong job satisfaction content. Taking again the example of banks, once cannot point at an area of personnel that has been decreased as a result of using computers. One can note, however, that banks now employ a large number of computer systems analysts. No one will disagree that this is a welcome trend. Thus, even though one sees a great proliferation of computing machinery which changes considerably the way in which some things are being done, the "revolution" is different in kind and tenor to the Industrial Revolution. It is more akin to the advent of the aeroplane which certainly has revolutionized transportation, but one does not talk of a "Flying Revolution"

Finally, what of the future ? There is no doubt that the next decade, at least, will see a major change in the role of automata in society in several ways. First, as already mentioned, internationally linked computer systems will emerge which will make an impact on the day-to-day trading and deployment of resources of nations. A second advance is likely to rely on the fact that electronic processing circuitry is becoming extraordinarily cheap and is allowing, through the construction of solid state microcircuits, vast quantities of electronics to be mass-produced. This results in making available quite sophisticated automata to the man in the street and even to children. Calculating machines are examples of this, and it will not be long before more advanced computers can be bought in supermarkets. A further effect of falling costs is that more "intelligent" machinery becomes ever more feasible, and it is likely that hardware will be manufactured which eventually might make computing utomata catch up with their "electronic br in" image.

BIBLIOGRAPHY

[1] ALEKSANDER, I., *"Microcircuit Learning Computers"*, Mills and Boon, London, 1971.

[2] KAUFFMAN, S.A., "Metabolic Stability and Epigenesis in Randomly Constructed Genetic Nets", *J. Theoret. Biol.*, 22 (1969) 437-467.

[3] FAIRHURST, M.C. and ALEKSANDER, I., "Natural Pattern Clustering in Digital Learning Nets", *Electronics Letters,* 7 (1971) 724-725.

[4] ZEEMAN, E.C., "Private Communication" to the 1972 Proc. of an Informal Meeting on Neutral Networks, UNESCO, Trieste.

[5] RYLE, G., *"The Concept of Mind"*, London, Hutchinson's University Library, 1949.

[6] LEE, S.G.M., and HAYES, M.R., *"Dreams and Dreaming"*, Penguin Modern Psychology Readings, London 1973.

[7] HILGARD, E.R., ATKINSON, R.L. and ATKINSON, R.C., *"Introduction to Psychology"*, Harcourt Brace and Jovanovich, New York, 1971.

[8] ALEKSANDER, I. and ATLAS, P., "Cyclic Activity in Nature : Causes of Stability", *Int. J. of Neuroscience*, 6 (1973) 45-50.

[9] ASHBY, R., *"Design for a Brain"*, Chapman and Hall, London, 1952.

[10] WIENER, N., *"God and Golem Incorporated"*, Chapman and Hall, London, 1964.